SELECTED WORKS OF MODERN CHINESE LEARNING

THE GROWTH AND INDUSTRIALIZATION OF SHANGHAI

D. K. LIEU

2015 · BEIJING

First Edition 2015

All rights reserved. No part of this publication may be reproduced or transmitted in any form or by any means, electronic or mechanical, now known or to be invented, without permission in writing from the publishers, except for brief quotations by reviewers.

ISBN 978-7-100-10490-6
ⓒ2015 The Commercial Press

Published by
The Commercial Press
  36 Wangfujing Road, Beijing 100710, China
  www.cp.com.cn

D. K. LIEU

(1891—1962)

Editorial Note

One hundred years ago, Zhang Zhidong tried to advocate Chinese learning by saying: "The course of a nation, be it bright or gloomy, the pool of talents, be it large or small, are about governance on the surface, and about learning at the root." At that time, the imperialist powers cast menacing eyes on our country, and the domestic situation was deteriorating. The quick infiltration of Western learning made the long-standing Chinese tradition come under heavy challenge. In those days, Chinese learning and Western learning stood side by side. Literature, history and philosophy split up, while many new branches of learning such as economics, politics and sociology were flourishing, which made many Chinese dazed. However, there appeared a vital and vigorous learning climate out of the confusing situation. It was at this critical moment that modern Chinese scholarship made the transition—by exchanging views, basing on profound contemplation and even with confrontation of idea and clash of views, the scholarship made continuous progress, bringing up a large number of persons of academic distinction and creating numerous innovative works. Changes in scholarship and in general modes of thinking made transition in all aspects of the society possible, thus laying a solid foundation for revitalizing China.

It's over a century since the journey of modern Chinese learning started, during which various schools of thought stood in great numbers, causing heated discussions. The journey sees schools of thought as well as relevant arguments rising and falling, waxing and waning instantly, leaving complicated puzzles to followers. By studying and reviewing the selected works, one may gain new insights into that journey; and it is the editor's sincere hope that readers would ponder over the future by recalling the past. That's why we have compiled "Selected Works of Modern Chinese Learning". The effort includes masterpieces of celebrated scholars from diverse fields of study and different schools of thought. By tracing back to the source and searching for the basis of modern Chinese learning, we wish to present the dynamics between thought and time.

The series of "Selected Works of Modern Chinese Learning" includes works (both in Chinese and in foreign languages) of scholars from China—mainland, Hong Kong, Macau, and Taiwan—and from overseas. These works are mostly on humanities and cover all fields of subjects, such as literary theory, linguistics, history, philosophy, politics, economics, jurisprudence, sociology, to name a few.

It has been a long-cherished wish of the Commercial Press to compile a series of "Selected Works of Modern Chinese Learning". Since its foundation in 1897, the Commercial Press has been privileged to have published numerous pioneering works and masterpieces of modern Chinese learning under the motto of "promoting education and enlightening people". The press has participated in and witnessed the establishment and development of modern Chinese learning. The series of "Selected Works of Modern Chinese Learning" is fruit of an effort to relay the editorial legacy and the cultural propositions of our senior generations. This series, sponsored by National Publication Foundation, would not be possible if there were no careful planning of the press itself. Neither would it be possible without extensive collaboration among talents of the academic circle. It is our deeply cherished hope that titles of this series will keep their place on the bookshelves even after a long time. Moreover, we wish that this series and "Chinese Translations of World Classics" will become double jade in Chinese publishing history as well as in the history of the Commercial Press itself. With such great aspirations in mind, fearing that it is beyond our ability to realize them, we cordially invite both scholars and readers to extend your assistance.

Editorial Department of the Commercial Press

December 2010

CONTENTS

FOREWORD   1

I. INTRODUCTION   3
Industrialization and the Breaking up of the Old Economic Organization—Factors Promoting Industrialization in China—Shanghai as the Principal Industrial Center of the Country.

II. BRIEF HISTORY OF INDUSTRIAL DEVELOPMENT IN SHANGHAI   17
Seven Periods in China's Industrial Development—The Golden Age—The Textile Industries—Apparel Manufacturing Industries—Manufacturing of Foodstuffs and Beverages—Machine Manufacturing—Leather and Rubber Goods—Chemical Industries—Paper Making and Printing.

III. RECENT DEVELOPMENTS AS REVEALED BY STATISTICAL SURVEYS   61
Growth of Shanghai Industries, 1931-1933—Tariff and Industrial Development—Some Comparative Figures—The Heavy Industries—The Textile Industries—The Foodstuff Industries.

IV SALIENT FEATURES OF SHANGHAI INDUSTRIALIZATION   87
Insufficient Capitalization—Small Size of Shanghai Factories—Extent of Mechanization—Raw Materials and Products.

V. LABOUR CONDITIONS IN SHANGHAI   111
Total Number of Workers—Wages and Earnings—Working

CONTENTS

Hours—The Labor Movement—Strikes and Lockouts—Labor Disputes.

VI. ECONOMIC EFFECTS OF INDUSTRIALIZATION   136
Growth of the City—Growth of Industrial Section—The Price Level—Foreign Trade—Transportation—The Money Market.

VII. THE SOCIAL EFFECTS OF INDUSTRIALIZATION IN SHANGHAI 161
Composition of Shanghai Population—Industrialization and the Family—Effects on the Housing Problem—Other Effects.

VIII. CONCLUSION   179

APPENDICES

A. STATISTICS OF SHANGHAI INDUSTRIES, 1931
    I. Business Organization   189
    II. Capital and Reserve   200
    III. Ownership of Factory Buildings   210
    IV. Officers and Workers   219
    V. Motive Power   229
    VI. Operating Time and Average Number of Years and Months in Operation   239
    VII. Statistics of the Preceding Year (1930)   251

B. STATISTICS OF SHANGHAI INDUSTRIES, 1933
    I. Business Organization and Capitalization   265
    II. Area and Ownership of Factory Site   276
    III. Officers and Workers   286
    IV. Motive Power   297
    V. Salaries and Wages   306
    VI. Operating Time and Average Number of Years and Months in Operation   315
    VII. Statistics of the Preceding Year (1932)   325

C. STATISTICS OF SHANGHAI INDUSTRIES, 1928-1934
    I. Capitalization and Number of Workers, 1928   337
    II. Working Hours and Wage Rates, 1928   341
    III. Number of Workers, 1929   344
    IV. Summary Figures for Shanghai Industries, 1931
    V. Summary Figures for Shanghai Industries, 1933
    VI. Statistics of Shanghai Industries, 1934   347

D. COMPARATIVE STATISTICS
    I. Comparison of Capitalization and Number of Workers of Individual Industries   358
    II. Comparison of Capitalization and Number of Workers of the Sixteen Industrial Groups   369
    III. Comparison of Major Statistical Data of the 1931 and 1933 Surveys   371

CONTENTS

IV.	Capitalization of Twelve Leading Industries	381
V.	Power Statistics of Twelve Leading Industries	382
VI.	Raw Materials and Output of Twelve Leading Industries	382

E. LABOUR STATISTICS
- I. Labour Statistics of Twelve Leading Industries — 383
- II. Wage Earnings in Different Industries — 384
- III. Working Hours Per Day in Different Industries — 385
- IV. Strikes and Lockouts—Industries and Services Affected, 1918-1932 — 386
- V. Strikes and Lockouts—Matters in Dispute, 1918-1932 — 387
- VI. Strikes and Lockouts—Results of Disputes, 1918-1932 — 387
- VII. Strikes and Lockouts—Nationality of Management, 1918-1932 — 388
- VIII. Strikes and Lockouts—Number of Cases, Number of Establishments and of Workers Involved, and Industrial Loss in the Form of Man-days and Wages, 1927-1932 — 388
- IX. Industrial Disputes—Number of Cases and Number of Establishments and of Workers Involved, 1928-1932 — 389
- X. Industrial Disputes—Matters in Dispute, 1928—1932 — 390
- XI. Industrial Disputes—Industries and Services Affected, 1928—1932 — 391
- XII. Industrial Disputes—Methods of Mediation, 1928-1932 — 392
- XIII. Industrial Disputes—Results of Disputes, 1928—1932 — 392
- XIV. Industrial Disputes—Nationality of Management, 1928—1932 — 393
- XV. Cost of Living and Wage Indices in Shanghai — 393

F. ECONOMIC AND RELATED STATISTICS
- I. Population of Shanghai — 394
- II. Population Movements in Shanghai Chinese Territory — 395
- III. Population Density in Shanghai — 395
- IV. Land Values in the International Settlement of Shanghai — 396
- V. Housing Statistics of the International Settlement of Shanghai — 397
- VI. Number of Houses in the French Concession of Shanghai — 398
- VII. Statistics of New Buildings in Chinese Territory of Shanghai — 398
- VIII. Statistics of New Buildings in the International Settlement of Shanghai — 399

CONTENTS

IX.	Statistics of New Buildings in the French Concession of Shanghai	399
X.	Mileage of Roads in Shanghai	400
XI.	Number of Vehicles in the International Settlement of Shanghai	401
XII.	Indices of Wholesale Prices in Shanghai	402
XIII.	Volume of Trade of Shanghai	403
XIV.	Net Value and Indices of the Foreign Trade of Shanghai	404
XV.	Net Value and Indices of Foreign Trade of China	405
XVI.	Net Value of Imports of Certain Manufactured Products into Shanghai and All China	406
XVII.	Net Value of Imports of Certain Industrial Raw Materials into Shanghai and All China	407
XVIII.	Net Value of Imports of Agricultural and Induserial Machinery into Shanghai and All China	408
XIX.	Gross Value of Exports of Certain Factory Products from Shanghai and All China	410
XX.	Vessels Entered and Cleared at the Port of Shanghai	411
XXI.	Inland Water Navigation Vessels Entered and Cleared at the Port of Shanghai	411
XXII.	Freight Statistics of the Nanking-Shanghai and Shanghai-Hangchow-Ningpo Railways	412
XXIII.	Passenger Statistics of the Nanking-Shanghai and Shanghai-Hangchow-Ningpo Railways	412
XXIV.	Revenue of the Nanking-Shanghai and Shanghai-Hangchow-Ningpo Railways	413
XXV.	Interest and Discount Rates in Shanghai	414
XXVI.	Business Statistics of Twenty-Eight Chinese Banks in Shanghai	414
XXVII.	Percentage Increases in the Business of Twenty-Eight Chinese Banks in Shanghai	415
XXVIII.	Silver Stock in Shanghai	415
XXIX.	Bank Clearings in Shanghai	416
XXX.	Volume of Transactions on Shanghai Exchanges	417
XXXI.	Volume of Buisness Done on the Shanghai Stock Exchange	418
XXXII.	Average Deflated Quotations of Government Bonds and Indices of Bonds and Stocks	418
XXXIII.	Spindlage of Cotton Mills in China, 1890-1935	419

G. SOCIAL STATISTICS

I.	Growth of Population in Shanghai	420
II.	Sex Ratio of Chinese Population in Shanghai	422
III.	Age Distribution of Population in Shanghai Chinese Territory in 1934	422
IV.	Nativity of Residents in Shanghai Chinese Territory	423

CONTENTS

V.	Increases in Land Values in the International Settlement of Shanghai, 1903-1933	424
VI.	Communistic Activities in Shanghai	424

H. EXPLANATORY NOTES ON THE VARIOUS SURVEYS

1.	Notes on the Survey of 1928	425
2.	Notes on the Survey of 1929	428
3.	Notes on the Survey of 1931	434
4.	Notes on the Survey of 1933	447
5.	Notes on the Survey of 1934	453

CHARTS

I.	Number of Chinese Factories in Shanghai, 1931 and 1933	456
II.	Capitalization of Chinese Factories in Shanghai, 1931 and 1933	457
III.	Number of Workers in Chinese Factories in Shanghai, 1931 and 1933	458
IV.	Motive Power of Chinese Factories in Shanghai, 1931 and 1933	459
V.	Value of Output of Chinese Factories in Shanghai, 1931 and 1933	460
VI.	Number of Shanghai Factory Workers by Sex, 1933	461
VII.	Statistics Reflecting the Growth of Shanghai	462
VIII.	Statistics Reflecting Growth in Trade and Finance, Shanghai	463
IX.	Statistics Reflecting Growth of Shanghai Industries	464

INDEX   465

FOREWORD

The study of Shanghai industrialization was started in May, 1931 when the Chinese Economic Society received a grant from the Institute of Pacific Relations for this purpose. A preliminary report was submitted to the Institute in July, 1933, as well as a special report on the silk reeling industry in Shanghai. Later in that year funds were received from a Chinese Government organization and the Sun Yat-sen Institute for the Promotion of Culture and Education for a second general survey of Shanghai industries, which was begun in 1933 and completed in the following year. The present volume is a result of the study, and in it the statistics collected in 1931 and 1933 are analyzed, compared and interpreted.

The work was first undertaken by a small staff under the direction of the Research Committee of the Chinese Economic Society. As the Chinese Statistical Society was also interested in such work, it appointed a few additional members to the directing committee and the office was reorganized into the China Institute of Economic and Statistical Research. The undersigned first served as the Chairman of the Research Committee, and then that of the Joint Committee and concurrently Director of the Institute. Under him Mr. Chung-pi Chang conducted the two surveys, with the assistance of Messrs. S. K. Kuo, T. L. Wu and some 30 investigators of the Institute and the various Government and private organizations which cooperated with it.

FOREWORD

Mr. Chong-chi Chen, with the assistance of several statistical workers, is responsible for the computation and presentation of all the statistical data contained in this volume, which include, besides those collected during the two surveys, figures relating to the industrial, economic and financial conditions in Shanghai as given in Appendices A-F. The statistics in Appendix G are supplied by Professor Charles C. L. Wu, who also contributes the chapter on the Social Effects of Shanghai Industrialization. Chapter II is prepared in Chinese by Mr. S. K. Kuo of this Institute and translated into English by Mr. Kingwell Tsha, who also translates some of the explanatory notes in Appendix H. Besides editing this chapter, the undersigned also writes all the remaining chapters of this volume. Miss Pearl Chan takes all the dictation and Miss S. T. King reads and corrects all the typewritten manuscripts.

Thanks are due to the National Government Directorate of Statistics, the Ministry of Industries, the National Tariff Commission, the Shanghai Bureau of Social Affairs, the Chiaotung University Research Institute, and the National Goods Advisory Board for their cooperation in carrying out the two surveys of 1931 and 1933. Those in the various organizations who rendered much help in the surveys have mostly been mentioned in the preliminary report. Thanks are also due to Professor J. T. Shotwell and Dr. J. B. Condliffe for providing the funds from the Institute of Pacific Relations for the study, without which it would probably not have been started, and to the various Chinese organizations and individuals who have contributed from time to time to complete the work.

D. K. LIEU.

Shanghai, July 7, 1936.

CHAPTER I

INTRODUCTION

To study industrialization and its effects, we must know first the meaning of the word. The following discussion is based on the definitions of various economists and what has actually happened in the industrialization of China and other countries.

1. Industrialization is represented by the existence of many factories where large numbers of workmen work together. Before the industrial revolution in England, the manufacturing establishments were all small, and the number of workers in them were small also, hence economists generally consider the working together of many labourers in the same establishment as one of the main features of modern industrialization. In recent years, the growth of large-scale production has accelerated this tendency of concentration.

2. Modern industries generally make use of motive power and modern machinery in the manufacturing of all kinds of products. This is a form of capitalist production termed by Baum-Bawerk "the round-about process of production". The greater the industrial development, the more complicated is the machinery used, and the longer the period for the attainment of the final aim of production.

3. In the handicrafts the employer and employees are in close touch with each other as master workman, journalists and apprentices.¹ Although the treatment of the apprentices might not always be desirable, yet the personal relationship is a compensation for many other defects of the system. With the emergence of modern industries, the relation between the employee and employer has become impersonal, and the chances of their coming into contact with each other are becoming fewer and fewer. In this we still refer to the managerial staff in the factories as representing the employers. If the reference is to the shareholders who really control the factories and own the property, and of the directors who direct the operations, there are even fewer chances for the workers to meet them and present personally whatever grievances they have. On the part of the employers, they also look upon the labourers as parts of the equipment of the factory, no better than machinery itself; there is no personal feeling between them. Although much has been done for the benefit of the labourers in recent years, yet the relation between capital and labour is quite different from what it is in the handicrafts.

4. The relation of the investors to the industries themselves has also become less and less personal. Although a small portion of the capitalists may take interest in the factories in which they invest their money and in a way direct their operations, yet the majority of the shareholders look upon their shares merely as a form of investment. If they receive good dividends, they are satisfied, and care no more for the management of the factories or for the future of the business. As Mr. Tawney points out in discussing the increasing separation of "business" from industry, "they (the business men) are pre-occupied, in fact, with financial results, and are interested in the actual making of goods only in so far as financial results accrue from it."²

---

1. We use the prestnt tense in referring to the handicrafts, because in China many of them are still in existence.
2. R. H. Tawney, *The Acquisitive Society*, p.213.

CHAPTER I INTRODUCTION

5. After the Industrial Revolution, the products of modern machinery are uniform in the same factory, where they are all manufactured with the same kind of machinery on a standardized basis. In recent years, with the further development of industrialization, the staple commodities have become more and more standardized, and those of the same grade must be exactly alike, although they are manufactured by different factories. This standardization of manufactured products is one of the main features of modern industrialization, and its effects are not limited to the manufacturing industries alone.

6. Wherever communications are convenient, localities which are suitable to industrial development generally have a large number of factories, and their products are marketed all over the world, while the raw materials also come from distant sources. This concentration of industries in a few places is the reason why industrial cities have risen in modern times, and has a particular bearing upon our present study.

Industrialization and the Breaking up of the Old Economic Organization

The industrialization of China, as is most strikingly shown in the city of Shanghai, has produced wide-reaching effects on the economic life and organization of the country. Of even greater consequences is the industrialization of the foreign countries with which we maintain trade relations. Although it is true that the process began there more than a century and a half ago, new developments are taking place all the time, and the rapid changes are making it more and more difficult for China even to maintain her position as an exporter of industrial raw materials, were she willing to be contented with that position. The result is the breaking down of the old Chinese economic organization which was based on small self-sufficient economic units. In its place a new organization has not yet taken shape, as the process of industrialization in China is much slower than that abroad, and in trying to catch up, everything is in a state of flux. We

SHANGHAI INDUSTRIALIZATION

shall first give a brief description of the old economic organization of China.

The object of the old economic organization of China was to preserve self-sufficiency. In each small economic unit the inhabitants were able to produce enough for their own consumption. If they had any surplus, which was usually in small quantities, they could exchange it with the surplus products of other villages or districts, or otherwise dispose of it themselves. The necessity of exchange was not so great; therefore, there was no need of extensive communication facilities. For the same reason, the commercial and financial organization in the country was also very simple. The main portion of the time of the farmers was engaged in producing foodstuffs which was to be consumed by their own families, or at least, by the local people. If they had surplus time, they would spend it in producing handicraft articles. The agricultural and handicraft products, if marketed at all, were marketed in the near-by towns or market centres. In these towns and centres there were also small handicraft shops which devoted their time to manufacturing articles for use of the near-by villages. Hence the small town together with the surrounding villages formed a small economic unit, which was self-sufficient to a large extent.

The life of the people was simple, and they consumed few things. The family was able to supply the foodstuffs for themselves and often also other articles of daily use. Whatever they could not supply themselves, they were able to buy from the near-by market towns. Where some special products became known to other parts of the country and were marketed to distant places, they were generally luxuries of which people were not in urgent need, such as the wine of Shaohing, the embroidery of Soochow, the silk of Hangchow, the satin of Nanking, the cloisonne of Peiping, the porcelain of Kiangsi, etc., etc.

The handicrafts and domestic industries did not need any standardized form of raw materials, but could always adapt themselves to the agricultural products of the locality. Hence agriculture and the handicrafts helped each other, and the whole

INTRODUCTION

economic organization was in itself adapted to the conditions of the rural folks. Although there were often wars and banditry in the country, and although the Government sometimes levied heavy taxes, the farmers were still able to maintain their living, and they did not come near bankruptcy.

Since the increased imports of manufactured products from abroad, and the gradual increase of factories in the country, the conditions described above have changed. Our farmers have become more and more accustomed to buying the products of modern factories, and the handicraft and domestic industries therefore have lost a good deal of their customers. What the rural districts can produce, and sell in exchange for factory products, include only such raw materials as cotton, wheat, tea, silkworm cocoons, beans, eggs, groundnuts, etc. Formerly silk was exported in large quantities to foreign countries, and the cotton and flour mills in the country also used native cotton and wheat to a large extent. The farmers were then still able to maintain a living by selling their products to these factories. In recent years, the market for silk and tea has been taken away from us by Japan, India and Italy, and the quantities of other products exported in these years have also diminished. This is because the industrial products of Europe and America have attained such high standards that the raw materials which we can usually supply them do not meet with their requirements. Even the cotton and flour mills in this country are now using large quantities of foreign cotton and wheat as their raw materials in addition to what is produced at home, because American cotton has longer staples and Canadian wheat produces more flour per bushel. This further limits the market of Chinese agricultural products.

At the same time, imported commodities and products of modern Chinese factories are sold in the interior districts to a larger and yet larger extent, and the small economic units of the market towns and rural districts which we have described above have broken down. In their trade with the industrial cities and the treaty ports, the terms of exchange are always against the rural districts, and there is always an unfavourable balance against the latter which they cannot make up except by sending silver to the cities or getting into debt to their merchants and banks. If the people in the cities and the treaty ports would invest their surplus capital in the interior, it will help the rural districts to a large extent, but unfortunately this has not been the case until very recently.

The great increase of the silver stock in Shanghai during the last number of years until the time when America began to buy silver is a proof that the interior towns have been sending specie to Shanghai for making up the difference between what they import and what they export. As if this were not enough, the industrial cities have gone further and tried to attract capital from the interior for investment in real estate and various enterprises of the cities. Consequently the funds in the interior are gradually drained away, and the rural districts are forced to insolvency. It is only in the last year or two that the large modern banks are beginning to invest their money in the rural districts, and in this way help to relieve the latter from bankruptcy.

A few years ago, the League of Nations invited the leading economists of various countries to form a committee to study the question of the world depression. In the report submitted by these economists, one important cause is stated to be the maladjustment of the supply of agricultural products to the demand and the consequent fall in their prices.[3] This refers to the countries of Europe and America. As the statistical data of China are incomplete, there is no reference to this country in their report. Yet the price level in China is always affected by the general world price level, and when the prices of foreign agricultural products fall, those of the Chinese products naturally go down with them, although there may be a lag in time. In the price index numbers of the National Tariff Commission for

---

3. *The Course and Phases of the World Depression*, p.38.

INTRODUCTION

Shanghai, this situation is clearly reflected. Since 1931 the gap between the prices of manufactured products and those of agricultural products has increased every year. The former still maintains a certain fairly high level, but the latter is falling rapidly. In such circumstances, the terms of exchange are very disadvantageous to the farmers.

At the same time, since the products of modern industries are widely marketed in the interior, the handicrafts there are driven out of competition. The farmers find it hard to earn extra income from such by-occupations as afforded by the handicrafts and domestic industries. They find it harder to maintain their living on this account. The small rural economic units of this country are thus affected by industrialization in two ways. First, it breaks up our old economic organization, and when the new organization is not yet perfected, the rural districts find it hard to tide over this transitional period. Second, because of the keen competition between modern industries on the one hand, and the handicrafts and domestic industries on the other, the latter are gradually being driven out of existence, thus reducing the income of the farmers as well as the rural districts as a whole. We consider these effects of industrialization as the fundamental causes of rural bankruptcy in China.

What, then, is the regime that has taken the place of the old economic organization of thousands of small self-sufficient units? We find that a few industrial cities have sprung up, and are continually growing, in a sense at the expense of the whole country. Instead of having a number of industrial centres well distributed in the different parts of the country, making use of the local natural resources and labour supply, and relieving agriculture of the burden which it has to shoulder for the supply of livelihood to the people, we have only a handful of large cities and a few more smaller ones concentrated mostly along the sea coast, especially in Kiangsu and Chekiang. There are large areas of the country not provided with any industrial centres at all, however small in size. Modern industries do not develop as they should, even in such centrally located cities as Hankow, Chengchow, Kiukiang, etc. Territorially speaking, the industrial development of the country is very much lop-sided.

Even in the few large industrial centres along the seacoast, including Shanghai itself, the development still lags far behind that in the West and Japan. What are often considered as modern plants in China would have long ago gone to the scrap heap in America or England. Rapid technical progress abroad is fast making the industrial equipment in China obsolete. Chinese cotton mills not only compare unfavourably with those of Lancashire, but also with the Japanese mills in Shanghai itself. Chinese factory management also leaves much to be desired, from the point of view of productive efficiency. Lacking the co-operation of foreign factory owners in China, we have not the opportunity of studying their mills in detail, but general observation shows that they are usually better equipped and managed than similar Chinese establishments, though still incomparable with the more advanced plants abroad. In the following study of Shanghai industrialization, we do not include any foreign establishments in it, because we have not the opportunity of collecting statistical data from any foreign factories here. The other thing to be borne in mind by the reader is to avoid conjuring up in his mind numerous up-to-date plants whenever we refer to the modern industries of China. They are modern only in a relative sense, as compared with the handicrafts of former times.

Factors Promoting Industrialization in China.

Our object is to study the industrialization of China. But as that subject is too big for a small volume like the present one, and as the statistical data which we have gathered for the modern industries of the whole country—at least all provinces except four in the Northeast, which are under Japanese military occupation, and a few in the Northwest and Southwest, where there are no modern industries—have been made for a Government

INTRODUCTION

organization which has not yet published the results, we shall, for the present, limit our discussion to Shanghai alone. In fact, this was the scope of the research project originally undertaken in collaboration with the Institute of Pacific Relations, and it is only proper that we limit the discussion within this scope. However, wherever reference to the whole country is necessary, such comparison will from time to time be made.

Shanghai is the most important industrial centre of this country. A special study of its industrialization will throw light not only on the economic problems of the city, but also of the country as a whole. At the same time, factors which affect the industrial development of the whole country necessarily affect this metropolis. From a previous study of the industrial development in China,[4] the following passage is taken:—

> Among the factors that promote industrial development in China, railways constitute one of the most important. For instance, Chowkiakow, Honan, was formerly a very important trading centre in the country, but now Chengchow is the leading city in that province, because it is at the junction of the Peking-Hankow and Lunghai Railways. Hsuchow, Kiangsu, where the Lunghai line traverses the Tientsin-Pukow Railway, has, due to the same reasons, superseded Tsingkiangpu on the Grand Canal as the most important city of northern Kiangsu. Although Tsingkiangpu is the northern terminus of steamship lines that navigate the Canal, the Lunghai Railway does not pass through that town, and there is little hope of future development. On the other hand, if a good harbor is constructed at Haichow, the eastern terminus of that railway, now that the line has reached the coast, that city may easily rival Nantung or Wusih, in southern Kiangsu, if not Shanghai itself. The development of Shihkiachwang at the juncture of the Peking-Hankow and Chengting-Taiyuan Railways, formerly a small market town, is another good example of the influence of railways on industrial development ....

---

4. D. K. Lieu, *China's Industries and Finance*, pp. 19-27.

SHANGHAI INDUSTRIALIZATION

The second factor in promoting China's industrial development is, according to our previous study, her foreign trade. This affects the development in three ways. In the first place, it is responsible for the industrialization of the treaty ports. In fact, our industrial centres are mostly also treaty ports, or very near to them. Shanghai is the largest port, and at the same time it is also the largest industrial city. This is because the people came into close contact with foreign influences in these ports and began to set up modern factories long before their compatriots did the same thing in the interior. Such an early start gathers momentum, which often brings about the concentration of certain industries in these ports, such as the cotton mills in Shanghai, Tsingtao and Tientsin, and the silk filatures in Shanghai, Wusih and Shunteh. The facilities offered by foreign trade organizations in the supply of modern machinery and industrial raw materials are also most convenient in the treaty ports.

Foreign trade exerts the greatest influence on the industrialization of the country through creation of a demand for the products of modern industries. Cigarettes, matches, canned food, cement, knitted hosiery, soap, tooth powder, leather and rubber shoes, etc., had all been first introduced into this country through foreign trade, and later factories came into existence here to meet the demand created by the habitual use of these imported articles, which have taken the place of the old-fashioned tobacco pipe, the flint and iron outfit, a mixture of lime and clay, Chinese old-fashioned cosmetics, etc., etc. Now, some of these old-fashioned articles have disappeared entirely, and with them the handicraft workshops which used to manufacture them. In other cases, their consumption has been much curtailed, and modernized Chinese use them no more. All these changes are due to foreign trade.

To a lesser extent, foreign trade has brought into existence industries which manufacture mainly, if not entirely, for export. The large number of bean oil presses in Manchuria is a case in point. A large proportion of the raw silk produced by the steam filatures of Shanghai, Wusih and Shunteh is for export

INTRODUCTION

also. With the growth of cotton mills in China, yarn is no more imported, but instead, certain quantities are exported to the South Seas. Silk hosiery produced by some high class knitting mills is marketed even in America. The Kiangnan Dockyard has constructed ships for foreign companies, and when the Hanyehping blast furnaces and rolling mills were in operation, pig iron and rails were shipped abroad. Such cases can be easily multiplied when modern industries develop further in this country.

While the growth of foreign trade promotes industrial development, its sudden interruption sometimes produces the same results, provided the imported articles have already a good market in this country. For instance, the European War gave a strong impetus to the growth of modern industries in China, especially cotton mills. Boycotts against the goods of certain countries have brought about similar results. The manufacture of modern umbrellas and parasols in Hangchow and Shanghai, to cite one among many pertinent examples, followed a boycott of Japanese goods.

A third important factor in the industrialization of China is the supply of cheap electric power. Although theoretically the relation between these two things is so apparent as to need no further comment, the fact was brought vividly to our attention during our industrial survey of the whole country in 1933-34. We found that districts well supplied with electric power to have many more modern factories than those equally well situated, but not adequately provided with electric power. Many Chinese towns have no power plants, and some which have them have only very small ones that are able to supply electric light but not power. Modern factories are concentrated largely in the provinces of Kiangsu and Chekiang, which also have the largest number of electric power plants. In Shanghai, the proportion of rented electric power consumed in the factories to power generated in the plants themselves is three to two, according to our survey of the same year.

Railways, foreign trade and cheap electric power have promoted industrialization all over the world. They have done so

SHANGHAI INDUSTRIALIZATION

in China, and in Shanghai, her industrial metropolis. Without the Shanghai-Nanking and Shanghai-Hangchow-Ningpo Railways, Shanghai could not have been what it is today. As the principal treaty port of the country through which over 50% of the total foreign trade is carried on, the effect of this factor is naturally felt first in this city. The Shanghai Power Company, the Compagnie Francaise de Tramways et d'Eclairage Electriques, and the three Chinese power plants in this city are important factors in its industrialization. In addition, its position as a treaty port near the mouth of the Yangtze River offers unparalleled facilities and inducements to foreigners to establish factories there. These are often larger in size than their Chinese prototypes, and their success usually brings about the establishment of similar factories by Chinese manufacturers. They demonstrate the profitableness of such industries, and serve besides to teach the Chinese workmen the process of manufacturing new products, except where secret processes are employed.

Other advantages also accrue to Shanghai in its industrial development. The climate is suitable to most kinds of manufacturing industries. Raw materials can be easily transported from any part of the country and of the world to this city, and at the same time its manufactures can be readily shipped to the interior as well as abroad. Some important raw materials, like cotton and silkworm cocoons, are found in the surrounding districts, and the dense population along the Yangtze Valley provides a good market for the industrial products of Shanghai. Once established as the principal industrial centre of the country, it further enjoys advantages which are denied other cities. Skilled workers are easily obtained here as they have more opportunities of acquiring such skill in the local factories, and when they are out of employment, they will rather stay in Shanghai where chances of their re-employment are greater than elsewhere. In fact, there are certain industries which are only found in Shanghai, and workers trained for such work have no chance of securing employment at all elsewhere, unless they are willing to give up the advantage of their former training. Facilities for the purchasing of materials, marketing of products, financing of the

INTRODUCTION

industries, securing the necessary business information, and keeping in close contact with the important commercial and industrial centres of the world, are all available in Shanghai to a degree which is unparalleled in other Chinese cities.

Shanghai as the Principal Industrial Centre of the Country.

As Shanghai is the most important industrial city of the country, the statistical study of the industrialization process is limited to Shanghai alone. In fact, this metropolis is so important in the economic life of the country that it had, according to a survey by the China Institute of Economic and Statistical Research, in 1933-34, about half of all the factories in the country which came up to the standard of the Chinese factory law. In that year the Institute was asked by a Chinese Government organization to make a survey of modern industries in 17 provinces and 128 counties and municipalities, including Shanghai, Tientsin, Hankow, Tsinan, Tsingtao, Canton, Amoy, Wusih, etc. Altogether there were 2,435 such factories of which about 1,200 were in Shanghai alone. This shows very clearly the position of Shanghai among the industrial cities of the country. When the statistical data are organized and classified into 16 large groups and over 150 smaller branches representing the different kinds of manufacturing industries, it is found that in other cities there were only industries that belonged to a few branches, at most, to a scores or two of them, while in Shanghai nearly all of the 150 odd branches were represented. Hence, in variety as well as in number, Shanghai is not paralleled by any other city.

Again, if we study the most important industries, such as cotton spinning, flour milling, tobacco and silk reeling, etc., the majority of factories in these industries are concentrated in Shanghai. There are 136 cotton mills in the whole country of which 64 are in Shanghai. There are 60 tobacco factories in all China, 46 of which are in Shanghai. If we compare the capitalization of all modern industries, then that of the factories in Shanghai amounts to 40% of the total capitalization in the whole country.

SHANGHAI INDUSTRIALIZATION

The number of labourers in Shanghai factories constitutes 43%, and the value of output of the Shanghai factories 50% of that of the whole country. All this indicates the industrial position of this city, which will be further made plain in the following chapters.

During the last five years the China Institute of Economic and Statistical Research, knowing the importance of Shanghai as the manufacturing center of the country, has spent much time in studying the process of industrialization as it takes place in this city. Many other organizations have also collected industrial statistics of Shanghai which we have analyzed in connection with the data we have collected ourselves, in order to study the development in the last few years. At the same time, other economic data have been studied to show their relation to the industrial development of Shanghai. The objective point of view is always maintained and no suggested solutions for industrial problems will be thrown out at random, because many of these problems are necessary evils of the industrialization process, and they cannot be solved separately. Besides, the breaking up of the old economic organization is the main result of industrialization, and before the new organization is perfected, serious economic problems are bound to occur during the transitional period, and the best solution in this sense is the acceleration of the process of industrialization and the concurrent establishment of a new economic regime through careful planning, rather than separate solutions for individual problems.

CHAPTER II

BRIEF HISTORY OF INDUSTRIAL DEVELOPMENT IN SHANGHAI

As the process of industrialization started in Shanghai several decades ago, it is necessary to give a brief historical account of it from its beginning. For such material we can draw upon a fairly large number of books on the subject as well as our own investigations. However, statistical data are available only to a very limited extent for the earlier periods, but since 1929 more comprehensive figures can be obtained. Lacking such data, we find, as a result of our statistical studies of Shanghai industrialization, that newspaper and magazine accounts of industrial developments from which authors on such subjects generally draw their information—in fact, even the so-called first hand information which we obtain from those now engaged in these industries—are often based on impressions rather than absolute facts, especially when they refer to general industrial conditions, and must be taken with more than a grain of salt. For instance, the prevailing opinion seems to be that Shanghai industries in general were already affected by the world depression in 1930 or 1931, whereas our statistics show that there was considerable development in most branches down to 1933.

SHANGHAI INDUSTRIALIZATION

The reason for such mistakes lies mainly in the frequency with which certain statements have been reiterated. As the silk reeling and cotton spinning industries are among the most important ones in Shanghai, their decline has been much talked about, as well as reported in the newspapers. This frequent reiteration has produced the general impression that Shanghai industries as a whole were badly hit by the depression as early as 1931, or even earlier. As a matter of fact, many other industries prospered till 1933, but their prosperity was not usually reported in the newspapers or talked about in general conversation. These industries, being usually run by single proprietorships or partnerships, did not care for publicity about their success, which would have only stirred up competition without any compensating advantages to themselves. An attempt on our part to collect information about the recent developments in the silk weaving industry, which was one of those that prospered in 1933, has convinced us of the meagreness of the available information about successful industries, especially when they do not produce staple commodities in which a large number of business men are interested. In the following, therefore, we will make use as much as possible of reliable statistical data, and the recounted facts have been checked with what may be considered the most reliable source books.

As Shanghai has always been the principal industrial center of the country, and its industrial development has been closely associated with that in the whole country, a cursory account of the latter should properly precede a historical résumé of the former. To the industrial development of China we should therefore first turn our attention.

Modern industry started in China at about 1862, hence the reign of Emperor Tungchi (同治) may be considered to have marked the beginning of China's industrialization. For convenience sake, the whole history from 1862 down to the present day may be divided into several periods, although authorities on the subject hold different opinions in regard to this matter. The following are the different ways of dividing Chinese industrial

CHAPTER II BRIEF HISTORY

history into periods as adopted by Yang Chien, Kung Ching, Yang Ta-ching, Hsu Yen-so and Yasuhara Besao (a Japanese writer, the author of "China's Industries and Raw Materials"), etc.:

Seven Periods in China's Industrial Development

Having considered the opinion of various writers on the subject, as well as the industrial history of China itself, we propose to divide the latter into 7 periods, as follows:

1. 1862-1877. Period of Ammunition Manufacturing
2. 1878-1894. Period of Commercial Commodities Manufacturing
3. 1895-1902. Period of Foreign Enterprises
4. 1903-1913. Period of Government Encouragement
5. 1914-1925. Period of Flourishing Private Enterprises
6. 1926-1933. Period of Co-operation between Government and People for Industrial Development
7. 1934-1936. Period of General Depression

The period of ammunition manufacturing. The period from 1862 to 1877 was characterized by the emphasis on arms and ammunition manufacturing. The Chinese Government, having been benefited by the use of modern arms in suppressing the Taiping Rebellion and having experienced their power of destruction in the Opium War, encouraged their manufacture by every possible means. In 1862, Li Hung-chang (李鴻章) built an ammunition factory in Shanghai which, in fact, marked the beginning of China's modern industry. Five years later, Tseng Kuo-fan (曾國藩) established the Kiangnan Dockyard (江南造船廠) at Kaochangmiao, Shanghai. Tso Chung-tang (左宗棠) founded in 1866 the Bureau of Shipping (福州航政局) in Foochow, and the next year, Li Hung-chang built the Kiangnan Arsenal in Shanghai.[5] In Szechuan, an arsenal was also built by Ting Pao-chen (丁寶楨) in 1877.[6] All these were important

---

5. Kung Chin, *A Sketch of China's Industrial Development*, pp. 14-21.
6. Yang Chien, *Chinese Industries in the Last Fifty Years*, an article in the *Fifty Years of Shun Pao*.

establishments for the manufacturing of arms and ammunition in the country. It may also be mentioned that during this period Tseng Kuo-fan and Li Hung-chang sent a number of youths abroad for technical training in connection with the manufacture of ammunition and the latter also founded a naval training school in Tientsin. All measures taken by the Government at that time were intended for military purposes, and few people seemed to give attention to the production of commercial commodities. This period may also be called that of government enterprises, inasmuch as the capital of all the above mentioned undertakings was furnished by the Government.

The period of the Commercial Commodities Manufacturing. The second period lasted from 1878 to 1894. The establishment of the Kansu Woollen Fabric Manufacturing Bureau by Tso Chung-tang (左宗棠) in that province on the former date marked the beginning of this period.[7] Four years later, Li Hung-chang started the construction of a cotton weaving factory in Shanghai, which was completed by 1890. Chu Ta-tsun (祝大椿), a Shanghai merchant, established, soon after, with a capital of $100,000 the Yuan Chang (源昌) Factory, producing machinery and metalware. In 1886 several German merchants founded the Chen Yu (正裕) Flour Mill in Shanghai and Li Hung-chang established the Leng Chang (倫章) Paper Mill in the same city. Simultaneously, Chang Chi-tung (張之洞), the then Viceroy of Hupeh and Hunan, established in the former province four factories for cotton weaving, spinning, ramie fibre preparing and silk reeling respectively. Shen Hsuan-hwei (盛宣懷) established in Shanghai the Hwa Shen Cotton Mill (華盛紗廠) in 1893. During this period, the manufacturing of articles of daily use, particularly the textile industries, flourished considerably. Industrial enterprises during this period were mostly initiated by the Government. However, as many of them did not produce satisfactory results, their operation was later turned over to private individuals, though the Government still exercised some degree of supervision. Con-

---

7. Kung, op. cit., pp. 26-27.

BRIEF HISTORY

sequently, this period is also designated by some as that of private operation under government supervision.

The period of foreign industrial enterprises in China. Consequent upon the signing of the Shimonoseki Treaty after the conclusion of the Sino-Japanese War of 1895, people of other nationalities were permitted to establish factories freely in the treaty ports of China. Many foreign merchants took this opportunity and a number of foreign-owned factories made their appearance. In Shanghai, cotton mills like Ewo (怡和) and Lao Kung Mao (老公茂) of British Nationality, Hung Yuan (鴻源), owned by American interests, and Jui Chi (瑞記), a German concern, came into existence one after another.[8] Flour mills followed in the wake of textile factories. The British-owned Chen Yu (增裕) Mill in Shanghai and the Russian-owned North Manchuria Mill in Harbin were founded. In other treaty ports, foreign owned dockyards, machine-manufacturing factories and oil mills were built. The influence of foreigners spread far and wide, until many Chinese, emulating the success of these foreign enterprises, began to raise funds for establishing similar modern factories. The Soo Leng (蘇綸) Cotton Mill of Soochow, the Yi Chen (業勤) Cotton Mill of Wusih, and the Tung Chiu Yuan (通久源) Cotton Mill of Ningpo appeared one after another, and "national salvation through industrialization" was the talk of the day. By 1896, there were 5 foreign and 7 Chinese cotton mills, with 417,000 spindles and 2,100 looms in China.[9] The Commercial Press of Shanghai, established in 1897, and the Ta Seng (大生) Cotton Mill of Nantung, established in 1898, were so well managed and rendered so much service to the public that they were regarded as models of modern industry in China. Many silk filatures were also established in Shanghai during this period. By 1902, there were 21 silk filatures with 7,306 reels in Shanghai.[10]

---

8. Kung, op. cit., p. 50.
9. These figures are based on Kung, *A Sketch of China's Industrial Development*, p. 51. Fong's *Cotton Spinning and Weaving Industries of China* gives 519,908 as the total spindlage of that year.
10. Ibid, p. 59.

SHANGHAI INDUSTRIALIZATION

The period of government encouragement. After the conclusion of the Boxer Uprising, the Manchu Government began to realize that military efforts could not make the nation powerful, and that it was necessary to promote commerce and industry. Consequently the Board of Commerce (商部) was established in 1903 for this purpose. Two years later, as the United States refused to admit Chinese laborers into that country, a movement to boycott American goods began in China, and more concrete measures of promoting home production were introduced. The Bureau of Industrial Technique (工藝總局) was established in Tientsin, while an exhibit for the purpose of encouraging modern industries was maintained in Peking. Plans for the building of technical high schools in various provinces, for giving rewards to successful industrialists and for the standardization of weights and measures were made. The Nanyang Tobacco Company of Hongkong was founded at this time. In 1906 the Ministry of Commerce was reorganized into the Ministry of Agriculture, Industry and Commerce, which promulgated regulations concerning rewards to Chinese industrialists. In 1909, the Nanyang Industrial Exposition (南洋勸業會), an unprecedented affair in China, was held in Nanking. By this time, modern industries like cotton spinning, flour milling and silk reeling had decidedly secured a foothold in China, while the manufacturing of woollen fabrics, matches, cement, paper, cigarettes, machinery, glassware, sugar, vegetable oil as well as ship-building and printing industries, had been more or less established. This period lasted eleven years from 1903 to 1913, during which both the Government and people had a better understanding of the importance of commerce and industry, and plans for the recovery of mining and other concessions from foreign firms and for the development of the natural resources by ourselves were made. Hence, this period may be also called the period of "recovering lost rights".

The Golden Age.

The period of flourishing private enterprises. When the World War began in 1914, imports from Europe and America

BRIEF HISTORY

stopped, while Japanese goods were boycotted in the next year on account of the Twenty-One Demands. The Chinese manufacturers therefore enjoyed almost a monopoly of the home market. When the War was over, Europe was so much worse off economically that it was not only unable to send its products to the Far East, but instead, had to import a good deal of Japanese manufactures, and thus diverted them from the Chinese market, where they had just recovered some of their popularity. The Student Movement of May 4, 1919, which resulted in the downfall of the Anfu Party, started a renewed boycott of Japanese goods and helped to drive them away from the Chinese market. These circumstances were most favorable to the development of Chinese industries, and many new factories were established during this period.

As cotton spinning and weaving have been the most important industries of China, and as cotton piece goods used to be our principal imports from England and Japan, the changes wrought by the European War and the Japanese boycott had also the greatest effect on these industries. The weaving mills in China are mostly small in size, and statistics for earlier years are unavailable. On the other hand, continuous statistics have been collected for the cotton spinning industry, which reflect very faithfully the development during the various periods, especially the one under consideration. As most spinning mills have also a large number of weaving looms, their growth indicates also a growth of the cotton weaving industry.

Starting with a very moderate spindlage of 114,712 in 1890 when the first cotton mill was established in Shanghai, the figure first exceeded the one million mark in 1914. By 1925 it went beyond four million, and by 1933, five million.[11] The devlopment during the twelve years before 1925 was of course most rapid, amounting to almost a four-fold increase in the number of spindles. Since that date it was more slow. What was true

---

11. See Table XXXIII, Appendix F, taken from Fong, *Cotton Spinning and Weaving Industries of China.*

of the cotton spinning industry was in general true of other manufacturing enterprises in China, although their development was not so great as that of the former. The period may therefore be considered as that of flourishing private enterprises in the industrial field.

The period of co-operation between Government and people for industrial development. In 1925, the May 30th incident of Shanghai aroused the entire nation. Civil strifes became fewer and encouragement of home-made products was once more the popular slogan. As a result, Chinese industries had another opportunity for development. Many modern factories, particularly those for manufacturing cigarettes, came into existence. After the northern expedition of the Nationalist Army in 1926, and the establishment of the National Government in Nanking the next year, the Ministry of Industries was organized. As it was then still in the time of military operations, the Ministry was not able to accomplish much. When the whole country was united under one government in 1928, political conditions became more stable. The National Government, with a view to carrying out its reconstruction program, organized the Ministry of Industry and Commerce as the highest government organization for the development of industry and commerce in this country. Measures such as the revision and drafting of laws and regulations for the promotion of industries, the organization of expositions, the establishment of manufacturers' banks and emporiums for home goods, were put into effect one after another. Many new Chinese factories appeared. About 4,000 manufacturers participated in the Chinese Home Products Exposition (中華國貨展覽會), but the actual number of existing factories, large and small, perhaps exceeded this number.

In 1929, the Government continued its efforts of encouraging and promoting modern industries. Regulations were promulgated, state industrial enterprises started and private factories encouraged. The system of weights and measures was standardized, industrial registration was enforced, and collection of industrial statistics began. All these measures were unprecedented in the history of

BRIEF HISTORY

Chinese industries. The abolition of the likin system and the gaining back of tariff autonomy particularly contributed to the progress of Chinese industries. However, on account of the world depression, certain industries underwent a decline, but on the whole, China's industries were still progressing. The cause of this, as will be explained in detail in the next chapter, was mainly attributable to the frequently revised tariff rates after the Government had secured tariff autonomy in 1929. Under the increased tariff rates, imported goods must necessarily be sold at higher prices, and it was evident that China's home industries were in a very favorable position for development. That they did develop, especially in Shanghai, can be readily seen from the statistical studies in the following chapters.

The period of general depression. Beginning in 1934, a general decline began to take place in Chinese industries. After the Japanese occupation of Manchuria in 1931, the extensive market of the Three Eastern Provinces was lost to Chinese manufacturers, while the incident also wrought havoc on the markets of South-east China. Next came the communistic disturbances in the Yangtze Valley and North China was constantly under threat of Japanese invasion [12]. In addition, the frequent famines due to droughts and floods aggravated the situation. Rural economy came near bankruptcy and the purchasing power of the people in general decreased. Many unsold commodities accumulated on the markets, and prices dropped to such an extent that manufacturers generally suffered heavy losses. Besides, the world wide economic depression had by this time penetrated China, and the American silver purchasing policy produced currency deflation in this country and destroyed what little hope of recovery on the part of the Chinese manufacturers. Last November, the Government, with a view to stabilizing the currency system and relieving the disintegrating industries, put into effect a currency reform which seemed to have the effect

---

12. This was the feeling prevailing among the Chinese people and was an important deterrent to private enterprises.

of stimulating home industries. The future, however, remains to be seen, and no prediction is yet possible at present.

The development of China's modern industries is in general as described above. In the course of this development, the position of Shanghai has been particularly prominent inasmuch as modern industries started earlier in Shanghai than in most other localities in China, and the number of factories here also much exceeds that of any other place. Consequently, the industrial development of Shanghai deserves a more detailed study. The following is a brief sketch of the development of the principal modern industries in Shanghai.

I. *The Textile Industries.*

The textile industries had a very early beginning in China. The ancient proverb, "Somebody will suffer from cold if any woman fails to weave", proves the antiquated origin of spinning and weaving in China. In former days, however, spinning and weaving were purely handicraft occupations. Modern textile industries did not start until several decades ago. The Kansu Woollen Fabric Manufacturing Bureau, founded by Tso Chung-tang in 1878 was a pioneer in this field. Later, machinery was introduced into cotton spinning, silk reeling and cotton and silk weaving. We will follow the historical development in each of these branches of the textile industry.

1. *Cotton spinning.*

The cotton mill equipped with modern machinery first appeared in Shanghai in 1890, when Li Hung-chang, then Viceroy of Chihli, realizing the importance of the cotton textile industry, established the Machine Cotton Weaving Bureau (機器織布局) and the New Cotton Spinning and Weaving Bureau (紡織新局) in this city. Unfortunately, the former was burnt down in 1893. As the Government did not wish to raise the necessary funds for the re-building of the factory, Li, assisted by Shen Hsuan-hwei, then Customs Superintendent of Tientsin, induced the public to invest in a new cotton mill, known as the Hwa Shen (華盛) Cotton Mill. This mill had 65,000 spindles and 600

BRIEF HISTORY

looms. It started operation in 1893. On account of business losses, it was reorganized several times, and its name changed from Hwa Shen to Yu Hsing (又新), Chi Cheng Yun Chi (集成永記) and San Hsing (三新). At present, it is known as the Shen Hsing 9th Mill (申新第九廠). The other mill, the New Cotton Spinning and Weaving Bureau, also changed its name to Fu Tai (復泰). Later it was bought by Nieh Chung-fu (聶仲甫) and is now called the Heng Feng Cotton Mill (恆豐).[13]

In 1895, the Ta Shun Cotton Mill (大純) was established and the Yu Yuan (裕源) and San Tai (三泰) Mills came into existence the next year. All of these three, however, failed, and were sold to Japanese merchants. Ta Shun became the 1st Mill of the Shanghai Cotton Manufacturing Company in 1920, and San Tai the 2nd Mill. Yu Yuan was reorganized into the 9th Mill of Naigai Wata Kaisha, Ltd.

After 1895, foreigners began to establish factories in China. The Shimonoseki Treaty, signed after the conclusion of the Sino-Japanese War, gave Japanese the right of building and operating factories in Chinese treaty ports. People of other nationalities, by virtue of the most favored nation clause in our treaties with their countries, acquired the same right. Many foreign cotton mills were started in Shanghai. In 1895, the British-owned Ewo Cotton Mill appeared. The next year, the British Lao Kung Mao Cotton Mill, and the German Jui Chi Cotton Mill came into existence. The Hung Yuan (鴻源) Mill, an American enterprise, followed in 1897. The ownership of this mill, however, went to some British interests, and later, to Japanese. It is now known as the 1st Mill of the Japan-China Spinning and Weaving Company. The Jui Chi Mill was bought by a British merchant and its name changed to Tung Fang (東方). In 1928, it came into Chinese hands, and its present name is the Shen Hsing 7th Mill. Lao Kung Mou Cotton Mill now becomes a Japanese factory under the name of Kung Dah 2nd Mill.

---

13. Fong, op. cit., p. 3.

SHANGHAI INDUSTRIALIZATION

In localities other than Shanghai, a number of cotton mills were also built, and the earliest was the Cotton Weaving Bureau (織布局) established by Chang Chih-tung at Wuchang in 1891, being one year after the first cotton mill came into existence in Shanghai. By 1899, there were in operation in China 17 cotton spinning mills. Of this total, 13 were located in the province of Kiangsu and 9 in Shanghai. Five of the nine Shanghai mills were owned by Chinese and the remaining four, by merchants of other nationalities.[14] No new mill appeared during the period from 1899 to 1904, on account of the scarcity of skilled labor and shortage of raw cotton supply, in addition to the then poor banking and communication facilities.

Consequent upon the conclusion of the Russo-Japanese War in 1905, the Far East began to undergo an economic recovery, Considerable progress in banking and communications was made in China, while the production of raw cotton and supply of trained labor also increased. Consequently, manufacturers of cotton goods came under much more favorable conditions. Thirteen cotton mills came into existence during the period from 1905 to 1913. Of this number, eleven were in Kiangsu, one in Chekiang and one in Honan. Six of the eleven Kiangsu mills—namely, Chiu Chen (九成 now Sen Sing No. 2), Cheng Hwa (振華 originally a Sino-British mill, now under Chinese management under the name of Cheng Hwa Li Kee), Kung Yih (公益, a British mill), Tung Chang ,(同昌), and the Naigai Wata Kaisha No. 2 and No. 4 Mills—were located in Shanghai. Two of these six were owned by Chinese interests, and three by foreigners, the remaining one being a Sino-British joint enterprise.

When the Great War broke out in 1914, import of cotton goods from Europe into China suddenly ceased, but Japanese piece goods were still imported to some extent. After its conclusion in 1918, when Japanese products were shipped to Europe to meet the urgent demands there, China was forced to reply on her home products. Chinese cotton goods manufacturers seized this golden opportunity and extended their business. As raw

---

14. Fong, op. cit., p. 5.

BRIEF HISTORY

cotton was then obtainable at low prices, while those of cotton yarn rose disproportionately, all cotton mills gathered very handsome profits. New mills appeared almost annually in the succeeding years. In 1925, 125 cotton mills, with a total spindlage of 3,429,922 were operating in China. Of these, 76, operating 1,897,682 spindles, were owned by Chinese; 45, with a total spindlage of 1,326,920, were Japanese mills and the remaining 4 with 205,320 spindles were British mills.[15] 58 of these mills, consisting of 22 Chinese, 32 Japanese, and 4 British were situated in Shanghai.[16]

The rapid progress made by Japanese mills in China, particularly during the five years after 1920, was the most remarkable feature of this period. From 1921 to 1925, 24 Japanese cotton mills were built in China, five in 1921, eight in 1922, four each in 1923 and 1924, and three in 1925. This rapid increase was largely caused by the revised tariff of 1919, in which the import duty on fine cotton yarn was raised.[17] Japanese manufacturers, in order to avoid paying the increased duty, began to establish mills in this country, especially in Shanghai. These Japanese mills, with their larger capital and higher productive efficiency, were in a much more favorable position than the Chinese mills, and they wielded a great influence in China's cotton industry.

After 1925, the golden age of the Chinese cotton industry was over, but as may be seen from the spindlage statistics in Appendix F, its development continued. However, most writers and many business men consider the industry to have been in a state of continuous decline ever since. What actually happened was that windfall profits were no more realizable, and business had to be carried on on a more conservative basis. While new mills were no more established every year, the existing ones were not losing

---

15. These figures are taken from Fong's book, Table 4 facing p. 13. They disagree with those in Kung, *A Sketch of China's Industrial Development*, p. 126.
16. Kung Chin, *A Statistical Analysis of Industrialization in Chinese Cities*, pp. 56-60.
17. At that time, when China was still under a conventional tariff, the increase consisted of revising the rates of the specific duties in order to make the tariff effective.

money, except when they indulged in speculation. That was really the cause of much of the trouble with this industry. The mill owners had been accustomed to huge profits during the postwar boom, and they could not be satisfied with the reasonable earnings of normal years. Hence they speculated in the cotton and yarn markets and often carried heavy stocks to facilitate such operations. Their interest was no more centered in production. In the case of some mills, speculation became their main business, although there were also mills which shunned such unsound practices. Some 1932, however, the industry has been hit by the general depression and operation has often been suspended.

Following the loss of the Three Eastern Provinces and the Shanghai "War", Jehol and Eastern Hopei were invaded and the former province was occupied by Japanese troops. The yarn market of North China, under such a grave menace, was extremely inactive, transactions being very few and unsold yarn accumulating. In Shanghai alone, accumulated stock once amounted to as much as 168,000 bales. Prices dropped rapidly and in April they reached a point considerably below the cost of production. Chinese cotton mill owners, being fully aware of the gravity of the situation, called a conference to discuss measures of relief. It was decided that, in order that the production of cotton yarn and the amount of unsold stock on the market might be reduced, all Chinese mills should, during the month from April 21 to May 20, 1933, curtail their working capacity by 23%. At the expiration of the period, however, the unfavorable conditions had by no means abated. Consequently, most mills continued to shorten their working hours voluntarily. According to statistics collected at the end of June, 12 Chinese cotton mills with 427,000 spindles were in complete suspension, five mills with 170,000 spindles, ceased to have night shifts, while a number of other mills also reduced their working periods now and then.

On July 1, 1933, the Chinese Cotton Mill Owners' Association proposed that all Chinese mills should suspend their night shifts. However, as the various mills were under diverse conditions, it was difficult to take unanimous action. The mills, therefore, con-

BRIEF HISTORY

tinued to operate under the system of voluntary reduction. It was also decided that no Chinese cotton mills should, either directly or indirectly, deliver yarn to the Chinese Cotton Goods Exchange in order to resist the downward trend of yarn prices. In September and October, the yarn market became more brisk and the accumulated stock began to decrease in quantity. On October 16, the Cotton Control Commission (棉業統制委員會) of the National Economic Council was formally inaugurated to carry out a price-controlling policy by absorbing the surplus yarn on the market and restricting speculation. As a result, yarn prices became more steady. Unfortunately, the Fukien Rebellion broke out. With the large South China market affected by the war, yarn prices again dropped rapidly. The standard yarn quotation went down in December to less than $170, the lowest record in the last ten years .

In 1934, the position of Chinese cotton mills was no better than in the previous year. The quotation of standard yarn fell further to $160.30 in April, a rarely seen phenomenon even in recent years. The principal northern market had gone with the loss of the Three Eastern Provinces, and through the Great Wall paths, which were now no longer in the hands of Chinese authorites, large quantities of cotton piece goods were being smuggled into North China. Consequently, not only the products of Shanghai mills could not be sold in that region, but the northern mills of Shantung and Hopei had to ship theirs southward in search of markets. The cotton yarn market was rendered still more inactive and the quantity of unsold stock, still greater. The heightened export duty on silver in the middle of October, coupled with brisk demands from South China, gave a firmer tone to the market. Owing to the active competition of Japanese mills, however, Chinese manufacturers still felt much difficulty in dealing with the situation.

However, as has been pointed out above, there has been some normal development of this industry even during the very recent period of general depression. It was naturally more rapid down to 1931, along with the development of other industries, but spindlage statistics showed slight increases even after that. The two years between 1931 and 1933 were better than the two following, some 620,000 spindles having been added during the interval. Between 1933 and 1935, on the other hand, the increase was only about half as great, being only 360,000 spindles.[18] Although these statistics refer to the whole country, they reflect also the conditions in Shanghai where a large proportion of the mills are concentrated. These figures disprove the general and often uncontradicted statement that the industry has been in a state of decline ever since 1925.

2. *Cotton weaving.*

On account of China's vast population and the prevailing custom of wearing cotton apparel her consumption of cotton piece goods is enormous. Cotton weaving had a very early beginning in China. Before she came into contact with Western countries in the modern era, the handicraft occupation of weaving had become the duty of almost every woman. Beginning with the reign of Emperor Kuang Hsu, machine weaving mills began to be established. The Machine Cotton Weaving Bureau (織布局) established in Shanghai by Li Hung-chang in 1890 marked the beginning of the modern cotton weaving industry in China, just as the New Cotton Spinning and Weaving Bureau was the first spinning mill. Meanwhile, several other weaving mills came into existence in other localities such as Wuchang, Hangchow, Chengtu, Chungking, Changchow, Kiangyin and Wusih. In the following years, cotton weaving industry progressed rapidly in the interior of China. In Shanghai, the San Yu Industrial Society (三友實業社), with its factory at Yinhsiangkang (引翔港),[19] was established in 1912 with a capital of $4000,000. This was, perhaps, the first large cotton weaving mill which was not a part of a spinning mill. The same year, the Ta Sen Weaving and Dyeing Factory (大森染織廠) came into existence at Tung-

---

18. See Table in Appendix E.
19. A section of Shanghai near Kiangwan.

BRIEF HISTORY

chiatu (董家渡), Pootung.[20] The Ta Feng Dyeing and Weaving Company (達豐染織公司) and the Chun Seng Weaving Factory (羣生布廠) started operations in 1913. The former, having a capital of half a million dollars, produced various varieties of fine cotton fabrics, which, in appearance and quality, compared favorably with imported goods.

After the War broke out in 1914, import of cotton piece goods from Europe and America diminished much in quantity, while the weaving industry in China flourished. Progress in Shanghai, the centre of China's cotton textile industries, was particularly marked. The establishment of new factories was frequent, and spinning mills established after this period were usually equipped with weaving looms. According to the statistics of 1915, the Chinese cotton mills had 2,254 weaving looms. The number increased to 16,381 in 1925, and the productive capacity was estimated at 99,623,000 yards of cotton fabrics annually.[21] These figures serve to prove the fact that the cotton weaving industry had a considerable development after the War. Since then the development of this industry was more or less parallel with that of the cotton spinning industry, although during very recent years the tendency seemed to point to opposite directions, especially in Shanghai.

3. *Silk reeling.*

Although hand-reeled raw silk was exported by China as early as 1516, modern silk filatures were not known to exist in the country until three centuries and a half later, when Chen Chi-yuan (陳啓元) established the first of its kind in 1867 at Namhoi, Kwangtung, after the French pattern. Preceded by two foreign enterprises, the one initiated by a French merchant in 1878 known as the Pao Chang Silk Filature (寶昌), and the other by some Italians in 1880, the first Chinese filature with 100 reeling basins

---

20. Pootung, Chapei, Kaochangmiao, Lunghwa, Hongkew, Zaukadoo, Yangtzepoo, Kiangwan, and Nantao are sections of the Shanghai city. In this chapter we shall refer to them from time to time without further explanations of their location.
21. Kung, op. cit., p. 150.

made its appearance in Shanghai in 1881 under the name of Kung Ho Yung (公和永). At about the same time, two British mills were brought into being by Jardine, Matheson & Company and the Kungping Company, each being installed with 108 reeling basins. Owing to poor management, however, these filatures all failed within a few years, and the Kungping Mill was reorganized into Chi Chang (旗昌). The silk industry became more prosperous by 1888. The Kung Ho Yung Mill was enlarged by the addition of 800 reels, and within the following eight years three more Chinese filatures were established, namely, Jui Lun (瑞綸), Hsin Chang (信昌) and Lun Hwa (綸華). The Hsin Chang, in spite of having gone through reorganization more than once, is still in operation and considered to be the best and largest filature in Shanghai, but the other two have both been dismantled.[22]

Prior to 1909, China's raw silk export had always been in excess of that from Japan and constituted from 20% to 30% of her total annual export trade, but beginning from that year, the situation has changed in favor of Japan. France had been the principal market for Chinese silk, but during the Great War, her purchasing power for luxuries was reduced to nil, and China's raw silk trade suffered accordingly. Meanwhile, Japan succeeded in developing the American market, which was least affected by the War, and her silk export trade thus greatly expanded. The industry in Shanghai nevertheless showed some development, the number of its silk filatures having increased from 35 with 11,085 reeling basins in 1909 to 61 with 16,692 reeling machines in 1916, but this was probably due to increased domestic demand for steam filature product in preference to handreeled silk.[23]

In 1917, under the joint sponsorship of the French Chamber of Commerce and the Kiangsu-Chekiang-Anhwei Silk and Cocoon Association (江浙皖絲繭公會), seconded by the British, American and Japanese Chambers of Commerce and other foreign silk interests in Shanghai, the International Committee for the Im-

---

22. D. K. Lieu, *The Silk Reeling Industry in Shanghai*, pp. 1 and 31.
23. Lieu, op. cit., p. 5.

provement of Sericulture (中國合衆蠶桑改良會) was formed, and received financial support from the Ministry of Finance for its maintenance. In the ten years from 1917 to 1926, the industry grew rather slowly from 70 filatures with 18,386 reeling basins to 81 filatures with 18,664 reeling basins, but the quality of their product was improved.[24]

After the inauguration of the National Government, many reforms were introduced on China's own initiative, and the number of Shanghai filatures continued to increase until in April, 1930, there were no less than 107 filatures and 25,395 reeling basins in operation, the highest record ever reached before or since.[25] For as an article of luxury, the demand for silk is very elastic, and foreign consumption was greatly curtailed on account of the depression. By November of the same year, all but one of the 107 filatures remained in operation. This was, of course, partly due to the seasonal character of the industry, which often had to suspend operations when the supply of cocoons from any crop, especially the spring one, was exhausted. In former years, however, a number of filatures usually continued to operate even in the winter by making use of cocoons kept in stock, and certainly when the next season began, nearly all of them would resume manufacturing activities. This time the industry was very badly hit by a sudden curtailment of foreign demand, and in 1931 only 70 filatures were in operation at the height of the season.

Thus, long before other Shanghai industries suffered from the effect of the world depression, the silk filatures had got into a very precarious position. This situation lasted several years until 1935, when a combination of circumstances brought about some revival in the industry. Prices of raw silk had gone up to a slight extent, due to economic recovery in the West, and the quality of cocoons had been much improved, thanks to the efforts of the National and Provincial Governments. The cocoons from the improve breeds were sold at $101 a picul (May, 1935), and due to their better quality, 20% more of raw silk could be reeled

---

24. Ibid.
25. Ibid.

from the same quantity, as compared with the cocoons raised by the old fashioned methods. Yet the latter used to fetch $219 a picul in May, 1930. The saving in the cost of production to the filatures was therefore as much as 61.6%. Hence, while other industries, especially cotton spinning, were suffering from the general depression since 1934, silk reeling, on the other hand, was gradually regaining its lost ground. Statistical data about this industry may be found in Chapters III and VI, as well as Appendix F.

4. *Silk weaving*.

Silk weaving as a modern industry in China, evolving from a family handicraft system of ancient origin, dates back only two decades and a half. While the Fu Hwa Silk Weaving Company (物華絲織股份有限公司), established in 1915, was the first of its kind to appear in Shanghai, followed by Ching Yun (錦雲), Chung Hwa Kung Yeh (中華工業), Wen Chi (文記), etc., the Mayar Silk Weaving Factory (美亞織綢廠), founded five years later, has the distinction of being the largest, not alone in Shanghai, but in whole China.[26] Its expansion has been such that it to-day operates 10 weaving mills jointly, besides the May Ni Finishing and Dyeing Works (美藝染煉廠), the Mei Chang Pattern Making co-operative Society (美章紋製合作社), and the Mei Ching Warp and Woof Factory (美經經緯廠).

As early as 1922, with the help of imported machinery, the Mayar concern began to turn out light silks and crepes after European and Ameican patterns, which enjoyed such good sales that it gave a strong impetus to other manufacturers to follow suit, heralding the beginning of a new era in the silk weaving industry. Unfortunately, in the autumn of the same year, the price of raw silk began to rise, until in September of the following year, the unprecedented figure of $1,950 per picul was reached, causing heavy losses to all silk weavers. Conditions became better in 1924 and improved the more in 1925 and 1926, when several new factories, including Wei Cheng (緯成), Yueh Hwa (悅

---

26. Kung, op. cit., p. 165.

BRIEF HISTORY

華), Tien Cheng (天成) and Yueh Hsin were established, and those in operation were all doing fairly good business. The silk weaving industry was then at its peak of prosperity in China.

From 1927 on to 1929 the industry suffered a decline due to high cost of production brought about by labor strikes, increase in French Indo-China's import duty on Chinese silk goods, and usurpation of the market by imported artificial silk goods, with shipments to French Indo-China alone dwindling from 3,822 piculs worth 4,504,077 Haikwan taels in 1926 to 1,361 piculs and 1,485, 590 Haikwan taels in 1929.

After 1929 the Chinese weavers began to import rayon from abroad, and produced a variety of fabric with cotton woof and rayon warp known as *ti* (綈), which became very popular on the market, returning handsome profits to the producers. New investors came to be interested in the industry, and new factories sprang into existence for the manufacture of this fabric. The situation was made still more favorable by the drop in the price of raw silk in April and June from 1,280 to 1,100 Haikwan taels per picul. After July, 1931, however, on account of the Great Yangtze flood, which affected more than 10 provinces and greatly reduced the purchasing power of the people in just as many provinces, the silk piece goods market was nearly in complete suspension, and unsold stock began to accumulate, forcing out of existence a great many small factories. The Mayar Mills, possessing other markets besides the Yangtze Valley one, was, on the other hand, able to increase its annual output to 192,794 pieces and its total business turnover to $5,600,000.[27]

In 1932 the situation was further aggravated by the Sino-Japanese conflict in Shanghai, which forced the many Chinese silk weaving factories situated in Hongkew, Yangtzepoo and Chapei to suspend operations, some being even burnt to the ground, as was the case of the Chen Yeh Wei Chi Silk Factory (振業維記織綢廠), a concern of considerable size situated

---

27. Information supplied by Mr. Tsai Sheng-pai, General Manager of the Mayar Mills.

near Kiangwan. Although the hostilities lasted only one month, most of the factories could not resume operations for a long time.

In the spring of 1933, demands from the South Seas were brisk, so many of the hitherto closed factories resumed work, showing some sign of revival in the silk weaving industry. Speculators, however, began to appear at this time, who, with rented buildings and machinery, operated only when the market was favorable, thus creating disturbance to the entire industry.

Conditions in 1934 became very bad. Prices of silk fabrics dropped by nearly 50%. The majority of the silk weaving factories were forced to wind up, and those which remained in operation were doing so at a loss, and were confronted with labor troubles because of proposed reductions in wages. By the end of February, there were only 200 factories actively engaged in production, of which the Mayar Mills, with 1,056 looms, were the most important.[28]

5. *Wool weaving and spinning.*

The manufacturing of woollen fabrics by means of machinery began in China when Tso Chung-tang founded in 1878 the Kansu Wool Weaving Bureau (甘肅織呢總局), a factory with 22 looms and 900 spindles. Cheng Hsiao-hsu (鄭孝胥) established the Jih Hui Woollen Fabrics Factory (日暉織呢廠), with 44 weaving looms and 1,750 spindles at Jih Hui Chiao (日暉橋), Shanghai.[29] This marked the beginning of wool weaving in this city. However, it was closed down in 1910. A little later it was taken over by the Government. In 1919, a number of merchants leased this factory from the Government at an annual rental of 14,000 taels, and operated it under the name of the First China Woollen Yarn Factory.[30] Only the spinning department, however, was in operation, while the weaving department was still left idle.

---

28. Number of looms taken from pamphlet of the Mayar Mills.
29. *Modern Industries of Shanghai,* published by the Shanghai Bureau of Social Affairs, p. 187.
30. Ibid, p. 188.

BRIEF HISTORY

In recent years, some development was apparent in the wool spinning and weaving industry here. The Chun An Woollen Yarn Factory (均安絨線廠) situated at Zonfeng Road, Hongkew, and the Wei I Woollen Yarn Factory (唯一絨線廠) on Chungking Road, were both established before 1921. After 1921 the industry progressed at a more brisk pace. The Sien Ta Wool Spinning and Weaving Factory (先達呢絨紡織廠) came into existence, immediately followed by Shen Ta (勝達), Wei Luen (緯綸) and Tien Hsiang (天祥). The principal product of these factories was camel wool linings. In order to avoid cutthroat competition among the various mills, a joint sales office was organized in 1929, and it accomplished much in resisting foreign competition and securing uniformity of prices. By 1930 the once very popular imported camel wool linings were almost entirely eliminated from Chinese markets.

The Ta Hwa Woollen Fabrics Factory (大華呢絨廠), which began to produce fabrics like serges, etc., appeared in 1929. All raw materials, such as wool and cotton yarn, used by this factory, were imported. The next year the Chang Hwa Company (章華毛絨公司) was established. This concern possessed a well equipped factory of considerable size. It spun woollen yarn and thread for its own use and produced all kinds of shirtings and coatings. In size and variety of products this concern ranked first in the Chinese wool weaving industry. In 1931 about a dozen wool weaving factories, Ta Chung Kuo (大中國), Ta Dah (大達), Chung Hwa (中華), etc., came into existence. After 1933, as the whole country has been in an economic depression, all of these factories have found it difficult to dispose of their products. Not only no new factories have appeared, but even the existing ones are in a precarious position.

II. *Apparel Manufacturing Industries*

1. *Knitting.*

The knitting industry did not begin in China until the middle of the reign of Emperor Kuang Hsu, when imported socks, singlets, etc., began to enjoy great popularity in China, and a number of hand knitting machines were brought into this country. The Ching Luen Knitting Factory (景綸針織廠), established in 1902, was the first of its kind in Shanghai. It specialized in the manufacture of singlets and shorts. The Su Luen (蘇綸) Knitting Factory, which specialized in the manufacture of hosiery, was established in Hangchow about the same time. In 1909, the Tung Hsing Hosiery Factory (東新襪廠), situated at Tangshan Road, Shanghai, started operations. Power driven knitting machines began to be imported into China in 1912, and the Ching Pu Hosiery Factory (進步襪廠), situated at Paoyuan Road, Chapei, was the first Shanghai manufacturer equipped with power driven machines. After Ching Pu, the Ching Hsing Knitting Factory (景星針織廠) appeared.

After the Great War broke out in 1914, as imported knitted goods disappeared from the market, the demand for home-made articles of this line far exceeded the supply, and new knitting factories sprang into existence in large numbers, not only in Shanghai, but also in other places like Tientsin, Hankow, Peiping, Wusih, Kiangyin, Tsingtao, Chungking, Wuchang, Liaoning and Yinkow. A great many varieties of articles, including lace, towels, scarfs, singlets and shorts, were produced, hosiery being the most important. Most of these new factories were very small in scale, and about 80% to 90% of them used only hand-operated machines. In addition to the factories, it was not infrequent that several families bought or rented a machine jointly and let their members produce knitting goods with it, as a hand machine cost only a comparatively small sum of money, while its monthly rental was only a dollar or two.

By 1926 there were more than 50 hosiery knitting mills, not including manufacturing families, in Shanghai alone. About a half of them, such as the Chung Hwa First Knitting Factory (中華第一針織廠), the Ching Pu Hosiery Factory (進步), the Kung Cho Hosiery Factory (工足襪廠), etc., were fairly large in size and equipped with power driven machines. By that time, machinery works in Shanghai were already able to produce knitting machines, which were much cheaper than imported articles. As a result,

BRIEF HISTORY

more knitting factories came into existence. In 1928, there were no less than 100 knitting factories in Shanghai, of which 35 were equipped with power driven machines.[31] The products of these factories are in no way inferior to imported articles, and consequently, they are not only poular at home, but also welcomed in markets abroad.

III. *Manufacturing of Foodstuffs and Beverages*
1. *Flour milling*.

Formerly, very crude methods were used in Chinese flour mills, and flour milling was regarded as one of the handicrafts. After China came into contact with the western countries, flour shipments into China increased steadily in quantity. Under the supposition that they supplied the need of the foreign residents in China, these shipments were exempt from Customs duty, but actually, considerable quantities were consumed by the Chinese. The value of flour imports in 1910 amounted to as much as 3,400,000 Haikwan taels in value, and the business of Chinese old style mills was seriously affected.

In 1886 some German merchants established the Chen Yu Flour Mill (正裕麵粉廠) in Shanghai,[32] while the Tsen Yu Flour Mill (增裕粉廠), a British enterprise, appeared shortly after the Sino-Japanese War. The latter produced the "Three Horses" brand flour, which was well received by consumers. After the establishment of this mill, many Chinese merchants became interested in flour milling. Sun To-seng (孫多森) of Shouchow organized the Pu Feng Flour Milling Company (阜豐麵粉公司), which had its factory on Mukanshan Road, Shanghai, in 1898. Other early mills in Shanghai were Hwa Hsing (華興), Yu Feng (裕豐), Shen Ta (申大) and Li Ta (立大).

During the Great War, when flour shipments from other countries were cut off, all Chinese mills prospered. Many of

---

31. Kung, op. cit., p. 177.
32. Foreign factories were allowed to be established in the foreign settlements in Shanghai even before the treaty ports were thrown open to them by the Shimonoseki Treaty.

them made extensions or built new mills. As a result, China became not only self-sufficient in this important foodstuff, but was able to dispose a surplus on foreign markets. Annual flour exports always exceeded imports. According to an investigation made between 1920 and 1921 by the British Chamber of Commerce in Shanghai, there were 51 flour mills distributed over various localities in the Yangtze Valley. Shanghai alone had 22 mills. The total number of flour mills in the country then amounted to 123.[33]

After 1921 all countries tried strenuously to regain their foreign markets, and China's flour milling industry began to come under less favorable conditions. Flour imports increased in quantity while exports decreased, and there was an excess of imports over exports every year. As wheat was then sold at a high price, while that of flour had fallen, a number of Chinese mills were reorganized or closed down. Although several new mills came into existence, they could not compare with those established in former years. According to the statistics concerning the distribution of flour mills in China published in 1928 by the former Bureau of Economic Information, there were in all 193 flour mills in the country. Of this number, 73 were in the Three Eastern Provinces, 71 in the Yangtze Valley and 49 in other places. Of the 71 in the Yangtze Valley, 27 were in Shanghai. In regard to the dates of their establishment, those of 176 mills were known. 37 were founded before the advent of the Republic, 117 during the period from 1912 to 1921 and 22 between 1922 and 1928.[34] From these figures it is clearly shown that the development of the flour milling industry in China was most rapid during the period from 1912 to 1921, and that progress has been much slower since the latter year. What was true of the whole country was also true of Shanghai.

The history of flour milling in Shanghai is briefly as stated above. Three stages may be seen in its course of development. The first period, from 1886 to 1911, was a time in which new

---
33. Kung, op. cit., p. 186.
34. *Chinese Economic Journal*, Vol. II, No. 6, pp. 533-541.

mills were constructed, production increased and the quality of products was being improved, resulting in wider markets and handsome profits to the mills. It may, therefore, be called the stage of start and development. The second period included those years between 1912 and 1921, corresponding roughly to the time of the European War. During this period, as most European and American countries were directing their efforts towards winning the War, and later towards rehabilitation, flourr import into China decreased much in quantity and Chinese flour was exported. From 1918 to 1921, the annual flour shipment from China usually amounted to more than 2,000,000 piculs, and in 1920 it rose to 4,000,000 piculs, valued at from 17,000,000 to 18,000,000 Haikwan taels.[35] Many new flour mills came into existence during this period.

The third period began with 1922 and continued to the present time. After the European War, the foreign trade of most countries began to recover. Meanwhile, China has been in a critical moment on account of internal disturbances and foreign invasion. Owing to bad crops, poor quality of native wheat and disrupted communication systems, which have prevented wheat produced in the interior to reach Shanghai and other flour milling centers, mills often experience a shortage of raw material. Consequently, wheat and flour imports have risen in amount and the latter has dominated the market. Chinese flour mills, thus seriously affected, have suffered heavy losses, and a number of them have closed down.

2. *Cigarette making.*

Cigarettes were unknown to China until she came into contact with western countries. After their introduction into this country, however, being at first regarded as a novelty, they have gained in popularity. In 1902 the British-American Tobacco Company established a factory in Shanghai for manufacture of cigarettes.[36] The

---

35. *Modern Industries of Shanghai*, p. 227. Elsewhere, all foreign trade figures cited in this and other chapters are directly quoted from the Chinese Customs Reports of the respective years.
36. Ibid, p. 248.

products of this factory, particularly the "Pinhead" and "'Pirate" brands, were widely sold. In addition to the one in Shanghai, factories were built by this company in Hankow, Tientsin, Liaoning, Harbin and Fangtze (Shantung).

Cigarette making by Chinese began in 1906. A boycott against American goods started about that time, and the movement of encouraging home industries gained strength. The Peiyang Tobacco Company (北洋烟草公司) was established in Tientsin, and the Nanyang Tobacco Company (南洋烟草公司) in Hongkong. Owing to its limited capital and poor products, which compared very unfavorably with imported articles, the former closed down not long after its establishment. The Nanyang Tobacco Company also failed, but later it was reorganized by Chien Chao-nan (簡照南) into the Nanyany Brothers Tobacco Company. According to the result of an investigation made in 1909, there were in this country 16 cigarette making factories of which 4 were owned by foreign interests.[37]

With a view to extending his business to the north, Chien Chao-nan, seizing the opportunity offered by the diminished cigarette imports during the European War, came to Shanghai and established in 1916 a factory of large size on Broadway Road. In 1919, he reorganized the Nanyang Brothers Tobacco Company, which had been an unlimited concern previously, into a corporation of limited liability with a capital of $15,000,000. After the May 30th incident of 1925, the movement for the encouragement of home-made goods came into full sway. The total output of existing Chinese owned cigarette factories fell far below the demand for home-made cigarettes. Consequently, many factories with small capitalization appeared in Shanghai. Statistics show that during the four year period from 1924 to 1927, the number of cigarette factories in Shanghai increased by 13 times, as there were 14 factories in 1924, 51 in 1925, 105 in 1926 and 182 in 1927.[38] Of these 182, only a small number, such as Nanyang, Hwa Chen (華成),

---

37. Hsu Yen-so, *A Brief History of Chinese Industries*, Vol. II, Chap. I, p. 23.
38. Kung Chin, *A Statistical Analysis of Industrialization in Chinese Cities*, p. 69.

BRIEF HISTORY

Chung Nan (中南), Ta Tung (大東), Fu Chang (福昌), etc., were comparatively large in scale, while the remaining ones each had a capital ranging from a few thousand dollars to between $10,000 and $20,000. During those years, sales of home-made cigarettes were very brisk, and all of these factories prospered.

The number of cigarette factories in Shanghai, however, began to decline gradually after 1928. It fell to 94 in 1928, 79 in 1929, 65 in 1930, 64 in 1931 (according to our own survey of that year, there were only 51 in operation) and 60 in 1932.[39] Our second survey in 1933 revealed the fact that only 45 cigarette factories were up to the standard set by the Factory Law. This great decrease in the number of factories did not really mean, as those in the business would have us believe, that the industry was declining. The simultaneous appearance of a large number of them several years ago was not a sign of healthy development in the industry. Like the cotton spinning mills, many small cigarette factories were established during the post-war boom to reap the unusual profits created by the circumstances. They were not in a position to stand any competition, and their closing down was to be reasonably expected.

In the later years, although the number decreased, those remained grew in size, or were otherwise put on a sounder basis. It was through such a process of elimination that the comparatively large mills, such as Hwa Chen, Ta Tung, Chung Nan, etc., have emerged from the multitude. Our 1933 survey showed that the value of output of this industry in that year was considerably higher than in 1931. The presence or absence of the small mills was of no consequence. We rather believe that even now there are still too many small factories which have neither adequate capital nor proper equipment to turn out cigarettes on a regular business basis. Most of them lead a precarious existence by manufacturing low grade cigarettes to the order of their customers, and in many cases they have only a machine or two for the final process of rolling the cigarettes, depending on the larger factories for the supply of all intermediate products. This is why they are so easily affected

---

39. Ibid.

SHANGHAI INDUSTRIALIZATION

by the recent appearance of hand-rolled cigarettes sold by small peddlers.

IV. *Machine Manufacturing.*

The development of machine manufacturing, the foundation of all other industries, is indicative of the degree of a country's industrialization. In Shanghai, where China's industries are concentrated, this industry has advanced considerably ahead. The Shanghai Dock and Engineering Company, Ltd., which specializes in shipbuilding and repairing of ship's machinery, was first established by British merchants in 1851. Chinese enterprise along this line began in 1862, when Li Hung-chang, realizing the power of modern ammunition in the suppression of the Taiping rebellion, founded a munition factory in Shanghai. Three factories of similar nature were built by him in Soochow, the management of them being estrusted to Ting Shih-chang (丁日昌), Han Tien-chia (韓殿甲), and a foreign engineer. In 1865 Ting Shih-chang bought a machinery factory in Shanghai which he merged with Li"s munition fcatory two years later.[40] This new mill, situated at Kao Chang Miao (高昌廟), was called the Kiangnan Manufacturing Bureau (江南製造總局) and is now known as the Kiangnan Dockard. It was purely a Government enterprise. The Yuan Chang Machinery Factory (源昌機器五金廠), established by Chu Ta-chun (祝大椿) in 1883, was the first private concern of its kind. Later the Yuan Chang Iron Works (遠昌鐵工廠) established by Li Yuan-yun (李遠篔) a Kwantung merchant, and the Chien Chang Iron Works (建昌鐵廠) by a man named Ling (林) appeared. The Kung Mou Machinery Factory (公茂機器廠), situated at Pai Lien Ching (白蓮涇), the Chih Feng Machinery Factory (熾豐機器廠) on Ward Road, the Tai Chu Yuan Iron Works (戴聚源鐵工廠) and the Jung Chang (鎔昌) Machinery Works all came into existence before 1901.[41] Owing to limited capital, the work of these factories was confined to the

---

40. Kung, *A Sketch of China's Industrial Development*, p. 15.
41. *Chinese Year Book*, 1935, p. 1132, and *Industrial Handbook of China Kiangsu*, p. 775.

BRIEF HISTORY

repairing of machines and the production of machine parts and accesories.

In 1902 the Ta Lung Iron Works (大隆鐵工廠) was established with a capital of $500,000 on the northern bank of Siao Sha Tu, Shanghai. This factory was able to produce textile machinery and Diesel engines and was thus the first Chinese manufacturer of complete machines.[42] The next year, Chu Chi-yao (朱志堯) established the Chiu Hsing Factory (求新廠), a shipbuilding and machine manufacturing works with a capital of 600,000 taels, at Nan Ma Tou (南碼頭). It failed in 1919 and became a Sino-French concern with its capital enlarged to 1,200,000 tales. The Wo Hsin Iron Works (和興鐵廠) at Pootung, which was closed down for many years but re-opened last year, also came into existence at about this time. It is the only machine works that has a smelting plant.

After Ta Lung and Chiu Hsin, many machine works and shops appeared. During the European War, when less machinery was imported, the development of this industry was particularly rapid. Among the notable works were the Hwa Seng Electric Manufacturing Factory (華生電器製造廠), established by Yi Yu-chai (葉友才) in Hongkew in 1916, and specializing in the manufacture of such electric machinery as generators, transformers, ect., and the Ming Tsing Machinery Factory (明精機器廠) built by Chang Ching-ling (章錦林) in Chapei in the same year and specializing in producing printing machines. The China Iron Works Company, Ltd. (中國鐵工廠), which produces textile machines, was founded by Nieh Yun Tai (聶雲台) in Woosung in 1921. A number of other factories are at present engaged in the production of machinery used by various industries, such as cigarette making, rubber manufacturing, knitting, cotton ginning and flour milling. A still larger number, being smaller in scale, do only repair work.

Although in regard to the number of factories, the growth of the machine manufacturing industry in Shanghai may be consider-

---

42. Ibid.

ed fairly rapid, most of the factories are very small in size and in capitalization, their principal work being repairing. Even the larger ones are often only able to produce machine parts. Only a very few of them can turn out complete sets of machinery. Consequently, machinery for cotton spinning, flour milling, paper making and sugar refining, needed by newly established factories, still have to be imported from abroad.

V. *Leather and Rubber Goods.*

1. *Tanning*

Tanning, with its origin dating back to 3,000 years ago, has had a very long history in China. In former days, it was a handicraft occupation, and the processes employed were very crude. Modern tanning did not begin until China came into contact with the western countries. Since then chemicals instead of natural products have been the principal tanning materials used in this industry. The Peiyang Tannery (北洋硝皮廠) of Tientsin, established by Wu Mou-ting (吳懋鼎) in 1898, was the first modern tanning factory in China. Others began to appear in Shanghai and Chengtu a little later. In 1904 a number of British merchants established the Shanghai Tanning Company, which was soon followed by three other tanneries, Yi Yuan (怡源), Lung Hua (龍華) and Chi Hsin (啓新). The Lung Hua Tannery was later bought over by Japanese merchants at a low price. Its name was changed to the Chung Hwa Tanning Factory (中華製革廠), and its capital increased to $800,000. The Way's Tannery (喊士皮廠), founded in 1909, was also a foreign enterprise, but it went into the hands of a group of Kwangtung merchants and was moved to Chueh Chia Chiao (屈家橋) of this city. In 1915 the Ching I Tanning Factory (精益製革廠) with a capital of $250,000 was built at Ku Chia Wan (顧家灣), Chapei. It soon established a branch factory at Pa Tze Kiao (八字橋). Other tanneries like Lau Yun Seng (老永森), and Ching Hsueh Chi (金燮記) came into existence in 1919.[43]

---

43. *Industrial Handbook of China, Kiangsu*, p. 726.

BRIEF HISTORY

The Kiangnan Tanning Factory (江南製革廠), a Sino-Japanese concern at first, was established at Tan Tsu Wan (潭子灣) with a capital of $150,000. It became later a pure Japanese concern, and its capital was enlarged to $500,000. This concern and the Chung Hua Tanning Factory, also Japanese-owned, had a total capital of $1,300,000, and were regarded as the leading tanneries in Shanghai. The Shanghai Tannery, an Italian concern, was established on Brenan Road with a capital of $140,000.[44] Although smaller than the two Japanese concerns, this factory was still much larger than most tanneries owned by Chinese. The Asia Tannery (亞州製革廠) was established on Kiangwan Road in 1924. The Ta Nan Tannery (大南皮革廠), which was reorganized into the Ta Chung Tanning Company (大中製革公司) in 1931 appeared in 1928. The next year, the Ta Hwa Tannery (大華製革廠) came into existence. This factory was also reorganized sometime later and its name changed to Ta Hwa Chang Chi (大華昌記). Among the Chinese Mills, Ching I (精益) is considered the largest one with Ta Hwa following next.

In addition to the modern tanneries mentioned above, many old style tanneries, known as *pi-chang* (皮廠) or *pi-fang* (皮坊) are in existence in regions around the West Gate and in Chapei. The number of these tanneries amounted in 1928 to more than 200, according to the result of an investigation made in that year by the Bureau of Social Affairs, while there were only ten modern tanning factories in Shanghai.[45] This shows that in this industry the latter has not yet displaced the former. It must also be remembered that although the *pi-fang* do not employ modern machinery, they generally use imported chemicals in the tanning process.

2. *Rubber goods manufacturing.*

Rubber goods manufacturing started in 1917 when the Kwangtung Brothers Rubber Goods Company (廣東兄弟樹膠公司) was established in Canton by several overseas Chinese. This con-

---
44. *Economic Year Book of China*, 1934, p. k. 515.
45. *The Industries of Shanghai*, pp. 48-49.

cern produced rubber overshoes as its principal line. In 1920 the Kiangwan Model Factory (江灣模範工廠) in Shanghai established a rubber goods department for the manufacture of toys, soles and overshoes. This marked the beginning of this industry in Shanghai. At that time, however, the market for Chinese rubber goods was not so good, and this factory failed a few years later on account of financial difficulties. Nevertheless, a number of new factories appeared later in Kwangtung. In Shanghai, no new factory came into existence until 1927, when the Yi Chang Rubber Goods Factory (義昌橡膠廠) was established by Shih Chih-shan (石芝珊), a student who had studied in Japan. This factory was situated on Tongshan Road. The "Pa Chi" (八吉牌華 brand overshoe, its principal product, was once very popular in the country. Sometime later, however, owing to the fact that prices of raw materials dropped severely, and the factory thus incurred large losses for having bought heavily when prices were high, it was sold to the Chen Tai Factory (正泰橡膠廠).[46]

In 1928 the Ta Chung Hwa Rubber Goods Factory (大中橡膠廠) was established by Hsueh Fu-chi (薛福基), upon his return from an investigation tour in Japan. This factory was large in scale and well equipped and is now regarded as the leading rubber goods manufacturer in Shanghai. Overshoes and sport shoes produced by this factory, bearing the "Double Coin" (雙錢牌) brand, have a very good market owing to their good quality. After 1928 a great many new factories came into existence in Shanghai. According to our investigation made in 1931, there were no less than 30 rubber goods factories in this city. The Sino-Japanese conflict of Shanghai in 1932 destroyed several of the factories situated in Chapei, such as Kuo Ming (國民), Teh Chang (德昌), Hou Seng (厚生) and Fu Sing (福星). However, as the Anti-Japanese boycott was at its height after the conflict, no Chinese would then buy Japanese rubber goods. Consequently the products of Chinese factories were in good demand and new factories continued to be established. According to our second investigation made in 1933, when only larger

---

46. *Economic Year Book of China,* 1934, p. k. 552.

mills were included, the number increased to 44. Since 1933 only the larger factories are able to carry on, while the smaller ones are in danger of being eliminated.

VI. *Chemical Industries.*

1. *Match maufacturing.*

In former years all matches used in China were imported. The earliest match shipments came to China after 1860. Being a convenient article of daily use, this imported article at once gained much popularity. Consequently the Chu Chang Match Factory (聚昌火柴廠), the shares of which were mostly held by the Government, was established in 1894 in Chungking, Szechuan. Thus started the match industry in China. The Ho Feng Match Factory (和豐) of Changsha and Hsueh Chang Match Factory (燮昌) of Hankow, two private concerns, both appeared in 1897. After that year a number of match factories came into existence in various localities. As the manufacturing of matches requires no great capital nor advanced technique, it is comparatively easy to set up a factory. Consequently, this industry is quite evenly distributed in China, factories being found in almost every province.

Match manufacturing in Shanghai began in 1904 when Yi Chen-chung (葉澄衷) established the Hsueh Chang Match Factory (燮昌火柴廠) on Tongshan Road. The Ying Chang Match Factory (熒昌火柴廠), situated at Luchiatu (陸家渡), Pootung came into existence in 1908. The Li Ming Factory (利民火柴廠) was established in 1918. The Chung Hwa Factory (中華廠) appeared in 1920, and the Yu Chang Factory (裕昌) in 1922.[47] After 1922 the Ta Hwa (大華), Hwa Ming (華明), and Chung Kuo (中國) factories were established. The Li Ming and Yu Chang factories failed not long after their establishment. The Ying Chang Factory built successively two branch factories in Chinkiang and Shanghai. In 1930, this factory, in order to secure the advantages of large scale production and enough strength to

---

47. Kung, op. cit. p. 204.

SHANGHAI INDUSTRIALIZATION

compete with foreign manufacturers, merged with the Chung Hwa Match Factory and the Hung Seng Match Factory of Soochow. The new concern was henceforth known as the Ta Chung Hwa Match Company (大中華火柴公司). Afterwards, this company further acquired control of Ying Chang of Hankow, Yu Seng (裕生) of Kiukiang, etc. Its capital has now been increased to $2,400,000, and it is now the leading match manufacturing concern in China.

The Hwa Chang Match Stick and Box Company (華昌梗片廠), established in 1915 at Chang Chia Pang (張家浜), Pootung, was the first of its kind in Shanghai. The Chiu Chi Match Stick Factory (久記製梗廠) was built in 1918, the Hsin Ming (新民製梗廠), in the next year, and the Hou Seng (厚生製梗廠) in 1927.[48] The Ta Chung Hwa Match Stick and Box Factory (大中華梗片廠) was established by the match company bearing the same name in 1934 at Tungkou (東溝), Pootung. Besides these, there were some foreign match factories in China, the Japanese being the most prominent. At present, however, there is only one foreign factory, Jui Seng (燧生廠) in Shanghai. This factory was originally a branch factory of the Jui Seng Match Company of Chinking (鎮江燧生火柴公司), but was later bought by the Japanese. In 1931 the management of this concern went into the hands of Mei Kwang Company, an American concern.

2. Enamelware manufacturing.[49]

Enamelware manufacturing is also an industry that came late into being in this country. During 1914 and 1915 the total annual import of enamelware always exceeded $3,000,000 in value. In 1916 an American merchant established at Ku Chia Wan, Chapei, the Kwang Ta Enamelware Factory (廣大搪磁廠), producing

---

48. Ibid.
49. This industry is classified under the chemical group because the manufacturing process is a chemical process, the metallic body being supplied by other factories. A special account is given of it here as its development involves some special features.

BRIEF HISTORY

cups, lunch holders, etc. This marked the beginning of the manufacture of enamelware in Shanghai. The Kwang Tah Enamelware Factory (廣達搪磁廠) came into existence after its inauguration and was later reorganized into the Yi Feng Factory (益豐). The Kwang Ta Factory also failed after that and went into the hands of Hsu Tao-seng (徐道生), a Chinese merchant, who reorganized it into the Chu Feng Enamelware Company (鑄豐搪磁公司). The erstwhile American owner was retained as engineer and extensions were made.[50] Basins and oil stoves manufactured by this concern were well received by the public.

The Ting Feng Factory (鼎豐搪磁廠), founded by Yao Mu-lien (姚慕蓮), and the Industrial and Commercial Company (工商公司), an enterprise of Wang I-ting (王一亭) and his Japanese friends, soon came into existence. The Chung Hwa Vocational School also set up an enamelware making department. Sometime later the Ting Feng Factory and the Industrial and Commercial Company both suspended operations owing to poor business while the Chung Hwa Vocational School reorganized its enamelware department into the Chung Hwa Enamelware Company, Ltd. (中華琺瑯股份有限公司).[51] After the May 30th incident of Shanghai, the movement of boycotting against imported goods and encouraging home-made products was at its very height, while overseas Chinese, with a view to helping their mother country economically, bought, whenever possible, Chinese made articles of daily use, including enamelware. In 1925 exports of Chinese enamelware began to be recorded in the Customs Returns and the import figures decreased. Owing to the large demands at home, the manufacturing of enamelware in China prospered more and more.

As the existing factories could not produce sufficient products to meet current demands, many new ones came into existence. The Chao Feng Factory (兆豐琺瑯廠) was built in 1925, the Wei Wei Factory (微微琺瑯廠) in 1926, the Hwa Feng Factory

---

50. *Special Pamphlet of Shanghai National Goods Exhibition.*
51. *Modern Industries of Shanghai*, pp. 118-119.

SHANGHAI INDUSTRIALIZATION

(華豐) in 1929 and the Chiu Hsing Factory (求新) in 1930. The Hwa Feng, Yi Feng, Chao Feng and Chu Feng Factories organized a joint sales office known as the Home-made Enamelware Business Office (國產搪磁營業所) at No. 64 Avenue Edward VII. Each of the factories was allotted a quota of business in accordance with its productive capacity. Under a single administration the business of these four factories began to attain common development. In 1931 the Li Feng (立豐) and Kiu Hsin (久新) factories appeared. According to our investigation conducted that year, the number of enamelware factories in Shanghai was 8. In 1933, 17 factories were found in existence in Shanghai according to our second investigation. The producers of the Chinese enamelware, after much improvement, are now in a position to drive out imported articles from home markets. The recent economic depression, however, has naturally been a serious obstacle to the further development of this industry.

VII. *Paper Making and Printing.*

1. *Paper making.*

Although paper making began at a very early date in this country, it has made little progress during the ages. Formerly all the paper used in China was made by hand. Paper making by machinery did not begin until 1891, when Li Hung-chang established the Lun Chang Paper Mill (倫章造紙廠), at Yangtzeopo, Shanghai. After this mill a number of others came into existence, and paper making began to become a modern industry in China. Taking the country as a whole, paper making by machinery flourishes most in the Yangtze Valley, with the Huang Ho and West River Valleys coming next in importance. The province of Kiangsu is the most prominent producing region along the Yangtze River, while Shanghai is again the center of this industry in Kiangsu.

After the establishment of Lun Chang a British paper mill came into existence in 1898, and the Lung Chang Paper Mill (龍章造紙廠) was established in 1905 by Pang Lai-chen (龐萊臣) with a nominal capital of 500,000 taels (the paid-up capital

BRIEF HISTORY

being about 300,000 taels) at Lunghwa (龍華).[52] During the ten year period after 1905, no new factory appeared owing to bad business conditions. The three existing mills also went through reorganizations and changed their names several times. The Lungchang Mill sustained losses amounting to nearly 46% of its total capital during the first two or three years after its establishment. After the management was taken over by Pang Yi-chai (龐怡齋), the original capital was gradually recovered. By strenuous effort the mill was put, after three or four years, on a better footing.[53] The Lung Chang Mill suspended operations shortly after its establishment, and in 1916, it was reorganized by Liu Pai-seng (劉柏森), who changed its name into Pao Yuan Mill (寶源造紙廠). Later, as an east branch mill was acquired, it was called Pao Yuan Paper Mill, West Branch, its principal products being *mao pien* (毛邊) and *lien-ssu* (連史), two kinds of Chinese writing paper. The British-owned paper mill became a Sino-Russian concern in 1914 and its name was changed into Hwa Chang Paper Mill (華章造紙廠). It came under the control of the Mitsubishi interests in 1915, but was bought in 1920 by Liu Pai-seng and reorganized into the Pao Yuan Paper Mill, East Branch (寶源東廠). Both branches of the Pao Yuan Mill, however, were again reorganized in 1924. The West Branch changed its name to Tien Chang West Mill (天章西廠), and the East Branch, to Tien Chang East Mill (天章東廠). At present, these two mills are producing principally M. F. printing paper and wrapping paper. Though other varieties, such as newsprint and *lien ssu* are also manufactured, they are of only secondary importance.

The Ching Cheng Paper Manufacturing Company, Ltd. (竟成造紙股份有限公司), with its mill on Chengtu Road, was established in the same year as Tien Chang. It produces various varieties of card board, packing and wrapping paper. Although its products cannot compare favorably with imported articles, a

---

52. *Modern Industries in Shanghai*, p. 259.
53. Kung, op. cit. p. 226.

large number of manufacturers and shops are using the card board of this mill for the making of paper boxes.

Yu Ya-ching (虞洽卿) and several of his associates founded the Kiangnan Paper Company (江南造紙公司) in 1925 with a capital of $400,000, which has been enlarged to $800,000 since. Its mill site was chosen at Zaukadoo and operations started in 1927. A branch mill was established in 1928 at Kaotze (高資), Kiangsu, to manufacture pulp from reed obtained from regions along the Yangtze River. This pulp is the principal material used for making paper by this mill, while the *lien ssu* and *mao pien* varieties of paper are its principal products.[54]

The Ming Seng Paper Mill (民生機器造紙廠) was established in 1928 with a capital of $100,000, packing and wrapping paper being its chief products. However, it was destroyed in the Sino-Japanese conflict in Shanghai in 1932. The Kung Hsing Card Board Company (公興卡紙公司) and the Paoshan Paper Mill (寶山造紙廠) were also situated in the Chapei area and, though not destroyed entirely, were seriously damaged. Even at present, these two mills have not quite recovered from these losses.

According to our investigation of 1931, there were altogether 11 paper mills in Shanghai, of which 7 produced ordinary varieties of paper, and the remaining were manufacturers of card board. During our second investigation in 1933, the number of mills had increased to 14. 8 of the number turned out ordinary paper, while 6 manufactured card board, etc. There was, therefore, some development in the paper making industry in Shanghai. Newsprint paper, the most widely used and urgently demanded variety in China, has, however, been little produced by Chinese paper mills. Almost all that is consumed in the country has to be imported from abroad. Consequently the Ministry of Industries is now carrying out a plan of building a mill at Wenchow, Chekiang, for the manufacture of this kind of paper.

---

54. Ibid.

BRIEF HISTORY

2. *Printing.*

The printing industry in China is divided into type printing and "color printing," which latter includes lithograph and offset. Both may be engaged in book or job printing, although newspapers are now printed only by the former process. As Shanghai is the commercial and cultural center of China, the printing business here is particularly well developed.

a. *News printing.*

The *North China Daily News Press* was the first concern of its kind in Shanghai, being established as early as 1850 for the publication of the English daily paper bearing that name. The *Shun Pao,* started in 1872, was the first Chinese daily in Shanghai. It was at first also a British enterprise, but later bought by Hsi Tze-pai (席子佩) at a price of 75,000 taels.[55] After *Shun Pao,* the *Sin Wan Pao* appeared in 1893, and the *China Times* in 1906. The Central Party Headquarters of Kuomintang established in 1916 the *Ming Kuo Jih Pao,* which, however, was discontinued in 1932. All other papers are now still in publication. The above mentioned are the leading newspapers of Shanghai and have their own printing presses. A large number of less important papers have been established after the advent of the Republic, and many of them are printed by printers on a contract basis.

b. *Book printing and job printing.*

The Mei Hwa Printing Office (美華印刷所), a foreign enterprise, was the first book printing concern in Shanghai and it can still be found in the Hongkew district. Chu Yi Tang (著易堂), situated at Shih Pi Lung (石皮弄) in the Chinese City, was the first Chinese enterprise along this line. It started business as early as 1843 or 1844, the founder being a man named Tu (杜). After this concern, Huei Wen Tang (會文堂), Chi Chen Book Company (集成書局) and Shao Yi Shan Fang (掃葉山房) came

---

55. *Fiftieth Anniversary of Shun Pao.*

into existence. The Commercial Press, although having a comparatively late start, was the first concern of large size and equipped with modern machinery. It was founded in 1897 by Hsia Tsui-fang (夏粹芳), Pao Yen-ung (鮑咸恩) and Pao Yen-shang (鮑咸昌). At first, it was small in scale and was destroyed by fire two years after its establishment. In 1903, it became a Sino-Japanese concern with Chang Yuan-chi (張元濟) as manager, and its business began to prosper. It was registered with the Ministry of Agriculture and Commerce in 1906. The Japanese shares were bought back and it became a purely Chinese concern again.[56] It has made rapid progress since then and is now the leading concern in China.

After the Commercial Press, the Wen Ming Book Company (文明書局) appeared in 1899, the Kuo Kwang Press (國光印刷局) in 1910, the Chung Hwa Book Company in 1914, the Ming Chih Book Company (民智書局) in 1921, the Ta Tung Book Company (大東書局) in 1922 and the World Book Company (世界書局) in 1925. All these did business on their own account. A number of printers who printed mainly for their customers also came into existence during those years, Hwa Feng (華豐), the Pacific (太平洋), Liang You (良友), Kuo Kwang (國光), Chung Hsin (中新) and the Science Press (科學) being the notable ones. Hwa Feng, established in 1915 on Lincoln Road, was comparatively the largest. During the Sino-Japanese conflict of 1932, the Printing Department of the Commercial Press, being situated in Chapei, was destroyed. The company, however, suspended operations only for a short period, and resumed them soon after. According to an investigation made by the Type Printers' Association, there were more than 500 job printers in Shanghai. In addition to this number, there were about 50 or 60 foreign concerns, mostly Japanese. In the year before last, as prices of raw materials rose on account of the rise of gold value, about 40 or 50 of the job printers in Shanghai were forced to close down.

---

56. *Fiftieth Anniversary of Shun Pao.*

BRIEF HISTORY

c. *"Color printing."*

The lithograph process was first used in China as early as 1876, when the San Wan Printing Office (山灣印刷所), a Sino-French enterprise, was established at Siccawei. Its publications consisted largely of religious literature of the Catholic Church. Tien Shih Chai (點石齋), a British concern, and Tung Wen Book Company (同文書局), an establishment founded by Hsu Yu-tse (徐裕子) in 1881, were engaged in the printing of books. The former, in addition to book printing, published a pictorial daily in three colors, which was the beginning of real color printing in China.[57] Proper color lithograph was started in 1904 by the Wen Ming Book Company. Japanese experts were employed to train apprentices and shaded printing began to appear. Much has been done in this line by the Commercial Press and colored lithography has become very popular in China.

Offset printing began in Shanghai in 1915. In 1922, the Commercial Press bought from America a double colored offset machine. After that, offset presses multiplied as cigarette factories came into existence in large numbers. In printing the brands and cigarette packages, the offset process turns out products five times as quick as lithography.

In addition to the above mentioned, subsidiary lines to printing, such as the engraving of zinc plates, half-tone, corotype, etc., have also been introduced into China. They are usually done by the larger printers such as the Commercial Press, but there are also small establishments which specialize in one or more of these lines.

Thus far we have dealt with only some of the leading industries. There is not enough space to cover all and every line, and it is thought that the brief résumé here given is sufficient to indicate the general process of industrial development in Shanghai. As developments in other cities often have a bearing on that in this city, especially when they refer to the beginning of a new

---

57. *Unpublished Report of the China Institute on the Printing Industry.*

industry, mention is often made of them. The same is true with foreign factories in Shanghai. They were often the precursors of Chinese industrial development, and as time went on, some of them were taken over by Chinese business men, while the foreign industrial promoters turned their attention to new lines. We have been unable to obtain statistical data about foreign factories in Shanghai; hence we will have to be satisfied with occasional references to them in connection with the above account.

The division of the history of Chinese industrial development into seven periods shows the nature of the development at different times, as well as the prosperity and decline of the industries in general. These changes apply to Shanghai as much as they apply to the whole country, inasmuch as Shanghai is the principal industrial center of China. They serve as a general background for the individual accounts of the development of various industries. In general, the modern industries in Shanghai have grown throughout all these periods, although there were slight ups and downs from time to time. In the last two years they were very much affected by the depression, but even then some industries continued to develop, and the whole situation, when compared with that of a couple of decades ago, certainly indicated marked growth. Bearing this general trend in mind, we shall go in detail in the next chapter into the developments of the last few years, especially the period between 1931 and 1933 which was covered by the two statistical surveys of this Institute.

CHAPTER III

RECENT DEVELOPMENTS AS REVEALED BY STATISTICAL SURVEYS.

While for the earlier years only descriptive accounts are available, with statistical data for a few special industries such as cotton mills and silk filatures, complete—or what are claimed to be complete—figures have been gathered since 1928. The pioneer work was done in that year by the Bureau of Social Affairs of the Shanghai City Government[58], and as such it was naturally not wholly satisfactory. Yet it made a beginning, and since then four other surveys have been made, two of which were made by the China Institute of Economic and Statistical Research in co-operation with other Government and private organizations. Although the figures of the various surveys are not entirely comparable, the two surveys of our own are, and even for the others, certain ideas may be obtained from them, if we keep in mind the nature and scope of these other surveys.

As has been pointed out, the 1928 survey is the first one. In a pamphlet published by the Bureau of Social Affairs on this sub-

---

58. By the "Shanghai City Government" we refer to the Chinese Administration which has jurisdiction over the Chinese territory (494.69 square km.) and to a limited extent over the International Settlement (22.60 square km.) and the French Concession (10.22 square km.).

SHANGHAI INDUSTRIALIZATION

ject, the total number of factories in existence in Shanghai in that year, including both Chinese and foreign establishments, was estimated at 1,781. Of these, 1,500 were covered by the survey, which therefore amounted to 84.2%. However, from the light which later surveys threw on this subject, the estimated total was apparently too low, but it probably included all the large establishments in Shanghai, together with some small ones. Before this estimate, there was not even the slightest idea as to how many factories were in Shanghai, whether they numbered a few hundred or a few thousand. In the same way, the total number of workers in the 1,500 surveyed factories was given as 223,691 which, though incomplete and inaccurate, also gave some idea where no idea had been obtainable.

That the figures were too low can be easily seen from a better and more scientific survey conducted by the same Bureau in the following year, in a different division, under the supervision of a well qualified statistician[59]. In that year the total number of factories in a number of specified industries was estimated at 2,326, and the number of labourers 285,700. Of these 1,593 factories were visited by investigators, and their names are given in the book. If the totals of a number of specified industries, important though they were, already amounted to such figures, that of all industries must have been even larger. And this survey was conducted less than a year later than the first one; hence the incompleteness of the earlier survey is evident.

Two years later the National Directorate of Statistics, the Ministry of Industries, the Shanghai Bureau of Social Affairs and the National Tariff Commission were all going to make surveys of Shanghai industries. At the same time the Chinese Economic Society had a research project financed by the Institute of Pacific Relations which called for a survey too. As the present writer was then in charge of the Chinese Economic Society project, and was serving as the Director-General of Statistics of the National

---

59. Mr. T. Y. Tsha of the Labor Division of the Bureau, the result of whose study is embodied in the *Wages and Hours of Labor of Greater Shanghai*, 1929.

CHAPTER III RECENT DEVELOPMENTS

Government, negotiations were initiated with the other organizations, which were convinced of the desirability of conducting a joint survey, instead of having each do its own work and repeat what would have to be done by the other institutions. As a result, a joint survey was carried out by the five organizations, plus the Research Institute of the Chiaotung University, a detailed account of which is given in the appendix and the Preliminary Report on Shanghai Industrialization published in 1933. The investigation was more thorough-going than the former two, as it amounted to a house-to-house survey. At the same time, a standard was set up so that only factories, employing more than ten workers or using motive power would be included. Altogether 1,672 were included in the statistics appended to the present volume, although over 2,000 mills were actually visited.[60] Those that are left out of account were either below the standard, or were visited after the lapse of a period of time, and had come into existence after the main period of the survey had expired.

A second chance of making an industrial survey of Shanghai was offered this Institute, which was jointly established by the Chinese Economic and the Chinese Statistical Societies after the 1931 survey, when it was asked by a Chinese Government Commission to carry out something like a census of modern industries of the whole country. As the ground to be covered was so extensive, the standard was set higher, and only factories that would be included in the meaning of that term as defined by the Chinese Factory Law of 1929 were to be investigated. This meant that the factories must use motive power *and* employ 30 or more workers. The total number in Shanghai, according to this standard, was found in 1933, the year of the second survey of this Institute, to be 1,186. Although this figure was much lower than that of 1931, yet the number of similar factories in the earlier year, according to our analysis, was only 710. Hence, the latter year had an increase of 476 large factories.[61]

---

60. Appendix A, Tables I-VII.
61. Appendix B. Tables I-VII.

SHANGHAI INDUSTRIALIZATION

Just as our second survey was nearing completion, the Bureau of Social Affairs of Shanghai started another survey, which was to include all and every factory in Shanghai, large or small, Chinese or foreign, but the number of items to be filled was limited to eight. This would have been more in the nature of a census, if all duplications could be avoided and really all factories were included. As it is, there is much doubt on these points. Besides the mistake of including some handicrafts and leaving out others seems to have been committed. In a piece of work of such large scope, mistakes could hardly be avoided when the time allowed was so short. If, on the other hand, a year or more were devoted to the survey, then more duplications would easily result, and there would have been too many changes during the period of the survey, which would make the result not so much of a census as of a continuous register. This is the special difficulty in Shanghai, where industrial changes are continually taking place. Yet when only the larger factories are included in a survey, the work is simpler, and mistakes are naturally fewer and can be easily rectified. It is apparently due to the very extensive scope of the 1934 survey and the inevitable duplication of factories that the total in that year is given as 5,418.[62] This very large number must not be mistaken to indicate a rapid growth of Shanghai industries since 1933.

Growth of Shanghai Industries, 1931-1933

Between the years 1931 and 1933 there was a real growth of modern industries in Shanghai. The figures for these two years are to a large extent comparable, because the two surveys were both conducted by the China Institute of Economic and Statistical Research (the 1931 survey was carried out by it before it had assumed its present name), and the schedules used were the same, with the exception of a few items. Most of the Institute investigators who took part in the first survey also participated in the second one. While the second survey was limited to factories that

---

62. *Directory of Shanghai Industries,* published by the Shanghai Bureau of Social Affairs. As shown in the book, only the particulars of 3,839 factories were ascertainable.

RECENT DEVELOPMENTS

came up to the standard of the Chinese Factory Law, those of the same size covered by the first survey are also separately shown in the tables in Appendix D. These two sets of figures are, therefore, comparable, and they show that the so-called modern industries in Shanghai had undergone much development during the interval.

While the details about the growth will be narrated industry by industry in the following sections, some summary figures may be given here. The number of factories in Shanghai that came up to the standard of the Chinese Factory Law in 1933 was about 60% larger than that in 1931, their capitalization and the number of workers employed in them about 20%, the value of their output 3% and the quantity of power consumed 18%. As the price level in China had begun to fall in 1932, which may be clearly seen from the wholesale price index numbers for Shanghai as well as many other kinds of statistics given in Chapter VI, the growth of Shanghai industries in these years needs some explanation. Why did industries continue to prosper in this city when the prices of commodities were rapidly falling? Did all industries prosper equally, or were some of them at least affected by the adverse effects of world economic forces? We will try to answer these questions in the following paragraphs.

To start with, we must first explain why the world depression was not felt in China until 1932. The decline began in Europe with the failure of a number of important banks on the continent in 1929, and in the United States there was the stock market crash. But the Chinese money market is not so sensitive with respect to changes in foreign countries of this nature, since Chinese banks are not in close contact with foreign banks, and neither Chinese holdings of foreign securities nor foreign deposits in China amount to such large sums that their sale or withdrawal would affect the Chinese money market. Besides, China was on the silver standard, and as the price of silver in London and New York experienced a great slump immediately after the depression, the value of Chinese currency fell with it. Consequently, commodity prices which fell abroad were, when converted into the more quickly depreciating Chinese silver currency, going up, as may be seen from the wholesale price index numbers of Shanghai till 1932.[63] As clearly indicated by these figures, the price level in China reached its peak two years after the depression had set in in other parts of the world. Under the stimulation of what amounted to involuntary inflation, Chinese business continued to be prosperous and manufacturing industries in Shanghai, with only a few exceptions, were still in the upward swing.

So far the growth of Shanghai industries may be attributed to monetary causes. In the latter part of 1931, however, England, Japan and a few other countries went off the gold standard, and silver began to appreciate in terms of these depreciating currencies. The price level in China began to fall, but in the decline, a gap appeared between the import and export prices. In 1927, 1928 and 1929 the difference between these two sets of index numbers was only two or three points, but since 1931 it increased by leaps and bounds until the import price index went 30 points above the wholesale price index two years later, and the export price index 20 points below the latter. The total discrepancy between the import and export price indexes was therefore as large as 50 points.[64] In such circumstances, the manufacturing industries were on the whole able to reap fairly large profits. The higher import prices set the limit to the prices which they might demand for their products, since the latter were in competition with imported goods. The prices of their raw materials, on the other hand, were kept low because they could not be higher than those of similar materials to be exported abroad.[65]

During the 1929 depression in America, the prices of raw materials fell more than those of finished products, agricultural products more than non-agricultural products, and consumption goods more than production goods.[66] In this country, when the

---

63. Appendix F, Table XII.
64. D. K. Lieu, *A Study of Our Price Level, 1926-1934*, in the Chinese Social and Political Science Review.
65. Ibid.
66. F. C. Mills, *Aspects of Recent Price Movements*, National Bureau of Economic Research Bulletin 48.

RECENT DEVELOPMENTS

effect of the depression began to be felt in 1931, the price changes followed the same course as that in America since 1929, with this exception, namely, that among commodities for export, production goods experienced a greater fall than consumption goods. This was naturally of greater advantage to the manufacturers who utilized indigent raw materials. At any rate, industrial raw materials are mostly agricultural products, and the greater decline in their prices lowered the cost of production to the manufacturers. Wages, as will be shown in greater detail in another chapter, generally constitutes a very small proportion of manufacturing cost in China, and its comparative inflexibility in a period of depression does not matter so much to Chinese industries as it does to those of other countries. That was perhaps why Shanghai industries continued to grow when the industries in America, where the price changes behaved in about the same way, were immediately affected by the depression of 1929. The stock market crash, which severely depressed the prices of American industrial securities, and the liquidation of numerous country banks also had no counterpart in China until 1934 and 1935. (There is practically no market for industrial securities of Chinese companies here, but the Shanghai manufacturers are more affected by the great decline in land values, as many of their loans are secured on factory site.)

Tariff and Industrial Development

One explanation of this gap was to be found in the continually increasing tariff rates since 1929. Before that, China was bound by unilateral treaties to levy only a nominal import duty of 5%, but as it was actually collected, the effective rate was not quite 4%. The latter was calculated from the value of net import and the revenue from the import duties. Although immediately before 1929 a surtax was agreed to by the treaty powers, yet it amounted only to about 2% in effective rate, and the duty and surtax together were below 6%.

In February, 1929, China first adopted a national tariff, at rates varying between 7-1/2 and 27-1/2 per cent, divided into 7 grades. The average effective rate in that year rose to 8.47%. It went up to 10.37% in 1930, 14.09% in 1931, 14.45% in 1932 and 19.74% in 1933.[67] Although such rates were incomparable with the high tariff walls of most other countries, yet they afforded quite a bit of protection to Chinese industries, especially as the rates on certain specific commodities were much higher. The *ad valorem* import duty on wines, for instance, was 80%.

In general, the import duty was higher on manufactured products than on raw materials, as is usually the case with most tariffs. This was naturally beneficial to the domestic industries. However, the tariff which was put in effect in July, 1934, slightly deviated from this rule. It brought about a reduction in the import duties on many kinds of cotton piece goods from 2% to 39% (with the duties which were enforced before July 1934 as 100%), and an increase in that on raw cotton of 43%. The severe depression in the cotton industry in 1934 and 1935 was perhaps due in part to these tariff measures. Whether it is desirable for the economic life of the Chinese nation as a whole to have tariff protection is a question which we cannot go into in this study, but there is no gainsaying the fact that in the years after 1929 the national tariff had been responsible for the growth of many Shanghai industries until they were overtaken by the depression in 1934.

Still another reason of the growth of Shanghai industries during a period of depression was perhaps this. The products of Chinese factories are mostly imitations of imported goods, but their quality is usually inferior to that of the latter. At the same time, their prices are generally much cheaper. Moreover, as will be seen from the statistical summaries in the appendix, most Chinese industries are engaged in the manufacture of goods for immediate consumption. When times were good, the people were inclined to spend more and buy the better products of foreign countries. After the depression set in, their income dropped, and they had to economize in their expenses. Hence more people began to buy the cheaper products of the local factories. In this way, we may say that the depression really helped the Shanghai

---

67. The New Tariff, in the *Chinese Economic and Statistical Review*, Volume I, No. 8.

RECENT DEVELOPMENTS

manufacturers. The increased output in most industries, as shown in the statistics of 1933 when compared with those of 1931, both of which are to be found in the appendices, is evidence of this peculiar development.

While the higher prices of imported European and American goods as compared with those of similar commodities manufactured in Shanghai, which difference was made greater by the increasing tariff rates, was instrumental in increasing the consumption of the products of local industries, the same factors were not enough to keep Japanese goods out of the Chinese market. The latter were equally cheap, and in some cases even cheaper than the products of Chinese factories. The yen has been continually dropping in recent years, and in addition to that, the Japanese manufacturers did their best to turn out cheap products for foreign consumption. Even India and other Asiatic and African markets felt the effect of this kind of competition.[68] China, being much nearer to Japan, and having been one of the most important markets of Japanese goods, must naturally feel the competition more keenly. However, the occupation of Manchuria in 1931 and the invasion of Shanghai in the following year aroused a good deal of anti-Japanese sentiment, which resulted in a nation-wide boycott of Japanese goods. According to a study by Professor Remer of Chinese boycotts, this was the biggest one on record, and its effectiveness was proved by trade and other statistics.[69] Hence, between 1931 and 1933, the Chinese manufacturers in Shanghai were protected against European and American competition by the tariff, and against Japanese competition by the boycott. When the boycott had spent its force, the effect of Japanese competition was then keenly felt, and Chinese industries in Shanghai suffered severe reverses.

The above observations, however, do not apply to all specific cases. Certain industries were affected more by the depression and by Japanese competition than others, and some felt the effect of

---

68. Hubbard, *Industrialization in the Far East*, pp. 12-24.
69. C. F. Remer, *A Study of Chinese Boycotts*, pp. 197-231.

SHANGHAI INDUSTRIALIZATION

the former much sooner. The silk reeling industry, for instance, was hit by the world depression almost as soon as it occurred abroad. As shown in a special study of that industry, the number of filatures and reeling basins both reached their zenith in April, 1930.[70] After that, a decline began, and the same prosperity has never been attained since. As the filatures in Shanghai are mostly rented, often for several months only, their operation is suspended from time to time, and the number of filatures and reeling basins in operation is a good indicator of the conditions of the industry. Also, the supply of cocoons is largest when the spring crop is harvested, which in Kiangsu and Chekiang takes place at about May. As soon as the supply is exhausted, production slackens, and many filatures suspend business. The industry is therefore subject to seasonal influences, but never before had so many filatures closed down as in November, 1930, when only one out of 107 filatures in Shanghai remained in operation. A detailed account of the decline is found in the book referred to above. As the product of this industry, raw silk, is to a large extent exported and is in the nature of luxury goods, the demand for which is very elastic, the fall in its price was very great and affected the industry very soon after the depression began abroad. This situation was clearly reflected by the greater fall of export prices when compared with the general price level in this country. Trade figures in Appendix F will show how far and how soon silk export dropped.

Another industry which was very badly hit in recent years was the cotton spinning industry. The papers were full of discouraging accounts. The loss of Manchuria in 1931, which had been the principal market of the products of the Shanghai cotton mills, was the first big blow to this industry. When later, the price of cotton was artificially maintained at a comparative high level in America and the price of yarn kept low through Japanese competition—the latter being usually controlled by the Osaka market—the cotton spinning industry in China experienced worse conditions. With the spinning of finer yarns in recent years,

---

70. D. K. Lieu, *The Silk Reeling Industry in Shanghai*, pp. 7-25.

RECENT DEVELOPMENTS

Chinese cotton mills are dependent on American cotton as raw material, as much as 40% of the cotton consumed in the Seng Sin Mills being from the United States. In addition, Chinese mills also use Indian cotton to some extent for coarse yarn. When import prices were high, the industry was naturally adversely affected. Indulgence on the part of many Chinese cotton mill owners in speculation, their indebtedness to banks for very large sums on comparatively short terms, and the keen competition of Japanese mills in Japan as well as in China, were additional causes of embarrassment to the industry. Since 1933, all Shanghai mills have suspended operation for various periods, and some of them have been closed down entirely.

Some Comparative Figures

In order to study the recent developments in detail in the different industries or groups of industries, three tables have been prepared to compare the results of the five statistical surveys mentioned at the beginning of this chapter. It should be borne in mind that the three surveys of 1928, 1929 and 1934 are generally not comparable with those of 1931 and 1933, as the former included both Chinese and foreign factories in Shanghai, and they were not limited to establishments of any definite size. Possibly they might be compared one with another, but the method of classification is not necessarily the same, and whenever there is any change in the figures, the conclusion cannot be drawn that changes actually occurred in the industries concerned. In particular is the 1928 survey incomparable with that of any other year, because even the main groupings are different from those of the others, which are based on the system adopted by the International Labor Office. We have therefore been obliged to re-arrange to a large extent the 1928 statistics so that those referring to the same industries as those in the other surveys, no matter how they were originally classified, appear side by side with the industries in the I.L.O. groupings. On account of this difference in the main groups, and the inclusion in the 1928 statistics of miscellaneous industries in each one of its groups, no totals can be given for any group after the re-arrangement in Table I, Appendix D, in which figures for 1929, 1931 and 1933 are also included.

SHANGHAI INDUSTRIALIZATION

Table D-II compares the figures of the four later surveys, by the main groups, according to the I.L.O. system of classification. As no separate data are given for the individual industries in this table, the 1928 figures cannot be inserted here. Because the scope of the 1929 and 1934 surveys differs one from the other, and also from that of the two surveys of this Institute, no hasty conclusions should be drawn from this table, any more than from the first one, although here the four surveys all adopt the same main groupings. These two tables are prepared with a view to presenting the results of the surveys of other organizations, rather than studying the growth or decline of the industries from the figures contained in them.

It has been suggested to the writer that, since the figures are not comparable, these tables had better be left out, as they may easily be misleading to the reader. This advice, however, has not been followed for many reasons. In the first place, in some industries the classification was the same in all years, the sizes of the factories were all large, and there were no foreign establishments in Shanghai. In such cases the figures are comparable. Second, although the much larger figures of 1928, 1929 and 1934 do not mean that the Shanghai industries were more prosperous in these years, they do mean that, in those industries where the figures far exceeded those of our own, the proportion of foreign and small factories was particularly large. Finally, this volume, being a study of Shanghai industrialization, must not leave out of account these other surveys, and these tables are perhaps the best way of presenting their results. While we naturally discuss in greater detail the results of our own surveys, other students of the same subject may have occasion to make use of the other figures. In these tables the merits as well as the defects of these surveys can be most readily seen.

In Table D-III, where only the figures for 1931 and 1933 are given, they are much more comparable. This is especially true with the two sets marked "b" and "c", since both refer to factories of particular sizes; namely, those using motive power and employing 30 or more workers. Hence this table is more elaborate, giving data for both individual industries and their totals by

RECENT DEVELOPMENTS

groups. The following discussion is based mainly on this table. Whenever reference is made to the figures of 1931, set "a", which represents all factories in the industry covered by that survey, is meant, unless special mention is made of the larger factories, i.e., those that come up to the standard of the Chinese Factory Law, as has been defined above. However, excepting the number of establishments, figures under "a" and "b" do not differ so very much, which means that the small factories add comparatively little to the total capitalization, number of workers, value of output, etc.

Although both the 1931 and 1933 surveys were conducted by this Institute, figures are sometimes incomplete for one industry in one year and another industry in another. The inability or unwillingness of one factory to supply a certain figure—say, capitalization or value of output—is sufficient to produce such a result. Also, in both years, a number of factories refused to supply any information at all. For these reasons, even the figures in Table III may be considered as not strictly comparable. Fortunately, the data are with few exceptions incomplete to a very small extent, and the non-co-operative factories are distributed among many industries, and are generally of comparatively small size. For the large ones, we have taken pains to secure their data by indirect methods, when direct investigation failed. Special mention will be made in the following discussion when the omission is comparatively significant. When the constituent industries are not very important, discussion will be confined to the group as a whole. Otherwise, observations are made for individual industries.

Under Group I, Woodworking Industries, are included saw mills and manufacturers of wood, bamboo and rattan articles. Although saw mills are the most important industry in this group, no statistics are available for 1928. In 1929 the number of these mills was given at 23 with 1,886 workers, including foreign as well as Chinese mills. The latter numbered only 8 in 1931, employing 392 workers. The very large number of laborers in 1929 was due to the larger size of the foreign mills, three of which had between them over 1,000 workmen. Besides, the 1929 survey, being made for the study of wages and labour hours, tried to include as many laborers in each industry as possible, and wherever their number is proportionally much larger in that year than in the other three surveys in Table I, we can be fairly sure that the industry concerned employs many hands for general instead of manufacturing work.

When the survey was limited to factories using power and employing more than thirty workers in 1933, we find that the number of Chinese saw mills that came up to that standard numbered only 4. In 1931 there were only two such factories. Furthermore, the number of workers in the 4 mills in 1933 was only slightly smaller than those of the 8 mills in 1931[71], while the quantity of power generated in the mills increased and rented electric power decreased. It means that some of the mills had grown in size during the interval of two years, and that as they grew, more use was made of power generated in the factory, instead of relying on rented power, as most small factories do. Had the scope of the 1933 survey been the same as that of 1931, the total number of laborers would have been much larger than in the former year. No comparison could very well be made with respect to capitalization and value of output, as these figures for 1931 were admittedly incomplete.

In the second group, Furniture Manufactories, there are only 3 divisions comprising industries manufacturing wooden furniture, iron and steel furniture, and rugs. None of them is of any special importance nor was there much significant change during these years.

The Heavy Industries

Metal Industries form the third group with two divisions: foundries and iron and steel works. The important Wo Hsin Iron Works at Pootung was not in operation during these years, and the data about the steel works of the Ministry of War are not available to private organizations. Hence the one establishment included in the latter division is the small experimental plant of the Academia Sinica.

---

71. Which included 6 small mills.

RECENT DEVELOPMENTS

Much development had apparently taken place in the founding industry, as the number of larger foundries had increased 2½ fold, with corresponding increases in capitalization, number of workers, value of output, as well as quantity of power employed. In the three other surveys the number of foundries is much larger, and it is due to the inclusion of very small establishments which we have left out.

Group IV includes industries that manufacture machinery and miscellaneous metallic products. There are now many mills in Shanghai which can manufacture steam engines, electric generators, motors, spindles, weaving machines for both cotton and silk industries, and equipment for rice and flour mills, tobacco factories, knitting mills and the printing press. Some of them have specialized in one line, and some in another. Many others can manufacture only machine parts, or specialize in repair work. Those which manufacture or repair machinery, except electric machinery, form the largest division in this group, those which manufacture metallic products come next and those producing electric machinery and utensils last. Products of the first and third divisions of this group are marketed all over the country.

In 1928 the number of factories in all three divisions, as we have re-arranged them, was 241, but in 1931 our survey included 288 of them, of which 82 came up to the standard of the Chinese Factory Law. The latter again increased to 173 in 1933, which was an increase of more than two-fold. Capitalization had increased two-and-half-fold, value of output three-fold, and number of workers 60%. When compared with the total figures of 1931, increases were also apparent, showing that this industry, which reflects best the general industrial development of Shanghai, had really grown considerably in these two years. More power was rented and less generated in the factories in 1933 than 1931, which was only natural since the lathes, drills and other machinery of these industries could best be operated by electricity.

Industries that construct boats, ships and vehicles for land transportation form the fifth group. The 1928 and 1929 surveys only covered ship-building works, of which there were 2 in the former, and 13 in the latter, year. In 1931 and 1933 this Institute covered also factories that built tramcars, fire engines, bicycles and rickshas. There were, of course, very many establishments producing the last two kinds of vehicles, but most of them were small in size, and therefore not included in our surveys. Motor car repair shops were also not included. The larger number of shipbuilding companies in 1929 is due to the inclusion of foreign establishments, which also explains the very large number of workers in that year. Comparing 1931 with 1933, we find that there were 21 Chinese establishments in the former year, of which 10 were up to the standard of the Factory Law, and 17 in 1933 up to the same standard. The capitalization, value of output and number of workers of these 17 establishments were all larger than those of the 21 in 1931.

The sixth group includes manufactories of (1) bricks, tiles and crucibles, (2) glassware, (3) cement and (4) stone, stone-powder and lime. The making of bricks, tiles and lime and the breaking of stone are industries that have long been in existence in China, but here we include only those which manufacture with modern machinery, except for 1934, the survey of which year probably covered also handicraft shops. There were 37 factories in this group in 1928, 30 in 1929, 44 in 1931, 41 in 1933 and 135 in 1934. In 1931 there were only 15 large factories (we will use the term "large factories" in this chapter to indicate factories that come up to the standard of the Chinese Factory Law), but in 1933 the number was almost as large as the total in 1931. In capitalization, value of output, motive power as well as number of workers, the figures for the 41 factories of 1933 far exceeded those for the 44 factories of two years ago.

Only the two surveys of this Institute have separate figures for Group VII, manufactories of construction material. In all other surveys they were either not covered, or classified under some other heading. Construction companies should, according to the International Labor Office classification, also come under this group, but as they are not manufactories, we have not included them in our surveys. There were only five manufactories of con-

RECENT DEVELOPMENTS

struction material in 1931 of which two were up to the legal standard. In 1933 the number was seven, and their capitalization and value of output were three times the figures for the two factories in 1931, and considerably larger than the five establishments of that year. The number of their workers was more than twice the total number in 1931.

In 1928 there were 8 public utility companies in Shanghai, including foreign corporations like the Shanghai Power Company and the Compagnie Francaise de Tramways et d'Eclairage Electriques. They were, however, not included in the 1929 study. The 1934 survey covered 13 establishments, and designated them as "motive power industries". As there were not so many suppliers of power in Shanghai, even when foreign establishments were included, the classification is therefore different from those in the other surveys. Hence the only comparison we can make is between the figures of 1931 and those of 1933. There were 5 suppliers of water and electricity in the former year and 3 in the latter. The smaller number in the latter case was due to the amalgamation of several electric works. Otherwise there had been little change between these two years, as evidenced by the figures representing capitalization, power, value of output and number of workers.

Group IX includes manufactories of matches, soda, soap and candles, enamelled ware, paint and printer's ink, cosmetics, medicine, celluloid articles and other chemical products. In 1933, thirteen factories in five new lines were added, viz., (1) acids,* (2) calcium and magnesium carbonate, (3) oxygen and acetylene, (4) dyes and (5) bakelite products. The total number also increased to 78 as against 60 in 1931, of which latter only 28 came up to the legal standard with respect to their size. In 1928 there were altogether 77 factories engaged in 7 industries in this group, in 1929 the number was 59 and in 1934 as many as 209. All these figures are, of course, incomparable with those of 1931 and 1933, except that the figures of 1928 and 1929, which

---

* There were acid factories before 1933, but they are classified under other divisions.

include foreign as well as very small Chinese establishments, are about the same as those of our own surveys, which in itself means that the industries in this group were gradually developing up to 1931. If we compare the figures of 1931 with the totals of 1933, then we see that capitalization and value of output had increased over 50%, power consumption 80%, and number of workers by 1700. The increase was much greater when compared with the figures for the large factories of 1931, the number of which was only about one-third that of 1933.

The Textile Industries

Now we come to the most important group of industries of Shanghai, the textile industries, which form Group X. We shall first enumerate its various branches as existed in Shanghai during the different surveys. They include cotton ginning, spinning and weaving, silk reeling and weaving, wool spinning and weaving, dyeing, printing of textiles, and the manufacturing of thread, gauze, mercerized yarn, ribbons and trimmings. In 1928 there were altogether 406 factories which could be classified under one or another of these headings. In 1929 there were 471; 1931, 546 (of which 264 were "large" factories); 1933, 391 and 1934, 1,006. If we compare the figures of 1931 and 1933, then the number of "large" factories had increased about 50%, capitalization and power consumption were greater and value of output about the same as the corresponding figures for all factories in the earlier year. The number of workers employed was smaller, not only when compared with the total figures of 1931, but also with those for the "large" factories of that date. It shows that although the size of some factories had increased, the industry was not as prosperous and furnished employment to a smaller number of laborers. A more detailed analysis of the textile industries is therefore necessary in studying the recent developments of Shanghai industries.

Occupying the most important position in the textile industries in Shanghai are the cotton mills. Their capitalization, value of output and number of workers constituted approximately 70%,

RECENT DEVELOPMENTS

60% and 50% respectively of those for the whole group, in both 1931 and 1933. We cannot compare the figures of these two years with those for the cotton spinning industry in the other years, as many foreign factories were included in the latter. But if we compare those of these two years, we shall see that although the capitalization and output figures were greater for 1933, those for 1931 were not complete. The number of laborers in 1931 was also not complete, yet it was larger than the 1933 figure by 2,318. This meant more unemployment in the latter year. Reasons for its decline, which became even worse after 1933, have been given in a previous connection.

Next in importance comes the cotton weaving industry. The number of factories in 1931 was not as large as that in 1928 or 1929 when foreign factories were included, but it was larger than that in 1933. On the other hand, the number of "large" factories was smaller by about a half. While capitalization in 1933 was smaller because the data were not complete, yet the value of output, power consumption and number of laborers had increased. Apparently this industry had prospered to a certain extent while cotton spinning suffered from the depression; perhaps because of it, as the low price of yarn must have been advantageous to the weaving mills.

The cotton weaving mills in Shanghai are generally small in size, and although many of them were also indebted to banks for working capital, yet the amounts of the loans were small, and were easily repaid when profits were for a while realized. With the lowering of their cost of production in the form of lower yarn prices, these mills did fairly good business. What has been said about the Japanese boycott and the tariff on western imports as protection to Shanghai industries applies to the cotton weaving industry. Its growth is apparent from the statistics of 1931 and 1933 in Table III, Appendix D.

Both 1931 and 1933 were bad years for the silk reeling industry, and the latter year was worse. While 66 out of 107 filatures were in operation during our survey of 1931, only 49 were running in 1933. If we compare these with the 104 of 1928 and 107 of 1929, the effect of the depression was very severe indeed. As studied in detail in our pamphlet on the Silk Reeling Industry in Shanghai, the zenith of the industry was reached in 1930, and in 1931 the 66 filatures kept only 17,238 reels in operation, as compared with the 25,395 reels in 1930 or even 24,906 in 1929. At the average of 234 workers per 100 reels, this means a loss of employment since 2929 to approximately 18,000 workers.[72] In Table III, Appendix D, the decrease in the number of laborers between these two years is shown as 11,000, because the 1929 figure is based on an estimate which is worked out quite differently from ours. There is a further decrease from 1931 to 1933, amounting to 10,629 workers. The capitalization and value of output also dwindled considerably in 1933, because in that year most filatures were operated on behalf of the creditors, and these figures did not represent the same kind of things as those in 1931.

Like the cotton weaving industry, the silk weaving industry was benefited by the cheap price of the raw material—silk. In addition, the increasing use of rayon also lowers its cost of production. Hence, while the 1928 and 1929 surveys listed only 46 and 48 such mills respectively, there were 250 of them in 1931, of which 77 were up to the legal standard. The number of the latter increased to 122 in 1933, with a larger number of workers and a greater output than the total number of factories in 1931, if we take the incomplete figures of these two years to be fairly representative of the general situation.

The wool spinning and weaving industry had undergone a significant development in these six years. There were only 7 such mills in the 1928 survey, but the number increased to 15 in 1931 and 26 in 1933. In capitalization the increase from 1931 to 1933 was almost two-fold, and in the number of workers, the value of output and power consumption, it was almost three-fold. Of course, most of the mills manufacture only woolen blankets and lining for Chinese garments, but at any rate, it indicates an increasing market for woolen products in this country.

---

72. Lieu, *The Silk Reeling Industry in Shanghai*, pp. 5 and 78.

RECENT DEVELOPMENTS

A new industry made its appearance in 1933. Serveral factories sprang into existence which manufactured mixtures of wool, cotton and silk waste. At the time of the investigation, it seemed that they were doing good business, and there was a chance for the industry to take root in this city.

Group XI includes all articles of apparel, except leather and rubber shoes, which we will put in the next group. Knitted hosiery, knitted underwear, straw and felt hats, handkerchiefs, buttons, umbrellas, etc., all belong to this group, but the first two are the most important. In 1928 there were 130 factories in this group, as far as we can re-classify the statistical data of that year. 102 mills were included under another group in 1929. 170 factories were in existence in 1931, of which 58 came up to the legal standard, but in 1933 those of the latter category numbered 89. In the very extensive and indiscriminating survey of 1934 the number went up to 473. If we compare the figures of 1933 with those of 1931, the number of large factories increased 50%. Their capitalization and value of output were not only larger than those of the large factories in 1931 but also of the total number.

As has been pointed out above, the two most important industries in this group are the hosiery and underwear manufactories. While the number of large factories in the former industry increasd by 8, the value of output increased by 50%, and was even greater than that of all knitting mills in 1931. Yet it was the mills which manufactured hosiery as well as other things (mostly underwear) and those manufacturing underwear in particular that experienced the greatest expansion during the interval. The number of large factories as well as the value of their output in both cases doubled in two years, while capitalization increased even more. It was perhaps due to the fact that the hosiery industry had already reached the peak of its development in the former year, while the underwear industry had not. Also, in the interior, hosiery knitting had become a domestic industry, many rural families renting hand-operated knitting machines for the making of hosiery. In these cases, the cotton yarn—for these families generally produce low grade stockings only—is generally supplied by certain commission houses or knitting mills, which also undertake to buy the products of this cottage industry or sell them at a commission. Knitted underwear is still made only in the mills, and the consumption is growing; hence the growth of this industry in Shanghai.

Leather, leather goods and rubber goods are included in Group XII. As the manufacture of leather articles, such as shoes, suitcases, etc., is usually done in very small establishments, none of them were included in the 1933 survey, and very few in that of 1931. There is yet no factory which manufacturers rubber in Shanghai, but many that produce rubber goods, especially shoes and over-shoes. Quite a few leather tanneries, however, are found in this city. Of these industries the one that experienced the greatest degree of expansion was that which manufactured rubber goods. In 1931 there were 29 such factories, of which 25 were up to the standard of the Chinese Factory Law. In 1933 the number of the latter category was 44, with their capitalization and number of workers doubled, and the value of their output quadrupled. It is a pity that the statistics for 1933 are not yet complete in some respects; otherwise the increase would be even more striking. The number of large leather tanneries increased from 7 to 10 during these two years, but the value of their output did not increase.

Taking the group as a whole, there were 150 factories in 1929; 57 in 1931, of which 33 were up to the legal standard; 55 in 1933 and 132 in 1934. The much larger number of factories in this group in 1929 and 1934 was probably due to the inclusion of numerous small establishments, especially those tanning with old-fashioned equipment or making leather shoes and bags.

The Foodstuff Industries

The manufactories of foodstuffs form Group XIII in our classification, including rice milling, flour milling, the manufac-

RECENT DEVELOPMENTS

ture of sugar, vegetable oil, cigarettes, cigars, liquor, refined salt, canned food, condiments, candy, casings, egg products and starch, the preparation of tea leaves and the refrigeration of meat, etc. Although there are many rice mills in Shanghai, they are mostly very small, or they belong to rice wholesalers whose principal business is the distribution of the product. The rice is milled only when it has not been sufficiently polished before being shipped to Shanghai and sold to these wholesalers. In the whole city, only one large rice mill was found both in 1931 and 1933. On the other hand, the flour mills were all large, and together with the cigarette factories and oil presses, they formed the three principal industries in this group, when the value of their output is taken as the criterion. There were a Chinese and a Japanese sugar refinery here, but the former never went into operation, and the latter was not included in our surveys of 1931 and 1933. Hence the few factories making sugar in these surveys were manufacturers of candy sugar.

A comparison of the statistics of the various years shows that there were 198 factories in this group in 1928; 103 in 1929; 175 in 1931 (of which 107 were up to the legal standard); 143 in 1933 and 323 in 1934. When we compare the figures of 1931 and 1933, we find that the capitalization and number of laborers were about the same in these two years, but the value of output increased by 60%. The largest increase was in the tobacco industry, where the value jumped from 46 million to 100 million dollars. The output of the flour mills also increased from 62 to 72 million dollars in value. The oil presses produced some 13 million dollars' worth of oil in both years. All other industries in the group did not come up to such large figures. Although the number of factories curing tea was much larger in 1933 than in 1931, it does not represent any real increase, because these plants are usually operated by tea exporters, and during the 1931 survey, some of them were mistaken to be business firms and were therefore left out from the investigation.

Group XIV comprises paper mills and printing establishments. The 1928 survey included 13 of the former, although only the

SHANGHAI INDUSTRIALIZATION

names of five of them were given. In 1929, 1931, and 1933 there were seven of them. As there has been little change in this industry in the recent years, the number should have been the same all through. With the printing business, the scale is often very small, and the inclusion or exclusion of small printing shops makes a good deal of difference in the total number. Hence, in 1928 the number was given as 210; 1929, 219; 1931, 106 (of which large ones numbered 52) and 1933, 92. Although the number of large printing establishments had increased in 1933, the number of workers employed as well as the value of output (in this case it generally represented the value of the work done) showed only slight changes, which shows that the business was not flourishing while competition was apparently keener. The value of output of the paper mills, on the other hand, increased about 40%. Book-binding, engraving, the manufacture of cartons and card-board, are also included in this group, but they are of very little significance. The total number of factories in the group was 238 in 1928; 226 in 1929; 155 in 1931 (of which 69 were large ones); 114 in 1933 and 577 in 1934. There was little difference between the capitalization and number of workers in 1931 and those in 1933, but the value of output had increased to some extent.

Ornaments, scientific apparatuses, musical instruments, educational supplies, etc., are the products of Group XV, which is one of the small and comparatively insignificant groups. In 1928 there were 18 establishments in this group; in 1931, 39 (of which 7 were large ones); in 1933, 18 and in 1934, 124. No industry of this group was included in the 1929 survey. There were some slight increases in capitalization and value of output from 1931 to 1933.

All miscellaneous industries not belonging to any previous groups are included in Group XVI, such as the manufacturing of tooth brushes, thermos bottles, coal briquettes, mirrors and ropes. There were 11 such factories in 1928, so far as we could classify them. No one was included in the 1929 survey. From 1931 to 1933 the number of large factories increased from 10 to 18, while the total of the former year was 32. In 1934 the number was given as 262, which must include many other industries not already

RECENT DEVELOPMENTS

enumerated above. We can hardly make any comparison in this group on account of the miscellaneous nature of the industries included.

In conclusion, we may say that there was much development in the Shanghai industries in recent years, especially between 1931 and 1933. With very few exceptions—notably the silk reeling industry—all Shanghai industries had grown during the period. The chemical and machine-making industries underwent the greatest development, the former because it was very well suited to Chinese requirements, and the latter because it was necessary to the development of all other industries. In the two most important groups—textiles and foodstuffs—the development was irregular. While the silk filatures were closed down in large numbers, the silk weaving mills enjoyed a certain degree of prosperity. Similarly, the cotton weaving industry seemed to have gained at the expense of the cotton spinning mills. The tobacco factories fared best, with the flour mills following, in the foodstuff group. Other industries in that group underwent only slight changes.

From another point of view it may be said that industries that produced ultimate consumption goods underwent greater development than those that turned out production goods, with, perhaps, the exception of the machine-making industry. This was only natural, since the demand for the latter products came from the former, and as industries developed, this demand grew with them. However, part of the demand might be satisfied with imported production goods, which were generally superior in quality to those produced by the Chinese factories. Hence the industries which specialized in those products could not catch up with those that produced goods for ultimate consumption. In fact, this is the natural process of industrialization, the development starting with the latter kind of industries, and extending backwards to those which make semi-finished products, and then again to those that supply industrial raw material and machinery.

The machine-making industry was an exception to this rule, because we classified factories that turned out all kinds of machines under this one heading. If the sub-divisions of this industry were examined separately, then some of them would be found to be making progress, and others lagging behind. In the other industries which produced industrial raw materials or semi-manufactured goods, the development was in most cases very slow during the interval, and some of them actually experienced setbacks. Tanning, cotton spinning and silk reeling were some industries which illustrated this situation.

Conclusions so far drawn are valid only for the period covered by our own surveys. After 1933, the depression in Shanghai has been very bad and business failures have been numerous. A partial survey of some Shanghai industries is being carried out at the time of writing, and before the work is completed, no definite statement can yet be made about the present industrial situation in this city. The general impression created by the newspaper reports, however, is that most industries are in difficult straits.

Again, it should be pointed out that the above conclusions have been based on statistics of Chinese factories only. The development of foreign industries may have been in different directions. As we have been unable to make a statistical study of it, we are not in a position to make comparisons. However, the most important foreign industry in Shanghai is, perhaps, cotton spinning, which is mainly under the control of Japanese interests. Although the competition of the Japanese cotton mills is keenly felt by the Chinese factories, yet their development has in many respects been more or less parallel. When the Japanese mills increased their spindles and looms, the Chinese mills were doing the same thing. On the other hand, when the latter were compelled last year to curtail production and suspend operation on certain days of the week, the former also followed suit. The Japanese mills were better off because of their superior equipment and larger capitalization, but the effect of the depression was not entirely unfelt.

CHAPTER IV

SALIENT FEATURES OF SHANGHAI INDUSTRIALIZATION

In the last chapter we have already made a vertical study of the industralization process in Shanghai to show how the various industries have prospered or declined. In the present chapter we shall make use of the same material and make a horizontal study to show the relative positions occupied by the different industries. In the case of the textile and foodstuff industries, something has already been said about this. Now we shall make use of statistical data and discuss them in connection with other industries.

The importance of the various industries can best be shown by making use of percentage figures to indicate the percentages which they constitute of the total. These percentages are presented in two tables in Appendix C. Although the percentages of the different industries differed slightly in 1931—1933, yet, since our attention is now focused on the relative positions of these industries, we shall not go into the changes in their positions. If there were changes during the interval, it might mean that the industry had prospered or declined, or that in 1931 there were more or less than the average proportion of small factories which were not included in the 1933 figures. However,

SHANGHAI INDUSTRIALIZATION

in most cases, the differences are not very large. If they are, we shall, as far as possible, make explanations for them.

From these percentages it is quite evident that the textile industries occupied the most important position in Shanghai with the foodstuff industries following next. In the two surveys, the number of factories in the former line constituted about 33% of the total number, and the capitalization from 38% to 39% of the total capitalization. In 1931 the number of laborers in the textile industries amounted to 60.1% of the total number of laborers in all industries, and in 1933 the percentage was 56. The value of output in the former year was 45% of the total and in the latter year 35.5%.[73] In the number of laborers and value of output, the percentages dropped quite significantly in the latter year, partly because the silk reeling industry was in a particularly bad situation during the latter year, and partly because the value of the products of the textile industries as a whole had fallen. As to the proportion of large to small factories, it was about the same in the textile industries as in all industries, and their exclusion should not make any difference with the percentages.

The number of laborers engaged in the textile industries was very large and among them the majority were female workers. Hence in the total number of laborers the number of female workers was also larger than that of the male workers. In 1931 the total number of female workers was 118,060, male workers 71,997, child workers 23,048 and the total 214,152, which last included a small number of workers whose sex was unknown. In 1933 these four figures were: female workers, 115,333; male workers, 75,693; child workers, 18,266 and the total, 214,736. Therefore, in both years the female workers were in the majority. In percentages of the total number, the female workers constituted 55% in 1931, and 53.7% in 1933. In both cases we have not taken into consideration the number of girls among the child workers.

---

73. For all detailed figures relating to the subject matter of this chapter, see Tables V and VI in Appendex C.

CHAPTER IV SALIENT FEATURES

In fact, they were also in the majority, and if their number were added to that of the female workers, the combined percentage would have been above 60% in both years.

If we analyze further the various industries in the textile group, then in 1933 the number of workers engaged in the cotton spinning industry was about 60,000; in the silk reeling industry, 30,000; in the cotton weaving industry, 9,000 and in the silk weaving industry, 10,000. As to the value of output, the cotton spinning industry produced $120,000,000, and cotton weaving and silk weaving each $20,000,000. The silk reeling industry used to have an output of very high value, but in this year, because the filatures were reeling on behalf of their creditors, and the business was also very bad, the total value of output was only $7,000,000. In 1931, when the conditions were better, the value was over $30,000,000, which must have been even larger in the earlier years when conditions were good.

In the matter of number of factories, capitalization and number of workers, the foodstuffs industries were not as important as the textile industries, but in the value of output, the former exceeded the latter in 1933. The number of factories in the foodstuff industries constituted of the total number only 10% to 12%; of the the total capitalization 19% to 23%; number of workers 11% to 13% and value of output 30% to 37%. In 1931 the value of output of the textile industries amounted to 45%, which was therefore higher than that of the food-stuff industries, but in 1933, as the cotton spinning and silk reeling industries declined, the percentage in the value of output dropped to 35.5%, while that of the foodstuff industries increased to 36.8%. Among the latter, the most important industries were naturally the flour milling and tobacco manufacturing branches. The value of output of the former reached $72,000,000 in 1933 and of the latter $100,000,000. As to the oil presses and rice mills, although they are also important in a sense, they include many handicraft workshops and otherwise small establishments. Large factories that come up to the Factory Law are very rare in these two industries;

SHANGHAI INDUSTRIALIZATION

hence from the point of view of modern industrialization, these two industries are not of much importance.

Besides the textile and foodstuff industries, those in Groups XI, XII and XIV come next in importance. Group XI includes the industries which produce clothing and other articles of apparel; Group XII, leather and rubber goods and Group XIV paper making and printing. The number of factories in Group XI constituted 10.2% of the total in 1931 and 7.5% in 1933. The value of output was 3.5% and 3.7% respectively. Group XII constituted in the number of factories 3.4% in 1931 and 4.6% in 1933 and the value of its output constituted 2.2% and 3.8% respectively. Similar percentages for Group XIV were 9.3%, 9.6%, 6.5% and 5.8% respectively. Besides these groups, all other industries came up to no more than 2% or 3% of the total.

Something has already been said in the last chapter concerning chemical industries. In 1933, although a small number of new factories were established to manufacture special chemicals, yet the majority consisted of factories producing matches, candles, cosmetics, etc. When the process of industrialization was still going on in this ountry, it was only natural that articles of daily use should first be manufactured while the more staple commodities would come later. The Yung Li Soda Factory in North China was organized more than ten years ago and in the beginning experienced great hardship in marketing its products. After many years of up-hill work, the factory finally took root, but it proved that before the other industries had developed to a certain extent, those that manufactured such basic commodities could not have had a very good market. Now as other chemical industries have prospered, and other kinds of industries demand more and more chemical raw materials, the factories that produce these materials will have a better market and consequently more and more of them will be established in Shanghai.

Although the development of machine-making and metallic products industries was quite striking, yet the factories were all comparatively small in size. Hence, although in numbers they

SALIENT FEATURES

constituted 14% to 18% of the total, in the value of output they amounted to only 2% to 3%, and in the number of workers about 5%. The capitalization was even smaller. So far as the value of output was concerned, the position occupied by these industries was even lower than that of the chemical industries, which in 1931 produced 3.7%, and in 1933 4.6%, of the total value of output. Similar percentages of the machine-making and metallic products industries were 2.6% and 3.9% respectively. Inspite of these small percentages, there was quite a bit of development in these as well as in the chemical industries.

The relation of the heavy industries to industries in general is the same as the chemical industries which produce acids, soda and other industrial raw materials. In recent years, the machine-making and metallic products industries developed to a large extent, although the position which they occupied in Shanghai industries as represented by the percentages they constituted of the total was not yet very important. The reason was that most of these factories were very small in size and they could not compare with the cotton spinning mills, flour mills, silk filatures and tobacco factories. This year the Wo Shin Iron Mill was reopened and at the same time the Central Machine Works of the Ministry of Industries has had its plant installed in Shanghai.[74] These two mills are fairly large in size, and if we add to them the steel mill of the Ministry of War, which we visited but were not able to secure any data for publication, there will be some change in the position of the heavy industries in Shanghai. As the importation of machinery has increased in recent years, the demand for machines and other products of the heavy industries is fairly great and there is much space for development in this line.

Insufficient Capitalization

The capitalization of Shanghai industries is, in most cases, insufficient. The men who established them generally raise only enough capital to buy the land, build the factory and instal the machinery—sometimes, the machinery only—while the working

---

74. *The Chinese Economic and Statistical Review*, Vol. III, No. 5.

SHANGHAI INDUSTRIALIZATION

capital depends almost entirely on loans from the modern and native banks. According to the industrial survey of this Institute in 1931, there were altogether 1,672 factories in Shanghai with a total capitalization of $142,329,494. The average capitalization was, therefore, about $80,000. In 1933, the scope of investigation was narrowed down to larger factories, and the total number was only 1,186. The total capitalization was $162,685,893, which gave an average of approximately $140,000. Although the capitalization data were not complete in both cases, yet the factories which failed to report their capitalization were usually the small ones, while the large factories, organized in the form of limited liability companies, generally reported their capitalization to us. Hence, even had the statistics been complete, the additions to the total capitalization would have been insignificant. If we study the various individual industries, the average capitalization would, in some cases, be larger than the general average and some smaller, as can be shown in the attached table. Hence, taking the Shanghai industries as a whole, there is no question about the insufficiency of their capitalization.

Two years ago we made a special study of the silk reeling industry in Shanghai. In 1929 and 1930 the total number of silk filatures in Shanghai was 104 and 107 respectively. In both years 65% of the filatures had only a capital between ₮10,000 and ₮25,000.[75] In 1931, on account of the world depression, most of the filatures in Shanghai were closed down, and the 66 that remained open had more capital to keep them going. Yet even then, 65% of them had only a capital between ₮20,000 and ₮35,000.[76] Of course the conditions in this industry are peculiar, because the factory as well as the machinery is rented, and hence less capital is needed.

If we compare the capitalization of the silk filatures with the value of the raw materials they purchase every month, then in 1931, of the total number of 63 filatures which supplied these

---

75. ₮ stands for taels, in this case Shanghai taels. Each Shanghai tael is equivalent to approximately $1.40 Chinese currency.
76. D. K. Lieu, *The Silk Reeling Industry in Shanghai*, p. 44.

SALIENT FEATURES

statistics, only 11 had enough capital to pay for the raw materials for one month. All the rest did not have enough for the purpose, and some of them had only enough money to buy one week's supply, which meant that the monthly outlay for raw materials was four times that of the total capital of the filature. If we compare the capitalization with the total amount needed for payment of salaries and wages during the year, then of the 58 filatures which supplied this kind of statistics, only 8 had sufficient capital for this purpose.[77] The capitalization of all the other filatures was smaller than the amount required for annual salary and wage payments. Although the factory and machinery in the case of silk filatures are generally not bought, yet when the capital is not sufficient even to pay for the raw materials or the wages and salaries in the year, the insufficiency of such capitalization is quite obvious.

We have also figured out the percentage relation between the capitalization on the one hand, and the value of output and value of raw materials on the other, for a number of important industries. Excepting the match industry, the capitalization was in most cases very small, while the value of output was comparatively large. Although this meant that the capital was being quite well utilized, yet when the value of output was large, the cost of production was naturally large too, and the capital was insufficient to meet the various expenses in some cases. If we take the year as a unit, most of these industries had to pay for the raw materials two or three times the amount represented by their capitalization, and in some cases as much as nine times. Hence most industries had to make loans from the native banks for these purposes. In Table D-IV the average capitalization of each factory in a number of important industries is given. It will be seen that in 1933 the cotton spinning industry had the largest average capital, being $1,600,000 per mill, and the foundries the smallest, about $8,000. Even the machine making industry had only an average capitalization of $47,000, while in 1931, when there were many smaller factories included in this group, the

---

77. *Ibid*, p. 46.

SHANGHAI INDUSTRIALIZATION

average capitalization was as low as $13,000.[78] These two are branches of the heavy industries, and with such low capitalization, their development was naturally very much limited.

Although in the case of cotton mills, the capitalization is fairly large, yet in the same way it is not quite sufficient. As a rule, almost all the cotton mills borrow money from the modern and native banks and the amounts are sometimes very large. Many of the mills have already been turned over to the banks to operate, and in some cases their accounts are supervised by the banks like the Sen Sing and Pu Yih mills. Although the reason why many cotton mills are in debt is often due to speculation, yet the insufficiency of the capitalization is also obvious.

Immediately after the European war, when this industry was most prosperous, many cotton mill managers expanded their business, increased the number of spindles and used up all their surplus cash. As soon as foreign competition began after the war, the cotton industry was badly affected and their products could not be easily marketed. These cotton mills therefore were unable to make money and had to go to the banks to borrow their circulating capital. A new mill, the Great China, which was established at that time, had an initial capital of $3,000,000, but all the money was used in buying land and machinery and constructing the plant. It began to borrow money from the banks before operation was started. As the boom was over almost immediately after the completion of the plant, there was no chance for it to make any money, and it had to get on on a hand-to-mouth basis, borrowing from the banks every now and then. The total amount of loans exceeded the value of the plant itself, and when it was compelled to liquidate and auction the plant, there was not even enough money to pay the creditors, and the total capitalization was wiped out.

An old factory is the Ta Sen Cotton Mill of Nantung, which has been in existence for several decades. Formerly it was making

---

78. See Appendix D, Table IV.

SALIENT FEATURES

money every year and its business policy was comparatively sound, while the profits made were distributed among the shareholders as dividends or used in the establishment of branch factories or other kinds of industries under Mr. Chang Chien (張謇). The machinery of old factories was not replaced and the capital for the new branches was also insufficient. Hence, as soon as the cotton boom was over, these factories were unable to distribute any more dividends. During the last decade or so, the campany was losing money, and the second branch mill was liquidated last year. The Sen Sing mills are also in the same plight, and a number of them have been put under the supervision of a banking syndicate consisting of the Bank of China, the Shanghai Commercial and Savings Bank and a few native banks. They supervise the payment of every cent, and also the purchase of the raw materials, the selling of the products, etc. Yet, after several years of such supervision, the money is still insufficient to repay the loans. Last year the No. 7 factory of those mills was auctioned, and a great deal of trouble was caused on account of the disagreement between the Chinese and foreign creditors of the company.[79] In the case of the Pu Yih Mills, they have long been put under the control of the creditor bank, the Kincheng Banking Corporation. The original shareholders have very little voice in the matter of management.

There is no market yet for industrial securities nor any institutions for underwriting them. When industries need money, they generally go to the ordinary commercial banks and the loans are made in one of two forms. Either it is made on the security of the *tsangchi*—including the factory site, the factory building and machinery—or it is secured on the raw materials or the finished products. In the first case, the time of the loan is longer, but as the machinery will depreciate in time, its price naturally goes down. Sometimes it becomes obsolete on account of technical improvements abroad. Hence, when the factory is unable to repay the loan, and the plant has to be sold out, the creditor will lose money on the machinery at least. The same is true with the

---

79. *The Chinese Economic and Statistical Review*, Vol. II, No. 2, p. 7.

factory building, which also depreciates with the years. On the other hand, the land on which the factory is built sometimes appreciates in value with the rise of land values in Shanghai. Formerly, this was the important factor which offset the possible losses in the two other items. Yet in recent years, on account of the depression, land values in Shanghai have also fallen, and loans on factory sites and machinery have become very unprofitable. The securities sometimes can not cover the loans made and interest accrued and the banks begin to demand repayment from the factories, which they are usually unable to do. At such a time like this, it is hard to find customers to buy the plants. Further loans from the banks are naturally out of the question, and the factories can not get any circulating capital to keep them going. As a matter of principle, such form of loans to the industries is also not proper. It should be based on the earning capacity of the industries and not secured on the immovable property. If the industry is not making money and the banks are compelled to take over the plant, they will not only stand heavy losses, but the transaction is also very troublesome.

Another kind of loans is secured either on the raw materials or on the finished products. The terms of these loans are shorter and the commodities are more easy to market. Yet their prices also rise and fall from time to time, and the banks are not commercial organizations that should be bothered with the sale of these goods when the factories are unable to repay their loans. Besides, during the term of the loan, the raw materials and the finished products have to be stored in the bank's warehouses. Whenever the factories need the raw materials for manufacturing purposes, they have to use the money obtained from previous sales of their products to repay a part of the loan and get out a portion of the raw materials used as its security. When this quantity of raw materials is manufactured and the products are sold out again, the money will be used to pay for a second instalment of the loan, and to get out a second instalment of the raw materials.[80]

---

80. *Shanghai*, a collection of lectures published in Chinese by the local Y.M.C.A., lecture on Shanghai Industries.

SALIENT FEATURES

Such a procedure is very inconvenient both for the banks and the industries themselves. If the loan is secured on the finished products, it is apparent that they are not quite saleable, because if they had a good market, there should have been no need of borrowing from the banks on their security. These loans are in the nature of commercial transactions, and as such, the securities should be in the form of credit instruments as it is in the case of most other countries. The advantage of credit instruments is that the time of the payment is certain, and that the commodities mentioned in them have already been sold before the bills are issued. When the bills are discounted by the banks, the only question is a matter of time. Those who sell the commodities are already assured of some form of payment, and unless there are special complications, they will always be able at the time specified to repay the loan. On the other hand, when goods are used as security, the banks will often be involved in commercial transactions when they have to sell these goods when the loan is not paid. For instance, in recent years, when the banks made loans to the silk industry on the security of the silk worm cocoons, the filatures were unable to repay these loans, and as the value of the cocoons fell considerably below the amount of loans, the banks were left with a large quantity of them on their hands which they could not sell without incurring a great loss. Hence they were compelled to rent filatures themselves, and make contracts with some silk merchants to run them on their behalf, thus making use of the cocoons they had taken over from other silk filatures. They were, therefore, drawn into industrial operations, just as they were often drawn into them on account of loans on factory sites and machinery.

The business organization of Shanghai industries usually takes the form of single proprietorships, partnerships or limited liability companies. Some other kinds of organizations also exist but they are very few in number. There are, for instance, a few factories operated by the Government. There are also some which are unlimited liability companies. In 1931 we investigated 1,672 factories, among which 3 were operated by the Government, 580 by single proprietorships, 700 by partnerships, 295 by limited liability companies, 51 by other forms of business organizations and 43, unknown. Of the 1,186 factories covered by the 1933 survey, there were 4 operated by the Government, 271 by single proprietorships, 443 by partnerships, 332 by limited liability companies, 43 by other forms of organization and 93, unknown. These figures show that the limited liability companies were not yet very popular in Shanghai, and other kinds of incorporated companies were even fewer. The majority still consisted of single proprietorships and partnerships. However, in 1933, because the factories were limited to those of larger size, the number of them which were operated by single proprietorships decreased and those operated by limited liability companies increased, yet the latter constituted no more than 28% of the total. In 1931 they constituted only 18%.[81]

Small Size of Shanghai Factories

The size of Chinese factories is usually small as it has already been reflected in the amount of capitalization. Even though the Chinese Factory Law puts the standard at a pretty low level, with 30 labourers as the minimum number, yet the Shanghai factories which come up to this standard form a very small proportion of the total. In 1931 when we made our first industrial survey of Shanghai, the number of factories that came up to this standard was 710 out of a total of 1672. The proportion was therfore 40%. That survey was still limited to factories which employed motive power or ten or more workers. If no limit was put on the scope, then the total number of factories must be even greater and the proportion of large ones lower. In 1933 our second survey covered 1186 factories which came up to the standard of the Factory Law. In the next year the Bureau of Social Affairs of the Shanghai City Government investigated the total number of factories in Shanghai and found the number to be 5,418.[82] It included some duplicates and some handicraft workshops, and according to our

---

81. See Appendix A, Table I, and Appendix B, Table I.
82. *Directory of Shanghai Factories,* published by the Bureau of Social Affairs.

SALIENT FEATURES

own investigations the total number should be about 4,000. Of these, those that came up to the standard set for our 1931 survey would probably number 2750.

In 1931, we included in the survey one item which was to show if the factory building was owned by the factory or rented, or if the land was rented while the building was constructed by the factory itself. Of the 1,672 factories covered by the survey, only 241 owned both factory and site. 110 owned the factory but the site was rented from others. 39 of them did not answer this enquiry, while the remaining 1,282 factories rented both land and building.[83] Although we also tried to find out if the factory building in each case was of the form which was especially adapted to the industry, or whether it was in the form of an ordinary house, the data collected were not suitable for the purpose because some of the investigators had some misunderstanding about the question. Yet, later, when we enquired from them about it, their impression was that most of the factories used dwelling houses of the type of the popular terrace buildings in Shanghai, where many houses are constructed side by side in rows. If one single house is insufficient for a factory, they will rent two or three of them. Any house would do so long as there is space to instal the machinery and allow the labourers to stand there and work. The factories do not care if the buildings are not adaptable to their special purposes. As the majority of the factories have rented buildings, and as the size is generally small, their establishment, suspension and removal can take place at any time. With the exception of the machinery, the factories hardly differ from ordinary business offices. It can move at any time. On one day it may be established in Chapei, and the next day when it is found that the rent is lower or that there are other conveniences in Nantao, it may be moved to the latter place immediately. When we investigated the factories a second time in 1933, we found that many of those that we covered in 1929 had moved in the interval, and they were usually the smaller factories.

---
83. See Appendix A, Table III.

SHANGHAI INDUSTRIALIZATION

On account of the small size, it is quite common for some industries to carry on only one stage of a manufacturing process, while other stages are carried out in separate industries. It is only in the larger factories that the whole process is carried out and many departments are maintained. For instance, although the silk weaving mills might buy the raw silk and manufacture the woof thread themselves, yet in most cases this is done by a different set of factories. While in the industrially advanced countries the silk reeling and weaving processes may go on under the same roof, in this country they are almost always separate. In the machine-making industry, there are special factories which cast the iron, others which turn them into machine parts, and still others which make boilers out of steel plates. The wooden models are made by another set of workshops. In a few cases, some large factories will combine their foundry and machine-making works in one, and sometimes they may have even a department for the making of models, but there are very few which combine all the processes mentioned above.

Not only that different branches of an industry are often kept independent, but in the same factory there is some sort of division of responsibility among several groups of people. For instance, if the motive power is supplied by steam engines, mechanics who are familar with this kind of machinery are sometimes employed who will supply a certain amount of motive power at a fixed sum. Such men will employ their own assistants and pay for the coal, the water and the lubrication oil. On the part of the factory, it buys the motive power on contract. This is the case with the silk filatures where the basis of such payments is the number of reels. Motive power which will be sufficient to supply 100 reels is paid at so much a month. When the man who contracts to supply this power buys coal, a similar procedure is adopted. The coal shops will supply so much coal a month which will be enough to produce so much power for so many reeling basins and they are also paid at fixed sums. As the silk filatures in Shanghai are mostly rented, several groups of men often run one single filature, each operating a part of it. The motive power sometimes comes from one single steam engine or a set of steam

SALIENT FEATURES

engines, and they are under the management of mechanics who are quite independent of the filature itself.[84]

In other cities cotton mills and knitting mills often rent their looms and knitting machines to the rural people, supply them with raw materials and let them carry on the manufacturing processes in their homes. The products are bought over by the factories at a price agreed upon beforehand. This is also because the size of the plants is so small that they are unwilling to expand and incur the responsibility of more rent and more risk. By renting out the machinery to the rural people, they are sure of an income in the form of rent, and the amount of expenses they have to pay out will be limited to the quantity of products they have agreed to buy.

In some cases the factories have raw materials supplied by their customers, and they charge only a sum equivalent to the cost of manufacturing plus profits. So when we try to find out the value of total output, we meet with certain difficulties. In the case of rice mills, although many of them buy rice and polish it for sale, yet there are also many of them which do the work for the customers entirely, while others do it partly for the customers and partly on their own account. In such circumstances it is very difficult to find out the value of total output, because a portion of the receipts represents only the value added by manufacture. It does not include the value of the raw materials. The same is true with the factories which manufacture machinery. In many cases they manufacture only on behalf of some customer and the raw material is supplied by the latter. Printers more often print for their customers, as it is true also in other countries. In Shanghai, many industries carry on their business under this system, while only the very large ones will buy the raw materials and manufacture on their own account.

Extent of Mechanization

Because the supply of electric power is abundant in Shanghai, and because the charges are comparatively low, the manufac-

---

84. *Shanghai,* lecture on industries.

turing industries here mostly use this form of power in preference to steam or oil engines. This also promotes small scale industries. When a factory has to buy its own steam engine or electric generator or even petrol engine, the cost is much higher. The small scale factories in Shanghai can generally buy a few motors and run their machinery with the use of rented electric power. Some of them do not usually operate all their machinery, and when a few of the machines are put in operation, only the motors attached to these machines need to be used, and no power is wasted in such circumstances. Hence the majority of Shanghai factories utilize rented electric power. In 1931, when the total quantity of power utilized by Shanghai factories was 158,389, rented electricity amounted to 90,214, horse power, or 60% of the total. In 1933, the total quantity of power consumed was 179,077 horse power, of which 108,782 horse power was rented. The ratio was also about 60%.[85] This shows the general use of electric power in Shanghai and explains the development of small scale industries here.

Although industrial development in Shanghai has gone further than any other part of the country, and although new industries are usually first established in this city, yet it does not mean that the plants here are modern and up-to-date. In fact, when they are compared with those in the industrially advanced countries, many of them would be considered as obsolete. For instance, the machinery in the cotton mills has mostly been used for over a decade. Formerly the Wing On 2nd Mill was considered as having very up-to-date machinery, but now it is already incomparable with that of many Japanese mills in Shanghai. The equipment of the other cotton mills is older, and their productive efficiency is therefore also lower. The yarn produced by Chinese cotton mills is generally of low count, and hence a larger quantity of yarn is produced in Shanghai per spindle than in England, America or Japan;[86] but if the same quality of cotton yarn is

---

85. See Appendix A, Table V and Appendix B, Table IV.
86. For production in English and Japanese mills see Freda Utley, *Lancashire and the Far East*, p. 202.

SALIENT FEATURES

compared, then we will see that the productive efficiency of the Chinese mills is much lower.

As the silk filatures are mostly rented, there is no hope of improving the reeling basins. Most of them still use those of the Italian type, although in recent years new filatures have been established in Wusih and Hangchow where the Japanese type of reeling basins are used, and where the quality of the product has been improved. Yet, in Shanghai little progress has been made in this line.

The machine making industry in Shanghai has developed to a greater degree than in other cities in the country. It can produce most kinds of machines after foreign patterns, and the price is generally low. They not only supply the need of Shanghai factories but also those in the interior. However, the machinery which these Shanghai factories are able to make are generally those which were used in the West some years ago. As to the most up-to-date machines, they have not yet learned how to make them. As these machines have to be bought from abroad, the price is generally very high. With the small scale industries, no inducement exists for them to buy such modern and expensive machinery.

The psychology of those people who promote industries in Shanghai is quite obvious. They prefer low costs in order to enable them to compete with other factories in the country. As there is a low tariff wall which makes imported goods sell at a slightly higher price than domestic products, with the exception perhaps of only Japanese goods, the competition is keenest among domestic industries themselves. To carry on such competition the Chinese industries generally sacrifice the quality of their products to lower prices. The general population which buys domestic products also prefers them on account of their cheaper prices. Hence there is no inducement for the manufacturers to utilize modern machinery and high quality raw materials which will not help in their competition with the other factories. Many of the manufacturers carry on their business on a speculative basis. They expect to make much money in a short period of time;

therefore they do not want to invest too much capital in their business. When they have made some money, they are ready to clear out at any time. Hence they prefer to rent their factory buildings, machinery and electric power. Anything that will lower the cost of production and make it unnecessary to invest large sums of money is always welcome to them.

This kind of speculative turn of mind is apparent from other things in the manufacturing industries, and in business in general. For instance, we have referred to the boom of the cotton industry during the European war, when a number of the old plants expanded their business to the utmost limit, and new mills were established in large numbers. During the May 30th Incident of 1925, when the boycott of English goods made the cigarettes of the B.A.T. Company very unpopular, many tobacco mills were established. This is the reason why even today almost all the cotton and tobacco mills are concentrated in Shanghai. Again in the rubber industry, there was for a time great profits in the making of rubber shoes and over-shoes. New factories were established and in 1933 the number was over 40. In the last two years, however, the business was not so good, any many of them closed down.

In other kinds of businesses also, like the large number of small banks established around 1921, and the 105 stock exchanges which came into existence in one single year, the same speculative nature is apparent.[87] All industries naturally involve some form of adventure and risk, yet this kind of short-sighted, cut throat competition is perhaps keenest in Shanghai. For this reason, the changes in Shanghai industries are very great, and many factories are closed down after having been in operation a year or two, while the re-organizing of industries takes place more often. In 1933, when we investigated the industries in Shanghai we calculated the length of time during which the factories had been in operation, and we found that the general average was eight years and four months, while in many industries it was as low

---

87. *Chinese Economic Monthly*, Vol. III, p. 21, and *Shanghai*, lecture on business.

SALIENT FEATURES

as two or three years. Yet these refer to the larger factories, because our survey was limited to them. Small scale industries change their management more often, and many of them seldom last over a couple of years.

The extent of mechanization can also be gauged by the number of horse power which is subject to control of each worker in the average, as well as by the average amount of power utilized by each factory, in the various industries. Concerning the latter, the cotton spinning mills had 2,133.2 horse power for each factory in the average, and the figure was the highest of all industries in 1933. Next came the flour mills, which used 815.7 horse power in each mill in the average, and after that the factories which manufactured rubber goods, with 168.6 horse power. All other industries employed less than 100 horse power each. Although foundries occupy a fairly important position in Shanghai industries, yet they use very little motive power. Their average in 1933 was 9.7 horse power.[88]

When we compare the quantity of motive power under control of each worker, we find that the largest amount was in the flour mill industry, where in 1933 each laborer used 4.86 horse power. Although the cotton spinning mills had the largest quantity of power per mill, yet they also employed a very large number of workers, and hence the number of horse power employed by one worker was only 1.02. All other industries in the same table had less than one horse power for each worker.[89]

The figures in the table referred to show the conditions in 1933. In that year we investigated only those factories which employed motive power, but some of them did not report according to our schedule, and we are compelled to leave them out in the calculation. When we figure out the average for all industries, we take all factories into consideration, whether their motive power was properly reported or not. The average per factory in this case was 151 horse power. In the same way, the number

---
88. See Appendix D, Table V.
89. Ditto.

of horse power at the command of each worker was 0.83. In other words, in the average for all industries, one worker did not employ as much as one horse power, and one factory only a little more than 150.

From the above it is seen that the utilization of motive power is very limited in Shanghai. Also utilization of modern machinery is very limited. Wherever hand operated machines can be used in place of power-driven ones, the former are preferred although modern manufacturing processes are adopted. The small scale tanneries mostly use old-fashioned instruments combined with modern chemicals in tanning leather. Of course, the quality of their products is naturally low, but at the same time the cost of production is also low, and they can be sold at low prices. In the manufacturing of cotton piece goods and underwear, or other knitted products, the looms and knitting machines are mostly operated by hand instead of electricity. In the same way the machines used in making matches are mostly operated by hand, although there are as many as 100 odd factories in this country. The running of printing presses is done in the same way, and only in some very large printing establishments and newspaper plants is motive power utilized.

Raw Materials and Products

The raw materials used by Shanghai industries are partly imported from abroad and partly supplied by the rural districts in the country. As the price of domestic raw materials fell in recent years, the industries in Shanghai reaped some profit, as we have pointed out in a previous chapter. However, the quality of the industrial materials produced in this country has not yet been fully improved, and transportation is still difficult. Hence in recent years Shanghai industries have been inclined to utilize more and more imported raw materials. For instance, China is the third largest cotton producing country and the neighboring districts of Shanghai are also cotton producing districts. However, the products of the surrounding districts are of low quality, because the staple is short, while the cotton of Shensi costs too much in transportation. Sometimes during the shipment, merchants adul-

SALIENT FEATURES

terate the cotton with water or other impure substances that destroy the quality of the cotton. Hence many Shanghai cotton mills depend on American cotton instead of domestic raw material. Some, like the Sen Sing Mills, utilize as much as 40% of American cotton. During the process of industrialization, the utilization of imported raw materials is unavoidable. Yet, since China is an agricultural country and produces large quantities of agricultural products, we should do our best to improve their quality, in order to meet the demands of modern industries. In this way, both agriculture and industry will be benefited. Otherwise, as we have pointed out in Chapter I, the results of industrialization will adversely affect the rural districts and cause their bankruptcy.

Shanghai flour mills also make use of foreign wheat to a large extent, although in northern Kiangsu, Shantung and Honan large quantities of wheat are produced every year. Hewever, the quality is not so good and adulteration by the merchants is a common practice. In calculating the cost of production, the flour mills find it cheaper to make use of Canadian or Australian wheat. In the last ten years the importation of foreign wheat increased considerably, as may be seen from the statistical table in Appendix F. The textile and foodstuff industries occupy very important places in Shanghai as has already been pointed out, and cotton spinning and flour mills are again important branches of these industries. It is therefore a great pity that these two industries, like many others, have to make use largely of imported raw materials.

For the improvement of agriculture, the Goverment has tried its best to introduce better breeds of cotton and to prevent adulteration. More has perhaps been done for the improvement of silk worm cocoons, and beneficial results have already been realized to a certain extent. In recent years, improved cocoons of Kiangsi and Chekiang have increased in quantity, and silk filatures are making use of them in manufacturing raw silk. Formerly 5.5 piculs of dried native cocoons could produce one picul of raw silk, but with the improved breed the ratio is lowered to 4.5 to 1. For this reason the cost of production of raw silk has been greatly lowered. Last year many silk filatures re-opened, partly because the price of silk abroad was rising, and partly because the improvement of the silk worm cocoons had lowered their costs. Hence for the development of industries, the production and improvement of industrial raw materials in the country is of great importance.

The tobacco industry occupies the first position in the foodstuff industries of Shanghai. Fortunately the raw material used in this industry can be drawn largely from inside the country, especially from the regions in Shantung, Honan and Anhwei. To a very small extent, American tobacco leaves are still imported for the manufacture of high grade cigarettes, but the quantity so imported has decreased very much since 1931. Shanghai is the centre of this industry. Most tobacco factories are located here. The British-American Tobacco Company has a factory in this city too, and it also makes use largely of Chinese raw material. Hence conditions in this industry, so far as raw material is concerned, are quite different from those in the cotton spinning and flour milling industries.

Other important industrial raw materials are different kinds of metals and chemicals. Although the heavy industries are making some progress in Shanghai, yet the quantity of iron reserve in China is very small, and the important iron mines are operated by Japanese, or have contracts with them to supply all iron to Japan.[90] The iron mills in China cannot have access to cheap raw material. The plants are also very old and heavily in debt to their creditors, and most of them have stopped operation. Although the Wo Shin Iron Mill has resumed operations, yet it is unlikely to be able to do very much in this line. Therefore, in the very important industrial raw materials of iron and steel, we have to depend a good deal on foreign imports.

---

90. *General Statement of the Mining Industry*, 5th Edition, a special report of the Geological Survey of China.

SALIENT FEATURES

As to chemical raw materials, with the development of the chemical industries we shall be able to produce a good deal for our own consumption in such things as soda and acids. However, the variety of chemicals is very large, and it is unlikely that we shall be able to produce all. What kinds of chemicals we shall try to produce will depend on the demand as much as on the extent of industrial development in this country.

On account of the low wage rates in China, the proportion which raw materials make up in the cost of production is usually very large. We have analyzed the cost of production of a few industries with respect to raw material, and find that in the cotton weaving industry, in 1933 for instance, raw materials constituted 88%, while in other industries they also amounted to somewhere between 70% and 80%. In the chemical industries alone they were as low as 55%. In the case of machine making and metallic products industries, because they did repair work to a large extent, the value of raw materials was comparatively low. The same was true of the tobacco industry, where, although we have left out those factories which specialized in production for their customers, we have been unable to separate the value of output from the value added by manufacture in the case of factories which both produced for themselves and for their customers. The low proportion of raw material cost in the factories making rubber products was one reason why that industry was very profitable in recent years.[91] In the case of foundries and machine making industries, the low percentage was partly made up with very high cost in fuel, and it did not mean that they made very large profits. If we take all industries into consideration, the average percentage which raw materials constituted of the value of output was about 60%.

As to the value of output, we have also calculated the average for each factory in a number of industries. The figure was highest in the flour industry, which amounted to $4,800,000. Next

---

91. See Appendix D, Table VI.

SHANGHAI INDUSTRIALIZATION

came cotton mills at $4,200,000; tobacco industry at $2,500,000, while all other industries were below $1,000,000, all in round numbers. The lowest figures were in the foundries and machine making industries, where the average value of output was less than half a million dollars.[92]

---

92. See Appendix D, Table VI.

CHAPTER V

LABOR CONDITIONS IN SHANGHAI

The total number of laborers in Shanghai, including the workers in the factories, the wharf porters and the ricksha coolies, was estimated by Mr. Tsha of the Shanghai Bureau of Social Affairs to be around 400,000. Among them the wharf coolies were said to be 20,000, based on an investigation by the Bureau in recent years. The number of ricksha coolies was estimated at 32,000 to 33,000 on the ground that there were 16,000 rickshas in Shanghai and about two men usually pulled one ricksha. As to the number of workers in the factories, Mr. Tsha based his figures on that supplied by the Bureau in 1934. That survey, as we have referred to, gave the total number of factories in Shanghai as 5,418, of which 3,839 factories reported a total number of workers of 299,000. Therefore, according to Mr. Tsha, the total number of workers of all factories should be about 300,000.[93] If, as we think, the 1934 survey of the Bureau of Social Affairs apparently included duplications and some handicraft industries, the total number of factories as well as workers needs revision.

That the two surveys of this Institute were both limited within a certain scope has already been explained in Chapter III. In

---

93. *Shanghai*, lecture on labor.

SHANGHAI INDUSTRIALIZATION

1933 we surveyed only those factories that came up to the standard of the Chinese Factory Law. Strictly speaking, since only establishments that came up to this standard could legally be considered as factories, the number of factory workers should be also limited to those working in these establishments. However, for the study of Shanghai industrialization according to the remarks in Chapter I, we do not emphasize the legal definition. All those establishments which employ modern machinery have some claim to our consideration. Hence, in 1931 our survey included more factories than would be considered as such by the Factory Law and the total number was 1,672. Of these 710 came up to the standard of the law and constituted 43% of the total. The total number of workers was 214,152, of whom 192,943 were in these 710 factories. The percentage which the latter constituted of the total was as much as 90. Had we not confined our survey to the scope we had chosen for 1931, we might have covered many more smaller factories, but the total number of laborers probably would not be increased by more than a few thousand.

Total Number of Workers

In 1933, although the number of large factories had increased to 1,186, the total number was not known. If we estimate the total on the basis of our 1931 survey, in which the large factories constituted 43% of the total, then the latter would be 2,759, and the number of workers, on the same basis of estimation, would be 235,567. Even if we should add to them factories which neither employed motive power nor had more than ten workers, but exclude the cottage industries, the very small workshops which produced for sale at their own premises, and those very small ones which were handicrafts in disguise, there were probably 1,000 more factories in 1933. Since none of these factories could have more than ten workers, the total number of workmen that we need include would not be as much as 10,000, and the grand total would not exceed 250,000. Of course our surveys were limited to the workers in Chinese factories. If their number was not quite complete, that has been made up by the liberality of

CHAPTER V LABOUR CONDITIONS

the estimates. However, foreign cotton mills had some 70,000 workers, and, with other foreign factories, would probably bring the grand total up to 350,000. The total number of factories would remain around 4,000.

In the section on labor movements in Shanghai, it will be stated that in the second period as many as 400,000 laborers took part in the movement. That naturally included all kinds of workers and was not confined to those in the factories. Even then the number was, perhaps, overstated, since during the labor movements the unions were anxious to report a larger number of workmen than they actually had, in order to show their importance. At the present time, the number of ricksha coolies was about the same as Mr. Tsha's estimate, because according to the special investigation of a committee on ricksha coolie welfare work, it was found that usually as many as three or four men would pull one ricksha. As will be given in the next chapter, the number of public rickshas is now 10,000, which means a total of about 35,000 coolies.

From the 1931 survey we obtained a total of 214,152 workers in the Shanghai factories, of whom 71,997 were men, 118,060 women, 23,048 children and 1,047 not classified. The percentages of the different kinds of laborers were 33.6%, 55.1%, 10.8% and 0.5% respectively. In 1933 the total number of workers was 214,736 and the figures for the male, female, child and unclassified workers were respectively 75,693, 115,333, 18,266 and 5,450. The percentages were respectively 35.3%, 53.7%, 8.5% and 2.5%. In both years the percentages of male, female and child workers did not change very much. However, as the child workers in the textile industries and industries making articles of apparel are mostly girls, about 15,000 should be added to female workers in 1931 and 11,000 in 1933. With this addition we shall find that workers of the female sex in both years exceeded 60% of the total.[94]

---

94. For all detailed data see Table III of Appendix D.

SHANGHAI INDUSTRIALIZATION

Taking the various main groups of industries, we find that the textile group had the largest number of workers in 1931, and their number constituted 60.1% of the total, and in 1933, 56%. The foodstuffs group constituted 10.9% of the total number of workers in 1931 and 12.7% in 1933. Since the total number of workers in both years was about the same, the changes in the percentages of these two groups should indicate absolute increases and decreases in the number of their workers. Besides these two groups, all other kinds of industries did not have more than 10% of the total number. The industry manufacturing articles of apparel, the paper making and printing industries and those producing machines and metallic wares had no more than 5% each. The leather and rubber group had about 4% and the chemical group 3½%. In 1933 the machine group had a slight increase and the apparel and paper groups had some decreases, while the chemical and leather and rubber groups increased most. The last was due to the significant development in the industry producing rubber goods.

The male workers were mostly engaged in the textile industries. After that came the foodstuffs industries, the machine making industries and the printing business. The women were almost entirely concentrated in the textile industries although some of them were, of course, in the foodstuffs group and the group producing articles of apparel. The concentration of child workers in the textile group was similar to the female workers, but otherwise they were engaged in the machine making industry and the printing business like the men. There were very few child workers in the foodstuffs group, although that group had many male and female workers. The children who worked in the textile group were mostly girls, while those in the machine making and printing industries were mostly boys.

If we take a number of important industries and calculate the average number of workers in each mill, then the cotton spinning industry would have the largest number. In 1933 each cotton mill had an average of 2,083 workers. Next came the silk filatures which had an average of 607 workers; the machine in-

LABOUR CONDITIONS

dustry with 402 workers; the tobacco industry with 388 workers and the rubber goods industry with 269 workers. All other leading industries had less than 200 workers. The average number in the foundry was the lowest, being only 36. In 1931, although the average figures differed from those in 1933, the order of importance of the industries was the same.[95]

When we divide the total value of output of these important industries by the total number of workers to arrive at the productive capacity of each workman, it is found that in most industries, with the exception of flour mills and cigarette factories, the figures were between $1,000 and $2,500. In the silk filatures the figure was very low, being only $241. This was due to the great depression in that industry. In the case of flour mills the large productivity of the workers was probably due to the greater extent of mechanization, which we have referred to in another chapter. In this industry each worker employed 4.86 horse power. The total number of workers not being very large, and the value of output being much larger, each worker was responsible for $28,888. This was the figure for 1933, while for 1931 the number was only slightly different. The high productive capacity of each worker in the tobacco industry was due to the very high amount of the total output. The figure for the productive capacity for each worker was over $6,000. In 1931 because many small mills were included in this industry, this figure was much lower, being only $4,484. Still it was much higher than that in other industries. In 1931 the lowest productive capacity of the average worker was also in the silk filatures, where the figures was only $762.[96]

Wages and Earnings

In 1929 the Shanghai Bureau of Social Affairs collected a large quantity of statistical data concerning wage earnings of Shanghai labourers.[97] The industries covered in this investiga-

---

95. See Appendix E, Table I.
96. Ditto.
97. This study is of earnings, while our own figures for 1933 refer to wage rates, although we have to use the word "wages" in both cases.

SHANGHAI INDUSTRIALIZATION

tion were the same as those referred to in connection with the industrial survey of 1929. However, in each industry the labourers were divided into a large number of groups according to the kind of work they did in the factories. For instance, in the shipbuilding industry the groups were woodsawing, foundry, iron work, copper work, work on the boat, work at the lathe, electric light mechanics, machinery work and accounting work. In the cotton mills the workmen were first divided into departments like the ginning department, the carding department, the coarse spinning department, the fine spinning department, the pattern department, etc., and in each department there were again a number of groups divided according to the kind of work done. Other industries were divided in a similar manner. At the same time the wages of the male, female and child workers were separately recorded and they were shown in different statistical groups giving the number of workmen receiving the wage from so much to so much in each statistical group. Then the average of all male workers in each industry was worked out for the hour and for the day. The same was done with regard to the female and child workers.

According to these statistical tables, the highest wages per hour for male workers was, in 1929, 14.6 cents. This was received in the printing industry, but because the working hours in that industry were short, the total earnings for the day were only $1.226 and were second highest among all industries.[98] In the silk weaving industry, although the male workers received only 12 cents per hour on the average, yet the average daily wage was $1.26, and was therefore higher than that in the printing industry. If we consider the wages of various groups of workers in these industries, we shall find that in the printing industry the engravers who were paid at piece rate received the highest wages, viz., 21.3 cents per hour and $1.775 per day. This was the average rate for all engravers. Among them there were some individuals who received even higher rates. When this Institute conducted the industrial survey of the whole country in 1933, we also found

---
98. See Appendix E, Table II.

LABOUR CONDITIONS

that the engravers in the printing industry received the highest wages. One particular workman in the Ministry of Finance Printing and Engraving Bureau in Peiping received more than $200 a month in wages. At first we thought he was a foreman or engineer, but after careful investigation it was found that he was just a skilled labourer. This shows that among the modern industries this kind of skilled labour receives the highest wages. In the silk weaving industry the highest wages were received by the weavers. Those who received piece rates were also better paid than those on time rates. The latter received an average wage of 4.5 cents, but that of the former was as high as 15.9 cents. Hence the daily wage of the former was as high as $1.6546. There were 1,002 male workers in the silk weaving industry covered by this survey of the Bureau of Social Affairs. Of this number, 617 were paid at piece rate, and only 22 weavers were paid at time rate. As the number of the former was very much larger than the latter, hence the average earnings of the male workers in this industry were comparatively high.

The lowest wages received by male workers were in the dyeing industry. The average daily wage was not more than 46.8 cents, which was due mainly to the short hours in this industry, being not more than eight hours a day. Otherwise, if the earnings by the hour were taken into account, the workers received as much as 6 cents per hour, which was not the lowest in all industries. The lowest per hour earnings were found in the cotton spinning industry, where the male workers received only 4.7 cents. This was because the semiskilled work in this industry was done mostly by women, hence the male wokers did not receive high wages. Some of them received as low as 3 or less than 3 cents per hour.

As to women workers, most of them were found in the cotton spinning and silk reeling industries. In the cotton spinning industry the average per hour earnings in 1929 were 3.8 cents and the average daily earnings 45.2 cents. In the silk reeling industry the average hourly amount was 4.9 cents and the average daily amount 53.9 cents. Both these sums were neither the highest nor the lowest in all industries in that year. The highest wages for female workers were in the silk weaving industry, where the per hour earnings were 8.6 cents and the daily amount 89.4 cents. The lowest was in the match industry, where the per hour amount was 2.7 cents and the daily earnings 24 cents.

Child workers received the lowest wages also in the match industry, where the per hour earnings were 2.5 cents and the daily amount 20.3 cents. The work of course was very simple, because they only put the match sticks in the boxes, and put on the chemicals on the outside of the boxes. In the cotton spinning industry, the child workers received also low per hour earnings of 2.5 cents, but as the working hours there were much longer, the average daily earnings were 30 cents. The highest wages for the child workers, according to the hour rate, was in the tobacco industry, where it was 4.2 cents. The number of working hours there, however, were short and the average daily earnings were only 41.6 cents. In the printing industry, although the child workers received only 4.1 cents an hour, the average daily earnings were as high as 41.8 cents.

From the above figures it will be seen that the printing industry pays the workers better than most other industries. This is not only because the work there requires more skill, but also because workers in this industry are more intelligent, and are in a position to bargain for better hours and wages for themselves. In the cotton spinning industry, on the other hand, the workers are mostly semi-skilled and unskilled, and at the same time the number is very large in Shanghai, as that industry is one of the most important industries in this city. Since there are so many workers who are in or try to get into this kind of semi-skilled or unskilled work, the labourers receive low wages. The very low wages of the female and child workers in 1929 were also found in this industry. The high wages in the silk weaving industry for both male and female workers was due to the skill required in that kind of work.

LABOUR CONDITIONS

The above is based on the study of the Bureau of Social Affairs.[99] The China Institute of Economic and Statistical Research also collected some wage data in its industrial surveys of 1931 and 1933. The 1931 figures were later organized and published in the Preliminary Report of Shanghai Industralization. As the way of summarizing the figures was not satisfactory in that report, we have adopted a different method of dealing with the figures for 1933, as given in Table V in Appendix B. Here, instead of finding out the median of the highest and lowest wage rates, we give the actual maxima and minima. As we had so many other items to cover in our survey, we were not able to collect the data on individual workers, as they did in the Bureau of Social Affairs, hence it was difficult to find out average hourly earnings for any class of workers. Where the wages were originally paid at piece rate, we converted them into time rates on the basis of the average number of pieces each worker could manufacture each day. Then we again converted the daily wages into monthly wages on the basis of the number of working days a month which was prevalent in that industry. As to the time rate workers, they were usually paid on the basis of the month and there was no need of conversion.

In many Shanghai industries, apprentices are hired and treated more or less like those in the old handicrafts. They are not given any wages, but only provided with board and lodging. Sometimes, in addition to the board and lodging, they are given a few dimes as pocket money. Hence the lowest wages in some industries are zero and in others less than a dollar. This does not represent the actual earnings of these workers, because their board and lodging should be considered in this connection. However, as the expenses in connection with board and lodging have been estimated at only about $6.00 and $0.50 respectively, the total earnings of such low paid workers are still very low.

From the data we collected in 1933, the highest wages sometimes exceeded $100 a month, as was the case in the shipbuilding industry, the railway machine shops, the electric plants, the silk

---

99. T. Y. Tsha, *Wages and Working Hours in Shanghai.*

weaving mills, the oil presses, the flour mills, the printing establishments and the manufacturers of thermos bottles and copper sheets.[100] The highest among them was $180 a month. In the industries which paid rather low wages, the highest rates were below $20 as in the manufactories of wooden boxes, metallic wares, bricks and tiles, stone works, dupion silk, dyed and printed cloth, and ribbons and trimmings.

As to the lowest wages in the various industries, the higest was $20 in the industries manufacturing lime with modern methods. Next to that came the manufacturing of aniline dyes, where the lowest wage was $16.50. The neon light, cement, crucible, and acid industries each paid the lowest rate of $15.00 a month. Other industries which paid above $10.00 were salt refining ($14.00), starch manufacturing ($13.00), frozen eggs ($12.60), alcohol ($12.00), cotton waste and other things ($12.00), water and electricity ($11.00), electric machinery and batteries ($10.50). With the exception of water supply and electric plants, all the other industries had only one factory each, and they were mostly very modern plants; hence the lowest wages were comparatively high. All the other industries paid less than $10.00 a month.

Many industries in Shanghai made use of apprentices, hence the lowest wages were sometimes below $1.00. Such industries included saw mills, iron furniture manufacturers, foundries, machine works, manufacturers of metallic products, electric machine works, shipbuilding works, factories producing construction materials, match factories, soap factories, enamel ware factories, varnish and paint works, manufacturers of bakelite, cotton weaving works, silk weaving works, woollen works, dyeing factories, knitting works, button factories, tanneries, canneries, oil presses, printing works and manufacturers of ornaments, scientific apparatuses, looking glasses and thermos bottles. The enumeration does not necessarily mean all the factories in the above industries employed apprentices, or even all factories in some

---

100. See Appendix B, Table V.

branches of these industries. It only means that there were some factories in these industries which utilized workers without any regular wage payments. In general, if the industry required skill, then there would be young people who were willing to serve as apprentices in order to learn the trade. The factories utilized such circumstances in order to save on wage payments. As the wage rates in China were low enough, this utilization of apprentices made them even lower, and hence the percentage which wage payments made of the cost of production was generally very small.

Mr. Tsha of the Shanghai Bureau of Social Affairs has compiled wage index numbers with 1930 as the base year. Although only figures for 5 years have been published, it can be seen that since 1930 the wage rates have been falling and they were lowest in 1934. 1933 was the highest year since 1930.[101] This seems to prove also that in that year industries were more prosperous, as may be seen from the statistics of our own surveys. Since the wholesale price and cost of living index numbers of Shanghai all began to fall in 1932, the earlier decline of the wage index numbers seems to be quite unusual, as it is the rule in most other countries for wages to lag behind prices. However, the index numbers of the wage rates were based on data of September 25th of every year. Towards the end of September, 1931, prices had already fallen, and it is not surprising that wages should fall with them. The reason why wages did not lag behind prices for at least a few months, if not a year or two, as it is usually the case in other countries, is probably because the Chinese workers in Shanghai have not organized and are unable to oppose any reduction in wages. Even if the workers of some industries actually opposed such reduction, it will not affect very much the general average of factory wages.

The cost of living index numbers of Shanghai were compiled with 1926 as the base year, and hence apparently they were higher than the wage rate index numbers. But if we change the base year of the former to 1930, then it will be seen that the decline in

---

101. *Chinese Economic and Statistical Review*, Vol. III, No. 3.

SHANGHAI INDUSTRIALIZATION

that series since 1933 was even greater than the decline in the latter. This means that although the Shanghai workers had their wages reduced, they were still able to maintain their living.

Index Number Base Year	Wage rates 1930	Cost of Living 1926	1930
1930	100.00	121.8	100.0
1931	96.61	125.9	103.4
1932	96.61	119.1	97.8
1933	98.31	107.2	88.0
1934	94.92	106.2	87.2
1935	—	106.6	87.5

If we study the wage payments in the more important industries investigated by this Institute in relation to the value of output, we shall see that the percentage was very low in almost all cases. In the silk weaving industry, where the percentage was high, it was only 14.2%, and this agrees with what we have said about the higher wage rates in that industry. Next came the match and knitting industries, while the low wage rates in the cotton spinning industry can also be seen from the low percentage which wage payments constituted of the cost of production in the same industry. The reason why the percentage was lowest in the flour mills was probably because that industry utilized more power and relatively fewer laborers and therefore the wage payments constituted only a small proportion of the value of output. It does not necessarily mean that the wages in that industry were very low. As most of the tobacco factories manufactured cigarettes for their customers, and conditions there were quite peculiar, the very low percentages of the wage rates were nothing unusual.

Working Hours

According to the investigation of the Shanghai Bureau of Social Affairs in 1929, the longest hours in the case of some laborers in certain industries exceeded 12 hours a day. The cotton spinning and weaving industries generally had such long hours, although the average working time was below that figure. The male workers in the silk reeling industry worked 12 hours a day

LABOUR CONDITIONS

in the average, but when we made a special investigation of this industry, we learned that the male workers there generally did very simple work as conveying silk and cocoons in the factory or janitor's work. Hence, even if they worked 12 hours, it was not so very strenuous. As to the cotton spinning and weaving industries, the situation was different, and 12 hours was really too long. The female and child workers in the silk reeling industry, the male and female workers of the silk weaving industry, the male workers of the knitting, tobacco, flour and paper making industries, the female workers of the paper making industry, and the child workers of the printing industry, all worked above 10 hours. In the enamel-ware, match, soap and egg industries, the male workers worked more than 9 hours a day. So also did the female workers in the soap and knitting industries and the child workers of the tobacco industry. Those that worked 9 hours a day were the male workers of the saw mills, foundries, machine works, shipbuilding works and tanneries; the female workers of the enamel-ware and egg products factories and the child workers of the enamel-ware industry. The male workers in the printing and oil industries, the female workers of the match, tobacco and printing industries and the child workers of the match industry worked in an average from 8 to 9 hours a day. In the glass industry, both men and boys worked only 8 hours. Their working hours were the shortest of all industries.[102]

According to the kind of work they performed in the industries, the shortest hours were those of the female workers who made the boxes in the tobacco industry, as they worked only 5½ hours a day. Similarly, the piece rate male workers in the oil presses also worked only 6 hours. However, in both cases they were paid by the piece, and the shorter the working hours, the less wages they received from the factory. It was of no advantage to the workers themselves. Those who worked above 12 hours were the boys in the printing industry. In the type-printing presses the boys who worked at time rate sometimes had to work 13½ hours a day. In the lithograph establishments the child

---
102. See Appendix E, Table III.

SHANGHAI INDUSTRIALIZATION

workers also worked more than 12 hours. Although the male and female workers in the printing industry had very short hours, apparently such privileges were not shared with the child workers. However, the child workers had to do rather simple wok, so the long hours might not be so hard on them.

In our own investigation, as we emphasized especially the process of industrial development, we were not able to distinguish between the different kinds of work done by the laborers, and the working hours in our statistical tables represent rather the hours during which the factories were in operation. In 1931, more emphasis was laid on this subject and the factories which occasionally had night shifts had the number of hours in the night shift given separately in the table, after a plus sign.[103] Those that had regular night shifts had the night hours added to the hours of work during the day. Hence, when the working hours in our table exceed 12, it means that these factories usually had night shifts. The figures given in our tables represent the average number of working hours of all factories in each industry. Since in no industry would all factories have night shifts, the average number of hours for the night shifts was usually from 3 to 5. It does not necessarily mean that the night shift was only so long. In a few industries, like cotton spinning, where all factories had night shifts, and where night shift was a regular part of the work, the total number of working hours was between 23 and 24.

In the 1933 statistics, although the main groups were the same as those in 1931, yet the subdivisions were slightly different, and in each subdivision the number of factories was also not quite the same. Hence the average hours of operation differed in these two years. Sometimes some of the factories actually increased the number of working hours and the difference between the two years represented actual changes. In some cases the difference was simply due to different methods of calculating the averages.[104] Still, in general, there were many similarities between the two

---
103. See Appendix A, Table VI.
104. See Appendix B, Table VI.

LABOUR CONDITIONS

years. For instance, the 23 to 24 hours in the cotton spinning industry and the very short hours in the printing industry, which also agreed with the study of the Bureau of Social Affairs.

Only a few factories in Shanghai give a holiday every Sunday but a number of them give the laborers one day or two a month as rest days. If, on these days, the laborers continue to work, they are entitled to additional wages known as "Shengkung." As the standard of living of the workers is very low, they are willing to sacrifice these rest days in order to increase their small income. Hence these rest days have more to do with the wage system than with the working time. The New Year and Festival Holidays are real holidays, but even then some workers might still continue to work while others might take more or fewer days for vacation. Hence in 1931 the number of days the factories were in operation often exceeded 360.[105]

As the workers in the printing industry are more intelligent, have higher wages and shorter working hours, they also enjoy more holidays during the year with the exception of the plate makers. Almost all kinds of workers in that industry work less than 340 days a year. Some of them have only 310 days. At the same time, more of them take part in strikes and labor disputes, which shows that the more intelligent the workers become, the more would they fight for their own rights and privileges.

The Labor Movement

According to a study by Mr. Tsha, the labor movement in Shanghai may be divided into four periods.[106] The May 4th movement of 1919 may be considered as the beginning of the first, the May 30th incident of 1925 that of the second, the occupation of Shanghai by the Nationalist Army in 1927 that of the third, and the January 28th incident in 1932 that of the

---

105. See Appendix A, Table VI.
106. *Shanghai*, lecture on labor.

SHANGHAI INDUSTRIALIZATION

fourth, period. He also gives an account of the development in the various periods which we will reproduce in brief below.

The first period: Although the labor movement started quite early in Shanghai, yet there had been no demonstration until the May 4th movement. Since then labor and capital formed two opposing camps. As the May 4th movement was started on account of an anti-Japanese boycott, the patriotic sentiment was very strong, and the labor organizations that came into existence at that time partook of this nature. There were about 50 labor unions in Shanghai at that time, and in 1922 an attempt was made to form a federation of these unions, but it did not succeed until the early part of 1925. More than 40 labor unions organized the Labor Federation of Shanghai, and it is reported that the membership of the federation was about 50,000. The officers of the Federation were mostly of the rather conservative type, and their organization was in touch with the right wing of the Nationalist party. However, the unions that were members of this Federation were of various kinds, and some of them were quite radical, hence the Federation was not in a position to control all its member unions. As to strikes, they also started in the early years of the Republic, but not until 1918 had there been statistical data concerning them. During the first period the number of strikes was small, ranging between 10 and 40 cases a year, as follows:

1918	21 cases
1919	23 "
1920	33 "
1921	19 "
1922	29 "
1923	14 "
1924	16 "

However, it was in 1922 that the new Penal Code first recognized the right of laborers to strike, and that may be considered the first step in the emancipation of the workers.

The second period: The May 30th incident also had its international complications. It was due, as we remember, to the

LABOUR CONDITIONS

shooting of certain Chinese by an English policeman in Shanghai, and it brought about a movement for the boycott of English goods. The workmen in the English factories in China began to strike, and as the sentiment ran high, the Labor Federation was not in a position to control the situation. Hence the radical elements overthrew the Federation and organized what was called the Shanghai General Labor Union. In July 1925, this Union reported and got registered 117 new labor unions with a membership of 217,000 workers. The size of this general union was, therefore, about 4 times that of the former Labor Federation. In September of the same year, however, the General Labor Union was dissolved by the Government, but its leading members still continued to carry out activities underground. During the expedition of the Nationalist Army against the Peiping Government the members of this General Labor Union tried to help the cause and carried out very big strikes. The first strike was participated in by 400,000 workers employed in 6,000 factories and the second by 300,000 laborers employed in 4,000 factories. When the Nationalist Army occupied Shanghai, some of the members of the General Labor Union took part in the fight. So far as the strikes were concerned, the number already increased to 75 in 1925, 257 in 1926, and 117 in 1927. At that time the Government gave quite free hand to the communist elements in the country, the radical wing took part in promoting the labor movement, and used Shanghai as the centre of the movement. Hence the laborers in Shanghai were inclined to the left, and strikes increased in number. As the Government was quite partial to laborers, they won in most cases against the capitalists.

The third period: The Kuomintang and Communist parties separated in July, 1927, but in April, the conservative elements among the Shanghai laborers had already taken away the power from the General Labor Union and organized an Association of Shanghai Labor Unions. At that time the military and government authorities in Shanghai were also of two groups. The conservative group was represented by the Provisionary Political Council of Shanghai and the radical group by the Provisionary City Government of Shanghai. The General Labor Union in conjunction with the radical elements among the military and government authorities tried to start some riots, but the conservative authorities took steps ahead of them, which enabled them to attack the General Labor Union, surround the Provisionary City Government, arrest the radical members of that government, and carry out a coup d'etat. The power was taken away from the radical groups.

In the remainder of that year there were as many as three organizations which were supposed to represent the labor interests. One was known as the Kungtunghwei (工統會). The second one was the Kungjentsunghwei (工人總會) and the third one the Tsungkunghwei (總工會). Each of them pretended to represent the whole labor organization in Shanghai and each fought against the two others. In May 1928 the central party organization appointed a re-organization committee to re-organize these labor organizations, but without success. After that, the Shanghai local party organization took over the matter and appointed a preparation committee for organizing a general labor union. Before anything was done by the preparation committee, however, the Nationalist Government had promulgated a Labor Union Law which prohibited the organization of federations of labor unions, hence nothing more was done in that line. As the Government had already driven out all communist members from the party, it took steps to prevent radical labor movements, and the relative positions of labor and capital were very much affected. Formerly, in all labor disputes, the laborers were usually victorious. Also there were only strikes by the laborers, while the capitalists never ordered any lockouts. In this period, however, lockouts were quite common, and the capitalists were sometimes successful in fighting against the laborers. The Government was anxious to control the labor movement and several laws were promulgated during this period, such as the Factory Law, the Labor Union Law and the Law Governing the Settlement of Labor disputes. Before the promulgation of the Labor Union Law there were in Shanghai altogether 427 labor unions with a total membership of 207,000 workers. According to Mr. Tsha's analysis, there were four special features in this period.

LABOUR CONDITIONS

(1) The labor movement turned from radical to conservative activities, (2) the movement to organize a labor federation failed, (3) the organization of individual labor unions was more uniform, and (4) the fight between labor and capital was on a more equal basis.

The fourth period: After the September 18th incident in Manchuria, when Japanese armies occupied Mukden, some of the Shanghai labor unions again organized a general labor union which was established in December, 1931. The individual labor unions which were reorganized again under the new Labor Union Law numbered by that time 68 with a total membership of over 60,000 laborers. In 1933 the number of labor unions increased to 76 and the next year to 84, while the total membership was increased in 1933 to 62,000 and in 1934 to 65,000. As the September 18th incident in Mukden and the January 28th incident in Shanghai were both incited by Japanese aggression, the labor movement in various parts of the country also concentrated its attention on opposing the Japanese. Hence in Shanghai the laborers organized the Anti-Japanese National Salvation Federation, the Shanghai Wharf Laborers' Anti-Japanese Association, the National Salvation Association of Seamen, the Anti-Japanese Punitive Army of Laborers in the newspaper business, and the Anti-Japanese Volunteers organized by the Post Office employees. On account of the international aspect of the movement of this period, the number of strikes was rather small, being only 82 cases in 1932, 88 cases in 1933 and about 63 cases in 1934.

Strikes and Lockouts

From 1918 to 1926 Dr. Ta Chen compiled statistics of labor strikes in Shanghai. After that the Bureau of Social Affairs continued to compile statistics of both strikes and lockouts from 1918 to 1932. However, the figures of the Bureau for the first nine years, although they cover the same period as that of Dr. Chen, do not agree with his figures as published in his book entitled "Chinese Labor Problems." Since the Bureau of Social Affairs is the administrative office in Shanghai which has charge of labor questions, its figures are naturally more official, and we therefore use their statistical data. Dr. Chen's figures were mostly collected from the newspaper reports. Their number was larger than that of the Bureau of Social Affairs, because some of the cases were not reported to that Bureau but only reported in the newspapers. Also Dr. Chen's study was confined to strikes only and did not include lockouts.[107]

Before 1927 the Bureau of Social Affairs had to collect figures retroactively, and therefore they were not quite complete. After that the Bureau has been in a position to collect first hand data, and it has published a book entitled "The Strikes and Lockouts in Shanghai in the Last 15 Years" which gives a detailed analysis of these cases. In our present chapter we shall utilize these figures to indicate the labor unrest in Shanghai.

Between 1918 and 1932 there were altogether 1,121 cases of strikes and lockouts, according to the Bureau of Social Affairs. Classified according to the kind of business or industry in which the laborers worked, then the textile industry had the largest number of cases, being 339, which was almost one-third of the total.[108] Next to that came communications, and next again the printing trade. The textile industry is the most important industry in Shanghai and has also the largest number of laborers, hence the large number of strikes in that industry. The communications group had so many strikes because there are the Nanking-Shanghai and Shanghai-Hangchow-Ningpo Railways, which employed a large number of workers, but this has nothing to do with manufacturing industries. Although the printing trade does not have so many laborers, yet, because the printers have more intelligence, they usually are the main force behind strikes and labor movements. The radical elements among the laborers are usually also workers in printing trades, hence the large number of strikes in this trade. If we limit the total number of strikes and lockouts to the manufacturing industries, then there were only 897 cases.

---

107. Ta Chen, *Chinese Labor Problems*, Table facing p. 150.
108. See Appendix E, Table IV.

LABOUR CONDITIONS

The percentage of cases in the textile industry becomes as high as 44% and that in the printing trade 12%. Although the foodstuff industry occupies a place in Shanghai manufacturing industries only second to that of the textile industry, yet the number of strikes and lockouts are not as many as those in the printing trade.

If we analyze the causes of the strikes and lockouts, then 1,024 cases were due to questions involving collective bargaining and only 97 had no such connections. The latter was less than 1/10th of the total. An analysis in greater detail shows that the disputes over wages came to 488 cases, or about 43% of the total. Questions concerning employment and discharge of laborers gave rise to 216 cases, about 19% of the total. Although the question of working hours is of great importance in foreign labor movements, in China it does not occupy a very important place, hence the number of strikes and lockouts due to this question was only 25 in the period of nine years.[109] Among the cases that had nothing to do with collective bargaining were some that were sympathetic strikes and others that were in connection with political questions. It is surprising to find that the number of strikes due to political reasons was rather small although in labor movements such political and international questions occupied an important place. Perhaps, in the Bureau's analysis, the causes were those given by the labor leaders in calling the strikes, while these men themselves might be motivated by political considerations. After all, the rank and file were more concerned with their own livelihood, and such questions as wages and employment were more important to them than political questions.

As to the results of such strikes and lockouts, in the majority of cases the demands of the laborers were accepted. In a total number of 1,121 cases, the demands of the laborers were accepted in 261 cases and partly accepted in 406 cases. The total of these two groups constituted about 60% of the grand total.[110] Where the demands of the capitalists were entirely accepted, the number of cases was only 6 and ten cases in which the demands were partly

---
109. See Appendix E, Table V.
110. Ditto, Table VI.

accepted. This was, of course, due to the small number of lockouts. Still, when we consider the number of cases where the laborers' demands were refused, they numbered only 281. It can be seen that the laborers were successful in their movement to the extent of about a half of all cases, because the number of cases in which their demands were entirely accepted was about the same as that in which they were entirely refused, while those demands which were partly accepted can be considered as compromises in which the laborers were partly successful. There were still 150 cases in which the question was not brought to a definite settlement, or the result of the settlement was not definitely known. If all data were available, we might be able to have full knowledge as to how far the laborers were successful in their strikes.

The statistical data representing strikes and lockouts not only included cases outside of manufacturing industries, but also cases in foreign factories and foreign business establishments. However, as the number of foreign factories and establishments in Shanghai was not very large, the number of cases was also small. The May 4th, May 30th and January 28th incidents all had to do with international questions in connection with Great Britain and Japan, hence the number of strikes in the factories and business houses of these two countries was larger than those of other countries. The total number of cases of Chinese nationality was 720, Japanese 159, English 136 and other countries less than 100.[111]

The number of man-days lost and the loss of wages due to strikes and lockouts could not be estimated for the 15 years, but figures are available since 1927. That year was before the separation of the communist party from the Kuomintang, and the radical laborers brought about a large number of strikes. Hence the number of man-days lost in that year was the largest of all years for which statistical data are available, and it amounted to 7,622,029 man-days. The year 1928 came next with 2,049,826 man days. None of the other four years had more than 1,000,000 man-days. As to the loss of wages, the largest was also in 1927, amounting to

---
111. Ditto, Table VII.

LABOUR CONDITIONS

$3,710,116.26. It was $835,962.73 in 1928 and below half a million dollars in all other years.[112]

The factories and commercial establishments suffering from strikes and lockouts since 1927 were 21,089. The largest number was also involved in 1927, being 11,698 cases. Next came 1928 with 5,433 factories. In the other years the number was very much smaller. As to the number of workers involved, the total was 1,361,122, of which male workers numbered 803,120, female workers 504,230 and child workers 53,772. The largest number of laborers was involved in 1927, being 881,289, making up about 60% of the total. In 1928 it was 204,563, and in all the other four years it was always below 100,000. It is a pity that no figures were available for 1926, when there were even more strikes and lockouts, and we ought to find more factories, establishments and workers involved and a larger number of man-days lost as well as a larger amount of wages.[113]

Labor Disputes

Statistics of labor disputes are available for 1928 to 1932 as published by the Bureau of Social Affairs. The number of cases was 1,491 and the number in each year was about the same.

The number of factories and establishments involved in the labor disputes totalled 11,799. The largest number was involved in 1929 and the smallest number in 1931. As to the number of laborers involved there were 196,910 men, 228,934 women and 58,937 child workers with a total of 484,781. The average number every year was larger than that of strikes and lockouts, but as these cases were all amicably settled through mediation or arbitration, the cases were not so serious as strikes and lockouts.[114]

The causes of labor disputes have been analyzed by the Bureau of Social Affairs into two groups: those having to do with collective bargaining and those having not. Among 1,491 cases,

---
112. See Appendix E, Table VIII.
113. Ditto.
114. See Appendix E, Table IX.

only 3 had nothing to do with collective bargaining. If the cases be further analyzed, then it will be found that the disputes were mostly caused by questions concerning employment or discharge, numbering 1,018 cases in these five years and constituting almost 70% of the total. Although the question of wages was very important in cases of strikes and lockouts, they did not occupy a very important position in labor disputes, and numbered only 163 cases.[115] This was probably due to the fact that the wage question was so important to the laborers that it generally gave rise to more serious disturbances, such as strikes. When the question concerned employment or discharge of a certain portion of the labourers, it could be more amicably settled.

Analyzed according to industry, the textile industry had the largest number of cases, being 490, which was about 33% of the total. Communications came next, with 250 cases, or about 17% of the total. The printing trade again occupied the third place and the foodstuff industry, the fourth place. If cases in modern manfacturing industries were alone considered, then the total number would be 1,154 cases, and the percentage of cases in the textile industry would be as high as 40.[116]

The methods of settling labor disputes were many. Some were settled through direct negotiation between the two parties, some through mediation or arbitration by a third party, while some others were settled without any discussion or mediation. The third party was either the Labor and Capital Mediation Committee or the Arbitration Committee or the Bureau of Social Affairs. The two Committees were also appointed by the City Government, and were therefore more or less official in nature. In these 5 years the cases that were settled through the mediation of the Bureau of Social Affairs or through its administrative orders were 849, amounting to 57% of the total. Cases settled by the Labor and Capital Mediation Committee numbered 394, and those by direct negotiations between the two parties 133. Besides these three groups, other cases were either settled through the media-

---

115. Ditto, Table IX.
116. Ditto, Table XI.

LABOUR CONDITIONS

tion of a third party or through arbitation or without negotiation or mediation.[117] Results of settlements show that the laborers were completely successful in 335 cases, complete unsuccessful in 195 cases and partially successful in 911 cases. If we consider the last as representing a half-and-half compromise, then the laborers were successful in more cases than they were unsuccessful.[118] Analyzed according to nationality, 1,401 cases were disputes in Chinese factories and establishments, while those in foreign factories did not number as much as 100.[119]

---

117. Ditto, Table XII.
118. Ditto, Table XIII.
119. Ditto, Table XIV.

CHAPTER VI

ECONOMIC EFFECTS OF INDUSTRIALIZATION

To study the process of industrialization in Shanghai we ought to know the economic background of the city on the one hand and the economic effects of the process on the other. The scope of the former is much bigger because it involves a study of the general economic forces of China as a whole as well as of the world. Yet, Shanghai is the most important industrial center of this country, and as our economic relations with the outside world mostly go through Shanghai, the economic background is itself, to a large extent, effect of the industrialization of the city. For instance, in the changes in population, trade and the money market, this situation is clearly reflected. We will refer to various kinds of economic statistics since 1925 or 1926 to show the economic development of Shanghai as well as the effect of the industrialization process on the city. It is a pity that in some of the series the figures for 1935 are lacking or not yet complete, because they have not yet been published.

If we analyze the various kinds of economic statistics in a cursory manner, we will find that they belong in general to two groups. Those in one group show continuous development and growth, although there have been in recent years important politi-

CHAPTER VI ECONOMIC EFFECTS

cal and economic changes, such as the removal of the National Capital to Nanking, the Japanese invasion of 1932, the world depression since 1929 and our going off the silver standard last year. These important changes have not affected the continuous development as represented by the statistics in this group. In the other group the figures show the varying prosperity and depression of the different years. If we make use of statistical methods and find out the trend lines, they will naturally also point upwards, but in the last decade or so the best year is not necessarily the last, as apparently is the case in the first group of statistical data. In fact the latest year is in some cases much worse than some of the previous years. Hence the first group of statistical figures show the general growth of industrial cities, while the second indicates more clearly the vicissitudes of the recent years.

Growth of the City

Population statistics will be discussed in greater detail in the next chapter on the Social Effects of Industrialization. In this chapter, since we are going to analyze various kinds of economic statistics, population data cannot be left out entirely. The population data in the next chapter are given for several decades, but only one figure is given for every five years. Here we will limit all series to the last ten years, while the population figures for every year are given to show the changes during the period when industrial surveys have been made in Shanghai.

Since there were no population statistics for the Chinese territory of Shanghai before 1930 and the 1935 figures for the French Concession are yet unavailable, the figures for the whole city are only for five years. For the other years they are not complete. Yet, as the International Settlement has a very large proportion of the population of Shanghai, and its growth is indicative of the industrial development of the city, its figures for the whole decade are very illustrative. If we take the last five years only, when the figures are complete for the three sections of the city, we find that in 1934 the

SHANGHAI INDUSTRIALIZATION

population figure was the highest. It exceeded 3½ million.[120] On the other hand, the figures of the International Settlement alone, throughout the ten years, show that the increase has been continuous. If a trend line is worked out by statistical methods for the figures of these ten years, the actual position of some years will be above the line and some below it. Hence the growth is not in the form of a compound interest curve, yet there is no doubt that every year the actual figures showed increases. The only exception is for the Chinese territory in 1932, when there was a sudden decrease on account of the Japanese invasion, but recovery was seen in the next year, and in 1934 it broke all former records.

The relation between population growth and industrial development is too obvious to need any comment. When industries develop, they will afford more employment to laborers, and more workers will come from other towns and provinces to Shanghai to earn their living. This is in addition to the natural increase due to excess of births over deaths among the local population. On the other hand, when population increases in the city, the demand for manufactured products, as well as the aggregate purchasing power increases, and industries naturally grow along with it. The almost continuous growth of Shanghai industries which is discussed elsewhere is a result of this development in addition to the other factors which are mentioned in that connection. This is the most fundamental effect of industrialization everywhere in the world. It explains the growth of cities and at the same time the continuous industrial development is also a result of the growth.

While Shanghai has already taken the fifth place among the large cities of the world, its future development is still unlimited. It has the chance of having a larger population alongside with the growth of other industrial cities of the world, and at the same time there is the possibility of its occupying even a higher position in the list of industrial cities on account of the large hinterland which offers a market for the products of Shanghai. Only a few large cities in America can compare with Shanghai, while the European

---

120. See Appendix F., Table I.

ECONOMIC EFFECTS

metropolises are generally handicapped by the political barriers which limit the territory they serve. The only drawback in the case of Shanghai is the low standard of living of the Chinese people, and consequently their low purchasing power. If the whole country is better developed economically, with better communications and better exploitation of natural resources, the future of Shanghai is bright indeed.

The statistical figures which reflect best the relation between population and land value are the density data. Hence in another table the population density of the three sections of Shanghai is given for the last ten years, showing its continuous increase in every case, while in a third one the rise of land values for the same period is also given.[121] As population density increases, and the industrial development of this city goes on, the value of land rises with it. The land value statistics of the International Settlement are given every three years by the Municipal Council on the basis of the assessed values of the four districts, East, West, North and Central. An average figure is also given for the four districts. The latest data are for 1933, because the next assessment will take place this year, and figures are not yet available.[122]

When we compare the assessed values of the last four dates since 1924, we can see that they were increasing steadily. The average assessed value per mow in 1933 was about two times that in 1924 and about 20% higher than that in 1930. Comparison between the figures for 1930 and 1927 shows that the increases during those three years was even greater. This is apparently unexpected because the world depression began in 1929, and yet land values in Shanghai went up in the following year instead of falling. It shows that the effects of the world depression in China came a little late, and it seems also to substantiate the statement made by the American Economic Mission that land speculation in

---

121. See Appendix F, Tables III and IV.
122. A detailed study of Shanghai land values has been made by Chang Hui. 張輝上海地價研究

SHANGHAI INDUSTRIALIZATION

Shanghai was one of the factors which brought about the depression in this country.

In fact, in every country, when business reaches the peak of prosperity, speculation must be very active. Only in other countries it takes place mostly on the stock market, and to a less extent on real estate and other things. In China, because the transactions on the stock exchange are mostly limited to Government bonds and treasury bills, which do not fluctuate so much when political conditions are stable, speculators are therefore compelled to turn to other things, such as real estate and gold bars. Of course there is also the foreign stock exchange in Shanghai where foreign companies' shares are transacted. However, they do not attract Chinese speculators so much as land and gold bars. Hence, although from other points of view, we find that this country had already got into a depression in 1932, yet the land values in Shanghai kept on going up till 1933.[123] This confirms the conclusion which we obtained from a study of industrial development, which was continued till 1933 and 1934 in spite of the falling price level.

The effect of population growth is also shown in the demand for housing facilities. Hence in another table we give the number and assessed values of houses of the International Settlement for a number of years. So far as the assessed values are concerned, those of 1934 were the highest (the 1935 figures are yet unavailable). In fact, the growth seems to be quite continuous throughout the whole period. In the table the houses are grouped into those that are occupied and those that are vacant, and we have figured out the percentages for the two. They show that although the assessed value was increasing, the number of vacant houses had also become greater during the last four years, especially the foreign style houses. In 1934 the latter kind of houses were vacant to the extent of 13.7% of the total number in the city, while only 6% of Chinese style houses were vacant. Therefore, the general average was only 7%. As the rental of the foreign style houses is

---

123. Some real estate agents are of the opinion that land values began to fall in 1932, but the Municipal Council statistics show that, if they had fallen below the 1931 level, they were at least higher than that in 1930.

ECONOMIC EFFECTS

generally higher, it is more difficult for their owners to get tenants during the depression.

From these figures it can be easily seen that the increased supply of houses was due to the landlords' speculative activities. They thought that the land values in Shanghai would still go up, and without taking due consideration of the depression, they kept on building, and thus added to the total assessed value of the houses. Yet, at the same time, the purchasing power of the tenants had decreased, and therefore vacant houses were increasing in proportion to the total, especially in the case of foreign style houses. In such bad times, it is only natural for tenants to move from the more expensive foreign style houses into the cheaper Chinese buildings, and to move from the bigger to the smaller houses. This tendency is not only shown clearly in the figures, but anyone who observes the general situation in Shanghai will come to the same conclusion. Everywhere the "To Let" signs are now in conspicuous display and they are good indications of bad times in the city. Statistics of the French Concession only give the numbers of Chinese and foreign styles houses in the territory.[124]

Growth of Industrial Section

Having already analyzed the assessed value of residence houses, we will now make a special study of building construction, especially factory buildings, to show the relation between industrial development and construction activities. In both the International Settlements and the French Concession, the statistics of new construction activities show that 1930 had the highest assessed values, and the number of buildings constructed was the largest of all years except 1925 in the former, and largest of all years in the latter. Of the buildings constructed, the number of factory buildings in the International Settlement was largest in 1934, with 1931 following. In the case of the Chinese territory, the number of new factory buildings in 1931 was largest, while the area of land occupied by such buildings was largest in 1932, and the assessed value in

---

124. See Appendix F, Tables V and VI.

1933. This quite agrees with the result of our industrial surveys of the city. In our survey we find that the number of large factories in 1931 was much smaller than that in 1933. From the building statistics we find that although the number of new factories constructed in the Chinese territory in 1931 was the largest, yet the area and assessed value were smaller than the two following years. This shows that the new factories constructed in that year were of smaller size than those in the later years. In 1934 all figures became smaller.[125]

If all kinds of new buildings in the Chinese territory be taken into consideration, the 1933 figure was highest as to the number of buildings and the area covered by them. In assessed value the 1934 figure was the highest, which was probably due to the increase in office buildings and apartment houses. In 1932, on account of the Japanese invasion, the people of the Chinese territory moved in large numbers into the settlements, but since that year the change has been in the other direction. While the population of the whole city has been growing, that in the Chinese territory has grown even faster, while at the same time more and more vacant houses are found in the settlements. As the rental in the Chinese territory is much lower, it is only natural for people in these hard times to move from the more expensive houses in the settlements to the less expensive ones in the Chinese territory. Hence the number and assessed value of new buildings in the settlements, with the exception of factories, are declining in recent years, while in the Chinese territory they are increasing.

As to factories, their number is much larger in the Chinese territory than in the settlements. Both land value and rental in the Chinese territory are much lower than in the settlements, and it is much more convenient as well as economical for the factories to be established there. For the same reason, the factories established in the Chinese territory can be much larger than those in the settlements, and that is why there were so many more large factories in 1933 than before. The building statistics of the Chin-

---

125. See Appendix F, Tables VII, VIII and IX.

ECONOMIC EFFECTS

ese City Government also show that in 1934 the growth of industries was arrested. Although this seems to contradict the impression given in a previous chapter by the very large number of factories in that year, the explanation is not far to seek. The industrial survey of 1934 as carried out by the Bureau of Social Affairs of the City Government included too many small factories and workshops and their large number is not indicative of industrial development. The total was probably not larger than that in 1931 or 1933 when we conducted our surveys, but as ours was limited to factories of certain sizes, the figures are therefore incomparable.

The construction of roads goes hand in hand with the growth of industrial cities. In the old fashioned cities of China the roads are not well constructed, and they are very narrow and crooked, like those of Mediæval Europe. On the other hand, good roads extend in all directions in all modern industrial cities, thus extending the city area, and providing space for industrial development. In Shanghai, the increase is greatest in the Chinese territory, where there had formerly been few macadamized roads over large areas of land. In the International and French Settlements, because the area is limited, new roads are fewer, yet there are additions from year to year.[126] As the factories of Shanghai are, to a large extent, situated in the Chinese territory, this increase of roads helps to a large extent their development, at the same time is made necessary by it. The large number of factories on such roads as Chungshan, Chunghsin, Kuoho, Chunghwa, etc. shows the concurrent development of public roads and manufacturing industries.

There has been a tendency in recent years for many factories to move out from the more valuable sites in the central district to the Chinese territory in Chapei. Although this tendency was checked for a while by the fear of renewed Japanese invasion after 1932, yet the re-building of the devastated section of Chapei has been going on very rapidly, and to-day we still find more factories there than in most other parts of the city. This is only

---

126. See Appendix F, Table X.

SHANGHAI INDUSTRIALIZATION

a natural tendency of urban development, since the industrial section ought to be in the outlying districts, while the central part of the city should be reserved for business premises. With the location of the railroad station in Chapei, where the Nanking-Shanghai and Shanghai-Hangchow-Ningpo railways meet, the future growth of Chapei is assured. It is a pity that the original plan of developing Kiangwan as the centre of Shanghai has not been carried out, on account of the Japanese invasion, otherwise the growth of Shanghai will be much faster, and a larger number of people will perhaps be attracted to this city than is already here.

Together with the increase of good roads, the increase of various kinds of vehicles is shown in another table. In Western cities, only motor cars and motor trucks need to be taken into account. But the conditions in Shanghai are quite peculiar, and besides motor vehicles, there are rickshas, carriages, bicycles, wheelbarrows and hand-trucks. Statistics of these vehicles are available only for the International Settlement, but from these figures we find that in 1934 the number of motor cars was over 9,300, almost twice as many as in 1926. The increase in the number of bicycles was about the same. One account of the limitation to the number of rickshas imposed by the Municipal authorities, the number remained during the last ten years around 10,000, in addition to a smaller number of private rickshas. Horse carriages and wheelbarrows were decreasing, as they were gradually driven out of existence through displacement by more modern forms of conveyance. This shows also the modernization of Shanghai. The number of carts increased two-fold in the last ten years.[127] It would otherwise be a very useful indicator of industrial development if we know what that included, for instance, if they included the motor trucks used by the factories, or if they were limited to carts pulled by human labor or pack animals.

The Price Level

Many of the series of statistical figures discussed in the preceding paragraphs are related to the population increase of Shang-

---

127. See Appendix F, Table XI.

ECONOMIC EFFECTS

hai, and hence their growth is almost constant. On the other hand, price, trade and financial statistics are of a slightly different nature. The wholesale price index numbers of Shanghai are the earliest ones compiled in this country. They were formerly prepared by the Bureau of Markets of the Peiping Finance Ministry. Under the National Government, the work has been taken over by the National Tariff Commission since 1926. The Commission and the Shanghai Bureau of Social Affairs have also compiled cost of living index numbers, and since 1930, wage index numbers. At the same time, the number of items included in the wholesale price index has also been increased. Those commodities which have close connection with modern indudstries are mostly found in the three groups: textiles, building materials and chemicals. Hence in the appended table we give, besides the general index number of wholesale prices, the index numbers of these three groups. In all cases the base year is 1926. In 1931, the general index reached the highest point, which was also true of the index numbers of textiles and building materials. In the case of chemicals, the peak was reached later in 1933, while textiles went down since 1931, and their fall was much greater than any other group. From these figures we may draw certain conclusions.[128]

The textile industries in Shanghai are the most important of all modern industries. As the prices of their products, as well as of their raw materials, fell suddenly after 1931, the effect on these industries has naturally been very great. Yet, it did not arrest the growth of other industries, and even in the textile group, the cotton and silk weaving industries, as we have pointed out in Chapter III, underwent further development after 1931. The general impression about the depression in Chinese industries is created mainly by the effects on the cotton mills and silk filatures. The index number of the textile group is computed mainly from the products of these factories. Hence it fell immediately after 1931. As we can prove with our statistical data, the decline was limited to these branches of the textile industries. In fact, even

---

128. See Appendix F, Table XII.

in the cotton mills, there have been additions to the spindlage since that year.

The continued rise in the prices of chemicals after 1931 reflects the continued growth of the chemical industries. In our survey of 1931, we found there were 60 factories in this industry, of which only 28 came up to the standard of the Chinese Factory Law. In 1933, our second survey covered as many as 78 factories, all of which were up to the legal standard. The capitalization and the value of output increased 50% during the two years, while the increase in power consumption was even greater. There was also a 25% increase in the number of workers engaged in this industry. This was for the industry as a whole. If we analyze the various kinds of factories in the industry, we shall find that several new chemical industries came into existence in Shanghai between 1931 and 1933. Factories were established since 1931 for the manufacture of oxygen, acetylene, dyes, bakelite, calcium and magnesium carbonate, etc. In all branches of chemical industries there were growth and development. The price index numbers confirm our findings.

Foreign Trade

The foreign trade of Shanghai also reflects the industrialization process very clearly.[129] As far as imports are concerned, the figures were largest in 1931. Since then they have decreased. The export figures were highest in 1930. Taking the totals of both imports and exports, and separating foreign trade from domestic trade, we find that 1931 was the best year for the first series and 1928 for the second. There is a third series showing the re-export of commodities to other treaty ports, which was also largest in 1928. The trend of foreign trade was therefore similar to that of the price level. It shows that the effects of the world depression reached China as late as 1932. However, trade statistics are based on value and value itself is affected by the fall in the price of silver. In 1930 and 1931 the world price of silver fell abruptly, and all foreign commodities, when their prices were con-

---

129. See Appendix F, Table XIII.

ECONOMIC EFFECTS

verted into the Chinese currency, naturally became higher than before, which accounted for the increase in the foreign trade figures of China. Since September 1931, when England and Japan went off the gold standard, the exchange rates of foreign currencies began to fall, and the prices of foreign commodities, when converted into the Chinese currency, also fell with them.[130] Hence both the foreign trade statistics and the wholesale price index numbers of China fell at the same time. The Shanghai index numbers were originally compiled for reference in tariff revision, and the commodities included have mostly been international goods. Thus the relation between the price indexes and our foreign trade is very close.

Computed into index numbers with 1926 as the base year, the exports from Shanghai fluctuated around 50 in the four years following 1931, while the imports only fell below the 1926 level in 1934 and 1935, and even then the index number was still above 80 in the latter year. Also, the peak was reached in 1929 in the case of the former, and in 1931 in the case of the latter, showing distinctly the effect of the world depression and silver depreciation on the value of the imports.[131] At the same time the index number of exports for all China dropped to as low as 42.8 in 1935, and imports, 52.5, both of which were lower than those for Shanghai alone. Similarly with the total value of foreign trade, the indexes of which were 68 for Shanghai and 48.2 for the whole country.[132] This means of course that Shanghai trade constituted in recent years a larger percentage of that of the whole country, as can be seen from the percent figures given in a separate column in the Shanghai table. However, it does not mean that Shanghai's foreign trade has proportionally increased, because since August, 1932, Manchurian imports and exports have been excluded from the totals for the whole country.[133]

---

130. cf. D. K. Lieu, *A Study of Our Price Level*, pp 10-11.
131. *Chinese Economic and Statistical Review*, Vol. III, No. 2, Table A, reproduced with addition as Table XIV, Appendix F.
132. See Appendix F, Table XV.
133. *Foreign Trade of China*, 1932, Part I.

SHANGHAI INDUSTRIALIZATION

In yet another way should we expect to see the close relation of foreign trade to industrialization. The more industrialized China is, the more the export of manufactured articles, and the less the import of the same commodities. At the same time, the importation of industrial raw materials and machinery increases. However, in the last six or seven years, so many extraordinary occurrences took place that these effects of industrialization were often modified by them. First, the world depression began in 1929, and our foreign markets were, to a large extent, cut off. As the demand for our products was, in some cases, more elastic than others, the effect of the depression also varied with the different commodities. Second, in 1930 and 1931, the world price of silver fell abruptly and resulted in a kind of inflation in China. Industries developed on that account, and our foreign trade was also maintained at a fairly high level until in 1931 England and Japan went off the gold standard and gradually worked towards economic recovery. China, on the other hand, was adversely affected by their monetary policies. Depression set in and our foreign trade dropped. The United States began to raise the price of silver since 1934, which caused a sort of deflation in our currency, further cut down our foreign trade, and affected our industrial development. On account of these special circumstances, the import and export figures do not represent very clearly the industrial development in this country. Yet, at the same time, they also show how industrialization is affected by other factors, and reflect the combined results of these two. We will now make use of some figures showing the importation and exportation of commodities which have a direct bearing on industralization and study their relations to our present subject.[134]

As has been mentioned in Chapter I, the importation of manufactured products is a factor which promotes industrial development in this country. Yet when our industries have developed to a certain extent, the importation of such articles naturally decreases. The most conspicuous instance is cotton yarn. Formerly this was imported in very large quantities, but during the last

---
134. See Appendix F, Tables XVI-XIX.

ECONOMIC EFFECTS

eleven years the quantity decreased greadually until in 1935, the total value was only 1/30th that of 1925, when we take the whole country into consideration. For Shanghai alone, the proportion was one to twelve. Again, in 1925, the value of imported cotton yarn was far greater than that of exported yarn, but since then the latter has increased much more rapidly, while by 1931 the import of yarn became very insignificant. When the two sets of figures are compared, with the exception of the first year or two, there has been always an excess of exports. This shows very clearly the development of our cotton spinning industry. It also shows that since 1925, this industry has developed to such an extent that the demand for yarn has been entirely supplied by domestic manufactures. The domestic product is even exported to foreign countries. However, since 1931, because of the world depression, and the fall of the pound sterling and the yen, the value of cotton yarn export has decreased.

In the importation of raw cotton, the peak was reached in 1931 as far as value is concerned. This is similar to the situation in the export of cotton yarn and for the same reasons. In the two following years, although other kinds of industries continued to develop, the cotton spinning industry was affected by the world depression, and the importation of raw cotton and the exportation of cotton yarn have decreased after that year. The same is true of the importation of textile machinery and machine parts. Although the number of spindles has still increased after that year, it is the result of contracts entered into before by the managers of cotton mills who are shortsighted enough to try to expand business at a time when depression has already been felt in the industry.

Silk reeling is also one of our most important industries. It is also to a large extent concentrated, like the cotton spinning industry, in Shanghai. Because its product constitutes luxury goods, and the foreign demand for it is more elastic, its exportation declined as soon as the world depression began. Since 1929 the Shanghai filatures were closed down to a large extent, and down to 1934, both for Shanghai and the whole country, the value of silk exported was only about 1/10th that of 1929. In the last

SHANGHAI INDUSTRIALIZATION

year or two, the Chinese Government did much to improve the silk worm breeds and to produce better and cheaper cocoons. Hence the cost of production of raw silk fell, and there was a slight recovery last year. As silkworm cocoons are produced in large quantities in China, and Japanese cocoons are used only to a very small extent, the importation of raw materials for this industry is negligible. Hence we will not reproduce the Customs statistics for cocoon import. The machinery for the silk reeling industry is not listed separately in the Customs reports, but is included under textile machines. As the silk industry has declined considerably, only a few new filatures have been established in other cities. In Shanghai all of them are old ones, and some of them have been closed down. Nothing has been added to their machinery equipment. If a detailed analysis of such machinery from the Customs reports were made, it would have only confirmed these facts.

Besides textile industries, the flour mills also occupy a very important place in Shanghai as well as in the whole country. In the Customs statistics, the products of the flour mills are listed under different headings. Before 1931 it was given as "wheat flour." After that the heading has been "machine milled wheat flour," but actually the difference is very little. During the last eleven years the largest quantity was exported in 1933, which shows that this industry had continued to develop for four years after the world depression began. In that year the value of flour exported from Shanghai was about the same as that exported from the whole country, which means that practically all the flour exported in that year came from Shanghai. This agrees with what we know of the actual conditions, because in recent years, the flour mills in other parts of the country were more affected than those in Shanghai. If we consider the statistics of the whole country, then the value of wheat flour imported was highest in 1929, but in Shanghai it was in 1932. The former is representative of the general situation with the other imports. The reason why there was a sudden increase in flour imports in Shanghai in 1932 was probably due to the Japanese invasion in that year. At that time there were so many troops in Shanghai that had to be rationed, and

ECONOMIC EFFECTS

as many flour mills were closed down temporarily, foreign flour had to be imported. So far as raw material was concerned, the importation of wheat was largest in 1931, both for Shanghai and the whole country. This is the same as that in other industries.

The tobacco industry is similar to the flour and cotton industries. The domestic market is, in these cases, more important than it is with steam filature silk. Hence, although the export of cigarettes dropped since 1928, the industry was not very much affected, and importation of raw materials increased until 1931. The importation of cigarettes was kept up until 1930, because, although production increased inside the country, and although exportation of cigarettes decreased, the consumption in this country had increased to such an extent that foreign cigarettes had to be imported in larger and larger quantities. The Customs statistics give figures about the import of cigarette machinery only after 1932, and the figure was largest for that year. According to those who are engaged in this industry, the effect of the consumption tax has been very great. Foremerly, cigarettes were divided into seven classes and taxed accordingly. As the cigarettes made in this country are mostly of the lower class, they were able to pay much less tax than the imported ones or those of the B.A.T., and were therefore able to compete with these products. Now the cigarettes are classified into two grades for taxation purposes, and the tax even on the lowest grade is higher than it was before. At the same time, the Chinese cigarette factories have been prohibited from giving prizes, and they find it harder to market their products in competition with those imported from abroad or those manufactured by the B.A.T.[135] As the competition has been greatest between the British American Tobacco Company and the Chinese factories, the market of the latter has been taken up by the former, while the importation of foreign cigarettes has decreased since 1930.

The position of Shanghai in the whole country can also be seen from the foreign trade statistics. For instance, in the case of

---

135. Unpublished Chinese report on the tobacco industry, prepared by this Institute.

cotton yarn, Shanghai takes in about 1/3 of what is imported into the whole country. The same is true with cigarettes. In the case of wheat flour, the proportion imported into Shanghai is only about 1/80th of that of the whole country at the lowest, and even in ordinary times it varies between 2% and 5%. This is because the people in the south do not consume wheat flour as much as those in the northern provinces. The fifteen flour mills in Shang hai utilize wheat of north Kiangsu, Australia and Canada to manufacture flour to supply the northern provinces, where they have to compete with the local mills. In the case of the tabacco industry on the other hand, practically all the factories are concentrated in Shanghai, and they are not subject to competition of the mills of other privinces.

Many of our people, in view of the increased importation of wheat in recent years, worry about the bankruptcy of the rural districts on this account. They believe that China has always been an agricultural country, and when she has to obtain supplies of rice and wheat from abroad, it means that her economic foundations are shaking. As a matter of fact, the imported wheat only takes the place of wheat flour imports, and is the result of industrialization of this country. The largest quantity of wheat flour was imported in 1929 when the value was $98,000,000. In the case of wheat imports, with the exception of 1931, the value has never exceeded this figure. Besides, the increase in wheat imports went hand in hand with the decrease in flour import, which shows that our flour mills are utilizing foreign wheat to produce flour, just as our cotton mills utilize foreign cotton to produce yarn. In the latter case, the highest record for cotton import was in the year 1931, when its value was 40 times that of yarn import. This is a definite proof of industrial development of this country. If the agricultural products can be improved and be adapted to the needs of modern industries, then although raw materials are being imported from abroad, both our agricultural and manufacturing industries can develop. Only when our agricultural products are of such a low quality that they can not be used at all in our manufacturing industries is the situation to be worried about.

ECONOMIC EFFECTS

If we study the statistics of foreign trade according to another classification, then we will find that the importation of industrial raw materials was highest in 1931. This was true also of the import of industrial machinery into Shanghai, although the highest record for the whole country was in 1930. Among the different kinds of industrial machinery, the most important ones consisted of textile machinery, prime movers, electric generators, agricultural machinery and lathes, and they were all imported in the largest quantities in 1931. It is a pity that the classification of machinery in the Customs reports was changed since 1931 and hence comparison is not so easy to make. In the case of imported manufactured products the highest record for Shanghai was generally the same as that for the whole country. At most the difference was only one year earlier or later. When the total value of the various imported commodities we have so far selected is taken into consideration, then for the whole country it reached the highest figure in 1929, which shows that, so far as these imports were concerned, the effect of the world depression was almost instantly felt in this country. Since that year, foreign industries were in no position to extend their market in the Far East, while the fall of silver price put another obstacle in the importation of foreign commodities. This situation is also clearly indicated by our industrial statistics, as well as the Shanghai price index numbers compiled by the National Tariff Commission.

Transportation

The steamship tonnage statistics of Shanghai are divided into two kinds, as given in the Customs reports. The first refers to the boats that sail between Shanghai and foreign ports as well as the treaty ports in China and the second between Shanghai and the small towns in the interior. Both the number and tonnage are given in the statistics.[136] In the figures for the first kind of vessels, the number was largest in 1930 and tonnage in 1931. For the second kind of vessels, the number was largest in 1933 and tonnage in 1934. Although figures for 1932 are unavailable,

---

136. See Appendix F, Tables XX and XXI.

SHANGHAI INDUSTRIALIZATION

it is not expected that that year would be a record year, as in all other statistical series the situation is about the same. The second kind of vessels which ply between Shanghai and the small towns in the interior are usually very small, and hence they are not of much importance. What are important are the figures for the other kind of vessels, and they show that the carrier trade was best in 1931, which was true also of foreign trade. These two sets of statistics should naturally correlate, but the tonnage figures prove that the quantity as well as value of our foreign trade has declined since that year.

Developments in land transportation can be seen from the statistics of the Nanking-Shanghai and Shanghai-Hangchow-Ningpo Railways.[137] So far as the transporting of goods is concerned, the ton-kilometrage of the former line was highest in 1926. In the four years from 1930 to 1933, it was lower than 1929, but in 1934 the figure was larger and almost compared favourably with that of 1926. In the case of the Shanghai-Hangchow-Ningpo Railway the record year was 1934, with 1930 following behind. The three years intervening were all below 1930. Hence from the statistics of goods transported on these two railways, it seems that the effect of the world depression was more immediately felt than shown by other statistical series. The recovery in 1934 was also similar to conditions in England and Japan. The statistics of goods transportation are given sometimes under several headings: agricultural products, animal products, forestry products and mineral products, but for these two lines recent figures under such headings are not available. Besides, when so classified, the figures given show the value of the goods transported and not the quantity or the ton-kilometrage. Hence, even if they were available, they would not show the traffic conditions of the railways. As to manufactured products transported over these two railways, it would be even harder to ascertain from the statistics that might be available.

Passenger traffic on these two lines attained the highest record in 1931, and in 1934 there was an indication of recovery. The

---
137. See Appendix F, Tables XXII, XXIII and XXIV.

ECONOMIC EFFECTS

situation is similar to that as shown by most other statistical series, while the recovery in 1934 also agrees with the goods transportation statistics. The revenue of the railway from both goods and passenger traffic was highest in 1931, in the case of the Shanghai-Hangchow-Ningpo line, and it also showed a tendency of recovery in 1934. In the case of the Nanking-Shanghai Railway, the 1934 revenue was higher than that of 1931.

The Money Market

To study the relation between Shanghai industrialization and the money market conditions, a few series of statistical data are available. The interest rate of the native banks, being more or less similar in its importance to the central bank discount rates in other countries, should have very great influence over the money market, and indirectly the industrial development in this city.[138] In fact, it has, as witness the embarrassment to the industries in the last two years when the interest rate often went up very high and banks were unwilling to make any loans to them. However, the rate usually fluctuates between quite wide limits from day to day, and the average rate for a month or a year, which is often used as its statistical summary, does not represent the situation satisfactorily. Especially the latter, which we must use in this connection since all other statistical series are represented by annual figures. Hence the very low rate in 1933 does not necessarily mean that money was very cheap in that year, and industries grew on that account. Figures showing the highest and lowest rates may add some information about the conditions of the money market, but even they do not tell everything. It should also be pointed out that the rate .05 in 1933 does not mean 5 per cent, but it means 5 cents per $1,000 per day, which, converted to the annual basis, is equivalent to 1.825 per cent.[139]

---

138. Since 1933 the Joint Reserve Board of Shanghai, which represents the modern banks here, has adopted official rates for discount and call loans, but their importance cannot yet compare with the "native rate".
139. See Appendix F, Table XXV.

SHANGHAI INDUSTRIALIZATION

The increases in bank deposits and loans, the issue of bank notes, the stock of silver in Shanghai, modern and native bank clearings, etc., are more indicative of the growth of Shanghai and its industrial development. Between 1925 and 1934, the loans of 28 Chinese banks, which have either their head or branch offices in Shanghai, increased 195 per cent; deposits, 251 per cent; note issue, 196 per cent; holdings of securities, 635 per cent; cash reserve, 143 per cent and capitalization, 123 per cent. In another column we have figured out the average increases every two years, on the assumption of an even development through-out the whole decade. Compared with these it will be seen that the growth of banking business from 1931 to 1933 was in most cases below the average percentages, and the exception was cash reserve.[140] Cash reserve includes both specie and bank notes, but specie holdings in Shanghai have also increased tremendously in recent years, reaching the highest record of 547 million dollars in 1933.[141] Compared with the 1926 figure, that of 1933 meant an increase of 272 per cent. Due to America's silver purchase program, large quantities of the white metal were exported in 1934 and 1935, and so the stock in Shanghai was considerably reduced. These changes have therefore no direct connection with industrial development.

Before 1933 there was no special clearing house for modern banks in Shanghai, although the native banks had had a clearing system for many years. In that year, however, the Shanghai Clearing House was organized by the modern banks, and they began to have their accounts cleared through this institution. The native banks still maintains their old clearing system, and the amount cleared through it is still much larger than that through the new Clearing House. When the two amounts are combined, certain duplications cannot be eliminated, but the resulting figure may be considered as more or less representing the total clearing transactions.[142] In the last decade, the total amount of clearings was largest in 1930, the year before trade reached its zenith in Shanghai.

---

140. Ditto, Tables XXVI and XXVII.
141. Ditto, Table XXVIII.
142. See Appendix F, Table XXIX.

ECONOMIC EFFECTS

Since then, the figure has become smaller—although in the new Clearing House more business has been done as more modern banks have joined the system—with a slight recovery in 1934. The situation is similar to most other statistical series which have direct relations with trade rather than industrial development. (Even in more recent years, the clearings were about twice as large as a decade ago.)

Transactions on the produce exchanges indicate the same tendency.[143] Trading was heaviest in 1931 in cotton, yarn, wheat, flour, beans, bean oil and bean cake. This was only natural, since it represented trade and its concomitant, speculation. Unlike bank clesrings, the growth of which is partly due to the increasing use of checks and native bank orders, and does not necessarily mean a larger volume of business in general, transactions on the produce exchanges in the earlier years were not always smaller than the later ones. For instance, there was in fact more transactions in wheat in 1928—the first year for which we have secured statistical data—than in 1932 or 1935. Dealings in wheat flour in 1926 were almost exactly the same as in 1935. Transactions in cotton and cotton yarn, especially the latter, increased. This was partly due to further development of the cotton industry of Shanghai in the last ten years, and partly due to increase in speculative activities in these commodities.

Gold bar transactions, which are mainly speculative, were heaviest in 1926, contrary to the trend in all other lines. Due to Government measures against such speculation, lest it should unduly affect the value of the national currency, they were at the lowest ebb last year. With the enforcement of the new currency system, the value of gold bars can no more fluctuate between wide limits, and transactions will never regain their former magnitude. Government bond transactions, on the other hand, have grown steadily except for 1932, when the value of the bonds was greatly affected by the Japanese invasion of Shanghai. Otherwise, the growth was quick as well as steady, as more and more bonds

---

143. Ditto, Table XXX.

SHANGHAI INDUSTRIALIZATION

and treasury notes were put on the market. Compared with the earlier years of the decade under consideration, the increase was more than ten-fold. This is parallel to the increase in the security holdings of the banks. Dealings in bonds and gold bars have no relation to the industrial or trade developments in Shanghai or the country. If there is any connection at all, gold bar transactions have something to do with fluctuations in foreign exchange rates, which themselves also have no direct bearing on Shanghai industrialization except through their effect on trade and cost of production as has been pointed out in Chapter III.

It is a pity that the Chinese stock exchange deals almost exclusively in Government bonds and treasury notes. Few industrial shares are listed on the exchange, and those that are listed are seldom dealt in. This situation is in part responsible for the difficulty in raising industrial capital and financing industrial development. Transactions on the foreign stock exchange and the index numbers of foreign company stocks in Shanghai are more indicative of the trade and industrial conditions of the city.[144] The former show that trading was brisk in 1931 and 1934, while in 1932 transactions during the whole year (i.e., excluding the first two months when all business was suspended on account of the Japanese invasion of the city) did not amount to as much as those in six months in 1933, not to mention the two good years. Worse still was the business in 1935, which was only about one-twentieth of that of the preceding year.

The heavy trading in 1934 was not, however, due to industrial or trade revival, as more than 90 per cent of the transactions were in the speculative rubber shares, while trading in common stocks was heaviest in 1931. Similarly, the stock index number, which does not take into account the rubber shares, shows a continuous decline since 1931.

Taking all in all, we find there are two main groups of economic activities or phenomena in Shanghai, as represented by

---
144. See Appendix F, Tables XXXI and XXXII.

ECONOMIC EFFECTS

various statistical series, one portraying the growth of the city and the other prosperity or depression in industry and trade. To the first group belong such things as population growth, the development of banking business, total assessed values of land and buildings, length of roads, etc., etc. The steady increases in transactions in Government securities and in the silver stock (except the last two years in the latter case) are of a similar nature, although they are subject to influences in as well as outside Shanghai. In a sense, however, we may also say that the growth of population is partly due to outside influences too, since it is the lack of employment and other discouraging conditions elsewhere that have driven people to this industrial center. Be that as it may, these developments may be considered as parallel to the general trend of industrial growth in Shanghai.

The other group of phenomena are more indicative of cylical changes in trade and industry. As trade began to decline in 1932, about two years ahead of industry, this group may be sub-divided into two smaller groups. Those which affect industrial development or are affected by it include the number of factory buildings constructed and their assessed value, the export of certain factory products like flour, the prices of certain groups of them like chemicals, not to mention the number of factories in operation, the number of workers engaged in them, the total value of their output, etc. The importation of industrial machinery and raw materials also has close connections with the industries, but it is more influenced by trade conditions in general, and therefore belongs to the second sub-group. The latter includes foreign trade in general, ocean and coastal shipping, freight traffic on the railways, bank clearings, transactions on the produce exchanges, and above all, the general price level. Building construction in general in Shanghai is more influenced by trade activities, as the more expensive buildings are office buildings or apartment houses. Hence such activities, as represented by their value, reached the peak in 1930 in the International Settlements. Average land values of all sections of the Settlement kept on rising till 1933, although in certain specific districts a fall in values began much earlier.

SHANGHAI INDUSTRIALIZATION

In most cases, the changes are quite reasonable in view of the general business conditions here.

A change for the better is seen in many lines in the second sub-group, and if we may assume that changes in trade conditions will soon have their effects felt in the industries, then we may reasonably expect recovery in the latter field in a year or two. The revival in the silk industry seems to confirm this forecast, but industrial development is influenced by many other factors, some f which are not economic, and predictions are therefore quite dangerous. For one thing, if the smuggling of Japanese goods, which is a very serious problem at the time of writing, should increase unchecked, the manufacturing industries in China in general, and in Shanghai in particular, may experience much worse things in the future.

CHAPTER VII

THE SOCIAL EFFECTS OF INDUSTRIALIZATION IN SHANGHAI

Industrialization is never a simple process. It involves radical changes in the methods of productive enterprises in the area affected —its effects reaching the entire life of the locality. And so it is very difficult, if not impossible, to separate the phases of social life which have been affected by industrialization from those which remain unaffected. In its early stages, the growth of Shanghai into a large city may be wholly attributed to the development of commerce, but later industrialization has become increasingly an important factor, though the social effects of the two intermingle and cannot be separated. Consequently it is not easy to ascertain the social effects of industrialization in Shanghai, as indeed there probably ar very few social conditions which can be said to be caused purely by industrialization. Thus the social facts mentioned in this chapter, though they are closely related with industrialization, are by no means the result of that phenomenon alone.

The population of Shanghai according to the report made in August, 1935, by the Bureau of Social Affairs, is 3,540,042. It

SHANGHAI INDUSTRIALIZATION

is the largest city in China. Its rapid growth, unequalled in China, is also unusual in the world.[145]

The reasons for this unusually rapid growth are of course very complex. But one of the principal reasons is the development of factories which has given rise to an ever increasing demand for workers; as a consequence, people hav poured in from all directions. According to our own investigations made in 1931, workers in factories alone reached the figure of 214,152 and in 1933 the number amounted to 214,736.[146] Among the individuals comprising this figure a large number are, of course, single, but there are many others who have brought their families to Shanghai. Often several members of a family engage in productive enterprises in different factories; but in most cases only the head of the family is the breadwinner. On an average, if one worker supports two people,[147] then the numbers of workers and their family members would amount to between 600,000 to 700,000. Their clothing, food, housing, communication and other needs of life would in turn give employment to at least another 100,000 people. It is vident therefore that industrialization is an important factor in the growth of population in Shanghai.

Composition of Shanghai Population

The distribution of sex in the population of Shanghai also bears the marks of industrialization. The distribution of sex is known as "sex ratio" (the number of males as compared with every hundred females). For example, the sex ratio of 105 to 100 means there are one hundred five males to every hundred females. It is customary among Chinese people who engage in business in cities to leave their families back in the country and so the sex ratios in large cities are usually rather high. In 1928 th sex ratios in six leading cities were as follows:[148]

---

145. See Appendix G, Table I.
146. See Appendix C, Table IV and V.
147. According to the recent findings of the Rickshaw Board of the International Settlement, one rickshaw man supports 2.67 family members.
148. Given in the *China Economic Year Book,* First Edition C. Page 32.

CHAPTER VII SOCIAL EFFECTS

Shanghai	135.0
Tientsin	161.9
Peiping	153.5
Canton	141.6
Hankow	155.1
Nanking	164.8

The population of Shanghai is the largest among the six leading cities and yet the sex ratio is the lowest; this phenomenon is due in a large measure to industrialization. Among the industries in Shanghai the cotton yarn and weaving industry is the most important, and in this kind of industry, mostly women workers are employed. According to our own investigations, Shanghai women workers reach the high figure of 115,333 (not including female child labor) while, on the other hand, the number of men workers is only 75,693. Among the one hundred thousand odd women workers, a part of them are members of workers' families, but a considerable number come to Shanghai singly to work in the factories. This serves to lower the rather high sex ratio in Shanghai. Moreover, the sex ratio among factory workers in the cities in China is always a little lower than what prevails in other trades. According to the investigations made by Chen Hua-ying, among the working families in Nanking and Hankow, the sex ratios are all below 115. Shanghai registers no exception in this respect. The factory workers constitute a fairly large portion of the whole populati n in the port city. In the area of Greater Shanghai Municipality, for example, it was 20.47% in 1932. The lower sex ratio obtaining among the factory workers has the effect, naturally, of lowering that of the whole city.

The a ove conclusions can be proved in a different way. From the reasons mentioned above, we can say that the higher the degree of industrialization, the lower becomes the sex ratio. While industrialization in Shanghai increases in intensity, its sex ratio drops lower and lower as the years go by. From the statistics

SHANGHAI INDUSTRIALIZATION

gathered in the International Settlement and the French Concession, this tendency is clearly shown.[149]

Industrialization has also a close relation with the distribution of age in the population of a city. Under ordinary circumstances, the distribution of age resembles a pyramid; the older the age, the less the number. According to the stimate of Leonard Hsu, the percentages of different age groups in relation to the total population are as follows:[150]

Age Group	Percentage
0-19	42-44
20-39	30-32
40-59	19-21
60-	5-7

But in a city where commerce and industry are highly developed, the situation is a little different. Workers engaged in various productive enterprises are eliminated when they become old. In America, in a survey of 40% of the factories employing 60% of the workers of the whole country, the highest age limit was forty-five. No extensive investigations of the ages of workers in Shanghai have yet been made, but according to our observations, the situation is probably not very different from that in the United States. If this is a fact, then the number of persons within the age group of 20-39 must be greatly increased and its percentage will be higher than any other group. If we take a look at the statistics of Shanghai population, it is clear that this is true. Taking Municipality of Greater Shanghai alone, the percentage of this age group is already higher than Hsu's estimate.[151]

Industrial development and the improvement of communications go hand in hand—the former promotes the latter and the latter facilitates the former. The communications of Shanghai have always been convenient because of its favorable

---
149. See Appendix G, Table II.
150. Hsu, *Introduction to the Study of Population*, Page 319.
151. See Appendix G, Table III. In this chapter the term "Municipality of Greater Shanghai" refers to the city area outside of the International Settlement and the French Concession.

SOCIAL EFFECTS

geographic position, and since the development of commerce and industry the port has become the leading center of communications in China. The improved means of communications have had a great effect upon the movement of population; not only the people in neighboring districts but also from the outlying provinces pour into Shanghai to seek their fortunes. According to the statistics of the Bureau of Navigation of the Ministry of Communications, there were 47,529 steamships entering and leaving the port of Shanghai in 1930, among which 23,790 were inland river boats and 23,739 were larger vessels passing Woosung. If we take 500 passengers as the average number of people carried by each vessel, the total number exceeds 23,000,000 and if we add the passengers carried by sailboats, th total amount will be greatly increased. This is, of course, by water alone. Communications by land bring to Shanghai also a goodly number. According to the statistics of 1931, the Nanking-Shanghai Railway carried 13,181,044 passengers; the Shanghai-Hangchow and Ningpo line carried 5,778,112 passengers.[152] From July, 1933, to June, 1934, the Nanking-Shanghai line carried 10,528,087 passengers; the Shanghai-Hangchow-Ningpo line carried 5,258,690 passengers.[153] Although not all the passengers carried by these two railways took Shanghai as the starting point or place of destination, yet if we assume that two-thirds of them did, it would be around 11,000,000 people coming into and leaving Shanghai through the railways. In recent years, the development of air lines and highways promotes further social movement. According to the statistics of 1931, the passengers carried by long-distance buses are as follows:[154]

Shanghai-Ming-Nai-Toa Long-distance Bus Co.	180,076
Shanghai-Tai Chong Long-distance Bus Co.	390,000
Shanghai-Nai Wei Long-distance Bus Co.	768,791
Shanghai-Chuen Sao Bus Co.	888,703

---

152. *The Statistics of Shanghai*, Section on Communication, page 19.
153. The *Year Book of Greater Shanghai Municipality*, page 26.
154. Ibid. pp. 11-12.

SHANGHAI INDUSTRIALIZATION

Recently the opening to traffic of highways linking Shanghai with Hangchow, Wusih, Soochow and other cities will undoubtedly further facilitate the movement of population of Shanghai.

As a result of this unusually mobile population, its composition is very complex. Classified according to native places, taking the area of the Greater Shanghai Municipality alone, it forms a model of China with every province and city represented.[155]

From the points of view of dialect, customs, ceremonials, one locality in China is quite different from others. Consequently, when people coming from diffrent localities reside together, there is more or less some feeling of remoteness. So in all big cities there is a special feeling of brotherhood among people coming from the same native place; and to promote co-operation and mutual assistance, native clubs and guilds are organized. In Shanghai there are several hundred of these organizations. Aside from this, people from the same native place have the tendency to settle down in one place; for example, the Cantonese living along North Szechuen Road, people from Changchow around Tsaokadoo and the Brenan Road district. Concentration of residence of the people from the same native place leads to the establishment of particular types of tea-houses, restaurants, amusement places, catering mostly to patrons of one particular place. These places, on the one hand, are informal places for gatherings and discussions, disseminating news and promoting friendliness among people from the same native place; but, on the other hand, they are often trouble-breeding centers and rallying grounds for feuds and conflicts between people of different native places.

The mobility of the population in Shanghai can also be seen from a minor matter. According to last year's report of the Municipal Council of the International Settlement, the number of deaths among Chinese residents was 15,688 and in that number 6,471 persons died without any responsible parties to take care of the burial. Now, in China, burial of the dead has always been looked upon as so important that even when the deceased is without imme-

---
155. See Appendix G, Table IV.

SOCIAL EFFECTS

diate members of his family, it is customary for his remote relatives and friends to take charge of the burial. Thus, for a man to have died without anyone to take care of his burial, is invariably a sign of his being a homeless destitute. And the presence of a large number of such characters is another proof of the mobility of the population of Shanghai.

Industrialization in a great metropolis does not only produce horizontal social mobility as mentioned above, but also causes vertical social movements—upheavals in the succession of professions and trades. When a society is in the process of industrialization, social strata are not permanent. Given ability and opportunity, within a few years after coming to Shanghai, a farmer from the country or a merchant from a small town might easily become a rich man or an important capitalist. The history of the earlier stages of the development of Shanghai abounds with such examples. It is still more common to see illiterate or ignorant parents with sons and daughters prominent in the professions while it is quite usual to find teachers in secondary schools, church workers, staff members of banks and companies, or movie stars, who have risen from a socially lower origin.

Industrialization and the Family

It is generally recognized that industrialization has a great deal to do with the family. One of the first effects of industrialization is the increase of factory workers who are drawn from the country. Most of these workers, if they are married, leave their wives and children behind on the farms. Being thus separated from their families, it is natural for these young working men to feel the need of sexual gratification, and as they have constant contact with female workers under conditions where the strength of social sanction is very weak, promiscuous affairs are inevitable. In the case of the female workers, these women, formerly only accustomed to the surroundings of the home, are not able to cope with or protect themselves against the large impersonal groups of factory environment. So with the breaking down of the customary standards of sex morality and restrictions of the relations between the sexes,

SHANGHAI INDUSTRIALIZATION

free co-habitation is almost the rule and seduction common among the working classes in Shanghai. If we look at the newspapers, we can see at once the prevalence of this condition. The following items of news are merely some examples.

Nye Chung-ti, aged twenty, a native of Tai Hsin, is employed in a silk factory. He is married to a girl from the same place and lives with her at 32 Li Chung-li, Chapei. His wife, having secured work in a factory, made the acquaintance of Hsieh Chun-lan, a member of the factory staff. Being of a romantic temperament she soon fell a victim to the wiles of Hsieh and had improper relations with him.[156]

Li Hsueh-tseng, a pretty young girl from Changchow, came to Shanghai with two brothers to work since in recent years farming in their native place was not sufficient to make a living. The girl secured work in a cotton mill and soon rented a house and lived with a man from Hopei.[157]

Wang Che-ling, a native of Pootung, lives in Chapei and earns his living as a workman. He has living with him a pretty young sister who works in a cotton mill. Recently she was seduced by a young man living in the same neighborhood and on July 26 eloped with him taking all her belongings. She is living with him in Wusih.[158]

Wang Gun-chuan, aged thirty, works as a foreman in a Japanese cotton mill on Ferry Road. He is married and has three children. But Wang likes feminine companionship and has since November of last year cohabited with a woman worker of the same factory.[159]

Whenever the Wing On cotton mill at Markham Road dismisses workers in the evening, men workers always tease and make fun of the women workers, resulting often in fights.

---

156. *The Evening News*, September 5, 1935.
157. *The Evening News*, September 17, 1935.
158. *The Evening News*, September 18, 1935.
159. *Shun Pao*, August 15, 1935.

SOCIAL EFFECTS

Pootoo Road and Gordon Road police stations in the neighborhood make it a practice to detail special police at such times to maintain order and prevent trouble. Yesterday the police had to use force to disperse a crowd of men workers who were troubling women workers. In escaping from the police a girl worker accidentally fell into Soochow Creek, and was drowned before she could be rescued.[160]

Although the lowering of the standard of sex morality is not all due to industrialization, yet industrialization is certainly a great factor. Last year the Protection of Children and Youth Advisory Commission of the League of Nations presented a report of its inquiry commission on the traffic in women and children in the Far East, in which it was pointed out that such traffic was mostly carried on in the Near East, Asia Minor and the Far East, and the women involved belonged mostly to the nationalities of the Far East among which Chinese women took the first place. The center of this nefarious activity was located in Shanghai.[161] These unfortunate women were usually lured from towns and villages around Shanghai, always on the pretext of finding highly remunerative work in factories; but as soon as the great metropolis was reached they were sold to houses of prostitution and eternal slavery. The following instances are but a few examples out of what must be innumerable occurrences.

Chen Mei-cheng, a pretty girl from Shaohsin, aged 18, went with her mother to live in Hangchow after the death of her father. Mei-cheng worked in a silk factory to help support the family. Last year some acquaintance of the mother paid the family a visit during which the mother was persuaded to send the daughter to work in Shanghai. The girl was sold to a house of prostitution in the International Settlement and made to receive guests.[162]

---

160. *Evening News,* July 25, 1935.
161. *Eastern Times,* April 6, 1933.
162. *Evening News,* March 27, 1935.

SHANGHAI INDUSTRIALIZATION

Kieng Wei-pao, a young girl, used to live in the country near Wusih. Her mother died and her father married again. But she could not get along with her step-mother. Taking advantage of this situation, a woman acquaintance of the father persuaded him to send the daughter to work in Shanghai. After a month of job hunting, she was coerced into leading the life of a prostitute. After a few months she contracted all the veneral diseases, but she was finally able to escape and with the help of some guest was sent to a hospital for treatment.[163]

Hsueh San-nan, a girl from Soochow, was engaged and about to be married, but she co-habited with another man by the name of Kwang Kin-pao. On the pretext of looking for work in Shanghai, she was led to the port city by Kwang and his friends, kept closely watched in a small inn, and finally sold to a house of ill fame and forced to be a prostitute.[164]

Chow Kwei-yin, aged 19, lived with her family in Changchow. A neighbor woman, seeing that Kwei-yin was a pretty, winsome girl, often told her stories of ease and luxury in Shanghai and how easy it was to earn high wages in the innumerable factories there. Being a young girl, Kwei-yin at last succumbed and got permission from her parents to seek her fortune in Shanghai—with the neighbor woman. On arriving, the latter immediately got in touch with agents of a house of prostitution and attempted to sell the girl.[165]

According to an investigation made by Hsu Wei-fang and Lin Ching-yu, out of 359 women criminals, 107 of them were factory workers, amounting to slightly over 29%, and among the crimes committed by factory workers, seduction occupied a large place, namely 23%.[166]

---

163. *Shun Pao*, April 27, 1935.
164. *Eastern Times*, April 12, 1935.
165. *Shun Pao*, July 12, 1935.
166. *The Continental Magazine*, Vol. I, No. 4. Hsu and Lin: *The Social Analysis of Women Criminals in Shanghai*.

SOCIAL EFFECTS

As cases of seduction are so common it is not strange that prostitutes, both public and private, are plentiful. According to a comparative study of prostitution in various countries made by a former professor of Yenching University, there was one prostitute in 960 persons in London, one in 580 persons in Berlin, one in 481 persons in Paris, one in 430 persons in Chicago, one in 250 persons in Tokyo, one in 250 persons in Peiping, one in 130 persons in Shanghai.[167] In other words, there were 25,000 prostitutes in Shanghai. According to some other estimates this figure is even higher. Taking only the International Settlement, it was reported that in 1933, as many as 1,167 prostitutes were arrested on the streets in Louza district alone, and from January to the end of May, 1934, 1,138 prostitutes were arrested in the same district. This figure did not include private prostitutes nor those found in hotels and amusement places.[168] Under the system where prostitutes are not subjected to compulsory examination, such a large number of loose women would naturally spread veneral diseases of all kinds. The importance of this problem can be realized easily if we glance at the ever present advertisements in the newspapers of the various kinds of medicines and doctors for diseases related to sex. According to the report of the Municipal Council of the International Settlement, there were 38,637 men treated for syphilis in the men's clinic in 1933 and 36,546 men treated in 1934. Recently owing to the prevalence of syphilis among the poor, the Chinese Medical Association has established temporarily, in the Epidemic Hospital on Tibet Road, a free clinic for the treatment of this dreadful disease. From the above, one can easily see that the spread of syphilis in Shanghai has reached a very alarming stage.

Effects on the Housing Problem

The increase in the value of land follows the development of industry and commerce. If we take the International Settlement as example, with the exception of a downward tendency which occurred during the last two years, there had always been a marked

---

167. *Shun Pao*, December 3, 1934.
168. *Eastern Times*, June 25, 1934.

rise in the value of land in the past thirty years.[169] The great majority of people cannot afford to purchase land nor are they able to build their own houses on leased land. The way out, therefore, is for the whole family to crowd together in very small quarters. For wage earners, however, even this is not possible; often five on six families have to share a little house. Sometimes one room about thirteen or fourteen feet by twenty feet is partitioned off for two families, and there they cook their food, nurse their babies, receive their guests, and carry on all their activities, so that the noise, dirt and confusion are beyond imagination; and as for safeguards against contagious diseases, or privacies that help to uphold the standards of morality, they are simply non-existent. But the rent these people pay often amounts to a quarter of their income!

But there are conditions even worse than those mentioned above. These are the mud-huts clustering around some factories, and the boat dwellers in the creeks. Not long ago, a reporter of the Evening News took a trip through the mud-huts located at the end of Ching Yu Road and Tsao Da Ju, Chapei, and wrote the following description.

"There you can discover shoulder high huts with any odds and ends such as broken pieces of wood, grass, reed or discarded iron sheets serving as tile for the roof; for windows there are little holes in the mud wall; rain or shine, summer or winter, the same darkness, dampness and dirty smells prevail. Some have a few pieces of broken-down furniture coated with slimy dust so that one cannot tell the material of which it is made, some even without what could be called a chair for the occupants not only sit on the ground but sleep on it as well!

"On the little narrow paths there are always puddles of muddy water; here men, women, children, pigs, dogs, chickens and ducks move and live. It is difficult to pick one's way through the dirt."

---

169. See Appendix G, Table V.

SOCIAL EFFECTS

We do not know how many mud-huts there are in Shanghai; probably not less than four or five thousand. In the districts where these mud-huts are located, there is always trouble. Only recently there were several incidents which made their appearance in the newspapers. For example, near Ching Kiang Road, Chapei, there is a vacant lot of about eight mow utilized by the poor from Verning and Yen-cheng as sites for their mud-huts. At the beginning of this year the owner of the lot wanted to build houses there for rent but these squatters refused to move giving one thing or another as excuses. After much negotiation and mediation through other parties, a written agreement was reached between the owner of the lot and all the squatters, that the former was to give each of the latter fifteen dollars and two "twans" of rice, and the latter were to move away by a set day. However, fifty-nine of them refused to move in spite of the agreement and as the contractor for the owner of the lot was anxious to start work, some persons were asked to talk to them. The squatters still refused to move, but instead got angry at the mediators and gathering a mob of some two hundred persons planned an attack. Only the timely arrival of the police averted troubles.[170] Another example: Opposite Yin Hua Li on Robson Road there is a vacant lot of about ten mow where for the last ten years "Kiang Pei" people (people from north of the Yangtze River) have lived in about six hundred mud-huts. Lately the owner of the lot wanted to use the land himself and notified the squatters to leave. Mediation by different organizations failed; finally through the efforts of the police station at Tsaokadoo, the squatters agreed to move by the end of the month upon payment by the owner of the land of three dollars to each family.[171]

The mud-hut districts are not only breeding places of trouble but are often causes of fire. Once fire gets started, it rages among these huts beyond control, and consequently several hundred of them may be burned down in a short time, leaving the occupiers homeless and devoid of whatever few worldly belongings they had. Within a month or two of this writing, several such fires

---

170. *Shun Pao*, September 28, 1935.
171. Ibid.

have occurred. At Tsao Ni Tang, Pootung, there were about six hundred working families living there in mud-huts. On the night of July 29 fire started and lasted more than two hours burning up practically the whole community. More than three thousand people were rendered homeless.[172] In the early morning of October 5, a fire broke out in a mud-hut located at Kwang Chao Road, Chapei. In a short time, the fire became uncontrollable and soon thirty-two huts and twenty-nine tiled houses were burned affecting one hundred and twenty families.[173]

Around these mud-huts there are always puddles of stagnant water, clouds of dust on good days and troughs of mud on rainy days. In the summer these places become the breeding places of mosquitoes and flies. The unhygienic conditions are beyond imagination. Such diseases as cholera, typhoid fever and malaria fever rage there and from there spread to other places, thus proving a difficult problem for authorities of public sanitation to tackle. Lately the City Government of Greater Shanghai has organized a Common People's Welfare Commission which is undertaking to build, on a larger scale, houses for the poor in order to solve this problem.

Other Effects

The Communists believe in class struggle and revolution by farmers and workers. At the beginning of their organization in China, they secretly participated in the labor movements and almost all the labor organizations in large cities were under their direction. The big labor demonstration in Shanghai on March 21, 1927, was their work. Later the internal dissension within the communist party became greater and greater, resulting in the split into two factions, which may be designated as the Stalin group and the Trotsky group; the former emphasizes land revolution, and the latter, labor revolution. Although the Stalin group has finally succeeded in coming to power, yet activities in the cities have never been abandoned. Thus

---
172. *Shun Pao*, July 30, 1935.
173. *The Evening News*, October 5, 1935.

SOCIAL EFFECTS

during the past years, the communists have always participated, and in some cases even taken active leadership, in labor strikes, disputes between capital and labor, students' strikes, assassinations and other activities subversive to social order and peace. A close watch over communists has been maintained by the authorities of Greater Shanghai. If we look at communistic activities discovered by the police of the International Settlement, we can easily recognize the possibility of their danger to society.[174]

We have said above that the dialects and customs from the various parts of China are sometimes quite different. Laborers coming from different localities have to depend upon those who come from their own native place to solve many problems. Coming from the same native place is a fact that shortens the "social distance" between the parties. Under the contract labor system prevailing in Shanghai, the development of labor groups into strong organizations is natural; but as there is a large number of laborers in a group, it is difficult to avoid mob psychology, and, with the addition of the activities of ambitious leaders, it results often in monopoly of a certain trade and the boycott of outsiders. For example, among carpenters, there are Wenchow, Kiangsi and local groups. The Wenchow group specializes mainly in making red wood and foreign style furniture; the Kiangsi group makes, principally, old style furniture, and the local group produces unpainted articles. This strict division of spheres often leads to fights whenever one group infringes upon the sphere of another, or even upon more minor issues. The following are some illustrations.

"At 5 o'clock yesterday afternoon, laborers of the Shantung group and the Hupei group, working at the wharf of the Butterfield and Swire Blue Funnel Line, in Pootung, had a fight because of a dispute about wages. The fight was stopped as leaders of both sides were willing to come to terms. However, after work was finished, some thirty odd laborers of the Shantung group went out of the west gate of the wharf and a like number of the Hupei group went out of the east gate of the wharf, and meeting in

---

174. See Appendix G, Table VI.

the vacant field west of the Yih Chung Machine Factory as if by appointment the two sides had another fight with iron bars, bamboo poles and knives. The fight lasted a long time and members of both sides received severe wounds." [175]

"The Shantung and Kiangpei Butcher groups, because of competition in the purchase of pigs had a grudge of long standing against each other and of late there have occurred many fights between the two groups. About 11 o'clock yesterday morning, Chen Tsin-ching and Hua Ching-hu, two butchers from the butchery located at 12 Tien How Li, Yochow Road, in the International Settlement, took trams to the southern part of the city and stopped at Yu Chai Wharf, planning to buy pigs from the wholesale stores in the neighborhood. However, as soon as they alighted from the tram they were suddenly attacked with axes and iron bars by more than thirty men of the Shantung group. In no time they received wounds all over their bodies and fell down in pools of blood." [176]

"At the little Nanyang Wharf in Lu Kia Ju, Pootung, is located the only ferry service for laborers, both men and women, who work in the factories of the Yangtzepoo district and live on the east side of the Whangpoo. Every morning and afternoon between five and seven o'clock, when the workers are going across the Whangpoo, to and from work, the ferry service has its busiest hours. All the boats engaged in this service are of old style, and of two different types. One type only takes the workers from their homes on the east side of the Whangpoo to the factories on the other side in the mornings; and the other type of boats takes the workers back from the factories to their homes in the evenings. This arrangement has avoided much trouble, but the rivalry between them has given rise to many quarrels and conflicts. Yesterday at a quarter to six in the morning, the two sides arranged to have a fight near the wharf. Both parties turned out in full force with whatever weapons they could get hold of, and as one side

---

175. *Shun Pao*, May 22, 1933.
176. *Shun Pao*, October 31, 1933.

SOCIAL EFFECTS

had the advantage of numbers, it carried the day. The leaders of the other side, Hu Kun-sheng, Yeh Ping-sheng and Chang Kang-chuan, were severely wounded."[177]

The existence of these labor groups organized according to native places not only causes feuds but is also a big hindrance to the development of the labor movement, since it counteracts much of the usefulness of the labor unions. Of course, it is still possible to organize labor unions, but the energy used to settle differences and prevent trouble between the different groups directly and indirectly hinders the activities and progress of the labor movement.

However, the growth of these labor groups has indirectly caused the lowering of the standards of morality between the sexes and the increase of crime. When a labor group from a certain locality has secured a degree of monopolistic privileges in a certain trade, it often absorbs more people—relatives, friends, old acquaintances—from the same locality to swell the ranks of that group. And as the economic conditions in the country districts in recent years have been none too good, a great many would strive to leave their native place and come to make a living in the city. In times of economic prosperity the hopes of these newcomers might be fulfilled but in times of depression they would soon be left destitute and then the men would turn to begging or thieving and the women would degenerate into the folds of vice.

Crime is always more prevalent in cities than in villages and towns. This tendency is even more noticeable in industrial cities because of the presence of a large number of laborers who, through their lack of education, and uncertainty in economic conditions, are far more liable to commit crimes. If we look at the 1930 Report of the Shanghai Special District Court, we can see at once the large number of crimes committed by laborers. In a total of 5,293 defendants of criminal prosecutions who received definite sentences, there were 1,738 laborers, amounting to 32.8%.[178]

---

177. *The Eastern Times*, May 4, 1933.
178. Computed from the *First Report of the Shanghai First Special Distirct Court*, page 248.

SHANGHAI INDUSTRIALIZATION

But if we compare this with the conditions of crime of the whole country, the percentage of crimes committed by laborers is entirely different. According to the statistics of the Ministry of Judicial Administration, the total number of defendants of criminal procedings during the first half of 1930 was 37,771 among which there were 5,615 laborers, amounting to 14.8%.[179]

This latter percentage is less than half of the 32.8% of Shanghai and from this comparison we may safely say that industrialization causes the increase of crime.

The effects of industrialization cannot be limited to one locality, indeed the effects of the industrialization of Shanghai are felt by the whol of China. What is mentioned in this chapter is, however, limited to Shanghai, and only a few social phenomena are given in order to show the close relation between industrialization and social life.

---

179. *Judicial Statistics,* January to June, 1930, Special Issue, Publication of the Ministry of Judicial Administration, page 338.

CONCLUSION

After having studied the industrialization processes in Shanghai from various angles, we will put together all the conclusions that we may draw from our study.

The development of Shanghai industries has been all the time going on although during some periods the development was slower than in others. It was affect d by many factors, such as the European War, the boycott of foreign goods, the National Tariff, the discrepancy between import and export prices, etc. As pointed out by another writer the three wars—Opium War, Sino-Japanese War and the European War—were closely related to the industrialization of China.[180] The first opened up China to foreign trade, and, as we have pointed out in Chapter I, it was the most important factor which promoted industrialization. After 1895 when the Shimonoseki Treaty allowed foreigners to establish factories in Chinese treaty ports modern industries began to spring up in various parts of China, especially Shanghai. They were responsible in promoting industrial development because

---

180. H. D. Fong, *Industrial Capital in China*, in *Nankai Social and Ecconomic Quarterly*, Vol. IX, No. 1, p. 27, et seq.

SHANGHAI INDUSTRIALIZATION

Chinese business men emulated the example and began to establish factories of their own. In Chapter II where we folllowed the history of the development of various Shanghai industries, it is quite apparent that many of them were started by foreigners. After the foreign factories had been established and had proven to be successful Chinese factories followed suit.

In the same chapter we also pointed out how the European War caused a boom in this country. Many factories were established immediately after the War began. As to the other factors which affected industrial development in this country we have already gone into th m in detail in Chapters I and III. They explain the development in particular during the period 1931 to 1933 which was covered by two industrial surveys conducted by this Institute. The recent depression in Shanghai industries was due to a few factors such as the raising of the price of silver by the American Government, the stoppage of the boycott of Japanese goods and the revised tariff of 1934 which reduced the import duty on many kinds of cotton piece goods and increased those on raw cotton.

In reviewing the development during the two years between 1931 and 1933 a few facts stood out prominently. The chemical industries and industries that manufacture machinery and metallic wares underwent the greatest development during the period although both of them do not yet occupy very important positions in the industries of Shanghai. Next to that was the growth of the factories manufacturing rubber goods as well as those that produced knitted under-wear and hosiery. The two groups to which these products belong are also of some importanc among Chinese industries although the most important groups are the textiles and foodstuffs industries. In the textile group, the cotton spinning and silk reeling industries experienced a decline since 1931 and 1929 respectively. The cotton and silk weaving industries on the other hand, kept on growing until 1933. The peculiar factors which affected these industries in such a diametrically opposite manner have also been explained in a previous connection In the foodstuffs group the greatest development was experienced

CHAPTER VIII CONCLUSION

in the tobacco mills and flour mills came next. Besides these, the paper making and printing industries hold also important positions but the latter has experienced a decline in recent years and the former has not changed very much.

From another point of view we may say that those industries which produce ultimate consumption goods experienced some development during the period under consideration while those that produced production goods did not grow so much. This is only natural since industrialization must begin at the end where goods are manufactured for consumption. However, the growth of a number of new chemical industries in Shanghai as well as the development in the machine-making industries indicate that the process of industrialization is going in that direction and very soon we may expect to see more balanced development in Shanghai industries.

Referring to the importance of the textile and foodstuffs industries, it can best be shown by the percentages which their capitalization, number of workers, value of output, etc., constituted of the total figures. In the former case, the capitalization constituted 39.1%, number of laborers 56% and value of output 35.5% in 1933. The latter did not have so much capitalization or so large a number of workers but its value of output was greater than that of the former. This was due to the greater mechanization of the flour mills where each worker had the use of 4.86 horse power as compared to the 1.02 horse power in the cotton mills. The latter, however, has larger factories and in each cotton mill over 2,000 horse power was utilized while the flour mills had only 800.

Concerning the nature of the power used in Shanghai industries, a large percentage consisted of rented electricity. In both 1931 and 1933 the percentage of rented electric power to total quantity of power consumed was 60%. This is due partly to the small size of the Shanghai factories and partly to the cheapness of electric power in Shanghai. The former fact was found demonstrated by the amount of capital of the average mill. Taking

SHANGHAI INDUSTRIALIZATION

all industries into consideration, the av rage capitalization in 1931 was as low as $80,000 and in 1933, $140,000. The majority of the factories, on the other hand, hardly had so much capital. It was due to the inclusion of large establishments as cotton and flour mills that the average was as high as given above. In fact, the most common size of capitalization in most industries was only about $20,000 to $30,000.

On account of this small capitalization it has been a practice for the Shanghai industries to rent the factory buildings. According to our survey of 1933, only 15% of the factories owned their own land and buildings, and 2% more rented their factory site and constructed buildings on it. That means that nearly 80% of the Shanghai factories rented buildings entirely and most of these buildings were not specially constructed for industrial purposes but were ordinary dwelling houses which were converted to such uses.

The small size of Shanghai factories can also be shown in the proportion of mills which come up to the standard of the Chinese Factory Law. That standard means only the utilization of motive power and the employment of 30 workers and certainly is not a very high standard, still of the 1,700 odd factories which we surveyed in 1931 only about 40% of them came up to the standard. All the rest, therefore, did not have even as much as 30 workers and according to our estimate probably 1,000 more factories were in Shanghai which employed less than 10 workers. For these reasons the type of business organization most prevalent in Shanghai industries was proprietorship and partnership. The limited liability companies were in the minority and they were those which operated the comparatively large mills. For instance, in 1931, 35% of the factories were run by proprietorships, 42% by partnerships and only 18% by limited liability companies. In 1933 when the survey was limited to larger factories 23% of them were run by proprietorships, 37% by partnerships and 28% by limited liability companies.

The laborers in Shanghai factories were mostly women because they made up the majority in the textile industries and these

CONCLUSION

industri s in turn employed a majority of all workers in Shanghai. The percentage of the female workers in 1931 was 55.1, and in 1933, 53.7, as against 33.6, and 35.3, respectively for the male workers. If we assume that the child workers in the textile industries and in those industries which manufacture articles of apparel in Group No. XI consist of girls, then we ought to add 7, to the 1931 figure and 5.5, to that of 1933. Then in both cases th proportion of femal workers would be above 60, of the total number of workers. The latter according to our estimate could not exceed 350,000 men, women and children.

In the matter of wages our study is based mainly on the investigation of Mr. Tsha of the Shanghai Bureau of Social Affairs in 1929 which was more comprehensive than ours in this respect. But according to his figures the highest wages received by male workers was in the silk weaving industry where the daily wage was $1.65. The lowest rate for men was 47 cents a day. For women the highest was 89 cents and the lowest 24 cents. The majority of the female workers in the textile industry received mostly 45 cents. The highest wage for women was also in the silk weaving industry and for both men and women the next highest was in the printing business. In the case of children the highest wage was 42 cents per day and the lowest 20 cents.

In the matter of working hours, the maximum for men was 12 hours a day in the silk reeling industry and the minimum 7-4/5 hours in the dyeing and bleaching industry. The maximum for women was 11-9/10 hours in the cotton spinning industry and the minimum 8-1/10 hours in the printing business. The child workers' longest hours were in the cotton spinning industry, being 12 hours a day, but in the glass manufactories they had the shortest hours, namely, 8. On the whole, it appears that the printing business treated both men and women better than most other industries both in the matter of wages and working hours.

Concerning labor disturbances and strikes, the number was largest in the textile industries which was only natural seeing that they had more than half of the workers in Shanghai factories. The strikes in those industries constituted 44% of all factory strikes which again constituted 80% of all strikes in Shanghai. The printing trade was responsible for 12% of all industrial strikes. The causes of the strikes were mostly disputes about wages which were responsible for 43% and employment and discharge of laborers were responsible for 19% of all the strikes. Long working hours furnished cause for more labor disputes, but they seldom ended in strikes as they do in the West. As the disputes were usually settled through mediation or direct negotiation between the two parties or arbitration, they did not bring about such serious effects or loss of wages as strikes did.

Although the wages of workers were quite low in Shanghai and although they were falling in recent years, yet the fall in the cost of living was even greater, especially since 1932. Hence the workers were able to get along in spite of their poor pay. These are clearly shown by the wage and cost of living index numbers compiled by two Government offices for this city.

Turning from the things in the industries themselves to general economic conditions, we find that the industrialization of Shanghai has produced certain results. It has caused a significant increase in the population of the city which has been almost continuous in spite of the various changes in political and economic conditions affecting the city. In the same way, the growth of the financial organizations has been steady. The imports of manufactured products to China, and in particular, Shanghai, has fallen with the development of native industries while the export of manufactured goods has increased. At the same time the import of machinery and industrial raw materials has also increased. That is what it should be since the industries during the beginning of their growth generally have to depend on imported raw materials and machinery. The statistics concerning cotton, cotton yarn, wheat, flour, tobacco, matches and the machinery used in these lines as given in the Customs statistics are exclusive proof of this statement.

CONCLUSION

The vicissitudes in the business and industrial development of Shanghai are reflected by two series of statistics. Those that have to do with general business have declined since 1932 because at that time the price level began to fall. Foreign trade, bank clearings, volume of transactions on the produce exchanges and railway traffic are some of the activities which are directly connected with general business conditions. All of them began to decline in 1932 although in the case of bank clearings and freight traffic there was a slight recovery in 1934. The effect of the business depression on construction activities seems to be quite immediate. Instead of having a lag for a couple of years, the number as well as assessed value of the buildings constructed in the International Settlements reached their peak in 1930. Land values, however, went up further three years later, as shown by the average land values in the records of the Municipal Council.

In the various kinds of activities which are indirectly connected with industrial development figures show that they kept on increasing until 1933 or 1934. For instance the number of new factory buildings in the International Settlement was largest in 1934, while in the Chinese territory, though the number was largest in 1931, their assessed value was highest in 1933. Export of wheat flour reached its highest in 1933 when Shanghai exported almost all that went abroad from China. Also the price index numbers of the chemical group kept on going up until 1934 while the textile group and the building material group began to fall in 1932. The transportation of goods on the Shanghai-Hangchow-Ningpo and Nanking-Shanghai Railways revived in 1934 which was probably due to the transportation of Shanghai factory products into the interior and the shipping of raw materials from the interior to Shanghai factories. Although we would expect that the importation of machinery and industrial raw materials should keep up with the industrial development in Shanghai till 1933, yet these two things were also affected by conditions in foreign countries as well as the price level in China. As the latter began to fall in 1932, the imports have also declined since.

SHANGHAI INDUSTRIALIZATION

Taking everything into consideration, we find that the importance of Shanghai as an industrial center of the country is unparalleled. Industrial development during the period 1931-1933, although it seems to be unexpected when we consider the business depression in the city, can also be very well explained by different reasons. For detailed information concerning the growth of Shanghai industries reference can be made to the figures in the appendices.

APPENDICES

APPENDIX A
STATISTICS OF SHANGHAI INDUSTRIES, 1931
TABLE A-I. BUSINESS ORGANIZATION

Code	Classification	(1) No. of Factories	(2) State-Ownership	(3) Single Proprietorship	(4) Partnership	(5) Limited Liability Company	(6) Others (1)	(7) Unknown
Group I. Woodworking Industries								
1-1	Saw mills	8		2	5			1
1-2	Manufacture of wooden boxes	1			1			
1-3	Manufacture of other wooden articles	2			2			
1-4	Manufacture of cork stoppers	3		3				
1-5	Manufacture of bamboo articles	1			1			
	Total for Group I.	15		5	9			1
Group II. Furniture Manufacturing								
2-1	Wooden furniture	3		2		1		
2-2	Steel furniture	9		5	3	1		
2-3	Rugs and carpets	5		4		1		
	Total for Group II.	17		11	3	3		
Group III. Metal Industries								
3-1	Founding							
3-1-1	Whole machines	3			3			
3-1-2	Machine parts and accessories	22		9	13			
3-1-3	Iron pipes	4		2	2			
3-1-4	Other articles	6		2	4			
3-2	Steel refining	1	1					
	Total for Group III.	36	1	13	22			
Group IV. Manufacture of Machinery and Miscellaneous Metal Products								
4-1	Manufacture and repairing of machines							
4-1-1	Printing machines							
4-1-1-1	Machines	13		9	2	1		1

Code	Classification	(1) No. of Factories	(2) State-Owneship	(3) Single Proprietorship	(4) Partnership	(5) Limited Liability Company	(6) Others	(7) Unknown
4-1-1-2	Machine parts	1			1			
4-1-2	Knitting machines							
4-1-2-1	Machines	23		18	5			
4-1-2-2	Machine parts	4		1	3			
4-1-3	Spinning and weaving machines							
4-1-3-1	Machines	20		7	9	4		
4-1-3-2	Machine parts	5		2	2	1		
4-1-3-3	Bobbins	7		3	1	2		1
4-1-4	Prime movers	21		8	9	4		
4-1-5	Other kinds of machines	8		6	1			1
4-1-6	Various kinds of machines	16		9	4	1	1	1
4-1-7	Various kinds of machine parts	9		7	2			
4-1-8	Manufacture and repairing of machines and machine parts	29		9	16	2		2
4-1-9	Repairing of machines and machine parts	24		12	11			1
4-2	Manufacture of metal products							
4-2-1	Boilers	5		5				
4-2-2	Weighing scales	4		3	1			
4-2-3	Nails	6		4	1	1		
4-2-4	Tins, boxes, etc.	23		7	14			2
4-2-5	Aluminumware	4		3			1	
4-2-6	Faucets, valves, etc.	5		2	3			
4-2-7	Lamps	6		4	1	1		
4-2-8	Miscellaneous articles	8		5	3			
4-3	Manufacture of electrical apparatus							
4-3-1	Electric light bulbs	5		1	2	2		
4-3-2	Neon light tubes	1					1	
4-3-3	Electric fans, heaters, etc.	3		1		1		1

Code	Classification	(1) No. of Factories	(2) State-ownership	(3) Single Proprietorship	(4) Partner-Ship	(5) Limited Liability Company	(6) Others	(7) Unknown
4-3-4	Electric supplies	7		2	2	2	1	
4-3-5	Flash lights	16		6	8	1		1
4-3-6	Dry batteries	8		4	3	1		
4-3-7	Electro-plating	13		8	4	1		
4-3-8	Electric welding	1					1	
	Total for Group IV.	295		146	108	25	5	11
Group V. Construction of Boats, Ships, and Vehicles for Land Transportation								
5-1	Shipbuilding							
5-1-1	Construction of ships	4	1	1		2		
5-1-2	Repairing of ships and manufacture of accessories	5		2	3			
5-2	Building of cars							
5-2-1	Railway workshops	1	1					
5-2-2	Tram cars (and ships)	1		1				
5-2-3	Bicycles	1			1			
5-2-4	Rickshas	8		5	3			
5-3	Building of fire engines	1		1				
	Total for Group V.	21	2	10	7	2		
Group VI. Manufacture of Bricks, Earthenware, Glass, etc.								
6-1	Bricks and tiles	5		1	1	3		
6-2	Glass							
6-2-1	Thermos bottles	2		1		1		
6-2-2	Bottles and lamp shades	14		7	5	2		
6-2-3	Glass bevelling	8		2	6			
6-3	Cement	1				1		
6-4	Stone powder and lime							
6-4-1	Lime	5		2	3			
6-4-2	Stone powder	9		4	2	2		1
	Total for Group VI.	44		17	17	9		1
Group VII. Building Material								
7-1	Building material	5		2	1	2		
	Total for Group VII.	5		2	1	2		

Code	Classification	(1) No. of Factories	(2) State-ownership	(3) Single Proprietorship	(4) Partner-Ship	(5) Limited Liability Company	(6) Others	(7) Unknown
Group VIII. Production and Transmission of Electricity and Supply of Water								
8-1	Electric and water works	5[2]				5		
Total for Group VIII.		5				5		
Group IX. Manufacture of Chemicals and Allied Products								
9-1	Matches							
9-1-1	Matches	3			1	2		
9-1-2	Shavings and splints	1			1			
9-2	Soap, washing soda and candles							
9-2-1	Soap	11		2	4	4	1	
9-2-2	Washing soda	1				1		
9-2-3	Soap, washing soda and candles	2		2				
9-3	Enamelled ware							
9-3-1	Enamelled ware	8		1	1	5	1	
9-3-2	Body of enamelled ware	2			1		1	
9-4	Varnish and printer's ink							
9-4-1	Varnish	4				4		
9-4-2	printer's ink	5		1	2	1	1	
9-5	Cosmetics	13		4	1	5	3	
9-6	Medicine	2			1	1		
9-7	Celluloid and other synthetic products	6		2	2	2		
9-8	Other chemical products	2		1		1		
Total for Group IX.		60		13	14	26	7	
Group X. Textile Industries								
10-1	Cotton spinning and weaving							
10-1-1	Cotton ginning	8		4	4			
10-1-2	Cotton fluffing	3		2	1			
10-1-3	Cotton spinning							
10-1-3-1	Yarn only	14			2	10	2	
10-1-3-2	Yarn and thread	3				2	1	

Code	Classification	(1) No. of Factories	(2) State-Ownership	(3) Single Proprietorship	(4) Partnership	(5) Limited Liability Company	(6) Others	(7) Unknown
10-1-3-3	Spinning and weaving	12		2	1	5	4	
10-1-4	Cotton weaving							
10-1-4-1	Using yarn only	23		15	4	2	1	1
10-1-4-2	Using yarn and thread	27		9	15	3		
10-1-4-3	Using thread only	6		1	5			
10-1-4-4	Making of knitted cloth	3			2	1		
10-1-4-5	Towels and bed sheets	4		1	1	1		1
10-1-5	Other cotton spinning and weaving	2		2				
10-2	Rayon fabrics	7		2	5			
10-3	Silk reeling and weaving							
10-3-1	Silk reeling							
10-3-1-1	Steam filature silk	66	1		54	2	1	8
10-3-1-2	Dupion silk	4			3	1		
10-3-1-3	Other special kinds of silk	3			1	2		
10-3-2	Silk weaving	35		9	22	2	1	1
10-4	Wool spinning and weaving							
10-4-1	Wool spinning	1			1			
10-4-2	Wool weaving	1			1			
10-4-3	Wool spinning and weaving	1				1		
10-5	Other animal tissue textiles	1			1			
10-6	Mixed fabrics							
10-6-1	Cotton and rayon	147		46	77	19	1	4
10-6-2	Cotton and silk	4		2	1	1		
10-6-3	Silk and rayon	44		11	29	3		1
10-6-4	Cotton, silk and rayon	16		6	8	2		
10-6-5	Cotton and wool	12			5	4	3	
10-6-6	Cotton, silk and wool	5		3	2			
10-7	Dyeing							
10-7-1	Mercerized yarn and thread	11		3	6	1	1	
10-7-2	Dyeing of cloth and							

Code	Classification	(1) No. of Factories	(2) State-Ownership	(3) Single Proprietorship	(4) Partnership	(5) Limited Liability Company	(6) Others	(7) Unknown
	woollens	7			3	4		
10-7-3	Dyeing of silk and cotton fabrics	4			3	1		
10-7-4	Dyeing of silk and woollen fabrics	7			4	2	1	
10-7-5	Dyeing of hosiery	1		1				
10-7-6	Dyeing for customers	2			1	1		
10-8	Printing of textiles							
10-8-1	Board printing	12		5	5	2		
10-8-2	Brush printing	7		4	2	1		
10-9	Thread							
10-9-1	Thread balls	7		3	4			
10-9-2	Waxed thread	2			1	1		
10-9-3	Warp and woof	2			1	1		
10-10	Trimmings and ribbons							
10-10-1	Trimmings							
10-10-1-1	Rayon entirely	12		8	3	1		
10-10-1-2	Cotton and rayon	6		2	4			
10-10-1-3	Silk and rayon	1			1			
10-10-1-4	Cotton yarn entirely	1		1				
10-10-2	Ribbons							
10-10-2-1	Cotton yarn entirely	5		4	1			
10-10-2-2	Cotton and rayon	1			1			
10-10-2-3	Cotton, rayon and rubber	3		2	1			
10-11	Cotton flannel finishing	2				1	1	
	Total for Group X.	545		149	286	77	17	16

Group XI. Clothing Industries Including Hosiery

Code	Classification	(1)	(2)	(3)	(4)	(5)	(6)	(7)
11-1	Knitted hosiery							
11-1-1	Cotton hosiery							
11-1-1-1	Cotton yarn only	11		5	4	2		
11-1-1-2	Cotton thread only	17		6	8	2	1	
11-1-1-3	Yarn and thread	5		4	1			
11-1-1-4	Raw material supplied by customers	1			1			
11-1-2	Silk and rayon hosiery							

Code	Classification	(1) No. of Factories	(2) State-ownership	(3) Single Proprietorship	(4) Partner-Ship	(5) Limited Liability Company	(6) Others	(7) Unknown
11-1-2-1	Silk only	2		1	1			
11-1-2-2	Silk and cotton	14		6	7	1		
11-1-2-3	Rayon and cotton	10		8	2			
11-1-2-4	Silk and rayon	1		1				
11-1-2-5	Silk, rayon and cotton	10		6	3	1		
11-1-3	Woollen hosiery (pure wool)	1		1				
11-1-4	Cotton, silk and wool combined	2		1	1			
11-1-5	Sewing of knitted hosiery	3		2	1			
11-1-6	Hosiery and other articles of apparel	24		7	13	3		1
11-2	Hats							
11-2-1	Straw hats	3		1	1	1		
11-2-2	Felt hats	1			1			
11-2-3	Chinese hats (silk, cloth, etc.)	1						1
11-2-4	Straw and felt hats	6		2	2	2		
11-2-5	Straw and Chinese hats	1		1				
11-3	Umbrellas							
11-3-1	Umbrella stems	1		1				
11-3-2	Umbrellas	13		7	6			
11-4	Handkerchiefs							
11-4-1	Handkerchiefs only	6		1		4		1
11-4-2	Handkerchiefs and other things	4		1	3			
11-5	Underwear and sweaters							
11-5-1	Silk only	3		1	1	1		
11-5-2	Cotton only	9		2	3	3		1
11-5-3	Cotton and wool	11		4	3	3	1	
11-5-4	Knitted fabric	1		1				
11-6	Other articles of of apparel							
11-6-1	Ties, scarfs and gloves	6		1	5			
11-6-2	Buttons	3		2	1			

Code	Classification	(1) No. of Factories	(2) State-ownership	(3) Single Proprietorship	(4) Partner-Ship	(5) Limited Liability Company	(6) Others	(7) Unknown
11-6-3	Silk and cloth shoes	1			1			
	Total for Group XI.	171		73	69	23	2	4
Group XII. Manufacture of Leather, Rubber Products, etc.								
12-1	Leather manufacturing							
12-1-1	Soft leather and uppers	4		1	1	2		
12-1-2	Hard leather and soles	7		2	5			
12-1-3	Others	7		3	4			
12-2	Leather goods							
12-2-1	Articles used by the military	3		1	2			
12-2-2	Leather trunks, cases, etc.	2		2				
12-2-3	Leather shoes	4		2	1	1		
12-3	Rubber goods							
12-3-1	Rubber shoes	24		1	11	8	2	2
12-3-2	Rubber soles, heels, etc.	5		1	1	3		
12-4	Glue	1				1		
	Total for Group XII	57		13	25	15	2	2
Group XIII. Preparation and Manufacture of Foods, Drinks and Tobacco								
13-1	Rice mills	12		3	8			1
13-2	Wheat flour mills	15		1	1	4	8	1
13-3	Rice and other flour mills	4		3	1			
13-4	Sugar refineries	4			4			
13-5	Biscuits, bread, candies and canned food							
13-5-1	Biscuits	9		3	5	1		
13-5-2	Bread	1			1			
13-5-3	Candies and sweetmeats	3		2			1	
13-5-4	Canned food	1			1			
13-5-5	Others	5			3	1	1	
13-6	Oil mills							
13-6-1	Bean oil	3			3			
13-6-2	Groundnut oil	3			3			
13-6-3	Cotton seed oil	5		1	1	3		

Code	Classification	(1) No. of Factories	(2) State-ownership	(3) Single Proprietorship	(4) Partner-Ship	(5) Limited Liability Company	(6) Others	(7) Unknown
13-6-4	Vegetable oil in general	2		1		1		
13-6-5	Lard manufacturing	1			1			
13-7	Tea							
13-7-1	By machine process	19		7	12			
13-7-2	By native process	12		4	7	1		
13-8	Tobacco							
13-8-1	Cigars	5		1	1	3		
13-8-2	Cigarettes	46		5	5	34	1	1
13-9	Wine and spirits	1				1		
13-10	Soda water and other soft drinks	2		1		1		
13-11	Condiments	8		1	2	4	1	
13-12	Casings	3		3				
13-13	Refined salt	1				1		
13-14	Frozen egg products	1		1				
13-15	Other food stuffs							
13-15-1	Starch	2		1	1			
13-15-2	Bean curd products	3		3				
13-16	Ice and cold storage	4			2	2		
	Total for Group XIII.	175		41	62	57	12	3
Group XIV. Manufacture of Paper, Book-Binding and Printing								
14-1	Paper manufacturing							
14-1-1	Paper	7		1	2	4		
14-1-2	Card board	1				1		
14-1-3	Tin foil	1			1			
14-2	Printing							
14-2-1	Newspaper printing and publishing	5		1	1	2	1	
14-2-2	Book printing and publishing	10			1	8		1
14-2-3	Printing with letter press[3]							
14-2-3-1	Full sheet press	13		5	5	3		
14-2-3-2	Half sheet press	9		4	5			

Code	Classification	(1) No. of Factories	(2) State-ownership	(3) Single Proprietorship	(4) Partner-Ship	(5) Limited Liability Company	(6) Others	(7) Unknown
14-2-3-3	Quarter and one-sixth size presses	10		3	4	2	1	
14-2-3-4	Small foot-operated presses	4		3	1			
14-2-3-5	Unclassified	4		2	1	1		
14-2-4	Rubber offset printing	7		4	2	1		
14-2-5	Lithographic printing	18		8	7	2		1
14-2-6	Lithographic and letter press printing	4		2	2			
14-2-7	Lithographic and offset printing	16		3	6	6	1	
14-2-8	Unclassified	6		2	1	3		
14-3	Book-binding	14		12	1			1
14-4	Paper manufactures							
14-4-1	Envelops and paper bags	3		2	1			
14-4-2	Cartons	20		7	10	1	1	1
14-4-3	Cards	2				2		
14-5	Engraving	1				1		
	Total for Group XIV.	155		59	51	37	4	4
Group XV. Manufacture of Scientific and Musical Instruments, Clocks and Watches, etc.								
15-1	Musical instruments							
15-1-1	Organs	9		2	7			
15-1-2	Pianos	2			2			
15-1-3	Gramophones and gramophone records	5		3	1		1	
15-1-4	Other musical instruments	2		1	1			
15-2	Educational supplies and toys							
15-2-1	Writing ink	4		2	2			
15-2-2	Writing outfit	5		2	1	1		1
15-2-3	Toys	6		2	1	3		
15-3	Scientific apparatus	5		2		3		
15-4	Clocks	1		1				
	Total for Group XV.	39		15	15	7	1	1

Code	Classification	(1) No. of Factories	(2) State-ownership	(3) Single Proprietorship	(4) Partner-Ship	(5) Limited Liability Company	(6) Others	(7) Unknown
Group XVI. Other Manufacturing Industries								
16-1	Tooth brushes	6		3	1	2		
16-2	Mirrors	4			2	2		
16-3	Coal briquettes	12		3	5	3	1	
16-4	Straw ropes	10		7	3			
	Total for Group XVI.	32		13	11	7	1	
	Grand Total for the Sixteen Groups	1,672	3	580	700	295	51	43

Notes: (1) This heading includes under it four forms of business organizations: (a) unlimited liability company, (b) limited partnership, (c) special form (e.g., a party subsidized factory), and (d) limited partnership company.

(2) Establishments which do not have power plants of their own to generate electricity but are engaged in selling electricity produced by other companies are not included.

(3) The sub-division of "Printing with letter press" is further divided into "Full sheet press", "Half sheet press", etc. It does not mean, however, that the factories thus classified have only full and half sheet presses. On the contrary, a "full sheet press" factory may be equipped with any number of machines of a smaller size, besides the full sheet press, while a "half sheet press" establishment may have other kinds also but not ones larger than the half sheet press, or, in other cases, not larger than what is specified in the titles of the sub-headings under which they are classified.

(4) Asterisks in the above table as well as in the tables following down to Table D-IV indicate that the data are incomplete or unavailable.

TABLE A-II. CAPITAL AND RESERVE

Code	Classification	(1) No. of Factories	(2) Capital ($)	(3) ($) Reserve
	Group I. Woodworking Industries			
1-1	Saw mills	8	79,333*	
1-2	Manufacture of wooden boxes	1	5,000	
1-3	Manufacture of other wooden articles	2	7,500	
1-4	Manufacture of cork stoppers	3	9,000	
1-5	Manufacture of bamboo articles	1	4,000	
	Total for Group I.	15	104,833*	
	Group II. Furniture Manufacturing			
2-1	Wooden furniture	3	420,000 [1]	
2-2	Steel furniture	9	371,800	
2-3	Rugs and carpets	5	43,700	
	Total for Group II.	17	835,500	
	Group III. Metal Industries			
3-1	Founding			
3-1-1	Whole machines	3	46,000	
3-1-2	Machine parts and accessories	22	95,600	616
3-1-3	Iron pipes	4	19,600	
3-1-4	Other articles	6	14,000	
3-2	Steel refining	1	200,000	
	Total for Group III.	36	375,200	616
	Group IV. Manufacture of Machinery and Miscellaneous Metal Products			
4-1	Manufacture and repairing of machines			
4-1-1	Printing machines			
4-1-1-1	Machines	13	100,400*	
4-1-1-2	Machine parts	1	1,600	
4-1-2	Knitting machines			
4-1-2-1	Machines	23	54,617	6,000
4-1-2-2	Machine parts	4	7,600	
4-1-3	Spinning and weaving machines			
4-1-3-1	Machines	20	435,479*	1,667
4-1-3-2	Machine parts	5	18,978	
4-1-3-3	Bobbins	7	302,309	*

Code	Classification	(1) No. of Factories	(2) Capital ($)	(3) Reserve ($)
4-1-4	Prime movers	21	861,000	13,560
4-1-5	Other kinds of machines	8	72,800	
4-1-6	Various kinds of machines	16	63,745*	
4-1-7	Various kinds of machine parts	9	67,800	400
4-1-8	Manufacture and repairing of machines and machine parts	29	213,611	1,500
4-1-9	Repairing of machines and machine parts only	24	81,489*	
4-2	Manufacture of metal products			
4-2-1	Boilers	5	18,000	
4-2-2	Weighing scales	4	12,900	
4-2-3	Nails	6	153,700	
4-2-4	Tins, boxes, etc.	23	283,433	15,000
4-2-5	Aluminumware	4	30,000*	
4-2-6	Faucets, valves, etc.	5	6,600*	
4-2-7	Lamps	6	47,000	
4-2-8	Miscellaneous articles	8	51,500	
4-3	Manufacture of electrical apparatus			
4-3-1	Electric light bulbs	5	160,000	30,000
4-3-2	Neon light tubes	1	60,000	3,000
4-3-3	Electric fans, heaters, etc.	3	106,000 [2]	
4-3-4	Electric supplies	7	485,478	42,778
4-3-5	Flash lights	16	191,744	
4-3-6	Dry batteries	8	26,350	
4-3-7	Electro-plating	13	24,800	
4-3-8	Electric welding	1	700	
	Total for Group IV.	295	3,939,633*	113,905*
Group V. Construction of Boats, Ships, and Vehicles for Land Transportation				
5-1	Shipbuilding			
5-1-1	Construction of ships	4	340,000*	
5-1-2	Repairing of ships and manufacture of accessories	5	44,500	
5-2	Building of cars			
5-2-1	Railway workshops	1	*	

Code	Classification	(1) No. of Factories	(2) Capital ($)	(3) Reserve ($)
5-2-2	Tram cars (and ships)	1	10,000	
5-2-3	Bicycles	1	50,000	
5-2-4	Rickshas	8	12,800	
5-3	Building of fire engines	1	2,000	
	Total for Group V.	21	459,300*	
Group VI. Manufacture of Bricks, Earthenware, Glass, etc.				
6-1	Bricks and tiles	5	1,137,000 [3]	20,000
6-2	Glass			
6-2-1	Thermos bottles	2	182,000	
6-2-2	Bottles and lamp shades	14	219,200	
6-2-3	Glass bevelling	8	15,839	
6-3	Cement	1	1,638,600	56,600
6-4	Stone power and lime			
6-4-1	Lime	5	60,133	
6-4-2	Stone powder	9	153,083*	
	Total for Group VI.	44	3,405,855*	76,600
Group VII. Building Material				
7-1	Building material	5	69,555*	417
	Total for Group VII.	5	69,555*	417
Group VIII. Production and Transmission of Electricity and Supply of Water				
8-1	Electric and water works	5	11,260,000	652,881
	Total for Group VIII.	5	11,260,000	652,881
Group IX. Manufacture of Chemicals and Allied Products				
9-1	Matches			
9-1-1	Matches	3	2,160,080 [4]	
9-1-2	Shavings and splints	1	80,000	
9-2	Soap, washing soda and candles			
9-2-1	Soap	11	896,667	
9-2-2	Washing soda	1	40,000	
9-2-3	Soap, washing soda and candles	2	65,555	
9-3	Enamelled ware			
9-3-1	Enamelled ware	8	784,000	15,073
9-3-2	Body of enamelled ware	2	30,000	

Code	Classification	(1) No. of Factories	(2) Capital ($)	(3) Reserve ($)
9-4	Varnish and printer's ink			
9-4-1	Varnish	4	571,000	13,800
9-4-2	Printer's ink	5	88,000	1,260
9-5	Cosmetics	13	3,291,000 [5]	3,096,332 [6]
9-6	Medicine	2	700,000	28,091
9-7	Celluloid and other synthetic products	6	167,944	
9-8	Other chemical products	2	520,000	10,000
	Total for Group IX	60	9,394,246	3,164,556
Group X. Textile Industries				
10-1	Cotton spinning and weaving			
10-1-1	Cotton ginning	8	87,000*	
10-1-2	Cotton fluffing	3	83,333	6,944
10-1-3	Cotton spinning			
10-1-3-1	Yarn only	14	10,252,221* [7]	523,611
10-1-3-2	Yarn and thread	3	4,088,888	
10-1-3-3	Spinning and weaving	12	23,611,111* [8]	819,444
10-1-4	Cotton weaving			
10-1-4-1	Using yarn only	23	2,476,300* [9]	171,927
10-1-4-2	Using yarn and thread	27	1,867,550	90,305
10-1-4-3	Using thread only	6	27,167	
10-1-4-4	Making of knitted cloth	3	7,778	
10-1-4-5	Towels and bed sheets	4	79,278*	
10-1-5	Other cotton spinning and weaving	2	15,000	
10-2	Rayon fabrics	7	27,600	
10-3	Silk reeling and weaving			
10-3-1	Silk reeling			
10-3-1-1	Steam filature silk	66	2,778,611	
10-3-1-2	Dupion silk	4	83,055	
10-3-1-3	Other special kinds of silk	3	362,311	10,417
10-3-2	Silk weaving	35	2,270,722*	500,000
10-4	Wool spinning and weaving			
10-4-1	Wool spinning	1	277,778	
10-4-2	Wool weaving	1	69,444	
10-4-3	Wool spinning and weaving	1	800,000	
10-5	Other animal tissue textiles	1	3,000	
10-6	Mixed fabrics			
10-6-1	Cotton and rayon	147	885,417*	

Code	Classification	(1) No. of Factories	(2) Capital ($)	(3) Reserve ($)
10-6-2	Cotton and silk	4	91,311	
10-6-3	Silk and rayon	44	720,044* [10]	3,294
10-6-4	Cotton, silk and rayon	16	584,400	
10-6-5	Cotton and wool	12	716,999	500
10-6-6	Cotton, silk and wool	5	214,889	500
10-7	Dyeing			
10-7-1	Mercerized yarn and thread	11	89,778* [11]	
10-7-2	Dyeing of cloth and woollens	7	1,001,889	10,000
10-7-3	Dyeing of silk and cotton fabrics	4	35,000	
10-7-4	Dyeing of silk and woollen fabrics	7	228,778 [12]	
10-7-5	Dyeing of hosiery	1	2,000	
10-7-6	Dyeing for customers	2	28,889	
10-8	Printing of textiles			
10-8-1	Board printing	12	63,100	5,000*
10-8-2	Brush printing	7	11,300	
10-9	Thread			
10-9-1	Thread balls	7	33,000	
10-9-2	Waxed thread	2	14,000	
10-9-3	Warp and woof	2	60,000 [13]	6,000
10-10	Trimmings and ribbons			
10-10-1	Trimmings			
10-10-1-1	Rayon entirely	12	25,000*	
10-10-1-2	Cotton and rayon	6	225,955	
10-10-1-3	Silk and rayon	1	600	
10-10-1-4	Cotton yarn entirely	1	1,600	
10-10-2	Ribbons			
10-10-2-1	Cotton yarn entirely	5	12,100	
10-10-2-2	Cotton and rayon	1	1,200	
10-10-2-3	Cotton, rayon and rubber	3	22,889	
10-11	Cotton flannel finishing	2	5,000	
	Total for Group X.	545	54,343,285*	2,147,942*
Group XI. Clothing Industries Including Hosiery				
11-1	Knitted hosiery			
11-1-1	Cotton hosiery			
11-1-1-1	Cotton yarn only	11	210,700	500

Code	Classification	(1) No. of Factories	(2) Capital ($)	(3) Reserve ($)
11-1-1-2	Cotton thread only	17	845,422*	16,000
11-1-1-3	Yarn and thread	5	49,667	
11-1-1-4	Raw material supplied by customers	1	500	
11-1-2	Silk and rayon hosiery			
11-1-2-1	Silk only	2	11,000	
11-1-2-2	Silk and cotton	14	1,197,772	2,000
11-1-2-3	Rayon and cotton	10	29,600	
11-1-2-4	Silk and rayon	1	200	
11-1-2-5	Silk, rayon and cotton	10	427,500	5,000
11-1-3	Woollen hosiery (pure wool)	1	4,167	
11-1-4	Cotton, silk and wool combined	2	11,944	
11-1-5	Sewing of knitted hosiery	3	4,500	
11-1-6	Hosiery and other articles of apparel	24	295,755	3,087
11-2	Hats			
11-2-1	Straw hats	3	106,000	
11-2-2	Felts hats	1	27,778	
11-2-3	Chinese hats (silk, cloth, etc.)	1	10,000	
11-2-4	Straw and felt hats	6	175,000	
11-2-5	Straw and Chinese hats	1	5,000	
11-3	Umbrellas			
11-3-1	Umbrella stems	1	*	
11-3-2	Umbrellas	13	33,000	17,500
11-4	Handkerchiefs			
11-4-1	Handkerchiefs only	6	112,944	
11-4-2	Handkerchiefs and other things	4	33,500	
11-5	Underwear and sweaters			
11-5-1	Silk only	3	146,889	
11-5-2	Cotton only	9	791,611	10,000
11-5-3	Cotton and wool	11	198,722	2,000
11-5-4	Knitted fabric	1	694	
11-6	Other articles of apparel			
11-6-1	Ties, scarfs and gloves	6	110,222	
11-6-2	Buttons	3	13,500	
11-6-3	Silk and cloth shoes	1	1,800	
	Total for Group XI.	171	4,855,387*	56,087

Code	Classification	(1) No. of Factories	(2) Capital ($)	(3) Reserve ($)
Group XII. Manufacture of Leather, Rubber Products, etc.				
12-1	Leather manufacturing			
12-1-1	Soft leather and uppers	4	180,450	4,240
12-1-2	Hard leather and soles	7	495,878	
12-1-3	Others	7	26,800	
12-2	Leather goods			
12-2-1	Articles used by the military	3	53,000*	10,000
12-2-2	Leather trunks, cases, etc.	2	8,000	
12-2-3	Leather shoes	4	54,600	2,500
12-3	Rubber goods			
12-3-1	Rubber shoes	24	2,262,112	100,000
12-3-2	Rubber soles, heels, etc.	5	86,000	
12-4	Glue	1	60,000	6,500
	Total for Group XII	57	3,226,840*	123,240
Group XIII. Preparation and Manufacture of Foods, Drinks and Tobacco				
13-1	Rice mills	12	116,722*	4,000
13-2	Wheat flour mills	15	6,463,889*	175,000
13-3	Rice and other flour mills	4	7,700	
13-4	Sugar refineries	4	86,778	2,000
13-5	Biscuits, bread, candies and canned food			
13-5-1	Biscuits	9	18,300	
13-5-2	Bread	1	3,600	
13-5-3	Candies and sweetmeats	3	9,972	
13-5-4	Canned food	1	10,000	
13-5-5	Others	5	503,800	4,875
13-6	Oils mills			
13-6-1	Bean oil	3	112,500	
13-6-2	Groundnut oil	3	92,500	
13-6-3	Cotton seed oil	5	587,222	5,000
13-6-4	Vegetable oil in general	2	555,556	
13-6-5	Lard manufacturing	1	3,000	
13-7	Tea			
13-7-1	By machine process	19	94,488	1,200
13-7-2	By native process	12	44,333	
13-8	Tobacco			

Code	Classification	(1) No. of Factories	(2) Capital ($)	(3) Reserve ($)
13-8-1	Cigars	5	119,167	
13-8-2	Cigarettes	46	21,111,705*	438,500
13-9	Wine and spirits	1	150,000	
13-10	Soda water and other soft drinks	2	310,000	12,500
13-11	Condiments	8	541,000	1,790
13-12	Casings	3	12,000	
13-13	Refined salt	1	240,000	
13-14	Frozen egg products	1	500,000	
13-15	Other food stuffs			
13-15-1	Starch	2	15,000	
13-15-2	Bean curd products	3	5,600	
13-16	Ice and cold storage	4	286,000	
	Total for Group XIII.	175	32,000,832*	644,865
Group XIV.	Manufacture of Paper, Book-Binding and Printing			
14-1	Paper manufacturing			
14-1-1	Paper	7	2,072,222	69,444
14-1-2	Card board	1	*	
14-1-3	Tin foil	1	7,600	
14-2	Printing			
14-2-1	Newspaper printing and publishing	5	3,900,000*	
14-2-2	Book printing and publishing	10	8,750,000*	1,335,611
14-2-3	Printing with letter press			
14-2-3-1	Full sheet press	13	222,000	
14-2-3-2	Half sheet press	9	79,600	
14-2-3-3	Quarter and one-sixth size presses	10	60,100	
14-2-3-4	Small foot-operated presses	4	10,000	
14-2-3-5	Unclassified	4	32,500	
14-2-4	Rubber offset printing	7	88,000	
14-2-5	Lithographic printing	18	146,100	8,011
14-2-6	Lithographic and letter press printing	4	36,000	
14-2-7	Lithographic and offset printing	16	1,085,889	51,564
14-2-8	Unclassified	6	186,000	11,863

Code	Classification	(1) No. of Factories	(2) Capital ($)	(3) Reserve ($)
14-3	Book-binding	14	11,700	
14-4	Paper manufactures			
14-4-1	Envelops and paper bags	3	6,500	
14-4-2	Cartons	20	120,000	
14-4-3	Cards	2	84,400	22,000
14-5	Engraving	1	*	
	Total for Group XIV.	*155*	*16,898,611**	*1,498,493*

Group XV. Manufacture of Scientific and Musical Instruments, Clocks and Watches, etc.

Code	Classification	(1) No. of Factories	(2) Capital ($)	(3) Reserve ($)
15-1	Musical instruments			
15-1-1	Organs	9	44,600	1,400
15-1-2	Pianos	2	8,400	
15-1-3	Gramophones and gramophone records	5	120,167	
15-1-4	Other musical instruments	2	6,000	
15-2	Educational supplies and toys			
15-2-1	Writing ink	4	20,500	1,000
15-2-2	Writing outfit	5	169,800	3,000
15-2-3	Toys	6	41,300	
15-3	Scientific apparatus	5	35,500	684
15-4	Clocks	1	7,000	
	Total for Group XV.	*39*	*453,267*	*6,084*

Group XVI. Other Manufacturing Industries

Code	Classification	(1) No. of Factories	(2) Capital ($)	(3) Reserve ($)
16-1	Tooth brushes	6	212,300	5,000
16-2	Mirrors	4	60,000	
16-3	Coal briquettes	12	422,000*	
16-4	Straw ropes	10	12,850	
	Total for Group XVI.	*32*	*707,150**	*5,000*
	Grand Total for the Sixteen Groups	*1,672*	*142,329,494**	*8,490,686**

Notes: (1) Including $300,000, which is the capital of the company which operates a factory in this division rather than that of the factory itself.

(2) Excluding the joint capitalization of one of the factories here with an electric light bulb factory, amounting to $100,000, which appears under 4-3-1 of Group IV.

(3) One of the factories has a branch factory in Chekiang and its capitalization of $1,000,000 includes that of the latter establishment.

(4) Including $1,910,000 which is the total capitalization of a company operating, besides a certain factory in this subdivision, several other establishments in other cities.

(5) Including $1,300,000 and $1,200,000 representing the capitalization of two Hongkong factories each of which has a branch in this division.

(6) Including the joint reserve of a factory in this division and its head factory in Hongkong, amounting to $3,000,000.

(7) One of the factories has a joint capitalization of $12,000,000 with two sister factories, which is given under "Cotton spinning and weaving", 10-1-3-3 of Group X.

(8) Including $12,000,000 referred to under (7).

(9) The capital of $2,000,000 of a factory here refers to that of the company which operates it.

(10) The capital of $2,000,000 of a company operating one of the factories in this and other subdivisions is given under the subdivision of "Silk weaving".

(11) One of the factories being a branch of another, its capital is included in the $10,000 given for the latter under 1-1-1 of Group XI (Cotton hosiery, cotton yarn only).

(12) Vide (10).

(13) Vide (10).

TABLE A-III. OWNERSHIP OF FACTORY BUILDINGS

Code	Classification	(1) No. of Factories	(2) Owned	(3) Rented	(4) Partly Owned and Partly Rented	(5) Unknown
Group I. Woodworking Industries						
1-1	Saw mills	8	3	2	2	1
1-2	Manufacture of wooden boxes	1	1			
1-3	Manufacture of other wooden articles	2		2		
1-4	Manufacture of cork stoppers	3		3		
1-5	Manufacture of bamboo articles	1		1		
	Total for Group I.	15	4	8	2	1
Group II. Furniture Manufacturing						
2-1	Wooden furniture	3	2		1	
2-2	Steel furniture	9		6	3	
2-3	Rugs and carpets	5		5		
	Total for Group II.	17	2	11	4	
Group III. Metal Industries						
3-1	Founding					
3-1-1	Whole machines	3		1	2	
3-1-2	Machine parts and accessories	22	2	18	2	
3-1-3	Iron pipes	4		3	1	
3-1-4	Other articles	6	1	3	1	1
3-2	Steel refining	1	1			
	Total for Group III.	36	4	25	6	1
Group IV. Manufacture of Machinery and Miscellaneous Metal Products						
4-1	Manufacture and repairing of machines					
4-1-1	Printing machines					
4-1-1-1	Machines	13	2	11		
4-1-1-2	Machine parts	1		1		
4-1-2	Knitting machines					
4-1-2-1	Machines	23	1	21	1	
4-1-2-2	Machine parts	4		4		
4-1-3	Spinning and weaving machines					
4-1-3-1	Machines	20	4	15	1	
4-1-3-2	Machine parts	5		5		

Code	Classification	(1) No. of Factories	(2) Owned	(3) Rented	(4) Partly Owned and Partly Rented	(5) Unknown
4-1-3-3	Bobbins	7	2	4	1	
4-1-4	Prime movers	21	5	14	2	
4-1-5	Other kinds of machines	8	1	7		
4-1-6	Various kinds of machines	16	2	13		1
4-1-7	Various kinds of machine parts	9	2	6		1
4-1-8	Manufacture and repairing of machines and machine parts	29	5	20	4	
4-1-9	Repairing of machines and machine parts only	24	2	20	1	1
4-2	Manufacture of metal products					
4-2-1	Boilers	5	1	2	1	1
4-2-2	Weighing scales	4		4		
4-2-3	Nails	6	2	4		
4-2-4	Tins, boxes, etc.	23	1	20	1	1
4-2-5	Aluminumware	4	1	3		
4-2-6	Faucets, valves, etc.	5		5		
4-2-7	Lamps	6		6		
4-2-8	Miscellaneous articles	8		8		
4-3	Manufacture of electrical apparatus					
4-3-1	Electric light bulbs	5	1	4		
4-3-2	Neon light tubes	1		1		
4-3-3	Electric fans, heaters, etc.	3		2	1	
4-3-4	Electric supplies	7	2	5		
4-3-5	Flash lights	16		16		
4-3-6	Dry batteries	8		8		
4-3-7	Electro-plating	13		13		
4-3-8	Electric welding	1		1		
	Total for Group IV.	*295*	*34*	*243*	*13*	*5*
Group V. Construction of Boats, Ships, and Vehicles for Land Transportation						
5-1	Shipbuilding					
5-1-1	Construction of ships	4	1	1	2	
5-1-2	Repairing of ships and manufacture of accessories	5	1	3	1	

Code	Classification	(1) No. of Factories	(2) Owned	(3) Rented	(4) Partly Owned and Partly Rented	(5) Unknown
5-2	Building of cars					
5-2-1	Railway workshops	1	1			
5-2-2	Tram cars (and ships)	1			1	
5-2-3	Bicycles	1			1	
5-2-4	Rickshas	8		8		
5-3	Building of fire engines	1		1		
	Total for Group V.	21	3	13	5	
Group VI. Manufacture of Bricks, Earthenware, Glass. etc.						
6-1	Bricks and tiles	5	4	1		
6-2	Glass					
6-2-1	Thermos bottles	2	2			
6-2-2	Bottles and lamp shades	14	6	7	1	
6-2-3	Glass bevelling	8		8		
6-3	Cement	1	1			
6-4	Stone powder and lime					
6-4-1	Lime	5	3	1	1	
6-4-2	Stone powder	9	2	1	5	1
	Total for Group VI.	44	18	18	7	1
Group VII. Building Material						
7-1	Building material	5	1	1	3	
	Total for Group VII.	5	1	1	3	
Group VIII. Production and Transmission of Electricity and Supply of Water						
8-1	Electric and water works	5	5			
	Total for Group VIII.	5	5			
Group IX. Manufacture of Chemicals and Allied Products						
9-1	Matches					
9-1-1	Matches	3	1		2	
9-1-2	Shavings and splints	1	1			
9-2	Soap, washing soda and candles					
9-2-1	Soap	11	4	4	3	
9-2-2	Washing soda	1		1		
9-2-3	Soap, washing soda and candles	2	1	1		
9-3	Enamelled ware					

Code	Classification	(1) No. of Factories	(2) Owned	(3) Rented	(4) Partly Owned and Partly Rented	(5) Unknown
9-3-1	Enamelled ware	8	1	2	5	
9-3-2	Body of enamelled ware	2		2		
9-4	Varnish and printer's ink					
9-4-1	Varnish	4	3	1		
9-4-2	Printer's ink	5	1	3	1	
9-5	Cosmetics	13	3	9	1	
9-6	Medicine	2	1	1		
9-7	Celluloid and other synthetic products	6		2	3	1
9-8	Other chemical products	2	1		1	
	Total for Group IX.	60	17	26	16	1
Group X. Textile Industries						
10-1	Cotton spinning and weaving					
10-1-1	Cotton ginning	8	1	1	1	5
10-1-2	Cotton fluffing	3		2	1	
10-1-3	Cotton spinning					
10-1-3-1	Yarn only	14	11	2		1
10-1-3-2	Yarn and thread	3	3			
10-1-3-3	Spinning and weaving	12	9	1	1	1
10-1-4	Cotton weaving					
10-1-4-1	Using yarn only	23	5	17	1	
10-1-4-2	Using yarn and thread	27	3	22	2	
10-1-4-3	Using thread only	6		5		1
10-1-4-4	Making of knitted cloth	3		3		
10-1-4-5	Towels and bed sheets	4	1	2		1
10-1-5	Other cotton spinning and weaving	2		2		
10-2	Rayon fabrics	7		7		
10-3	Silk reeling and weaving					
10-3-1	Silk reeling					
10-3-1-1	Steam filature silk	66	5	58		3
10-3-1-2	Dupion silk	4		4		
10-3-1-3	Other special kinds of silk	3		1	2	
10-3-2	Silk weaving	35	7	27		1
10-4	Wool spinning and weaving					
10-4-1	Wool spinning	1			1	
10-4-2	Wool weaving	1		1		

Code	Classification	(1) No. of Factories	(2) Owned	(3) Rented	(4) Partly Owned and Partly Rented	(5) Unknown
10-4-3	Wool spinning and weaving	1	1			
10-5	Other animal tissue textiles	1	1			
10-6	Mixed fabrics					
10-6-1	Cotton and rayon	147	2	144		1
10-6-2	Cotton and silk	4		3	1	
10-6-3	Silk and rayon	44	5	38		1
10-6-4	Cotton, silk and rayon	16	1	15		
10-6-5	Cotton and wool	12	2	8	2	
10-6-6	Cotton, silk and wool	5	1	3		1
10-7	Dyeing					
10-7-1	Mercerized yarn and thread	11		9	2	
10-7-2	Dyeing of cloth and woollens	7	3	3	1	
10-7-3	Dyeing of silk and cotton fabrics	4		4		
10-7-4	Dyeing of silk and woollen fabrics	7	2	5		
10-7-5	Dyeing of hosiery	1		1		
10-7-6	Dyeing for customers	2		2		
10-8	Printing of textiles					
10-8-1	Board printing	12		12		
10-8-2	Brush printing	7		6		1
10-9	Thread					
10-9-1	Thread balls	7		5	2	
10-9-2	Waxed thread	2		2		
10-9-3	Warp and woof	2		1	1	
10-10	Trimmings and ribbons					
10-10-1	Trimmings					
10-10-1-1	Rayon entirely	12	1	11		
10-10-1-2	Cotton and rayon	6	1	5		
10-10-1-3	Silk and rayon	1		1		
10-10-1-4	Cotton yarn entirely	1		1		
10-10-2	Ribbons					
10-10-2-1	Cotton yarn entirely	5		4	1	
10-10-2-2	Cotton and rayon	1		1		
10-10-2-3	Cotton, rayon and rubber	3		3		
10-11	Cotton flannel finishing	2		2		
	Total for Group X.	545	65	444	19	17

Code	Classification	(1) No. of Factories	(2) Owned	(3) Rented	(4) Partly Owned and Partly Rented	(5) Unknown
Group XI. Clothing Industries Including Hosiery						
11-1	Knitted hosiery					
11-1-1	Cotton hosiery					
11-1-1-1	Cotton yarn only	11	1	10		
11-1-1-2	Cotton thread only	17	3	12	2	
11-1-1-3	Yarn and thread	5		5		
11-1-1-4	Raw material supplied by customers	1		1		
11-1-2	Silk and rayon hosiery					
11-1-2-1	Silk only	2		2		
11-1-2-2	Silk and cotton	14	1	13		
11-1-2-3	Rayon and cotton	10		10		
11-1-2-4	Silk and rayon	1		1		
11-1-2-5	Silk, rayon and cotton	10	1	8	1	
11-1-3	Woollen hosiery (pure wool)	1		1		
11-1-4	Cotton, silk and wool combined	2		2		
11-1-5	Sewing of knitted hosiery	3		3		
11-1-6	Hosiery and other articles of apparel	24		24		
11-2	Hats					
11-2-1	Straw hats	3		3		
11-2-2	Felt hats	1		1		
11-2-3	Chinese hats (silk, cloth, etc.)	1		1		
11-2-4	Straw and felt hats	6	1	5		
11-2-5	Straw and Chinese hats	1		1		
11-3	Umbrellas					
11-3-1	Umbrella stems	1				1
11-3-2	Umbrellas	13		13		
11-4	Handkerchiefs					
11-4-1	Handkerchiefs only	6		6		
11-4-2	Handkerchiefs and other things	4		4		
11-5	Underwear anad sweaters					
11-5-1	Silk only	3	1	2		
11-5-2	Cotton only	9	3	5	1	
11-5-3	Cotton and wool	11	1	10		

Code	Classification	(1) No. of Factories	(2) Owned	(3) Rented	(4) Partly Owned and Partly Rented	(5) Unknown
11-5-4	Knitted fabric	1		1		
11-6	Other articles of apparel					
11-6-1	Ties, scarfs and gloves	6		6		
11-6-2	Buttons	3		3		
11-6-3	Silk and cloth shoes	1		1		
	Total for Group XI.	*171*	*12*	*154*	*4*	*1*
Group XII. Manufacture of Leather, Rubber Products, etc.						
12-1	Leather manufacturing					
12-1-1	Soft leather and uppers	4	2	2		
12-1-2	Hard leather and soles	7	3	1	2	1
12-1-3	Others	7	2	4	1	
12-2	Leather goods					
12-2-1	Articles used by the military	3		3		
12-2-2	Leather trunks, cases, etc.	2	1	1		
12-2-3	Leather shoes	4		3		1
12-3	Rubber goods					
12-3-1	Rubber shoes	24	5	16	2	1
12-3-2	Rubber soles, heels, etc.	5	1	3	1	
12-4	Glue	1	1			
	Total for Group XII.	*57*	*15*	*33*	*6*	*3*
Group XIII. Preparation and Manufacture of Foods, Drinks and Tobacco						
13-1	Rice mills	12	1	11		
13-2	Wheat flour mills	15	10	4	1	
13-3	Rice and other flour mills	4	1	2		1
13-4	Sugar refineries	4		4		
13-5	Biscuits, bread, candies and canned food					
13-5-1	Biscuits	9		9		
13-5-2	Bread	1		1		
13-5-3	Candies and sweetmeats	3		3		
13-5-4	Canned food	1		1		
13-5-5	Others	5		3	2	
13-6	Oil mills					
13-6-1	Bean oil	3		2	1	
13-6-2	Groundnut oil	3		3		

Code	Classification	(1) No. of Factories	(2) Owned	(3) Rented	(4) Partly Owned and Partly Rented	(5) Unknown
13-6-3	Cotton seed oil	5	1	3	1	
13-6-4	Vegetable oil in general	2	2			
13-6-5	Lard manufacturing	1		1		
13-7	Tea					
13-7-1	By machine process	19		18		1
13-7-2	By native process	12		12		
13-8	Tobacco					
13-8-1	Cigars	5	1	4		
13-8-2	Cigarettes	46	6	33	6	1
13-9	Wine and spirits	1	1			
13-10	Soda water and other soft drinks	2	1	1		
13-11	Condiments	8	2	2	4	
13-12	Casings	3		3		
13-13	Refined salt	1		1		
13-14	Frozen egg products	1		1		
13-15	Other food stuffs					
13-15-1	Starch	2	1		1	
13-15-2	Bean curd products	3		3		
13-16	Ice and cold storage	4	2	1	1	
	Total for Group XIII.	175	29	125	19	2
Group XIV. Manufacture of Paper, Book-Binding and Printing						
14-1	Paper manufacturing					
14-1-1	Paper	7	5	1	1	
14-1-2	Card board	1		1		
14-1-3	Tin foil	1		1		
14-2	Printing					
14-2-1	Newspaper printing and publishing	5	3	2		
14-2-2	Book printing and publishing	10	3	6		1
14-2-3	Printing with letter press					
14-2-3-1	Full sheet press	13	1	12		
14-2-3-2	Half sheet press	9		9		
14-2-3-3	Quarter and one sixth size presses	10		10		
14-2-3-4	Small foot-operated presses	4		4		
14-2-3-5	Unclassified	4		4		
14-2-4	Rubber offset printing	7		7		

Code	Classification	(1) No. of Factories	(2) Owned	(3) Rented	(4) Partly Owned and Partly Rented	(5) Unknown
14-2-5	Lithographic printing	18	1	17		
14-2-6	Lithographic and letter press printing	4		4		
14-2-7	Lithographic and offset printing	16	4	11		1
14-2-8	Unclassified	6	1	5		
14-3	Book-binding	14		14		
14-4	Paper manufactures					
14-4-1	Envelops and paper bags	3		3		
14-4-2	Cartons	20	2	18		
14-4-3	Cards	2	2			
14-5	Engraving	1		1		
	Total for Group XIV.	*155*	*22*	*130*	*1*	*2*
Group XV. Manufacture of Scientific and Musical Instruments, Clocks and Watches, etc.						
15-1	Musical instruments					
15-1-1	Organs	9		7	2	
15-1-2	Pianos	2	1	1		
15-1-3	Gramophones and gramophone records	5		5		
15-1-4	Other musical instruments	2		2		
15-2	Educational supplies and toys					
15-2-1	Writing ink	4	2	2		
15-2-2	Writing outfit	5		5		
15-2-3	Toys	6		5		1
15-3	Scientific apparatus	5	1	4		
15-4	Clocks	1		1		
	Total for Group XV.	*39*	*4*	*32*	*2*	*1*
Group XVI. Other Manufacturing Industries						
16-1	Tooth brushes	6	1	5		
16-2	Mirrors	4		3		1
16-3	Coal briquettes	12	3	7	2	
16-4	Straw ropes	10	2	4	1	3
	Total for Group XVI.	*32*	*6*	*19*	*3*	*4*
	Grand Total for the Sixteen Groups	*1672*	*241*	*1282*	*110*	*39*

TABLE A.IV. OFFICERS AND WORKERS

Code	Classification	(1) No. of Factories	(2) Male Officers	(3) Female Officers	(4) Total No. of Officers	(5) Male Workers Time	(6) Male Workers Piece	(7) Female Workers Time	(8) Female Workers Piece	(9) Child Workers Time	(10) Child Workers Piece	(11) Total No. of Workers Time	(12) Total No. of Workers Piece	(13) Time & Piece	(14) Total No. of Workers Required for Full Time Operation
	Group I. Woodworking Industries														
1-1	Saw mills	8	60*		60*	390				2		392		392	429
1-2	Manufacture of wooden boxes	1	8		8	15						15		15	15
1-3	Manufacture of other wooden articles	2	5		5	13				7		20	10	30	37
1-4	Manufacture of cork stoppers	3	5		5	34	11			12		46		46	50
1-5	Manufacture of bamboo articles	1	2		2	11	11	15	10	7		33	11	44	44
	Total for Group I.	15	80*		80*	463	11	15	10	28		506	21	527	575
	Group II. Furniture Manufacturing														
2-1	Wooden furniture	3	11		11	368	321					368	321	689	803
2-2	Steel furniture	9	66		66	351	76			164		515	76	591	546*
2-3	Rugs and carpets	5	13		13		163			145		145	163	308	318
	Total for Group II.	17	90		90	719	560			309		1,028	560	1,588	1,667*
	Group III. Metal Industries														
3-1	Founding														
3-1-1	Whole machines	3	8		8	52				32		84		84	55*
3-1-2	Machine parts and accessories	22	36		36	301				173		474		474	478*
3-1-3	Iron pipes	4	10		10	74				42		116		116	120
3-1-4	Other articles	6	9		9	71				28		99		99	123*
3-2	Steel refining	1	3		3	29				1		30		30	*
	Total for Group III.	36	66		66	527				276		803		803	776*
	Group IV. Manufacture of Machinery and Miscellaneous Metal Products														
4-1	Manufacture and repairing of machines														
4-1-1	Printing machines														
4-1-1-1	Machines	13	21		21	138				159		297		297	249*
4-1-1-2	Machine parts	1	1		1	4				1		5		5	5
4-1-2	Knitting machines														
4-1-2-1	Machines	23	32		32	194	12			208		402	12	414	485
4-1-2-2	Machine parts	4	7		7	59	32	43	7	13	10	115	49	164	171
4-1-3	Spinning and weaving machines														
4-1-3-1	Machines	20	109		109	1,110	15			440		1,550	15	1,565	1,947*
4-1-3-2	Machine parts	5	7		7	29				50		79		79	109

Code	Classification	(1) No. of Factories	(2) Male Officers	(3) Female Officers	(4) Total No. of Officers	(5) Male Workers Time	(6) Male Workers Piece	(7) Female Workers Time	(8) Female Workers Piece	(9) Child Workers Time	(10) Child Workers Piece	(11) Total No. of Workers Time	(12) Total No. of Workers Piece	(13) Total No. of Workers Time & Piece	(14) Total No. of Workers Required for Full Time Operation
4:1-3-3	Bobbins	7	40		40	153	207		40	58		211	247	458	571
4:1-4	Prime movers	21	130		130	798		100		358		1,256		1,256	1,713
4:1-5	Other kinds of machines	8	9		9	85				81		166		166	160*
4:1-6	Various kinds of machines	16	37		37	214	24			200		414	24	438	560*
4:1-7	Various kinds of machine parts	9	20		20	137				115		252		252	297
4:1-8	Manufacture and repairing of machines and machine parts	20	91		91	534				380		914		914	817*
4:1-9	Repairing of machines and machine parts only	24	34		34	195				160		355		355	371*
4:2	Manufacture of metal products														
4:2-1	Boilers	5	12		12	99				12		111		111	90*
4:2-2	Weighing scales	4	11		11	34				16		50		50	65
4:2-3	Nails	6	15		15	113				16		129		129	70*
4:2-4	Tins, boxes, etc.	23	133		133	566	35	131		455	4	1,152	39	1,191	1,264*
4:2-5	Aluminumware	4	10		10	112		3		35		150		150	149*
4:2-6	Faucets, valves, etc.	5	6		6	32				32		64		64	72
4:2-7	Lamps	6	21		21	82	24	8		26	15	116	39	155	209
4:2-8	Miscellaneous articles	8	17		17	101	4			20		121	4	125	84*
4:3	Manufacture of electrical apparatus														
4:3-1	Electric light bulbs	5	44	1	45	121	37	82	65	92	10	295	112	407	492
4:3-2	Neon light tubes	1	10		10	18				14		32		32	32
4:3-3	Electric fans, heaters, etc.	3	28		28	305²				33		338		338	460
4:3-4	Electric supplies	7	49		49	327	39	149	3	79		555	42	597	644*
4:3-5	Flash lights	16	85		85	334	55	30		118		482	55	537	503*
4:3-6	Dry batteries	8	31		31	122		31		25		178		178	218
4:3-7	Electro-plating	13	18		18	117	3			74		191	3	194	197*
4:3-8	Electric welding	1				5				3		8		8	*
	Total for Group IV.	295	1,028	2	1,030	6,138	487	577	115	3,273	39	9,988	641	10,629	12,004*

Group V. Construction of Boats, Ships, and Vehicles for Land Transportation

Code	Classification	(1)	(2)	(3)	(4)	(5)	(6)	(7)	(8)	(9)	(10)	(11)	(12)	(13)	(14)
5-1	Shipbuilding														
5:1-1	Construction of ships	4	248		248	1,765	200			63		1,828	200	2,028	6,200*
5:1-2	Repairing of ships and manufacture of accessories	5	28		28	161				60		230		230	455

Code	Classification	(1) No. of Factories	(2) Male Officers	(3) Female Officers	(4) Total No. of Officers	(5) Male Workers Time	(6) Male Workers Piece	(7) Female Workers Time	(8) Female Workers Piece	(9) Child Workers Time	(10) Child Workers Piece	(11) Total No. of Workers Time	(12) Total No. of Workers Piece	(13) Total No. of Workers Time & Piece	(14) Total No. of Workers Required for Full Time Operation
5-2	Building of cars														
5-2-1	Railway workshops	1	20		20	40									*
5-2-2	Tram cars (and ships)	1	14		14	38								1,037[4]	150
5-2-3	Bicycles	1	7		7	42	7			30		73		73	*
5-2-4	Rickshas	8	9		9					3		38		38	68*
5-3	Building of fire engines	1	1		1	7						72	7	79	30
	Total for Group V.	21	327		327	2,053	207			198		10	207	10	6,903*
												2,251		3,495[5]	
	Group VI. Manufacture of Bricks, Earthenware, Glass, etc.														
6-1	Bricks and tiles	5	61[6]		61	633	16	150	42	23		806	58	864	902
6-2	Glass														
6-2-1	Thermos bottles	2	9		9	146		4		53		203		203	207
6-2-2	Bottles and lamp shades	14	65		65	535		7		589		1,131		1,131	1,096*
6-2-3	Glass bevelling	8	22		22	106	28			26		132	28	160	138*
6-3	Cement	1	56		56	220						220		220	318
6-4	Stone powder and lime														
6-4-1	Lime	5	18		18	133	25					133	25	158	212
6-4-2	Stone powder	9	43		43	111	19					111	63	174	151*
	Total for Group VI.	44	274		274	1,884	88	161	44 86	691		2,736	174	2,910	3,024*
	Group VII. Building Material														
7-1	Building material	5	28		28	139	30			26		165	30	195	150*
	Total for Group VII.	5	28		28	139	30			26		165	30	195	150*
	Group VIII. Production and Transmission of Electricity and Supply of Water														
8-1	Electric and water works	5	360	1	361	1,079[7]						1,079		1,079	1,111
	Total for Group VIII.	5	360	1	361	1,079						1,079		1,079	1,111
	Group IX. Manufacture of Chemicals and Allied Products														
9-1	Matches														
9-1-1	Matches	3	82		82	260	178	109	722	32	117	401	1,017	1,418	1,430
9-1-2	Shavings and splints	1	15		15	50	266		270			50	536	586	586
9-2	Soap, washing soda and candles														
9-2-1	Soap	11	123	1	124	347		150		11		508	85	593	764*
9-2-2	Washing soda	1	3		3	20			85			20		20	20
9-2-3	Soap, washing soda and candles	2	18		18	42				3		45		45	62

Code	Classification	(1) No. of Factories	(2) Male Officers	(3) Female Officers	(4) Total No. of Officers	(5) Male Workers Time	(6) Male Workers Piece	(7) Female Workers Time	(8) Female Workers Piece	(9) Child Workers Time	(10) Child Workers Piece	(11) Total No. of Workers Time	(12) Total No. of Workers Piece	(13) Total No. of Workers Time & Piece	(14) Total No. of Workers Required for Full Time Operation
9-3	Enamelled ware	8	196	8	204	1,278	50	215	19	217		1,710	69	1,779	2,445*
9-3-1	Enamelled ware	2	10		10	14	6			18		32	6	38	49
9-3-2	Body of enamelled ware														
9-4	Varnish and printer's ink	4	39		39	183[8]		16				199		199	239*
9-4-1	Varnish	5	17		17	48*						48*		48*	50*
9-4-2	Printer's ink	13	270	32	302	346	86	653	314	6		1,005	400	1,405	1,886
9-5	Medicine	2	43		43	90		50	70	6		146	70	216	320
9-6	Cosmetics														
9-7	Celluloid and other synthetic products	6	49		49	149	59	68	30	10		227	89	316	317
9-8	Other chemical products	2	46	1	47	290	50	100	400	31	30	421	480	901	1,030
	Total for Group IX.	60	911	42	953	3,117*	695	1,361	1,910	334	147	1,812*	2,752	7,564*	9,198*
Group X. Textile Industries															
10-1	Cotton spinning and weaving														
10-1-1	Cotton ginning	8	110		110	181					10	181	341	522	*
10-1-2	Cotton fluffing	3	19		19	130		130				260		260	250*
10-1-3	Cotton spinning														
10-1-3-1	Yarn only	14	728	9	737	3,805	1,042	5,862	10,249	715	120	10,382	11,411	21,793	21,169
10-1-3-2	Yarn and thread	3	189		189	1,419	232	886	3,750	46	416	2,351	4,398	6,749	6,749
10-1-3-3	Spinning and weaving	12	1,268	2	1,270	5,249*	1,210	6,043*	20,563	1,088*	29	12,380*	21,802	34,182*	29,407*
10-1-4	Cotton weaving														
10-1-4-1	Using yarn only	23	296	4	300	1,969[9]	193	185	745	109	20	2,263	958	3,221	1,718*
10-1-4-2	Using yarn and thread	27	396	13	409	,603	402	75	1,428	69	139	747	1,969	2,716	2,545*
10-1-4-3	Using thread only	6	38	3	41		77	10	152	6	16	16	245	261	298
10-1-4-4	Making of knitted cloth	3	10		10		33		22	2		2	55	57	89
10-1-4-5	Towels and bed sheets	4	48		48	8	100		46	28		36	146	182	172*
10-1-5	Other cotton spinning and weaving	2	10		10	21	45	6	16	1	9	22	70	92	92
10-2	Rayon fabrics	7	19		19		64		13		17	6	94	100	117
10-3	Silk reeling and weaving														
10-3-1	Silk reeling														
10-3-1-1	Steam filature silk	66	1,676	193	1,869	1,487		24,830	4,879	8,994	167	35,311	5,046	40,357	38,937*
10-3-1-2	Dupion silk	4	116	11	127	22		1,596		107		1,725		1,725	1,725
10-3-1-3	Other special kinds of silk	3	43	1	44	278		405	60	40		723	60	783	130*
10-3-2	Silk weaving	35	318	2	320	124	1,021[10]	91	560[11]	389[12]	195	604	1,776	2,380	3,303*
10-4	Wool spinning and weaving														

Code	Classification	(1) No. of Factories	(2) Male Officers	(3) Female Officers	(4) Total No. of Officers	(5) Male Workers Time	(6) Male Workers Piece	(7) Female Workers Time	(8) Female Workers Piece	(9) Child Workers Time	(10) Child Workers Piece	(11) Total No. of Workers Time	(12) Total No. of Workers Piece	(13) Total No. of Workers Time & Piece	(14) Total No. of Workers Required for Full Time Operation
10-4-1	Wool spinning	1	14		14	120		56				200		10[18]	160
10-4-2	Wool weaving	1	31		31	130		70	65			200	65	200	200
10-4-3	Wool spinning and weaving	1	40		40	5		*		24		200		265	450
10-5	Other animal tissue textiles	1	2		2						87	5*		5*	37
10-6	Mixed fabrics														
10-6-1	Cotton and rayon	147	541	9	550	433	1,774	123	1,062	173		729	2,923	3,652	3,939*
10-6-2	Cotton and silk	4	23		23	15	43	11	20	2	151	28	63	91	96
10-6-3	Silk and rayon	44	320	1	321	338*	708	396	793*	136	11	870*	1,562*	2,432*	1,882*
10-6-4	Cotton, silk and rayon	16	185		185	61	623	52	303*	29		142	937*	1,079*	1,416
10-6-5	Cotton and wool	12	120	1	121	278	6	188	262	88		554	268	822	756*
10-6-6	Cotton, silk and wool	5	86	1	87	91	224	54	70	11		156	294	450	509
10-7	Dyeing														
10-7-1	Mercerized yarn and thread	11	60		60	229	270[14]			1		230	270	500	543*
10-7-2	Dyeing of cloth and woollens	7	213		213	715	34		30	107		822	64	886	664*
10-7-3	Dyeing of silk and cotton fabrics	4	34		34	70				22		92		92	75*
10-7-4	Dyeing of silk and woollen fabrics	7	90		90	297[15]	50			47[16]		344	50	394	351*
10-7-5	Dyeing of hosiery	1	2		2	10						10		10	20
10-7-6	Dyeing for customers	2	20		20	28	60			6		34	60	94	96
10-8	Printing of textiles														
10-8-1	Board printing	12	88		88		142*		1	43	160*	43	303*	346*	456
10-8-2	Brush printing	7	70		70	37	118		10	10	21	47	149	196	181*
10-9	Thread														
10-9-1	Thread balls	7	32		32	25	8		151	23	2	25	161	186	202*
10-9-2	Waxed thread	2	13		13		22		32	2		2	54	56	61
10-9-3	Warp and woof	2	54		54	252[17]		148[18]		260[19]		660		660	1,000
10-10	Trimmings and ribbons														
10-10-1	Trimmings														
10-10-1-1	Rayon entirely	12	20		20	60[20]	26	4	6	20		84	32	116	114*
10-10-1-2	Cotton and rayon	6	95		95	72	175	96	216	12	4	180	395	575	697
10-10-1-3	Silk and rayon	1				6						6		6	*
10-10-1-4	Cotton yarn entirely	1	1		1					5		5		5	5
10-10-2	Ribbons														
10-10-2-1	Cotton yarn entirely	5	11		11	38	22	16	3	28		82	25	107	107*
10-10-2-2	Cotton and rayon	1	1		1	2			2			2	2	4	4

Code	Classification	No. of Factories	Male Officers	Female Officers	Total No. of Officers	Male Workers Time	Male Workers Piece	Female Workers Time	Female Workers Piece	Child Workers Time	Child Workers Piece	Total No. of Workers Time	Total No. of Workers Piece	Total No. of Workers Time & Piece	Total No. of Workers Require for Full Time Operation
10-10-2-3	Cotton, rayon and rubber	3	39		39	32	63		14	2	2	34	79	79	79
10-11	Cotton flannel finishing	2	7	1	8									34	37
	Total for Group X.	545	7,496	251	7,747	18,640*	8,787*	41,333*	45,764*	12,622*	1,576*	72,595*	56,127*	128,732[21]*	120,838*
Group XI.	Clothing Industry														
	Including Hosiery														
11-1	Knitted hosiery														
11-1-1	Cotton hosiery														
11-1-1-1	Cotton yarn only	11	76	1	77	73	49		365	57[22]	2	130	416	546	635*
11-1-1-2	Cotton thread only	17	200	2	202	503	503	117	1,916	184	78	804	2,497	3,301	2,316*
11-1-1-3	Yarn and thread	5	23		23	120	23		299	25		145	322	467	470
11-1-1-4	Raw material supplied by customers	1	3		3		14		8				22	22	24
11-1-2	Silk and rayon hosiery														
11-1-2-1	Silk only	2	17		17		14		53				67	67	88
11-1-2-2	Silk and cotton	14	151		151	80	62	133	474	23	14	236	550	786	831*
11-1-2-3	Rayon and cotton	10	49	2	51		95		397	14	3	14	495	509	667
11-1-2-4	Silk and rayon	1					19		13				32	32	32
11-1-2-5	Silk, rayon and cotton	10	74	3	77	51	131	115	309	7	13	173	453	626	480*
11-1-3	Woollen hosiery (pure wool)	1	3		3				8		7		15	15	50
11-1-4	Cotton, silk and wool combined	2	20		20		32		84		15		131	131	174
11-1-5	Sewing of knitted hosiery	3	15		15				67	2	10	2	77	79	79
11-1-6	Hosiery and other articles of apparel	24	245	6	251	13	469	8	696	30	43	51	1,208	1,259	2,336
11-2	Hats														
11-2-1	Straw hats	3	9		9	15	20	3	4	16		34	24	58	60
11-2-2	Felt hats	1	3		3	10			7			10	7	17	20
11-2-3	Chinese hats (silk, cloth, etc.)	1	2		2		18		8[23]			10	26	36	36
11-2-4	Straw and felt hats	6	44		44	125	25	25	68	38		188	93	281	352
11-2-5	Straw and Chinese hats	1	10		10	25	20		12	10		35	32	67	70
11-3	Umbrellas														
11-3-1	Umbrella stems	1				12						12		12	*
11-3-2	Umbrellas	13	38		38	103	12	46	105	48	4	197	121	318	380
11-4	Handkerchiefs														
11-4-1	Handkerchiefs only	6	85	3	88	24		40	440	3		67	440	507	621
11-4-2	Handkerchiefs and other things	4	33		33	17			32	6		23	32	55	70
11-5	Underwear and sweaters														

Code	Classification	(1) No. of Factories	(2) Male Officers	(3) Female Officers	(4) Total No. of Officers	(5) Male Workers Time	(6) Male Workers Piece	(7) Female Workers Time	(8) Female Workers Piece	(9) Child Workers Time	(10) Child Workers Piece	(11) Total No. of Workers Time	(12) Total No. of Workers Piece	(13) Time & Piece	(14) Total No. of Workers Required for Full Time Operation
11·5-1	Silk only	3	32		32	55	34	3	188	34		92	222	314	342
11·5-2	Cotton only	9	192	3	195	164	177	431	487	46	2	641	666	1,307	1,617*
11·5-3	Cotton and wool	11	76	2	78	163	100	20	345	12		195	445	640	710*
11·5-4	Knitted fabric	1					4		4				8	8	10
11·6	Other articles of apparel														
11·6-1	Ties, scarfs and gloves	6	46		46		18	15	82	31		46	100	146	174
11·6-2	Buttons	3	11		11		39		31				70	70	21
11·6-3	Silk and cloth shoes	1	4		4		17				4		21	21	21
	Total for Group XI.	171	1,461	22	1,483	1,553	1,895	956	6,502	596	195	3,105	8,592	11,697	12,735*

Group XII. Manufacture of Leather, Rubber Products, etc.

Code	Classification	(1)	(2)	(3)	(4)	(5)	(6)	(7)	(8)	(9)	(10)	(11)	(12)	(13)	(14)
12·1	Leather manufacturing														
12·1-1	Soft leather and uppers	4	25		25	84	12			15		99	12	111	246*
12·1-2	Hard leather and soles	7	43		43	276				20		296		296	279*
12·1-3	Others	7	10		10	78	13			8		86	13	99	113
12·2	Leather goods														
12·2-1	Articles used by the military	3	36		36	800	8	60		4		864	8	872	872
12·2-2	Leather trunks, cases, etc.	2	4		4	20	54		3	30		50	57	107	124
12·2-3	Leather shoes	4	51²⁴		51	32	130			60		92	130	222	246
12·3	Rubber goods														
12·3-1	Rubber shoes	24	477	10	487	1,805	575	333	3,869	60	6	2,198	4,450	6,648	4,970*
12·3-2	Rubber soles, heels, etc.	5	20		20	89	6	8	6	5		102	6	108	131*
12·4	Glue	1	8		8	78		15				93		93	105
	Total for Group XII.	57	674	10	684	3,262	792	416	3,878	202	6	3,880	4,676	8,556	7,086*

Group XIII. Preparation and Manufacture of Foods, Drinks and Tobacco

Code	Classification	(1)	(2)	(3)	(4)	(5)	(6)	(7)	(8)	(9)	(10)	(11)	(12)	(13)	(14)
13·1	Rice mills	12	120²⁵		120	10	156			16		26	156	182	215*
13·2	Wheat flour mills	15	506		506	2,114	289					2,114	289	2,403	2,383*
13·3	Rice and other flour mills	4	7		7	19				1		20		20	24
13·4	Sugar refineries	4	28		28	138		4		2		144		144	157
13·5	Biscuits, bread, candies and canned food														
13·5-1	Biscuits	9	26		26	67		51		35		153		153	160
13·5-2	Bread	1	4		4	10				4		14		14	14
13·5-3	Candies and sweetmeats	3	18		18	29			47	6		35	47	82	104
13·5-4	Canned food	1	3		3	6				6		6		6	6

Code	Classification	(1) No. of Factories	(2) Male Officers	(3) Female Officers	(4) Total No. of Officers	(5) Male Workers Time	(6) Male Workers Piece	(7) Female Workers Time	(8) Female Workers Piece	(9) Child Workers Time	(10) Child Workers Piece	(11) Total No. of Workers Time	(12) Total No. of Workers Piece	(13) Total No. of Workers Time & Piece	(14) Total No. of Workers Required for Full Time Operation
13-5-5	Others	5	58		58	310	23	282		69	1	661	24	685	459*
13-6	Oils mills														
13-6-1	Bean oil	3	23		23	362	20					362	20	382	382
13-6-2	Groundnut oil	3	32		32	165	1,320			10		175	1,320	1,495	1,330*
13-6-3	Cotton seed oil	5	116		116	390	81					390	81	471	516
13-6-4	Vegetable oil in general	2	68		68	464						464		464	864
13-6-5	Lard manufacturing	1	1		1	12				1		13		13	13
13-7	Tea														
13-7-1	By machine process	19	47		47	267^26		467^26				734^26		734^26	983*
13-7-2	By native process	12	23		23	238		399				637		637	746
13-8	Tobacco														
13-8-1	Cigars	5	36		36	8	18	78	252			86	270	356	363
13-8-2	Cigarettes	46	745	92	837	2,448*	65	128	10,749*	215	180	2,791*,	10,994*	13,785*	13,933*
13-9	Wine and spirits	1	10		10	20						20		20	100
13-10	Soda water and other soft drinks	2	27		27	188				8		196		196	208
13-11	Condiments	8	72	2	74	337		103	20	6		446	20	466	505*
13-12	Casings	3	11		11	52		13				65		65	80
13-13	Refined salt	1	18		18	40				2		42		42	200
13-14	Frozen egg products	1	42	2	44	150		200				350		350	*
13-15	Other food stuffs														
13-15-1	Starch	2	4		4	35						35		35	45
13-15-2	Bean curd products	3	4		4	50						50		50	57
13-16	Ice and cold storage	4	28		28	86						86		86	74*
	Total for Group XIII.	175	2,077	96	2,173	8,015*	1,972	1,725	11,068*	375	181	10,115*	13,221*	23,336*	23,921*
Group XIV. Manufacture of Paper, Book-Binding and Printing															
14-1	Paper manufacturing														
14-1-1	Paper	7	86		86	764	4	482		4		1,250	4	1,254	1,446
14-1-2	Card board	1	18		18	137		28		4		169		169	169
14-1-3	Tin foil	1	7		7		13		20		33		33	33	50
14-2	Printing														
14-2-1	Newspaper printing and publishing	5	588	2	590	840						840		840	230*
14-2-2	Book Printing and Publishing	10	463	4	467	2,444	339	738		371	71	3,553	410	3,963	1,221*

Code	Classification	(1) No. of Factories	(2) Male Officers	(3) Female Officers	(4) Total No. of Officers	(5) Male Workers Time	(6) Male Workers Piece	(7) Female Workers Time	(8) Female Workers Piece	(9) Child Workers Time	(10) Child Workers Piece	(11) Total No. of Workers Time	(12) Total No. of Workers Piece	(13) Time & Piece	(14) Total No. of Workers Required for Full Time Operation
14-2-3	Printing with letter press														
14-2-3-1	Full sheet press	13	101		101	344	113²⁷			276	15	620	128	748	565*
14-2-3-2	Half sheet press	9	35	3	38	111	51			91	18	202	69	271	289
14-2-3-3	Quarter and one-sixth size presses	10	34		34	118				78		196		196	209*
14-2-3-4	Small foot-operated presses	4	9		9	49				21		70		70	74
14-2-3-5	Unclassified	4	14		14	87				17		104		104	104
14-2-4	Rubber offset printing	7	22		22	101		6		55		162		162	167
14-2-6	Lithographic and letter press	18	60		60	224	96			69	46	293	142	435	462*
14-2-7	Lithographic printing	4	13		13	62				19		81		81	84
14-2-7	Lithographic and offset printing	16	146		146	651	37	29	6	220		900	43	943	1,065
14-2-8	Unclassified	6	69		69	212	41	32		106	6	350	47	397	388*
14-3	Book-binding	14	17		17	34	136	19	129	49		102	265	367	354*
14-4	Paper manufactures														
14-4-1	Envelops and paper bags	3	7		7	17	6			8		25		25	30*
14-4-2	Cartons	20	66		66	190	124	41	19	66	2	297	25	525	619
14-4-3	Cards	2	13		13	48		12	102	12		72	228	72	72
14-5	Engraving	1	6		6	12						12		12	15
	Total for Group XIV.	155	1,774	9	1,783	6,445	960	1,387	276	1,466	158	9,298	1,394	10,692	7,613*
Group XV. Manufacture of Scientific and Musical Instruments, Clocks and Watches, etc.															
15-1	Musical instruments														
15-1-1	Organs	9	20		20	109	51			67		176	51	227	266
15-1-2	Pianos	2	7		7	8	49			5		13	49	62	66
15-1-3	Gramophones and gramophone records	5	32		32	90	35			22		112	35	147	158*
15-1-4	Other musical instruments	2	1		1	40				15		55		55	50*
15-2	Educational supplies and toys														
15-2-1	Writing ink	4	25		25	23	43	10		3		36	43	79	98
15-2-2	Writing outfit	5	14		14	50			48	10		60	48	108	69*
15-2-3	Toys	6	19		19	162	24			47	3	209	27	236	284
15-3	Scientific apparatus	5	13	2	15	60				46		116		116	130
15-4	Clocks	1	3		3	27		10		14		41		41	41
	Total for Group XV.	39	134	2	136	569	202	20	48	229	3	818	253	1,071	1,162*

Code	Classification	(1) No. of Factories	(2) Male Officers	(3) Female Officers	(4) Total No. of Officers	(5) Male Workers Time	(6) Male Workers Piece	(7) Female Workers Time	(8) Female Workers Piece	(9) Child Workers Time	(10) Child Workers Piece	(11) Total No. of Workers Time	(12) Total No. of Workers Piece	(13) Total No. of Workers Time & Piece	(14) Total No. of Workers Required for Full Time
	Group XVI. Other Manufacturing														
	Industries														
16-1	Tooth brushes	6	64	3	67	32	165	1	150	33	51	66	366	432	55
16-2	Mirrors	4	28		28	159	28			34		193	28	221	2
16-3	Coal briquettes	12	84		84	300	17					300	17	317	44
16-4	Straw ropes	10	6		6		7		301				308	308	32
	Total for Group XVI.	32	182	3	185	491	217	1	451	67	51	559	719	1,278	1,54
	Grand Total for the Sixteen Groups	1,672	16,962*	438	17,400*	55,094*	16,903*	1,952*	70,108*	20,692*	2,356*	123,738*	89,307*	214,152²⁸*	210,30

Notes: (1) That the number of workers required for full time operation in some of the industries appear to be smaller than the number of workers actually employed in these same industries is due to the failure on the part of certain factories to furnish the necessary data in the former case.
(2) Including 30 laborers doing odd jobs in one of the factories.
(3) Exclusive of the number of workers hired through labor contractors, which is unknown.
(4) Separate figures for male, female, and child workers are not available.
(5) Including 1,037 persons whose sex is not known.
(6) In the case of a certain factory, the number of officers of its affiliated factory in Chekiang is included.
(7) Including 50 workers doing odd jobs in one of the factories.
(8) Including 40 workers doing odd jobs in one of the factories.
(9) Of the 1,270 workers of a factory included in this figure, some are piece rate workers.
(10) Time rate workers form a part of the 319 workers of seven factories included in this figure.
(11) Time rate workers form a part of the 344 workers of seven factories included in this figure.
(12) Piece rate workers form a part of the 266 workers of eight factories included in this figure.
(13) Separate figures for male, female and child workers in this case are not available.
(14) Time rate workers form a part of the 56 workers of a certain factory included in this figure.
(15) Piece rate _____ form a part of the 58 workers of a certa factory included in this figure.
(16) Piece rate workers form a part of the 24 workers of a cera factory included in this figure.
(17) Piece rate workers form a part of the 230 workers of a certa factory included in this figure.
(18) Piece rate workers form a part of the 100 workers of a certa factory included in this figure.
(19) Including some piece rate workers.
(20) Three of the employees of a certain factory are half labore and half officers.
(21) Including 10 persons whose sex is not known.
(22) Some of the 17 workers of two factories are piece rate worke
(23) All these workers worked outside of the factory.
(24) Three of the factories have their shop employees mixed wi their factory staff. Similar is the case with some of the ri mills, handkerchief manufacturers, and canned food factories
(25) In the case of rice mills, all except one put their time rate ma workers with the regular factory officers, and as there is no wa to separate the two, this industry shows more staff membe than time rate factory hands.
(26) The number of contracted laborers in one of the factories is n known.
(27) Including 25 persons hired by contract.
(28) Including 1,047 persons whose sex is not known.

TABLE A-V. MOTIVE POWER

Code	Classification	(1) No. of Factories	(2) Power of Prime Movers (H. P.)	(3) Rented Electric Power (H. P.)	(4) Total (H. P.)
Group I. Woodworking Industries					
1-1	Saw mills	8	35.0	578.0	613.0
1-2	Manufacture of wooden boxes	1		50.0	50.0
1-3	Manufacture of other wooden articles	2		5.0	5.0
1-4	Manufacture of cork stoppers	3			
1-5	Manufacture of bamboo articles	1		10.0	10.0
	Total for Group I.	15	35.0	643.0	678.0
Group II. Furniture Manufacturing					
2-1	Wooden furniture	3			
2-2	Steel furniture	9		270.0	270.0
2-3	Rugs and carpets	5			
	Total for Group II.	17		270.0	270.0
Group III. Metal Industries					
3-1	Founding				
3-1-1	Whole machines	3		15.0	15.0
3-1-2	Machine parts and accessories	22		107.5	107.5
3-1-3	Iron pipes	4		20.5	20.5
3-1-4	Other articles	6		19.0	19.0
3-2	Steel refining	1		130.0	130.0
	Total for Group III.	36		292.0	292.0
Group IV. Manufacture of Machinery and Miscellaneous Metal Products					
4-1	Manufacture and repairing of machines				
4-1-1	Printing machines				
4-1-1-1	Machines	13	18.0	97.5	115.5
4-1-1-2	Machine parts	1		5.0	5.0
4-1-2	Knitting machines				
4-1-2-1	Machines	23		82.0	82.0

Code	Classification	(1) No. of Factories	(2) Power of Prime Movers (H.P.)	(3) Rented Electric Power (H.P.)	(4) Total (H.P.)
4-1-2-2	Machine parts	4	2.5	7.0	9.5
4-1-3	Spinning and weaving machines				
4-1-3-1	Machines	20	294.0	1,389.3	1,683.3
4-1-3-2	Machine parts	5		26.0	26.0
4-1-3-3	Bobbins	7	130.0	86.0	216.0
4-1-4	Prime movers	21	68.0	234.2	302.2
4-1-5	Other kinds of machines	8		34.5	34.5
4-1-6	Various kinds of machines	16		135.5	135.5
4-1-7	Various kinds of machine parts	9		64.0	64.0
4-1-8	Manufacture and repairing of machines and machine parts	29		226.5	226.5
4-1-9	Repairing of machines and machine parts only	24		112.5	112.5
4-2	Manufacture of metal products				
4-2-1	Boilers	5		21.0	21.0
4-2-2	Weighing scales	4		6.5	6.5
4-2-3	Nails	6		148.0	148.0
4-2-4	Tins, boxes, etc.	23		205.0	205.0
4-2-5	Aluminumware	4		62.0	62.0
4-2-6	Faucets, valves, etc.	5		31.0	31.0
4-2-7	Lamps	6		65.0	65.0
4-2-8	Miscellaneous articles	8		41.0	41.0
4-3	Manufacture of electrical apparatus				
4-3-1	Electric light bulbs	5		61.0	61.0
4-3-2	Neon light tubes	1		6.0	6.0
4-3-3	Electric fans, heaters, etc.	3		127.0	127.0
4-3-4	Electric supplies	7	25.0	115.8	140.8
4-3-5	Flash lights	16		141.5	141.5
4-3-6	Dry batteries	8		11.0	11.0
4-3-7	Electro-plating	13		103.0	103.0
4-3-8	Electric welding	1		2.0	2.0
	Total for Group IV.	295	537.5	3,646.8	4,184.3

Code	Classification	(1) No. of Factories	(2) Power of Prime Movers (H. P.)	(3) Rented Electric Power (H. P.)	(4) Total (H. P.)
Group V. Construction of Boat, Ships, and Vehicles for Land Transportation					
5-1	Shipbuilding				
5-1-1	Construction of ships	4	40.0	2,822.3	2,862.3
5-1-2	Repairing of ships and manufacture of accessories	5	75.0	60.5	135.5
5-2	Building of cars				
5-2-1	Railway workshops	1	400.0		400.0
5-2-2	Tram cars (and ships)	1		19.5	19.5
5-2-3	Bicycles	1		9.0	9.0
5-2-4	Rickshas	8		22.5	22.5
5-3	Building of fire engines	1		3.0	3.0
	Total for Group V.	21	515.0	2,936.8	3,451.8
Group VI. Manufacture of Bricks, Earthenware. Glass, etc.					
6-1	Bricks and tiles	5	205.0	55.0	260.0
6-2	Glass				
6-2-1	Thermos bottles	2	24.0	35.0	59.0
6-2-2	Bottles and lamp shades	14		14.0	14.0
6-2-3	Glass bevelling	8		38.5	38.5
6-3	Cement	1	2,060.0		2.060.0
6-4	Stone powder and lime				
6-4-1	Lime	5		5.0	5.0
6-4-2	Stone powder	9		328.0	328.0
	Total for Group VI.	44	2,289.0	475.5	2,764.5
Group VII. Building Material					
7-1	Building material	5	50.0	6.0	56.0
	Total for Group VII.	5	50.0	6.0	56.0
Group VIII. Production and Transmission of Electricity and Supply of Water					
8-1	Electric and water works	5	51,581.3	1,512.9	53,094.2
	Total for Group VIII.	5	51,581.3	1,512.9	53,094.2
Group IX. Manufacture of Chemicals and Allied Products					

Code	Classification	(1) No. of Factories	(2) Power of Prime Movers (H.P.)	(3) Rented Electric Power (H.P.)	(4) Total (H.P.)
9-1	Matches				
9-1-1	Matches	3	84.0	58.0	142.0
9-1-2	Shavings and splints	1	60.0		60.0
9-2	Soap, washing soda and candles				
9-2-1	Soap	11	76.0	93.0	169.0
9-2-2	Washing soda	1	5.0		5.0
9-2-3	Soap, washing soda and candles	2		5.0	5.0
9-3	Enamelled ware				
9-3-1	Enamelled ware	8	244.0	432.3	676.3
9-3-2	Body of enamelled ware	2		28.0	28.0
9-4	Varnish and printer's ink				
9-4-1	Varnish	4		364.0	364.0
9-4-2	Printer's ink	5		107.0	107.0
9-5	Cosmetics	13		63.5	63.5
9-6	Medicine	2		52.4	52.4
9-7	Celluloid and other synthetic products	6		179.5	179.5
9-8	Other chemical products	2	50.0	700.0	750.0
	Total for Group IX.	60	519.0	2,082.7	2,601.7
Group X.	Textile Industries				
10-1	Cotton spinning and weaving				
10-1-1	Cotton ginning	8	275.0	40.0	315.0
10-1-2	Cotton fluffing	3		468.3	468.3
10-1-3	Cotton spinning				
10-1-3-1	Yarn only	14	3,750.0	16,717.3	20,467.3
10-1-3-2	Yarn and thread	3		4,833.3	4,833.3
10-1-3-3	Spinning and weaving	12	1,735.0	17,921.3	19,656.3
10-1-4	Cotton weaving				
10-1-4-1	Using yarn only	23	40.0	882.5	922.5
10-1-4-2	Using yarn and thread	27	100.0	1,021.2	1,121.2
10-1-4-3	Using thread only	6		41.0	41.0
10-1-4-4	Making of knitted cloth	3		2.0	2.0
10-1-4-5	Towels and bed sheets	4		18.0	18.0
10-1-5	Other cotton spinning and weaving	2		11.5	11.5

Code	Classification	(1) No. of Factories	(2) Power of Prime Movers (H. P.)	(3) Rented Electric Power (H. P.)	(4) Total (H. P.)
10-2	Rayon fabrics	7		35.5	35.5
10-3	Silk reeling and weaving				
10-3-1	Silk reeling				
10-3-1-1	Steam filature silk	66	1,331.0		1,331.0
10-3-1-2	Dupion silk	4	156.0		156.0
10-3-1-3	Other special kinds of silk	3	150.0		150.0
10-3-2	Silk weaving	35	35.0	492.2	527.2
10-4	Wool spinning and weaving				
10-4-1	Wool spinning	1		180.0	180.0
10-4-2	Wool weaving	1		50.0	50.0
10-4-3	Wool spinning and weaving	1	350.0		350.0
10-5	Other animal tissue textiles	1		5.0	5.0
10-6	Mixed fabrics				
10-6-1	Cotton and rayon	147		1,095.8	1,095.8
10-6-2	Cotton and silk	4		20.0	20.0
10-6-3	Silk and rayon	44	105.0	711.5	816.5
10-6-4	Cotton, silk and rayon	16		221.7	221.7
10-6-5	Cotton and wool	12	14.0	224.5	238.5
10-6-6	Cotton, silk and wool	5		194.6	194.6
10-7	Dyeing				
10-7-1	Mercerized yarn and thread	11		79.0	79.0
10-7-2	Dyeing of cloth and woollens	7	100.0	780.0	880.0
10-7-3	Dyeing of silk and cotton fabrics	4		13.0	13.0
10-7-4	Dyeing of silk and woollen fabrics	7		167.5	167.5
10-7-5	Dyeing of hosiery	1		3.0	3.0
10-7-6	Dyeing for customers	2		31.5	31.5
10-8	Printing of textiles				
10-8-1	Board printing	12		24.0	24.0
10-8-2	Brush printing	7		12.0	12.0
10-9	Thread				
10-9-1	Thread balls	7		39.0	39.0
10-9-2	Waxed thread	2		55.0	55.0

Code	Classification	(1) No. of Factories	(2) Power of Prime Movers (H. P.)	(3) Rented Electric Power (H. P.)	(4) Total (H. P.)
10-9-3	Warp and woof	2	150.0	35.0	185.0
10-10	Trimmings and ribbons				
10-10-1	Trimmings				
10-10-1-1	Rayon entirely	12		50.0	50.0
10-10-1-2	Cotton and rayon	6		309.5	309.5
10-10-1-3	Silk and rayon	1		3.0	3.0
10-10-1-4	Cotton yarn entirely	1		3.5	3.5
10-10-2	Ribbons				
10-10-2-1	Cotton yarn entirely	5		28.0	28.0
10-10-2-2	Cotton and rayon	1		2.5	2.5
10-10-2-3	Cotton, rayon and rubber	3		11.0	11.0
10-11	Cotton flannel finishing	2		23.0	23.0
	Total for Group X.	545	8,291.0	46,856.7	55,147.7
Group XI.	Clothing Industries				
Including Hosiery					
11-1	Knitted hosiery				
11-1-1	Cotton hosiery				
11-1-1-1	Cotton yarn only	11		79.5	79.5
11-1-1-2	Cotton thread only	17	25.0	405.0*	430.0*
11-1-1-3	Yarn and thread	5		50.0	50.0
11-1-1-4	Raw material supplied by customers	1			
11-1-2	Silk and rayon hosiery				
11-1-2-1	Silk only	2			
11-1-2-2	Silk and cotton	14		101.5	101.5
11-1-2-3	Rayon and cotton	10		10.0	10.0
11-1-2-4	Silk and rayon	1			
11-1-2-5	Silk, rayon and cotton	10		24.5	24.5
11-1-3	Woollen hosiery (pure wool)	1			
11-1-4	Cotton, silk and wool combined	2			
11-1-5	Sewing of knitted hosiery	3		2.2	2.2
11-1-6	Hosiery and other articles of apparel	24		45.7	45.7
11-2	Hats				

Code	Classification	(1) No. of Factories	(2) Power of Prime Movers (H. P.)	(3) Rented Electric Power (H. P.)	(4) Total (H. P.)
11-2-1	Straw hats	3		1.0	1.0
11-2-2	Felt hats	1		5.0	5.0
11-2-3	Chinese hats (silk, cloth, etc.)	1			
11-2-4	Straw and felt hats	6	*	146.0	146.0*
11-2-5	Straw and Chinese hats	1			
11-3	Umbrellas				
11-3-1	Umbrella stems	1			
11-3-2	Umbrellas	13		30.0	30.0
11-4	Handkerchiefs				
11-4-1	Handkerchiefs only	6		28.5	28.5
11-4-2	Handkerchiefs and other things	4		8.5	8.5
11-5	Underwear and sweaters				
11-5-1	Silk only	3		102.0	102.0
11-5-2	Cotton only	9		577.0	577.0
11-5-3	Cotton and wool	11		150.5	150.5
11-5-4	Knitted fabric	1		1.0	1.0
11-6	Other articles of apparel				
11-6-1	Ties, scarfs and gloves	6		19.0	19.0
11-6-2	Buttons	3		8.0	8.0
11-6-3	Silk and cloth shoes	1			
	Total for Group XI.	171	25.0*	1,794.9*	1,819.9
Group XII. Manufacture of Leather. Rubber Products, tc					
12-1	Leather manufacturing				
12-1-1	Soft leather and uppers	4	70.0	77.5	147.5
12-1-2	Hard leather and soles	7	107.5	209.0	316.5
12-1-3	Others	7		82.0	82.0
12-2	Leather goods				
12-2-1	Articles used by the military	3			
12-2-2	Leather trunks, cases, etc.	2			
12-2-3	Leather shoes	4			
12-3	Rubber goods				
12-3-1	Rubber shoes	24	941.7	3,168.7	4,110.4
12-3-2	Rubber soles, heels, etc.	5	35.0	73.0	108.0

Code	Classification	(1) No. of Factories	(2) Power of Prime Movers (H.P.)	(3) Rented Electric Power (H.P.)	(4) Total (H.P.)
12-4	Glue	1	32.0	70.0	102.0
	Total for Group XII	57	1,186.2	3,680.2	4,866.4
Group XIII. Preparation and Manufacture of Foods, Drinks and Tobacco					
13-1	Rice mills	12		627.0*	627.0*
13-2	Wheat flour mills	15	325.0	11,365.8	11,690.8
13-3	Rice and other flour mills	4		25.0	25.0
13-4	Sugar refineries	4		6.0	6.0
13-5	Biscuits, bread, candies and canned food				
13-5-1	Biscuits	9		37.0	37.0
13-5-2	Bread	1			
13-5-3	Candies and sweetmeats	3			
13-5-4	Canned food	1		5.0	5.0
13-5-5	Others	5		60.5	60.5
13-6	Oils mills				
13-6-1	Bean oil	3	290.0		290.0
13-6-2	Groundnut oil	3	60.0	8.0	68.0
13-6-3	Cotton seed oil	5	432.0	373.0	805.0
13-6-4	Vegetable oil in general	2	175.0	543.0	718.0
13-6-5	Lard manufacturing	1			
13-7	Tea				
13-7-1	By machine process	19		107.5	107.5
13-7-2	By native process	12		55.5	55.5
13-8	Tobacco				
13-8-1	Cigars	5		5.0	5.0
13-8-2	Cigarettes	46		2,721.5	2,721.5
13-9	Wine and spirits	1			
13-10	Soda water and other soft drinks	2	3.0	83.0	86.0
13-11	Condiments	8	68.0	95.5	163.5
13-12	Casings	3			
13-13	Refined salt	1		*	*
13-14	Frozen egg products	1		200.0	200.0
13-15	Other food stuffs				
13-15-1	Starch	2		10.5	10.5

Code	Classification	(1) No. of Factories	(2) Power of Prime Movers (H.P.)	(3) Rented Electric Power (H.P.)	(4) Total (H.P.)
13-15-2	Bean curd products	3		9.5	9.5
13-16	Ice and cold storage	4	200.0	190.0	390.0
	Total for Group XIII.	175	1,553.0	16,528.3*	18,081.3*
Group XIV. Manufacture of Paper, Book-Binding and Printing					
14-1	Paper manufacturing				
14-1-1	Paper	7	1,337.0	2,641.0	3,978.0
14-1-2	Card board	1		2,500.0	2,500.0
14-1-3	Tin foil	1		8.0	8.0
14-2	Printing				
14-2-1	Newspaper printing and publishing	5		887.7	887.7
14-2-2	Booking printing and publishing	10		1,771.8	1,771.8
14-2-3	Printing with letter press				
14-2-3-1	Full sheet press	13		92.5	92.5
14-2-3-2	Half sheet press	9		45.5	45.5
14-2-3-3	Quarter and one-sixth size presses	10		19.5	19.5
14-2-3-4	Small foot-operated presses	4			
14-2-3-5	Unclassified	4		12.0	12.0
14-2-4	Rubber offset printing	7		85.5	85.5
14-2-5	Lithographic printing	18		147.0	147.0
14-2-6	Lithographic and letter press printing	4		25.5	25.5
14-2-7	Lithographic and offset printing	16		425.0	425.0
14-2-8	Unclassified	6		100.5	100.5
14-3	Book-binding	14			
14-4	Paper manufactures				
14-4-1	Envelops and paper bags	3		7.0	7.0
14-4-2	Cartons	20		90.0	90.0
14-4-3	Cards	2		15.0	15.0
14-5	Engraving	1			
	Total for Group XIV.	155	1,337.0	8,873.5	10,210.5

Code	Classification	(1) No. of Factories	(2) Power of Prime Movers (H. P.)	(3) Rented Electric Power (H. P.)	(4) Total (H. P.)
	Group XV. Manufacture of Scientific and Musical Instruments, Clocks and Watches, etc.				
15-1	Musical instruments				
15-1-1	Organs	9		3.0	3.0
15-1-2	Pianos	2			
15-1-3	Gramophones and gramophone records	5		35.0	35.0
15-1-4	Other musical instruments	2			
15-2	Educational supplies and toys				
15-2-1	Writing ink	4		8.0	8.0
15-2-2	Writing outfit	5		15.5*	15.5*
15-2-3	Toys	6		9.9	9.9
15-3	Scientific apparatus	5		22.0	22.0
15-4	Clocks	1		8.0	8.0
	Total for Group XV.	39		*101.4*	*101.4*
	Group XVI. Other Manufacturing Industries				
16-1	Tooth brushes	6		105.0	105.0
16-2	Mirrors	4		70.0	70.0
16-3	Coal briquettes	12	256.0	338.0	594.0
16-4	Straw ropes	10			
	Total for Group XVI.	32	*256.0*	*513.0*	*769.0*
	Grand Total for the Sixteen Groups	*1,672*	*68,175.0**	*90,213.7**	*158,388.7**

TABLE A-VI. OPERATING TIME AND AVERAGE NUMBER OF YEARS AND MONTHS IN OPERATION

Code	Classification	(1) No. of Factories	(2) No. of Operating Hours per Day (1)	(3) No. of Operating Days per Year (2)	(4) Average No. of Years & Months in Operation (3)
Group I. Woodworking Industries					
1-1	Saw mills	8	10.7+2.2	343.7	9/7
1-2	Manufacture of wooden boxes	1	10.0+ *	360.0	4/
1-3	Manufacture of other wooden articles	2	10.0+4.0	324.0	8/9
1-4	Manufacture of cork stoppers	3	9.3+2.2	340.0	17/
1-5	Manufacture of bamboo articles	1	9.5+3.0	*	5/
	Totals and Averages for Group I.	*15*	*10.4+2.4*	*341.1*	*3/11*
Group II. Furniture Manufacturing					
2-1	Wooden furniture	3	9.2+4.3	365.0	36/
2-2	Steel furniture	9	10.6+4.3	357.7	7/9
2-3	Rugs and carpets	5	9.8+0.6	362.0	12/9
	Totals and Averages for Group II.	*17*	*10.1+3.1*	*360.2*	*14/2*
Group III. Metal Industries					
3-1	Founding				
3-1-1	Whole machines	3	9.3+3.8	360.0	7/9
3-1-2	Machine parts and accessories	22	9.9+2.4	352.2	8/2
3-1-3	Iron pipes	4	9.0+3.6	357.0	9/5
3-1-4	Other articles	6	9.9+1.5	360.0	13/1
3-2	Steel refining	1	8.0+ 0	306.0	/7
	Totals and Averages for Group III.	*36*	*9.7+2.6*	*353.4*	*8/10*
Group IV. Manufacture of Machinery and Miscellaneous Metal Products					
4-1	Manufacture and repairing of machines				
4-1-1	Printing machines				

Code	Classification	(1) No. of Factories	(2) No. of Operating Hours per Day	(3) No. of Operating Days per Year	(4) Average No. of Years & Months in Operation
4-1-1-1	Machines	13	10.4+2.4	355.7	11/1
4-1-1-2	Machine parts	1	10.0+3.0	365.0	3/
4-1-2	Knitting machines				
4-1-2-1	Machines	23	9.2+2.6	341.2	11/
4-1-2-2	Machine parts	4	12.6+ 0	322.0	1/4
4-1-3	Spinning and weaving machines				
4-1-3-1	Machines	20	9.9+3.3	344.1	7/7
4-1-3-2	Machine parts	5	12.1+1.4	349.6	11/9
4-1-3-3	Bobbins	7	9.2+3.6	330.3	6/1
4-1-4	Prime movers	21	10.2+2.5	352.6	11/7
4-1-5	Other kinds of machines	8	9.8+3.6	360.6	10/8
4-1-6	Various kinds of machines	16	9.8+2.1	350.2	10/9
4-1-7	Various kinds of machine parts	9	9.8+3.1	360.0	11/
4-1-8	Manufacture and repairing of machines and machine parts	29	9.1+3.9	357.0	11/4
4-1-9	Repairing of machines and machine parts only	24	9.6+3.1	353.9	8/6
4-2	Manufacture of metal products				
4-2-1	Boilers	5	8.8+1.0	361.0	18/10
4-2-2	Weighing scales	4	9.0+2.2	360.0	7/3
4-2-3	Nails	6	11.2+2.3	356.5	4/10
4-2-4	Tins, boxes, etc.	23	10.0+3.1	338.7	5/11
4-2-5	Aluminumware	4	9.6+2.6	356.5	6/
4-2-6	Faucets, valves, etc.	5	11.0+2.8	362.0	8/3
4-2-7	Lamps	6	10.0+2.6	344.8	6/11
4-2-8	Miscellaneous articles	8	10.0+3.4	355.2	7/6
4-3	Manufacture of electric apparatus				
4-3-1	Electric light bulbs	5	10.3+1.9	336.0	3/1
4-3-2	Neon light tubes	1	8.0+3.0	312.0	1/6

Code	Classification	(1) No. of Factories	(2) No. of Operating Hours per Day	(3) No. of Operating Days per Year	(4) Average No. of Years & Months in Operation
4-3-3	Electric fans, heaters, etc.	3	10.3+2.3	348.0	12/
4-3-4	Electric supplies	7	9.8+4.1	345.3	14/4
4-3-5	Flash lights	16	9.7+3.2	351.5	2/11
4-3-6	Dry batteries	8	8.2+2.0	319.2	5/2
4-3-7	Electro-plating	13	10.3+3.1	348.5	5/9
4-3-8	Electric welding	1	9.0+ 0	365.0	1/7
	Totals and Averages for Group IV.	295	9.8+2.9	348.7	8/9
Group V. Construction of Boats, Ships, and Vehicles for Land Transportation					
5-1	Shipbuilding				
5-1-1	Construction of ships	4	10.0+1.7	348.0	23/7
5-1-2	Repairing of ships and manufacture of accessories	5	9.6+3.0	362.0	12/5
5-2	Building of cars				
5-2-1	Railway workshops	1	10.0+ 0	280.0	25/
5-2-2	Tram cars (and ships)	1	9.0+5.0	360.0	4/5
5-2-3	Bicycles	1	8.0+ 0	260.0	1/
5-2-4	Rickshas	8	10.5+3.9	351.0	7/1
5-3	Building of fire engines	1	9.0+3.0	360.0	14/
	Totals and Averages for Group V.	21	9.8+3.0	345.7	12/3
Group VI. Manufacture of Bricks, Earthenware, Glass, etc.					
6-1	Bricks and tiles	5	10.9+2.0	336.4	7/5
6-2	Glass				
6-2-1	Thermos bottles	2	9.7+ 0	348.0	9/6
6-2-2	Bottles and lamp shades	14	10.6+ 0	284.9	6/7
6-2-3	Glass bevelling	8	9.3+3.4	328.8	3/7
6-3	Cement	1	21.0+ 0	*	8/4
6-4	Stone powder and lime				
6-4-1	Lime	5	13.1+0.7	285.6	7/2

Code	Classification	(1) No. of Factories	(2) No. of Operating Hours per Day	(3) No. of Operating Days per Year	(4) Average No. of Years & Months in Operation
6-4-2	Stone powder	9	10.1+2.2	345.5	4/9
	Totals and Averages for Group VI.	44	10.8+2.3	314.0	6/1
Group VII. Building Material					
7-1	Building material	5	9.2+ 0	357.0	12/11
	Totals and Averages for Group VII.	5	9.2+ 0	357.0	12/11
Group VIII. Production and Transmission of Electricity and Supply of Water					
8-1	Electric and water works	5	15.2+1.0	345.0	17/6
	Totals And Averages for Group VIII.	5	15.2+1.0	345.0	17/6
Group IX. Manufacture of Chemicals and Allied Products					
9-1	Matches				
9-1-1	Matches	3	10.0+ *	344.3	2/6
9-1-2	Shavings and splints	1	8.0+ 0	*	16/7
9-2	Soap, washing soda and candles				
9-2-1	Soap	11	8.8+1.9	311.1	10/4
9-2-2	Washing soda	1	24.0+ 0	336.0	1/9
9-2-3	Soap, washing soda and candles	2	8.5+ 0	362.5	18/10
9-3	Enamelled ware				
9-3-1	Enamelled ware	8	16.1+1.1	325.9	4/10
9-3-2	Body of enamelled ware	2	9.7+3.2	324.0	1/10
9-4	Varnish and printer's ink				
9-4-1	Varnish	4	12.0+0.7	337.5	9/10
9-4-2	Printer's ink	5	10.8+0.8	344.0	5/9
9-5	Cosmetics	13	8.8+1.6	307.1	6/11
9-6	Medicine	2	8.0+3.7	324.0	6/
9-7	Celluloid and other synthetic products	6	9.7+0.4	350.4	3/5
9-8	Other chemical products	2	15.0+5.0	315.5	8/4

Code	Classification	(1) No. of Factories	(2) No. of Operating Hours per Day	(3) No. of Operating Days per Year	(4) Average No. of Years & Months in Operation
	Totals and Averages for Group IX.	60	10.8+1.6	325.2	7/2
Group X.	Textile Industries				
10-1	Cotton spinning and weaving				
10-1-1	Cotton ginning	8	11.7+ 0	215.5	14/6
10-1-2	Cotton fluffing	3	13.0+3.3	344.3	6/3
10-1-3	Cotton spinning				
10-1-3-1	Yarn only	14	22.8+ 0	326.2	8/7
10-1-3-2	Yarn and thread	3	23.3+ 0	328.0	10/11
10-1-3-3	Spinning and weaving	12	22.4+ 0	320.2	15/7
10-1-4	Cotton weaving				
10-1-4-1	Using yarn only	23	11.6+3.5	344.4	7/5
10-1-4-2	Using yarn and thread	27	10.4+2.2	336.6	7/6
10-1-4-3	Using thread only	6	10.9+0.5	362.5	5/1
10-1-4-4	Making of knitted cloth	3	10.7+10.0	268.0	2/3
10-1-4-5	Towels and bed sheets	4	8.7+1.3	279.3	7/8
10-1-5	Other cotton spinning and weaving	2	11.5+ 0	360.0	6/5
10-2	Rayon fabrics	7	14.7+3.0	329.4	3/1
10-3	Silk reeling and weaving				
10-3-1	Silk reeling				
10-3-1-1	Steam filature silk	66	10.7+ 0	234.2	4/2
10-3-1-2	Dupion silk	4	11.0+ 0	307.0	5/4
10-3-1-3	Other special kinds of silk	3	14.7+0.7	312.7	6/7
10-3-2	Silk weaving	35	13.7+1.2	335.2	2/11
10-4	Wool spinning and weaving				
10-4-1	Wool spinning	1	10.0+ 0	336.0	/8
10-4-2	Wool weaving	1	9.0+8.0	336.0	13/
10-4-3	Wool spinning and				

Code	Classification	(1) No. of Factories	(2) No. of Operating Hours per Day	(3) No. of Operating Days per Year	(4) Average No. of Years & Operations Operation
	weaving	1	20.0+ 0	336.0	2/2
10-5	Other animal tissue textiles	1	10.5+ 0	360.0	8/
10-6	Mixed fabrics				
10-6-1	Cotton and rayon	147	12.9+1.8	331.3	2/
10-6-2	Cotton and silk	4	15.4+1.4	335.0	2/
10-6-3	Silk and rayon	44	14.6+2.6	333.9	2/3
10-6-4	Cotton, silk and rayon	16	14.2+1.3	329.7	2/8
10-6-5	Cotton and wool	12	12.9+1.4	318.5	2/6
10-6-6	Cotton, silk and wool	5	11.1+2.5	340.0	2/11
10-7	Dyeing				
10-7-1	Mercerized yarn and thread	11	8.9+1.4	346.0	5/
10-7-2	Dyeing of cloth and woollens	7	13.3+2.6	332.0	2/5
10-7-3	Dyeing of silk and cotton fabrics	4	11.0+3.0	296.0	8/
10-7-4	Dyeing of silk and woollen fabrics	7	10.1+3.0	346.1	8/2
10-7-5	Dyeing of hosiery	1	10.0+ 0	*	10/
10-7-6	Dyeing for customers	2	23.0+ 0	313.5	3/11
10-8	Printing of textiles				
10-8-1	Board printing	12	9.3+2.8	321.4	3/7
10-8-2	Brush printing	7	11.3+1.7	318.3	8/5
10-9	Thread				
10-9-1	Thread balls	7	9.8+1.3	305.0	4/6
10-9-2	Waxed thread	2	10.0+3.2	318.0	10/
10-9-3	Warp and woof	2	10.5+6.7	339.0	1/5
10-10	Trimmings and ribbons				
10-10-1	Trimmings				
10-10-1-1	Rayon entirely	12	11.8+3.8	307.8	5/9
10-10-1-2	Cotton and rayon	6	15.5+2.0	331.5	6/6
10-10-1-3	Silk and rayon	1	10.0+ 0	*	5/6
10-10-1-4	Cotton yarn entirely	1	12.0+ 0	360.0	1/2
10-10-2	Ribbons				
10-10-2-1	Cotton yarn entirely	5	11.8+0.6	328.2	8/9
10-10-2-2	Cotton ond rayon	1	13.0+ 0	308.0	2/6

Code	Classification	(1) No. of Factories	(2) No. of Operating Hours per Day.	(3) No. of Operating Days per Year.	(4) Average No. of Years & Months in Operation.
10-10-2-3	Cotton, rayon and rubber	3	12.8+1.5	353.7	4/6
10-11	Cotton flannel finishing	2	15.0+1.5	264.0	/3
	Totals and Averages for Group X.	545	13.1+2.1	328.3	4/3
Group XI. Clothing Industries Including Hosiery					
11-1	Knitted hosiery				
11-1-1	Cotton hosiery				
11-1-1-1	Cotton yarn only	11	12.9+2.2	290.0	4/3
11-1-1-2	Cotton thread only	17	16.4+1.0	330.6	6/5
11-1-1-3	Yarn and thread	5	11.4+ 0	280.0	7/1
11-1-1-4	Raw material supplied by customers	1	8.0+2.0	280.0	/9
11-1-2	Silk and rayon hosiery				
11-1-2-1	Silk only	2	11.0+ 0	324.0	13/
11-1-2-2	Silk and cotton	14	9.7+3.1	301.5	6/5
11-1-2-3	Rayon and cotton	10	10.0+3.2	327.8	6/5
11-1-2-4	Silk and rayon	1	10.0+ 0	360.0	/11
11-1-2-5	Silk, rayon and cotton	10	9.8+2.9	300.7	9/
11-1-3	Woollen hosiery (pure wool)	1	9.0+3.0	290.0	4/
11-1-4	Cotton, silk and wool combined	2	8.0+ 0	342.0	3/6
11-1-5	Sewing of knitted hosiery	3	9.0+2.5	342.0	6/
11-1-6	Hosiery and other articles of apparel	24	9.8+2.6	316.2	6/4
11-2	Hats				
11-2-1	Straw hats	3	10.0+ 0	228.7	3/1
11-2-2	Felt hats	1	10.0+4.0	180.0	2/7
11-2-3	Chinese hats (silk, cloth. etc.)	1	11.0+4.0	300.0	5/
11-2-4	Straw and felt hats	6	10.2+1.5	267.0	6/11
11-2-5	Straw and Chinese hats	1	10.0+3.0	280.0	20/

Code	Classification	(1) No. of Factories	(2) No. of Operating Hours per Day	(3) No. of Operating Days per Year	(4) Average No. of Years & Months in Operation
11-3	Umbrellas				
11-3-1	Umbrella stems	1	*+*	*	3/
11-3-2	Umbrellas	13	11.3+0.7	213.2	6/7
11-4	Handkerchiefs				
11-4-1	Handkerchiefs only	6	9.3+2.8	344.0	5/7
11-4-2	Handkerchiefs and other things	4	10.0+2.6	315.7	7/5
11-5	Underwear and sweaters				
11-5-1	Silk only	3	9.7+ 0	344.0	2/1
11-5-2	Cotton only	9	11.8+2.7	310.0	6/6
11-5-3	Cotton and wool	11	10.2+1.8	290.7	4/3
11-5-4	Knitted fabric	1	(4)	360.0	2/7
11-6	Other articles of apparel				
11-6-1	Ties, scarfs, and gloves	6	9.3+1.7	287.3	3/1
11-6-2	Buttons	3	10.0+1.6	304.0	5/8
11-6-3	Silk and cloth shoes	1	10.0+ 0	280.0	2/9
	Totals and Averages for Group XI.	*171*	*10.9+2.2*	*300.8*	*6/*
Group XII. Manufacture of Leather, Rubber Products, etc.					
12-1	Leather manufacturing				
12-1-1	Soft leather and uppers	4	9.4+0.9	337.2	8/4
12-1-2	Hard leather and soles	7	9.3+1.1	346.4	9/5
12-1-3	Others	7	10.1+0.3	338.8	6/2
12-2	Leather goods				
12-2-1	Articles used by the military	3	15.0+ 0	360.0	9/5
12-2-2	Leather trunks, cases, etc.	2	11.0+2.0	336.0	8/3
12-2-3	Leather shoes	4	9.9+2.4	345.0	15/6
12-3	Rubber goods				
12-3-1	Rubber shoes	24	12.1+1.8	328.6	2/
12-3-2	Rubber soles, heels, etc.	5	9.7+3.0	350.4	4/3
12-4	Glue	1	24.0+ 0	180.0	11/
	Totals And Averages for				

Code	Classification	(1) No. of Factories	(2) No. of Operating Hours per Day	(3) No. of Operating Days per Year	(4) Average No. of Years & Months in Operation
	Group XII.	57	11.1+1.6	334.4	5/11
	Group XIII. Preparation and Manufacture of Foods, Drinks and Tobacco				
13-1	Rice mills	12	9.4+1.8	361.7	8/2
13-2	Wheat flour mills	15	20.7+1.0	303.1	15/4
13-3	Rice and other flour mills	4	10.0+ 0	363.3	4/3
13-4	Sugar refineries	4	8.5+1.7	332.7	2/5
13-5	Biscuits, bread, candies and canned food				
13-5-1	Biscuits	9	9.9+1.0	352.1	5/11
13-5-2	Bread	1	20.0+ 0	360.0	3/11
13-5-3	Candies and sweetmeats	3	9.3+0.7	260.0	3/3
13-5-4	Canned food	1	10.0+ 0	324.0	7/
13-5-5	Others	5	12.7+2.0	354.0	10/9
13-6	Oil mills				
13-6-1	Bean oil	3	11.7+6.3	281.7	3/6
13-6-2	Groundnut oil	3	12.0+6.0	340.0	17/
13-6-3	Cotton seed oil	5	13.4+2.5	271.8	13/6
13-6-4	Vegetable oil in general	2	19.5+ 0	294.0	31/
13-6-5	Lard manufacturing	1	* + *	365.0	11/
13-7	Tea				
13-7-1	By machine process	19	10.0+4.4	180.0	7/7
13-7-2	By native process	12	10.0+4.6	166.0	5/10
13-8	Tobacco				
13-8-1	Cigars	5	9.2+ 0	308.8	10/3
13-8-2	Cigarettes	46	9.8+5.5	319.3	4/11
13-9	Wine and spirits	1	9.0+ 0	360.0	8/
13-10	Soda water and other soft drinks	2	9.0+2.5	240.0	15/
13-11	Condiments	8	16.3+0.6	322.7	3/11
13-12	Casings	3	9.3+4.0	361.7	8/
13-13	Refined salt	1	16.0+ 0	336.0	2/5
13-14	Frozen egg products	1	8.0+ *	*	1/
13-15	Other food stuffs				

Code	Classification	(1) No. of Factories	(2) No. of Operating Hours per Day	(3) No. of Operating Days per Year	(4) Average No. of Years & Months in Operation
13-15-1	Starch	2	9.5+1.0	362.5	3/4
13-15-2	Bean curd products	3	13.7+ 0	328.0	4/6
13-16	Ice and cold storage	4	8.7+ 0	353.7	4/8
	Totals and Averages for Group XIII.	175	11.4+3.5	319.0	7/5
Group XIV.	Manufacture of Paper, Book-Binding and Printing				
14-1	Paper manufacturing				
14-1-1	Paper	7	20.8+ 0	321.7	9/1
14-1-2	Card board	1	20.0+ 0	336.0	9/7
14-1-3	Tin foil	1	* + *	360.0	7/6
14-2	Printing				
14-2-1	Newspaper printing and publishing	5	12.3+ *	321.6	33/6
14-2-2	Book printing and publishing	10	8.3+3.7	316.0	11/11
14-2-3	Printing with letter press				
14-2-3-1	Full sheet press	13	9.3+2.7	324.0	7/4
14-2-3-2	Half sheet press	9	9.0+4.0	329.3	10/4
14-2-3-3	Quarter and one sixth size presses	10	9.0+4.1	308.9	11/3
14-2-3-4	Small foot-operated presses	4	9.0+4.0	318.0	15/9
14-2-3-5	Unclassified	4	9.7+2.2	318.0	11/1
14-2-4	Rubber offset printing	7	9.0+3.7	315.4	4/10
14-2-5	Lithographic printing	18	8.8+4.0	321.9	7/6
14-2-6	Lithographic and letter press printing	4	8.7+4.9	318.0	5/5
14-2-7	Lithographic and offset printing	16	9.6+3.8	320.2	9/1
14-2-8	Unclassified	6	8.7+2.7	328.0	7/2
14-3	Book-binding	14	9.7+2.1	339.4	12/1
14-4	Paper manufactures				
14-4-1	Envelops and paper bags	3	9.7+2.7	344.0	1/5

Code	Classification	(1) No. of Factories	(2) No. of Operating Hours per Day	(3) No. of Operating Days per Year	(4) Average No. of Years & Months in Operation
14-4-2	Cartons	20	9.7+2.6	332.2	5/11
14-4-3	Cards	2	9.5+3.2	322.0	12/9
14-5	Engraving	1	11.0+3.5	360.0	2/
	Totals and Averages for Group XIV.	155	9.9+3.3	325.6	9/7
Group XV. Manufacture of Scientific and Musical Instruments, Clocks and Watches, etc.					
15-1	Musical instruments				
15-1-1	Organs	9	9.7+2.8	347.8	12/2
15-1-2	Pianos	2	10.0+3.2	348.0	8/6
15-1-3	Gramophones and gramophone records	5	9.0+3.3	336.0	9/11
15-1-4	Other musical instruments	2	9.7+4.0	365.0	4/4
15-2	Educational supplies and toys				
15-2-1	Writing ink	4	9.7+1.6	346.2	14/9
15-2-2	Writing outfit	5	9.8+1.2	339.4	5/7
15-2-3	Toys	6	9.7+2.8	348.2	5/3
15-3	Scientific apparatus	5	9.6+2.6	355.2	10/1
15-4	Clocks	1	9.5+3.0	308.0	1/1
	Totals and Averages for Group XV.	39	9.6+2.6	346.2	9/
Group XVI. Other Manufacturing Industries					
16-1	Tooth brushes	6	10.7+ .5	314.7	10/11
16-2	Mirrors	4	9.6+1.6	321.0	4/2
16-3	Coal briquettes	12	11.0+2.5	310.6	3/11
16-4	Straw ropes	10	9.8+ 0	304.1	0/6
	Totals and Averages for Group XVI.	32	10.5+1.6	311.4	7/4
	Grand Totals and Averages for the Sixteen Groups	1672	11.2+2.5	329.4	6/10

Notes: (1) Figures before the plus sign (+) in this column denote the average fixed or customary number of operating hours per day, while those following stand for the everage extra number of operating hours per day over and above the customary operating time temporarily put in as circumstances required.

(2) The number of operating days per year of each industry is worked out by multiplying, factory by factory, the usual number of operating days in a month by the number of months during which it operates. It does not necessarily mean that all the workers work on all operating days.

(3) The "average number of years and months in operation" means the average length of time from the first month of operation, actual or calculated (usually from the time of establishment and sometimes re-organization), until December, 1931.

(4) No definite operating hours on account of the "contract system" adopted.

TABLE A-VII. STATISTICS OF THE PRECEDING YEAR (1930)

Code	Classification	(1) No. of Factories	(2) Salary Payments ($)	(3) Wage Payments ($)	(4) Value of Output ($)
	Group I. Woodworking Industries				
1-1	Saw mills	8	12,887.00*	52,230.00*	1,605,555.55*
1-2	Manufacture of wooden boxes	1	940.00	1,800.00	69,750.00
1-3	Manufacture of other wooden articles	2	1,030.00	1,803.00	18,064.00
1-4	Manufacture of cork stoppers	3	984.00	4,380.00	60,000.00
1-5	Manufacture of bamboo articles	1	156.00	4,500.00	20,000.00
	Total for Group I.	15	15,997.00*	64,713.00*	1,773,369.55*
	Group II. Furniture Manufacturing				
2-1	Wooden furniture	3	2,160.00*	23,328.00	1,150,000.00
2-2	Steel furniture	9	20,308.00	53,719.00	535,800.00*
2-3	Rugs and carpets	5	2,388.00	18,185.20*	151,343.95*
	Total for Group II.	17	24,856.00*	95,232.20*	1,837,143.95*
	Group III. Metal Industries				
3-1	Founding				
3-1-1	Whole machines	3	1,704.00	12,560.00	52,830.00
3-1-2	Machine parts and accessories	22	8,168.00*	74,661.00*	553,700.00*
3-1-3	Iron pipes	4	2,906.00	17,971.00	152,000.00
3-1-4	Other articles	6	920.00*	5,576.00*	31,000.00*
3-2	Steel refining	1	(1)	(1)	(1)
	Total for Group III.	36	13,698.00*	110,768.00*	789,530.00*
	Group IV. Manufacture of Machinery and Miscellaneous Metal Products				
4-1	Manufacture and repairing of machines				
4-1-1	Printing machines				

Code	Classification	(1) No. of Factories	(2) Salary Payments ($)	(3) Wage Payments ($)	(4) Value of Output ($)
4-1-1-1	Machines	13	1,740.00 [2]*	11,750.00 [2]*	229,580.00*
4-1-1-2	Machine parts	1	48.00	670.00	4,000.00
4-1-2	Knitting machines				
4-1-2-1	Machines	23	6,886.00*	35,372.00*	164,653.15*
4-1-2-2	Machine parts	4	530.00	3,750.00	9,934.00
4-1-3	Spinning and weaving machines				
4-1-3-1	Machines	20	40,976.00*	245,600.00*	995,133.33*
4-1-3-2	Machine parts	5	2,180.00	5,402.00	59,450.00
4-1-3-3	Bobbins	7	7,218.00	65,224.67	430,077.77*
4-1-4	Prime movers	21	41,009.50*	176,913.51*	1,192,980.00*
4-1-5	Other kinds of machines	8	2,700.00*	24,204.00*	134,800.00*
4-1-6	Various kinds of machines	16	21,011.00	73,042.00	439,088.89*
4-1-7	Various kinds of machine parts	9	8,292.00	48,530.00	283,000.00
4-1-8	Manufacture and repairing of machines and machine parts	29	39,792.00 [3]*	149,564.00 [3]*	1,110,750.00
4-1-9	Repairing of machines and machine parts only	24	14,955.00	51,727.54*	213,777.27*
4-2	Manufacture of metal products				
4-2-1	Boilers	5	2,424.00	18,500.00	134,611.11
4-2-2	Weighing scales	4	3,480.00	8,160.00	52,000.00
4-2-3	Nails	6	6,544.00	20,680.00	303,507.78*
4-2-4	Tins, boxes, etc.	23	49,115.53*	130,103.99	1,747,822.22
4-2-5	Aluminumware	4	1,596.00	22,986.00	293,555.56
4-2-6	Faucets, valves, etc.	5	1,606.00	6,792.00	50,000.00*
4-2-7	Lamps	6	3,258.00	13,420.00	87,500.00*

Code	Classification	(1) No. of Factories	(2) Salary Payments ($)	(3) Wage Payments ($)	(4) Value of Output ($)
4-2-8	Miscellaneous articles	8	3,240.00	17,044.00	209,917.77
4-3	Manufacture of electric apparatus				
4-3-1	Electric light bulbs	5	14,376.00*	71,800.00*	754,000.00*
4-3-2	Neon light tubes	1	4,900.00	7,700.00	105,000.00
4-3-3	Electric fans, heaters, etc.	3	8,033.33*	85,500.00	660,666.67
4-3-4	Electric supplies	7	41,050.00	202,523.00	898,102.22
4-3-5	Flash lights	16	10,036.00*	65,900.00*	356,159.96
4-3-6	Dry batteries	8	4,908.00	11,400.00*	281,000.00
4-3-7	Electro-plating	13	3,310.00	18,624.00*	118,502.00
4-3-8	Electric welding	1	*	*	*
	Total for Group IV.	295	344,314.36*	1,592,882.71*	11,419,569.70*
Group V. Construction of Boats, Ships, and Vehicles for Land Transportation					
5-1	Shipbuilding				
5-1-1	Construction of ships	4	330,442.63	1,637,087.88	5,752,012.84
5-1-2	Repairing of ships and manufacture of accessories	5	15,793.00	43,773.44*	317,200.00
5-2	Building of cars				
5-2-1	Railway workshops	1	36,960.00	558,748.56	1,065,416.18
5-2-2	Tram cars (and ships)	1	5,304.00	24,000.00	190,000.00
5-2-3	Bicycles	1	*	*	*
5-2-4	Rickshas	8	324.00	4,372.00*	51,060.00*
5-3	Building of fire engines	1	192.00	1,102.40	14,777.78
	Total for Group V.	21	389,015.63*	2,269,084.28*	7,390,466.80*

Code	Classification	(1) No. of Factories	(2) Salary Payments ($)	(3) Wage Payments ($)	(4) Value of Output ($)
Group VI.	Manufacture of Bricks, Earthenware, Glass, etc.				
6-1	Bricks and tiles	5	20,205.00*	66,359.00	631,411.10 [4]
6-2	Glass				
6-2-1	Thermos bottles	2	1,945.15	18,754.20*	200,000.00* [5]
6-2-2	Bottles and lamp shades	14	17,842.00	82,452.60*	613,614.00*
6-2-3	Glass bevelling	8	3,760.00*	19,228.00*	73,044.00*
6-3	Cement	1	86,145.88	73,919.18	1,804,320.42
6-4	Stone powder and lime				
6-4-1	Lime	5	3,824.00	35,022.00	370,806.40
6-4-2	Stone powder	9	7,759.00	17,765.32*	322,500.00*
	Total for Group VI.	44	141,481.03*	313,500.30*	4,015,695.92*
Group VII.	Building Material				
7-1	Building material	5	13,240.00	43,507.78	425,555.55*
	Total for Group VII.	5	13,240.00	43,507.78	425,555.55*
Group VIII.	Production and Transmission of Electricity and Supply of Water				
8-1	Electric and water works	5	293,834.07*	491,301.72*	6,778,300.24
	Total for Group VIII.	5	293,834.07*	491,301.72*	6,778,300.24
Group IX.	Manufacture of Chemicals and Allied Products				
9-1	Matches				
9-1-1	Matches	3	27,600.00*	254,952.00*	2,160,000.00
9-1-2	Shavings and Splints	1	5,400.00	60,000.00	429,861.11
9-2	Soap, washing soda and candles				

Code	Classification	(1) No. of Factories	(2) Salary Payments ($)	(3) Wage Payments ($)	(4) Value of Output ($)
9-2-1	Soap	11	45,784.03*	75,282.74*	3,763,166.55
9-2-2	Washing soda	1	2,400.00	4,800.00	144,000.00
9-2-3	Soap, washing soda and candles	2	5,501.00	6,352.00	310,833.33
9-3	Enamelled ware				
9-3-1	Enamelled ware	8	69,327.87 [6]*	282,046.79 [6]*	2,746,666.67
9-3-2	Body of enamelled ware	2	450.00	1,200.00	30,000.00
9-4	Varnish and printer's ink				
9-4-1	Varnish	4	7,949.00*	29,242.26*	1,050,000.00*
9-4-2	Printer's ink	5	5,580.00	6,386.00*	246,180.00
9-5	Cosmetics	13	33,686.00*	83,045.00*	3,103,154.97
9-6	Medicine	2	21,480.00	24,540.00	942,080.00
9-7	Celluloid and other synthetic products	6	4,220.00*	26,650.00*	425,555.56
9-8	Other chemical products	2	46,000.00	47,600.00	1,000,000.00*
	Total for Group IX.	60	275,377.90*	902,096.79*	16,351,498.19*
Group X. Textile Industries					
10-1	Cotton spinning and weaving				
10-1-1	Cotton ginning	8	17,992.00	37,349.00	5,543,585.00
10-1-2	Cotton fluffing	3	5,170.00	40,850.00	814,868.89
10-1-3	Cotton spinning				
10-1-3-1	Yarn only	14	277,625.17*	2,417,187.31*	38,550,837.50*
10-1-3-2	Yarn and thread	3	82,600.00*	1,035,000.00*	8,538,266.67
10-1-3-3	Spinning and weaving	12	369,782.17*	3,851,628.42	70,032,226.89
10-1-4	Cotton weaving				
10-1-4-1	Using yarn only	23	105,624.52*	454,741.43*	6,037,825.45*
10-1-4-2	Using yarn and thread	27	76,980.25*	451,363.29*	6,000,232.78*

Code	Classification	(1) No. of Factories	(2) Salary Payments ($)	(3) Wage Payments ($)	(4) Value of Output ($)
10-1-4-3	Using thread only	6	4,700.00*	14,800.00*	140,555.55*
10-1-4-4	Making of knitted cloth	3	1,100.00	3,800.00	85,666.67
10-1-4-5	Towels and bed sheets	4	12,800.00*	22,500.00*	366,911.11*
10-1-5	Other cotton spinning and weaving	2	1,100.00	2,611.00*	42,480.00
10-2	Rayon fabrics	7	4,588.00	31,350.00	268,694.45
10-3	Silk reeling and weaving				
10-3-1	Silk reeling	66	278,461.40 [7]	1,574,076.50 [7]	29,129,307.78*
10-3-1-1	Steam filature silk	4	20,700.00*	189,333.33*	1,369,298.36
10-3-1-2	Dupion silk	3	30,091.00	79,440.20	665,403.01
10-3-1-3	Other special kinds of silk	35	133,317.67*	493,818.55*	5,390,095.12*
10-3-2	Silk weaving		(8)	(8)	(8)
10-4	Wool spinning and weaving				
10-4-1	Wool spinning	1	7,800.00	30,000.00	440,277.78
10-4-2	Wool weaving	1	19,974.53	25,252.51	244,444.44
10-4-3	Wool spinning and weaving	1	600.00	548.00	8,333.33
10-5	Other animal tissue textiles				
10-6	Mixed fabrics				
10-6-1	Cotton and rayon	147	65,360.00*	413,833.80*	4,628,672.40*
10-6-2	Cotton and silk	4	3,332.00*	15,800.00*	130,327.76*
10-6-3	Silk and rayon	44	88,659.00 [9]*	415,502.00 [9]*	6,311,911.68*
10-6-4	Cotton, silk and rayon	16	60,135.00	103,999.60	2,155,991.44
10-6-5	Cotton and wool	12	20,710.00*	35,684.00*	1,686,111.10*
10-6-6	Cotton, silk and wool	5	29,200.00	185,000.00	705,555.55*
10-7	Dyeing				
10-7-1	Mercerized yarn and thread	11	7,618.00*	71,940.00*	829,305.55 [10]*
10-7-2	Dyeing of cloth and woollens	7	101,228.00*	136,470.00*	4,121,388.89*

Code	Classification	(1) No. of Factories	(2) Salary Payments ($)	(3) Wage Payments ($)	(4) Value of Output ($)
10-7-3	Dyeing of silk and cotton fabrics	4	4,570.00	10,440.00	109,600.00
10-7-4	Dyeing of silk and woollen fabrics	7	31,263.00*	51,186.00*	722,000.00 [11]
10-7-5	Dyeing of hosiery	1	*	*	9,000.00
10-7-6	Dyeing for customers	2	*	*	131,000.00
10-8	Printing of textiles				
10-8-1	Board printing	12	12,590.00*	22,300.00*	134,210.00*
10-8-2	Brush printing	7	12,696.00	17,668.00*	95,000.00
10-9	Thread				
10-9-1	Thread balls	7	2,686.00*	11,976.00*	144,140.00*
10-9-2	Waxed thread	2	1,960.00	9,356.00	216,000.00
10-9-3	Warp and woof	2	6,000.00*	14,600.00*	555,555.55 [12]
10-10	Trimmings and ribbons				
10-10-1	Trimmings				
10-10-1-1	Rayon entirely	12	3,376.00	12,424.00*	287,100.93*
10-10-1-2	Cotton and rayon	6	32,697.76*	87,435.47*	1,935,221.76
10-10-1-3	Silk and rayon	1		540.00	2,600.00
10-10-1-4	Cotton yarn entirely	1	40.00	*	*
10-10-2	Ribbons				
10-10-2-1	Cotton yarn entirely	5	2,400.00	6,924.00	123,302.22
10-10-2-2	Cotton and rayon	1	120.00	*	*
10-10-2-3	Cotton, rayon and rubber	3	6,600.00	22,900.00	99,999.99*
10-11	Cotton flannel finishing	2	(13)	(13)	(13)
Total for Group X.		545	1,944,247.47*	12,401,628.41*	197,903,305.60*
Group XI. Clothing Industries Including Hosiery					
11-1	Knitted hosiery				

Code	Classification	(1) No. of Factories	(2) Salary Payments ($)	(3) Wage Payments ($)	(4) Value of Output ($)
11-1-1	Cotton hosiery				
11-1-1-1	Cotton yarn only	11	15,820.00*	95,949.22*	1,152,361.06*
11-1-1-2	Cotton thread only	17	36,982.24*	269,779.45*	3,294,106.68*
11-1-1-3	Yarn and thread	5	720.00*	5,360.00*	365,002.78*
11-1-1-4	Raw material supplied by customers	1	(14)	(14)	(14)
11-1-2	Silk and rayon hosiery				
11-1-2-1	Silk only	2	3,316.00	13,700.00	89,222.22
11-1-2-2	Silk and cotton	14	28,039.50*	86,128.71*	1,210,620.84*
11-1-2-3	Rayon and cotton	10	10,268.00*	91,860.00*	472,730.00
11-1-2-4	Silk and rayon	1	(15)	(15)	(15)
11-1-2-5	Silk, rayon and cotton	10	32,738.00	114,700.00	693,736.11
11-1-3	Woollen hosiery (pure wool)	1	852.00	6,000.00	*
11-1-4	Cotton, silk and wool combined	2	3,292.00	23,400.00	291,666.67
11-1-5	Sewing of knitted hosiery	3	1,260.00	5,000.00	6,860.00*
11-1-6	Hosiery and other articles of apparel	24	42,432.00*	194,790.60*	1,460,134.75*
11-2	Hats				
11-2-1	Straw hats	3	2,976.00	2,248.00	45,650.00
11-2-2	Felt hats	1	*	*	69,444.44
11-2-3	Chinese hats (silk, cloth, etc.)	1	480.00	3,600.00	45,000.00
11-2-4	Straw and felt hats	6	16,200.00	54,588.00	801,888.89
11-2-5	Straw and Chinese hats	1	2,400.00	12,390.00	105,000.00
11-3	Umbrellas				
11-3-1	Umbrella stems	1		*	1,008.00
11-3-2	Umbrellas	13	5,948.00	16,712.00*	530,900.00
11-4	Handkerchiefs				

Code	Classification	(1) No. of Factories	(2) Salary Payments ($)	(3) Wage Payments ($)	(4) Value of Output ($)
11-4-1	Handkerchiefs only	6	17,770.00*	39,103.33	1,043,333.32
11-4-2	Handkerchiefs and other things	4	4,296.00*	11,400.00*	654,600.00
11-5	Underwear and sweaters				
11-5-1	Silk only	3	11,111.11*	47,222.22*	574,995.55
11-5-2	Cotton only	9	36,544.00[16]	118,200.00[16]*	1,579,124.44
11-5-3	Cotton and wool	11	16,155.30	85,395.67*	1,278,800.00
11-5-4	Knitted fabric	1		1,500.00	72,000.00
11-6	Other articles of apparel				
11-6-1	Ties, scarfs, and gloves	6	3,540.00	7,970.00	131,500.00
11-6-2	Buttons	3	1,720.00	3,880.00	31,520.00
11-6-3	Silk and cloth shoes	1	624.00	3,300.00	36,000.00
	Total for Group XI.	171	295,484.15*	1,314,177.20*	16,037,205.75*

Group XII. Manufacture of Leather, Rubber Products, etc.

Code	Classification	(1) No. of Factories	(2) Salary Payments ($)	(3) Wage Payments ($)	(4) Value of Output ($)
12-1	Leather manufacturing				
12-1-1	Soft leather and uppers	4	12,648.00	15,915.30	334,300.00
12-1-2	Hard leather and soles	7	16,398.00*	42,458.00*	1,510,723.67
12-1-3	Others	7	1,044.00*	8,100.00*	505,600.00*
12-2	Leather goods				
12-2-1	Articles used by the military	3	14,600.00	163,400.00	1,960,000.00
12-2-2	Leather trunks, cases, etc.	2	792.00	17,700.00	120,100.00
12-2-3	Leather shoes	4	15,888.00	63,700.00	325,000.00
12-3	Rubber goods				
12-3-1	Rubber shoes	24	108,834.00*	679,251.70*	4,506,149.99*
12-3-2	Rubber soles, heels, etc.	5	3,968.00*	7,755.49*	162,000.00

Code	Classification	(1) No. of Factories	(2) Salary Payments ($)	(3) Wage Payments ($)	(4) Value of Output ($)
12-4	Glue	1	3,600.00	1,570.00	120,000.00
	Total for Group XII.	57	177,772.00*	999,850.49*	9,543,873.66*

Group XIII. Preparation and Manufacture of Foods, Drinks and Tobacco

Code	Classification	(1) No. of Factories	(2) Salary Payments ($)	(3) Wage Payments ($)	(4) Value of Output ($)
13-1	Rice mills	12	9,468.00*	7,080.00*	977,400.00*
13-2	Wheat flour mills	15	137,189.78*	338,979.00*	62,728,355.33*
13-3	Rice and other flour mills	4	80.00	549.00	12,060.00
13-4	Sugar	4	4,500.00*	17,800.00*	838,888.88
13-5	Biscuits, bread, candies and canned food				
13-5-1	Biscuits	9	5,566.00*	13,830.00*	166,466.67*
13-5-2	Bread	1	1,104.00	1,798.00	54,000.00
13-5-3	Candies and sweetmeats	3	2,980.00	5,290.00	71,000.00
13-5-4	Canned food	1	600.00	360.00	20,000.00
13-5-5	Others	5	12,828.00[17]*	56,955.60[17]*	1,030,000.00*
13-6	Oil mills				
13-6-1	Bean oil	3	7,182.00	75,834.00	5,062,500.00
13-6-2	Groundnut oil	3	3,040.00*	76,896.00*	3,024,222.22
13-6-3	Cotton seed oil	5	29,696.67	69,929.67	2,974,191.65
13-6-4	Vegetable oil in general	2	10,000.00*	70,000.00*	2,800,000.00*
13-6-5	Lard manufacturing	1		2,160.00	80,000.00
13-7	Tea				
13-7-1	By machine process	19	5,670.22*	25,315.55*	621,737.50*
13-7-2	By native process	12	2,830.00*	13,735.95*	227,116.10*
13-8	Tobacco				
13-8-1	Cigars	5	17,700.00	76,060.00	269,200.00

Code	Classification	(1) No. of Factories	(2) Salary Payments ($)	(3) Wage Payments ($)	(4) Value of Output ($)
13-8-2	Cigarettes	46	291,135.00[18]*	1,698,211.00[18]*	46,575,769.00*
13-9	Wine and spirits	1	3,000.00	4,000.00	50,000.00
13-10	Soda water and other soft drinks	2	20,150.00	21,440.00	421,000.00
13-11	Condiments	8	32,280.00	94,496.00	3,811,840.00
13-12	Casings	3	1,088.00*	4,560.00*	118,756.00
13-13	Refined salt	1	10,080.00	9,200.00	300,000.00
13-14	Frozen egg products	1	(19)	(19)	(19)
13-15	Other food stuffs				
13-15-1	Starch	2	288.00	3,000.00	64,180.00
13-15-2	Bean curd products	3	360.00	4,444.00	86,000.00
13-16	Ice and cold storage	4	12,900.00	17,527.00	72,200.00
	Total for Group XIII.	175	621,715.67*	2,709,450.77*	132,456,883.35*

Group XIV. Manufacture of Paper, Book-Binding and Printing

Code	Classification	(1) No. of Factories	(2) Salary Payments ($)	(3) Wage Payments ($)	(4) Value of Output ($)
14-1	Paper manufacturing				
14-1-1	Paper	7	68,176.44	280,976.44	3,509,583.34
14-1-2	Card board	1	8,760.00	39,600.00	651,388.89
14-1-3	Tin foil	1	1,250.00	2,040.00	24,000.00
14-2	Printing				
14-2-1	Newspaper printing and publishing	5	423,000.00*	384,000.00*	4,468,000.00*
14-2-2	Book printing and publishing	10	65,490.08*	388,435.51*	15,001,395.75*
14-2-3	Printing with letter press				
14-2-3-1	Full sheet press	13	32,364.00*	117,680.00*	498,400.00
14-2-3-2	Half sheet press	9	11,232.00	34,928.00	185,635.00
14-2-3-3	Quarter and one sixth size presses	10	13,000.00	21,672.00	207,000.00

Code	Classification	(1) No. of Factories	(2) Salary Payments ($)	(3) Wage Payments ($)	(4) Value of Output ($)
14-2-3-4	Small foot-operated presses	4	3,768.00	13,233.00	58,900.00
14-2-3-5	Unclassified	4	1,370.00*	5,150.00*	69,145.00
14-2-4	Rubber offset printing	7	10,280.00*	49,770.00*	695,000.00*
14-2-5	Lithographic printing	18	13,206.75*	72,181.01*	324,231.57*
14-2-6	Lithographic and letter press printing	4	3,888.00	17,467.20	140,000.00
14-2-7	Lithographic and offset printing	16	45,584.00*	171,726.00*	1,866,000.00*
14-2-8	Unclassified	6	4,080.00*	20,941.00*	99,000.00*
14-3	Book-binding	14	1,892.00	27,332.00	56,909.00
14-4	Paper manufactures				
14-4-1	Envelops and paper bags	3	450.00	1,150.00*	12,923.00
14-4-2	Cartons	20	16,224.00*	67,721.50*	447,892.00
14-4-3	Cards	2	2,912.00	6,550.00*	141,000.00
14-5	Engraving	1	*	*	5,000.00
	Total for Group XIV.	155	728,927.27*	1,722,553.66*	28,461,403.55*

Group XV. Manufacture of Scientific and Musical Instruments, Clocks and Watches, etc.

Code	Classification	(1) No. of Factories	(2) Salary Payments ($)	(3) Wage Payments ($)	(4) Value of Output ($)
15-1	Musical instruments				
15-1-1	Organs	9	6,900.00	45,299.77	204,225.00
15-1-2	Pianos	2	3,216.00	21,500.00	123,000.00
15-1-3	Gramophones and gramophone records	5	46,540.00	29,920.00	407,500.00
15-1-4	Other musical instruments	2	*	3,600.00	30,000.00
15-2	Educational supplies and toys				
15-2-1	Writing ink	4	3,984.00	9,327.00	242,000.00
15-2-2	Writing outfit	5	6,252.00	15,422.00	246,220.00
15-2-3	Toys	6	567.00	9,150.00	53,000.00*

Code	Classification	(1) No. of Factories	(2) Salary Payments ($)	(3) Wage Payments ($)	(4) Value of Output ($)
15-3	Scientific apparatus	5	4,050.00*	15,660.00*	84,000.00
15-4	Clocks	1	*	*	*
	Total for Group XV.	39	71,509.00*	149,878.77*	1,389,945.00*
Group XVI.	Other Manufacturing Industries				
16-1	Tooth brushes	6	17,600.00*	55,540.00*	398,800.00
16-2	Mirrors	4	6,635.00	30,340.00	281,500.00
16-3	Coal briquettes	12	23,862.00*	41,225.00*	2,023,800.00*
16-4	Straw ropes	10	348.00*	13,804.00*	50,980.00*
	Total for Group XVI.	32	48,445.00*	140,909.00*	2,755,080.00*
	Grand Total for the Sixteen Groups	1672	5,399,914.55*	25,321,535.08*	439,328,826.81*

Notes: (1) As the factory was not established until May, 1911, it had no output in 1930.
(2) The combined amount of salary and wage payments in 1930 of one of the factories is given as $20,800 but separate figures are not available.
(3) One of the factories does not give separate figures for its salary and wage payments in 1930 which amounted in total to $15,000.
(4) Including $500,000 which is the combined value of output of a factory in this division and its branch in Chekiang.
(5) Excluding the value of output of a factory which is affiliated to a factory included in the subdivision of "Tins, boxes, etc."
(6) No separate figures are given by one of the factories for its salary and wage payments in 1930 which amounted to $45,346 altogether.
(7) Thirty of the factories here do not furnish separate figures for their salary and wage payments in 1930 which aggregated $2,370,623.35.
(8) No output value in 1930 as the factory was established in April, 1931.
(9) The salary and wage payments in 1930 of one of the factories amounted to $25,700, but separate figures are not available.
(10) One of the factories being a branch of a hosiery knitting mill and its value of output of $64,000 is included in that of the latter appearing under "Cotton hosiery, cotton yarn only".
(11) The value of output of one of the factories here, about $240,000, is included in that of its sister factories under "Silk weaving" and "Mixed fabrics, silk and rayon".
(12) Not including $10,000,000, the value of output of one factory in this subdivision whose product is used as raw material by its affiliated factories under "Silk weaving" and "Mixed fabrics, silk and rayon", to save double count in the group total.
(13) As the two factories were both established in 1931, there are no figures for 1930.
(14) No 1930 statistics as the factory was established in March, 1031.
(15) No 1930 statistics as the factory was established in January, 1931.
(16) The combined amount of salary and wage payments in 1930 of one of the factories is given as $9,840, no separate figures being available.
(17) The combined amount of salary and wage payments in 1930 of one of the factories is given as $44,500, no separate figures being available.
(18) The combined amount of salary and wage payments in 1930 of one of the factories is given as $6,000, no separate figures being available.
(19) No 1930 statistics as the factory did not come into being until 1931.

APPENDIX B
STATISTICS OF SHANGHAI INDUSTRIES, 1933
TABLE B-I. BUSINESS ORGANIZATION AND CAPITALIZATION

		(1)	(2)	(3)	(4)	(5)	(6)	(7)	(8)
					Business Organization				
Code	Classification	No. of Factories	State Ownership	Single Proprietorship	Partnership	Limited Liability Co.	Others	Unknown	Amount of Capital ($)
Group I. Woodworking Industries									
1-1	Saw mills	4		2	1	1			345,944
1-2	Manufacture of wooden articles								
1-2-1	Wooden boxes	1		1					30,000
1-2-2	Bobbins	5		2		2	1		236,531
	Total for Group I.	10		5	1	3	1		612,475
Group II. Furniture Manufacturing									
2-1	Steel furniture	6				4	2		368,500
2-2	Rugs and carpets	1		1					10,000
	Total for Group II.	7		1		4	2		378,500
Group III. Metal Industries									
3-1	Founding								
3-1-1	Machines and machine parts	17		7	10				113,000
3-1-2	Iron pipes	4		2	1	1			48,000
3-2	Steel refining	1	1						200,000
	Total for Group III.	22	1	9	11	1			361,000
Group IV. Manufacture of Machinery & Miscellaneous Metal Products									

Code	Classification	(1) No. of Factories	(2) State-Ownership	(3) Single Proprietorship	(4) Partnership	(5) Limited Liability Co.	(6) Others	(7) Unknown	(8) Amount of Capital ($)
			Business Organization						
4-1	Manufacture and repairing of machines								
4-1-1	Printing machines	6		4	1	1			88,000
4-1-2	Knitting machines	6		3	3				62,000
4-1-3	Spinning and weaving machines	13		8	2	3			387,000*
4-1-4	Prime movers	13		5	4	4			397,000
4-1-5	Various kinds of machines	22		9	9	4			1,022,889*
4-1-6	Machine parts								
4-1-6-1	Axes, etc.	1		1					9,500
4-1-6-2	Knitting needles	7		2	5				19,600
4-1-6-3	Fancets, valves, etc.	2		1	1				55,000
4-1-7	Repairing of machines	11		5	6				81,500*
4-2	Manufacture of metal products								
4-2-1	Boilers and water tanks	1		1					25,000
4-2-2	Tins								
4-2-2-1	Tins only	5		1	3			1	72.000
4-2-2-2	Tins and printing	4		1	2	1			140,000
4-2-2-3	Tins and other products	4		1	2	1			470,000
4-2-3	Aluminumware	4		1	3				100,000
4-2-4	Nails								
4-2-4-1	Nails only	4		2	2				200,902
4-2-4-2	Nails and other products	2				2			320,000
4-2-5	Lamps	3		3					25,000
4-2-6	Copper sheets	4		1	1	1	1		330,000
4-2-7	Iron bars	1			1				41,958
4-2-8	Other metal products	5			3	1		1	98,000

		(1)	(2)	(3)	(4)	(5)	(6)	(7)	(8)
			\multicolumn{6}{c}{Business Organization}		
Code	Classification	No. of Factories	State-Ownership	Single Proprietorship	Partner-ship	Limited Liability Co.	Others	Unknown	Amount of Capital ($)
4-3	Manufacture of electric machines and apparatus								
4-3-1	Electric machines and apparatus	3			2	1			114,790
4-3-2	Electric machines and dry batteries	1	1						500,000
4-3-3	Electric fans, heaters, utencils, etc.	5		1	1	3			1,880,000 [1]
4-3-4	Electric supplies	4		2	1	1			92,000
4-3-5	Electric supplies and other products	2		1	1				13,000
4-3-6	Electric light bulbs	13		2	5	4		2	667,986*
4-3-7	Neon light tubes	1					1		60,000
4-3-8	Dry batteries	3		1	1	1			120,000
4-3-9	Dry batteries and flash lights	1			1				*
4-3-10	Flash lights	8		2	5	1			177,244
4-3-11	Electric welding	1				1			30,000
4-4	Foundry works								
4-4-1	Spinning and weaving machines	3		1	2				70,000
4-4-2	Various kinds of machines	3		1	1	1			50,000*
4-4-3	Metal products	1			1				4,000
	Total for Group IV.	167	1	60	69	31	2	4	7,724,369*
Group V.	Construction of Boats, Ships and Vehicles for Land Transportation								
5-1	Shipbuilding								
5-1-1	Construction of ships	1	1						*
5-1-2	Construction of ships and other instruments of transportation	5		3	1	1			380,000

Code	Classification	(1) No. of Factories	(2) State-Ownership	(3) Single Proprietorship	(4) Partnership	(5) Limited Liability Co.	(6) Others	(7) Unknown	(8) Amount of Capital ($)
				Business Organization					
5-1-3	Repairing of ships	7		4	2			1	73,000*
5-2	Building of cars								
5-2-1	Railway workshops	1	1						*
5-2-2	Bicycles	1						1	50,000
5-2-3	Charcoal gas trucks	1			1				20,000
	Total for Group V.	16	2	7	4	1		2	523,000*
Group VI. Manufacture of Bricks, Earthenware, Glass, etc.									
6-1	Bricks and tiles								
6-1-1	Bricks and tiles in general	2				2			1,040,000 [2]
6-1-2	Glazed tiles	2				2			180,000
6-2	Glass								
6-2-1	Glassware	21		7	5	7		2	431,000*
6-2-2	Glass bevelling	3		2	1				12,500
6-3	Cement	1				1			1,638,600
6-4	Stone, stone powder, and lime								
6-4-1	Lime	1			1				20,000
6-4-2	Stone powder	3		1	1	1			203,000
6-4-3	Stone breaking	1		1					3,000
6-5	Crucibles								
6-5-1	Crucibles only	1					1		100,000
6-5-2	Crucibles and fire bricks	2				2			150,000
6-5-3	Crucibles, glassware, and fire bricks	1				1			100,000
6-6	Coal briquettes	6			2	3		1	390,000*
	Total for Group VI.	44		11	10	19	1	3	4,268,100*
Group VII. Building Material									
7-1	Building Material	7		5	1	1			165,000*
	Total for Group VII.	7		5	1	1			165,000*

		(1)	(2)	(3)	(4)	(5)	(6)	(7)	(8)
					Business Organization				
Code	Classification	No. of Factories	State-Ownership	Single Proprietorship	Partnership	Limited Liability Co.	Others	Unknown	Amount of Capital ($)
Group VIII. Production and Transmission of Electricity and Supply of Water									
8-1	Electric and water works	3[3]				3			11,290,000
	Total for Group VIII.	3				3			11,290,000
Group IX. Manufacture of Chemicals and Allied Products									
9-1	Matches								
9-1-1	Matches	4			1	3			3,320,000 [4]
9-1-2	Shavings and splints	3				3			216,900
9-2	Soap								
9-2-1	Soap only	4		2		1		1	145,000
9-2-2	Soap, washing soda, and candles	1		1					10,000
9-3	Enamelled ware								
9-3-1	Enamelled ware only	13		3	1	7	1	1	1,032,500
9-3-2	Enamelled ware and other products	4		1		3			280,000
9-3-3	Body of enamelled ware	2		1		1			15,000
9-4	Dyes, varnish, and printer's ink								
9-4-1	Varnish	3				3			570,000
9-4-2	Printer's ink	2		1		1			150,000
9-4-3	Dyes	1				1			100,000
9-5	Cosmetics	13		1	2	7	2	1	5,213,916 [5]
9-6	Medicine								
9-6-1	Medicine in general	6			1	5			1,070,000
9-6-2	Medicine and soap	1				1			500,000
9-7	Artificial resin								
9-7-1	Celluloid products	6		3	1	2			260,000
9-7-2	Beetle and bakelite	7		1	1	4		1	229,000
9-8	Acids								
9-8-1	Acids only	1				1			750,000

Code	Classification	(1) No. of Factories	(2) State-Ownership	(3) Single Proprietorship	(4) Partnership	(5) Limited Liability Co.	(6) Others	(7) Unknown	(8) Amount of Capital ($)
			Business Organization						
9-8-2	Acids, caustic soda, and bleaching powder	1				1			400,000
9-9	Calcium and magnesium carbonates	3				2		1	650,000
9-10	Oxygen and acetylene	1				1			250,000
9-11	Other chemical products	2			2				37,778
	Total for Group IX.	*78*	*14*	*9*	*47*	*3*		*5*	*15,200,094*
Group X. Textile Industries									
10-1	Cotton spinning and weaving								
10-1-1	Cotton ginning	5		3	2				43,000*
10-1-2	Cotton fluffing								
10-1-2-1	Cotton fluffing only	7		5	1	1			83,889*[6]
10-1-2-2	Cotton fluffing and manufacture of other products	1			1				5,000
10-1-3	Cotton spinning								
10-1-3-1	Spinning only	12			1	8	2	1	15,583,562 [7]
10-1-3-2	Spinning and weaving	16				11	5		33,254,192 [8]
10-1-3-3	Spinning and making of cotton blankets	1	1						279,720
10-1-4	Cotton weaving								
10-1-4-1	Weaving only	69		15	31	18	2	3	3,976,898*
10-1-4-2	Weaving and manufacture of machinery	1				1			300,000
10-1-5	Medicicated gauze and cotton	3		1	1	1			68,000
10-2	Silk reeling and weaving								
10-2-1	Silk reeling								
10-2-1-1	Steam filature								

		(1)	(2)	(3)	(4)	(5)	(6)	(7)	(8)
			\multicolumn{6}{c}{Business Organization}		
Code	Classification	No. of Factories	State-Ownership	Single Proprietorship	Partner-ship	Limited Liability Co.	Others	Unknown	Amount of Capital ($)
	silk	49			6	1		42	214,930*
10-2-1-2	Dupion silk	2	1					1	37,000
10-2-1-3	Silk waste	1				1			347,225
10-2-2	Silk weaving	122		24	62	24	3	9	4,026,855*
10-3	Wool spinning and weaving								
10-3-1	Wool weaving only	21	2	13		5	1		906,675*
10-3-2	Wool spinning and weaving	2				2			1,100,000
10-3-3	Wool bowing	1	1						2,000
10-4	Spinning and weaving of waste cotton, wool, and silk	3	1	1	1				1,430,000
10-5	Dyeing								
10-5-1	Mercerized yarn and thread	16	4	11		1			128,000
10-5-2	Dyeing in general	30	3	20	4		3		623,000*
10-5-3	Dyeing and printing of textiles	1				1			600,000
10-6	Printing of textiles	6	3	2	1				42,000
10-7	Thread making								
10-7-1	Warp and woof	4		1	2			1	140,000
10-7-2	Thread balls	3	1	2					16,000
10-7-3	Other kinds of of thread	3	1	2					11,000
10-8	Making of trimmings and ribbons								
10-8-1	Ribbons	2	1	1					60,000
10-8-2	Elastic belts	3	2	1					38,000
10-8-3	Trimmings and ribbons	2	1	1					16,000
10-8-4	Trimmings, ribbons, and chopsticks	1		1					200,000

Code	Classification	(1) No. of Factories	(2) State-Ownership	(3) Single Proprietorship	(4) Partnership	(5) Limited Liability Co.	(6) Others	(7) Unknown	(8) Amount of Capital ($)
			Business Organization						
10-9	Cotton flannel finishing								
10-9-1	Cotton flannel finishing only	2		1	1				60,000
10-9-2	Cotton flannel finishing and dyeing and printing of textiles	2			2				31,000
	Total for Group X.	391		71	164	83	13	60	63,623,946*
Group XI. Clothing Industries, Including Hosiery									
11-1	Knitted hosiery								
11-1-1	Knitted hosiery only	38		10	22	3	1	2	1,960,749
11-1-2	Knitted hosiery, underwear and sweaters, and other articles of apparel	14		5	5	4			1,466,710
11-2	Hats	7		2	4	1			238,000
11-3	Umbrellas	2			2				61,500
11-4	Hankerchiefs	7		2	2	2		1	113,000
11-5	Underwear and sweaters	16		4	6	5		1	1,013,167
11-6	Woollen and cotton blankets	1			1				5,000
11-7	Other articles of apparel								
11-7-1	Buttons	3		1	2				33,000
11-7-2	Scarfs, gloves, etc.	1			1				83,333
	Total for Group XI.	89		24	45	15	1	4	4,974,459
Group XII. Manufacture of Leather, Rubber Products etc.									

		(1)	(2)	(3)	(4)	(5)	(6)	(7)	(8)
				Business Organization					
Code	Classification	No. of Factories	State-Ownership	Single Proprietorship	Partnership	Limited Liability Co.	Others	Unknown	Amount of Capital ($)
12-1	Leather manufacturing								
12-1-1	Leather manufacturing only	9		2	5	2			965,000
12-1-2	Leather manufacturing and manufacture of glue	1		1					15,000
12-2	Manufacture of rubber goods	44	4	16	11	9		4	4,023,888*
12-3	Manufacture of glue	1			1				60,000
	Total for Group XII.	55	6	22	14	9		4	5,063,888*
Group XIII. Preparation and Manufacture of Foods, Drinks, and Tobacco
13-1	Rice mills	1		1					10,000
13-2	Wheat flour mills	15			8	7			6,249,650
13-3	Sugar refineries	4		3				1	256,000
13-4	Manufactured foodstuffs								
13-4-1	Canned food	7		2	4	1			1,473,600
13-4-2	Bean curd products	1	1						4,000
13-4-3	Candies	2	2						24,000
13-5	Oil mills	10	1	5	4				1,271,056
13-6	Tea	44	14	29	1				248,200
13-7	Cigarettes	46	4	9	29	2		2	19,002,667*
13-8	Alcohol	1			1				70,000
13-9	Soda water and other soft drinks								
13-9-1	Soda water	1		1					50,000
13-9-2	Soda water and manufacture of ice	1			1				300,000
13-10	Condiments	5	2		1	1		1	870,000
13-11	Starch	1			1				100,000
13-12	Refined salt	1			1				240,000
13-13	Frozen egg products	1	1						500,000

Code	Classification	(1) No. of Factories	(2) State-Ownership	(3) Single Proprietorship	(4) Partnership	(5) Limited Liability Co.	(6) Others	(7) Unknown	(8) Amount of Capital ($)
			Business Organization						
13-14	Ice and cold storage	2				2			424,000
	Total for Group XIII.	143		25	50	53	11	4	31,093,173*
Group XIV. Manufacture of Paper, Book-Binding and Printing									
14-1	Paper manufacturing								
14-1-1	Paper	7		1	1	5			2,306,389
14-1-2	Card-board	1				1			400,000
14-1-3	Tin foil	1			1				7,600
14-2	Printing								
14-2-1	Printing only	85		19	33	30		3	9,494,000*
14-2-2	Printing and type casting	7		2		5			3,655,000*
14-3	Paper manufactures								
14-3-1	Cartons	10		3	4	3			14,000
14-3-2	Cards, etc.	3			1	2			76,400
	Total for Group XIV.	114		25	40	46		3	16,073,389*
Group XV. Manufacture of Scientific and Musical Instruments, Clocks and Watches, etc.									
15-1	Musical instruments	2		1		1			105,000
15-2	Educational supplies	6		2	1	3			261,000
15-3	Scientific apparatus	5			1	2	1	1	148,500
15-4	Clocks and flash lights	1				1			50,000
15-5	Toys	4			1	3			60,000
	Total for Group XV.	18		3	3	9	2	1	624,500
Group XVI. Other Manufacturing Industries									
16-1	Tooth brushes								
16-1-1	Tooth brushes only	5		2	1	1		1	100,000
16-1-2	Tooth brushes and tooth powder	1				1			160,000

Code	Classification	(1) No. of Factories	(2) State-Ownership	(3) Single Proprietorship	(4) Partner-ship	(5) Limited Liability Co.	(6) Others	(7) Unknown	(8) Amount of Capital ($)
				Business Organization					
16-2	Mirrors	4		3	1				54,000
16-3	Thermos bottles								
16-3-1	Whole bottle	2		1		1			170,000
16-3-2	Tin outside cover only	7		1	4			2	66,000
16-3-3	Vacuum bottles only	3		1	2				160,000
Total for Group XVI.		22		5	10	4		3	710,000
Grand Total for the Sixteen Groups		1186	4	271	443	332	43	93	162,685,893*

Notes: (1) One of the factories in this subdivision is affiliated with another establishment and their joint capitalization of $300,000 appears with the latter in the subdivision of "Electric light bulbs".

(2) The capital of $1,000,000 of a factory here includes that of its affiliated factory in Chekiang.

(3) Not including establishments which sell electricity for other companies and do not themselves generate electricity.

(4) Including $3,000,000 which is the total capitalization of a company operating besides a certain factory in this subdivision, several other establishments in other cities.

(5) Including $2,400,000 and $1,300,000, representing the capital of two Hongkong factories each having a branch classified under this division.

(6) One of the factories being a branch of another, its capitalization of $699,300 appears with that of the latter in 10-1-3-2, "Cotton, spinning and weaving".

(7) The joint capitalization of a certain factory here with two sister factories, amounting to $12,000,000, is shown in 10-1-3-2, "Cotton, spinning and weaving".

(8) Including $12,000,000, the joint capitalization of two sister factories under this heading and another in 10-1-3-1, "Cotton, spinning only".

TABLE B-II. AREA AND OWNERSHIP OF FACTORY SITE

		(1)	(2)	(3)	(4)	(5)	(6)
				\multicolumn{4}{c}{Ownership of Factory Site}			
Code	Classification	No. of Factories	Average Area per Factory (Mow)	Owned	Rented	Partly Owned and Partly Rented	Unknown
Group I. Woodworking Industries							
1-1	Saw mills	4	6.20	2	1		1
1-2	Manufacture of wooden articles						
1-2-1	Wooden boxes	1	3.00	1			
1-2-2	Bobbins	5	3.00	1	3		1
	Totals and Averages for Group I.	10	4.62	4	4		2
Group II. Furniture Manufacturing							
2-1	Steel furniture	6	2.10		6		
2-2	Rugs and carpets	1	*		1		
	Totals and Averages for Group II.	7	2.10		7		
Group III. Metal Industries							
3-1	Founding						
3-1-1	Machines and machine parts	17	0.62	1	16		
3-1-2	Iron pipes	4	2.12	1	3		
3-2	Steel refining	1	2.12	1			
	Totals and Averages for Group III.	22	1.00	3	19		
Group IV. Manufacture of Machinery and Miscellaneous Metal Products							
4-1	Manufacture and repairing of machines						
4-1-1	Printing machines	6	1.43	1	4		1
4-1-2	Knitting machines	6	0.55		6		
4-1-3	Spinning and weaving machines	13	5.27	3	9		1
4-1-4	Prime movers	13	2.37	4	8	1	
4-1-5	Various kinds of machines	22	1.52	3	19		

Code	Classification	(1) No. of Factories	(2) Average Area per Factory (Mow)	(3) Owned	(4) Rented	(5) Partly Owned and Partly Rented	(6) Unknown
				\multicolumn{4}{c}{Ownership of Factory Site}			
4-1-6	Machine parts						
4-1-6-1	Axes, etc.	1	2.00		1		
4-1-6-2	Knitting needles	7	0.10		5		2
4-1-6-3	Faucets, valves, etc.	2	*		1		1
4-1-7	Repairing of machines and machine parts	11	1.00		8		3
4-2	Manufacture of metal products						
4-2-1	Boilers and water tanks	1	4.00			1	
4-2-2	Tins						
4-2-2-1	Tins only	5	0.20				1
4-2-2-2	Tins and printing	4	1.50		3	1	
4-2-2-3	Tins and other products	4	5.67	1	3		
4-2-3	Aluminumware	4	4.00		4		
4-2-4	Nails						
4-2-4-1	Nails only	4	3.85	1	3		
4-2-4-2	Nails and other products	2	4.50	1	1		
4-2-5	Lamps	3	0.95		3		
4-2-6	Copper sheets	4	2.25	1	3		
4-2-7	Iron bars	1	4.00		1		
4-2-8	Other metal products	5	0.85	1	3		1
4-3	Manufacture of electric machines and apparatus						
4-3-1	Electric machines and apparatus	3	0.25	1	2		
4-3-2	Electric machines and dry batteries	1	10.00				1
4-3-3	Electric fans, heaters, utensils, etc.	5	3.47	4	1		
4-3-4	Electric supplies	4	0.63		4		
4-3-5	Electric supplies and other products	2	0.50	1	1		

Code	Classification	(1) No. of Factories	(2) Average Area per Factory (Mow)	(3) Owned	(4) Rented	(5) Partly Owned and Partly Rented	(6) Unknown
				\multicolumn{4}{c}{Ownership of Factory Site}			
4-3-6	Electric light bulbs	13	3.19	1	10		2
4-3-7	Neon light tubes	1	*		1		
4-3-8	Dry batteries	3	3.17	1	2		
4-3-9	Dry batteries and flash lights	1	0.40		1		
4-3-10	Flash lights	8	1.87	1	7		
4-3-11	Electric welding	1	3.50	1			
4-4	Foundry works						
4-4-1	Spinning and weaving machines	3	0.90		3		
4-4-2	Various kinds of machines	3	5.45		3		
4-4-3	Metal products	1	1.50		1		
	Totals and Averages for Group IV.	167	2.56	26	125	3	13
\multicolumn{8}{l}{Group V. Construction of Boats, Ships and Vehicles for Land Transportation}							
5-1	Shipbuilding						
5-1-1	Construction of ships	1	*	1			
5-1-2	Construction of ships and other instruments of transportation	5	11.25	1	4		
5-1-3	Repairing of ships	7	2.75	2	4	1	
5-2	Building of cars						
5-2-1	Railway workshops	1	118.00	1			
5-2-2	Bicycles	1	*		1		
5-2-3	Charcoal gas trucks	1	1.00		1		
	Totals and Averages for Group V.	16	17.50	5	10	1	
\multicolumn{8}{l}{Group VI. Manufacture of Bricks, Earthenware, Glass, etc.}							
6-1	Bricks and tiles						
6-1-1	Bricks and tiles in general	2	104.00	2			

Code	Classification	(1) No of Factories	(2) Average Area per Factory (Mow)	(3) Owned	(4) Rented	(5) Partly Owned and Partly Rented	(6) Unknown
				Ownership of Factory Site			
6-1-2	Glazed tiles	2	8.33	1	1		
6-2	Glass						
6-2-1	Glassware	21	2.83	7	11		3
6-2-2	Glass bevelling	3	0.30		3		
6-3	Cement	1	100.00	1			
6-4	Stone, stone powder, and lime						
6-4-1	Lime	1	*	1			
6-4-2	Stone powder	3	10.00	1	1		1
6-4-3	Stone breaking	1	1.00		1		
6-5	Crucibles						
6-5-1	Crucibles only	1	2.30		1		
6-5-2	Crucibles and fire bricks	2	4.90		2		
6-5-3	Crucibles, glassware, and fire bricks	1	14.00		1		
6-6	Coal briquettes	6	2.63		5		1
	Totals and Averages for Group VI.	44	12.60	13	26		5
Group VII. Building Material							
7-1	Building material	7	1.56		4		3
	Totals and Averages for Group VII.	7	1.56		4		3
Group VIII. Production and Transmission of Electricity and Supply of Water							
8-1	Electric and water works	3	*				3
	Totals and Averages for Group VIII.	3	*				3
Group IX. Manufacture of Chemicals and Allied Products							
9-1	Matches						
9-1-1	Matches	4	20.27	1	1	1	1
9-1-2	Shavings and Splints	3	26.25		1	1	1
9-2	Soap						
9-2-1	Soap only	4	2.13	1	1		2

Code	Classification	(1) No. of Factories	(2) Average Area per Factory (Mow)	(3) Owned	(4) Rented	(5) Partly Owned and Partly Rented	(6) Unknown
				\multicolumn{4}{c}{Ownership of Factory Site}			
9-2-2	Soap, washing soda, and candles	1	2.00		1		
9-3	Enamelled ware						
9-3-1	Enamelled ware only	13	4.57	2	8		3
9-3-2	Enamelled ware and other products	4	4.67	1	3		
9-3-3	Body of enamelled ware	2	2.50		2		
9-4	Dyes, varnish, and printer's ink						
9-4-1	Varnish	3	20.00				3
9-4-2	Printer's ink	2	1.00		1		1
9-4-3	Dyes	1	6.00	1			
9-5	Cosmetics	13	8.68	2	3	4	4
9-6	Medicine						
9-6-1	Medicine in general	6	5.10		3		3
9-6-2	Medicine and soap	1	*		1		
9-7	Artificial resin						
9-7-1	Celluloid products	6	2.62	1	5		
9-7-2	Beetle and bakelite	7	0.40		6		1
9-8	Acids						
9-8-1	Acids only	1	46.00	1			
9-8-2	Acids, caustic soda, and bleaching powder	1	*				1
9-9	Calcium and magnesium carbonates	3	14.00		2		1
9-10	Oxygen and acetylene	1	2.77	1			
9-11	Other chemical products	2	2.00		2		
	Totals and Averages for Group IX.	78	8.06	11	40	6	21
Group X.	Textile Industries						
10-1	Cotton spinning and weaving						
10-1-1	Cotton ginning	5	2.83	1	2		2
10-1-2	Cotton fluffing						
10-1-2-1	Cotton fluffing only	7	1.42	1	6		

Code	Classification	(1) No. of Factories	(2) Average Area per Factory (Mow)	(3) Owned	(4) Rented	(5) Partly Owned and Partly Rented	(6) Unknown
				Ownership of Factory Site			
10-1-2-2	Cotton fluffing and manufacture of other products	1	12.00		1		
10-1-3	Cotton spinning						
10-1-3-1	Spinning only	12	30.67	7	2		3
10-1-3-2	Spinning and weaving	16	39.19	15	1		
10-1-3-3	Spinning and making of cotton blankets	1	21.00	1			
10-1-4	Cotton weaving						
10-1-4-1	Weaving only	69	3.53	3	52	6	8
10-1-4-2	Weaving and manufacture of machinery	1	14.75			1	
10-1-5	Medicicated gauze and cotton	3	1.50		3		
10-2	Silk reeling and weaving						
10-2-1	Silk reeling						
10-2-1-1	Steam filature silk	49	2.50		47		2
10-2-1-2	Dupion silk	2	7.00		2		
10-2-1-3	Silk waste	1	*	1			
10-2-2	Silk weaving	122	1.77	3	94		25
10-3	Wool spinning and weaving						
10-3-1	Wool weaving only	21	0.87		19		2
10-3-2	Wool spinning and weaving	2	*				2
10-3-3	Wool bowing	1	*		1		
10-4	Spinning and weaving of waste cotton, wool, and silk	3	11.10	1	2		
10-5	Dyeing						
10-5-1	Mercerized yarn and thread	16	1.35	1	15		
10-5-2	Dyeing in general	30	1.66	3	23	1	3

Code	Classification	(1) No. of Factories	(2) Average Area per Factory (Mow)	(3) Owned	(4) Rented	(5) Partly Owned and Partly Rented	(6) Unknown
				\multicolumn{4}{c}{Ownership of Factory Site}			
10-5-3	Dyeing and printing of textiles	1	*				1
10-6	Printing of textiles	6	0.67		5		1
10-7	Thread making						
10-7-1	Warp and woof	4	0.60		3		1
10-7-2	Thread balls	3	1.80		3		
10-7-3	Other kinds of thread	3	0.29		3		
10-8	Making of trimmings and ribbons						
10-8-1	Ribbons	2	2.00		1		1
10-8-2	Elastic belts	3	1.25		3		
10-8-3	Trimmings and ribbons	2	*		1		1
10-8-4	Trimmings, ribbons, and chopsticks	1	11.00	1			
10-9	Cotton flannel finishing						
10-9-1	Cotton flannel finishing only	2	0.65		2		
10-9-2	Cotton flannel finishing and dyeing and printing of textiles	2	1.00		2		
	Totals and Averages for Group X.	391	5.37	38	293	8	52
Group XI.	Clothing Industries, Including Hosiery						
11-1	Knitted hosiery						
11-1-1	Knitted hosiery only	38	1.39	4	32		2
11-1-2	Knitted hosiery, underwear and sweaters, and other articles of apparel	14	2.94	3	10		1
11-2	Hats	7	2.35	3	2		2
11-3	Umbrellas	2	0.70		2		
11-4	Handkerchiefs	7	0.54		7		
11-5	Underwear and sweaters	16	2.25	4	11		1

Code	Classification	(1) No. of Factories	(2) Average Area per Factory (Mow)	(3) Owned	(4) Rented	(5) Partly Owned and Partly Rented	(6) Unknown
				\multicolumn{4}{c}{Ownership of Factory Site}
11-6	Woollen and cotton blankets	1	0.40		1		
11-7	Other articles of apparel						
11-7-1	Buttons	3	1.20		3		
11-7-2	Scarfs, gloves, etc.	1	*		1		
	Totals and Averages for Group XI.	89	1.69	14	69		6
Group XII. Manufacture of Leather, Rubber Products, etc.							
12-1	Leather manufacturing						
12-1-1	Leather manufacturing only	9	6.00	6	3		
12-1-2	Leather manufacturing and manufacture of glue	1	2.00		1		
12-2	Manufacture of rubber goods	44	2.66	8	21		15
12-3	Manufacture of glue	1	*				1
	Totals and Averages for Group XII.	55	3.36	14	25		16
Group XIII. Preparation and Manufacture of Foods, Drinks, and Tobacco							
13-1	Rice mills	1	2.00		1		
13-2	Wheat flour mills	15	17.67	10	4	1	
13-3	Sugar refineries	4	2.70		3		1
13-4	Manufactured foodstuffs						
13-4-1	Canned food	7	3.95	1	6		
13-4-2	Bean curd products	1	*		1		
13-4-3	Candies	2	1.00	1			1
13-5	Oil mills	10	11.33	1	8		1
13-6	Tea	44	0.45	2	42		
13-7	Cigarettes	46	2.30	8	35		3
13-8	Alcohol	1	7.20		1		

Code	Classification	(1) No. of Factories	(2) Average Area per Factory (Mow)	Ownership of Factory Site			
				(3) Owned	(4) Rented	(5) Partly Owned and Partly Rented	(6) Unknown
13-9	Soda water and other soft drinks						
13-9-1	Soda water	1	5.00		1		
13-9-2	Soda water and manufacture of ice	1	*				1
13-10	Condiments	5	7.49	2	2		1
13-11	Starch	1	10.00		1		
13-12	Refined salt	1	30.00	1			
13-13	Frozen egg products	1	*		1		
13-14	Ice and cold storage	2	*	1			1
	Totals and Averages for Group XIII.	143	4.41	27	106	1	9
Group XIV.	Manufacture of Paper, Book-Binding and Printing						
14-1	Paper manufacturing						
14-1-1	Paper	7	18.00	4	1		2
14-1-2	Card-board	1	5.50	1			
14-1-3	Tin foil	1	*		1		
14-2	Printing						
14-2-1	Printing only	85	0.67	2	76		7
14-2-2	Printing and type casting	7	4.55		6		1
14-3	Paper manufactures						
14-3-1	Cartons	10	1.30		8		2
14-3-2	Cards, etc.	3	1.80	2	1		
	Totals and Averages for Group XIV.	114	1.52	9	93		12
Group. XV.	Manufacture of Scientific and Musical Instruments, Clocks and Watches, etc.						
15-1	Musical instruments	2	0.60		2		
15-2	Educational supplies	6	0.83		5		1
15-3	Scientific apparatus	5	2.50	1	3		1
15-4	Clocks and flash lights	1	1.50		1		

Code	Classification	(1) No. of Factories	(2) Average Area per Factory (Mow)	(3) Owned	(4) Rented	(5) Partly Owned and Partly Rented	(6) Unknown
				\multicolumn{4}{c}{Ownership of Factory Site}			
15-5	Toys	4	0.45		3		1
	Totals and Averages for Group XV.	18	1.17	1	14		3
Group XVI. Other Manufacturing Industries							
16-1	Tooth brushes						
16-1-1	Tooth brushes only	5	1.35		4		1
16-1-2	Tooth brushes and tooth powder	1	2.70	1			
16-2	Mirrors	4	0.45		3		1
16-3	Thermos bottles						
16-3-1	Whole bottle	2	2.50	1	1		
16-3-2	Tin outside cover only	7	0.60		5		2
16-3-3	Vacuum bottles only	3	0.70		3		
	Totals and Averages for Group XVI.	22	1.03	2	16		4
	Grand Totals and Averages for the Sixteen Groups	1,186	4.55	167	851	19	149

TABLE B-III. OFFICERS AND WORKERS

Code	Classification	(1) No. of Factories	(2) Male Officers	(3) Female Officers	(4) Total No. of Officers	(5) Male Workers	(6) Female Workers	(7) Child Workers	(8) Total No. of Workers
	Group I. Woodworking Industries								
1-1	Saw mills	4	30		30	376		2	378
1-2	Manufacture of wooden articles								
1-2-1	Wooden boxes	1	7		7	70			70
1-2-2	Bobbins	5	28		28	296	17	28	341
	Total for Group I.	10	65		65	742	17	30	789
	Group II. Furniture Manufacturing								
2-1	Steel furniture	6	69		69	403		141	544
2-2	Rugs and carpets	1	8		8	75	300	75	450
	Total for Group II.	7	77		77	478	300	216	994
	Group III. Metal Industries								
3-1	Founding								
3-1-1	Machines and machine parts	17	40		40	328		219	547
3-1-2	Iron pipes	4	19		19	156		49	205
3-2	Steel refining	1	5		5	33		2	35
	Total for Group III.	22	64		64	517		270	787
	Group IV. Manufacture of Machinery and Miscellaneous Metal Products								
4-1	Manufacture and repairing of machines								
4-1-1	Printing machines	6	36		36	124		79	203
4-1-2	Knitting machines	6	35		35	136		100	236
4-1-3	Spinning and weaving machines	13	76		76	464		284	748

Code	Classification	(1) No. of Factories	(2) Male Officers	(3) Female Officers	(4) Total No. of Officers	(5) Male Workers	(6) Female Workers	(7) Child Workers	(8) Total No. of Workers
4-1-4	Prime movers	13	86		86	412		272	684
4-1-5	Various kinds of machines	22	166		166	1,302		465	1,767
4-1-6	Machine parts								
4-1-6-1	Axes, etc.	1	5		5	15		20	35
4-1-6-2	Knitting needles	7	15		15	156	76	65	297
4-1-6-3	Faucets, valves, etc.	2	11		11	36		34	70
4-1-7	Repairing of machines and machine parts	11	38		38	324		232	556
4-2	Manufacture of metal products								
4-2-1	Boilers and water tanks	1	3		3	65		5	70
4-2-2	Tins								
4-2-2-1	Tins only	5	19		19	150	33	55	238
4-2-2-2	Tins and printing	4	39		39	221	96	50	367
4-2-2-3	Tins and other products	4	77		77	531	112	130	773
4-2-3	Aluminumware	4	33		33	194	24	25	243
4-2-4	Nails								
4-2-4-1	Nails only	4	18		18	78		24	102
4-2-4-2	Nails and other products	2	34		34	260		7	267
4-2-5	Lamps	3	10		10	73	60	15	148
4-2-6	Copper sheets	4	46		46	255		6	255
4-2-7	Iron bars	1	9		9	40		6	46
4-2-8	Other metal products	5	32		32	132	10	112	254
4-3	Manufacture of electric machines and apparatus								
4-3-1	Electric machines and apparatus	3	59		59	316		80	396

Code	Classification	(1) No. of Factories	(2) Male Officers	(3) Female Officers	(4) Total No. of Officers	(5) Male Workers	(6) Female Workers	(7) Child Workers	(8) Total No. of Workers
4-3-2	Electric machines and dry batteries	1	1		1	143			143
4-3-3	Electric fans, heaters, utencils, etc.	5	81		81	675	99	123	897
4-3-4	Electric supplies	4	26	1	27	124	40	58	222
4-3-5	Electric supplies and other products	2	11		11	78	44	24	146
4-3-6	Electric light bulbs	13	151	6	157	578	364	186	1128
4-3-7	Neon light tubes	1	26		26	40			40
4-3-8	Dry batteries	3	24		24	83	65	8	156
4-3-9	Dry batteries and flash lights	1	6		6	30	10		40
4-3-10	Flash lights	8	68		68	314	22	85	421
4-3-11	Electric welding	1	7		7	25		9	34
4-4	Foundry works								
4-4-1	Spinning and weaving machines	3	20		20	73		70	143
4-4-2	Various kinds of machines	3	22		22	164		38	202
4-4-3	Metal products	1	4		4	26		26	52
	Total for Group IV	167	1,294	7	1,301	7,637	1,055	2,687	11,379

Group V. Construction of Boats, Ships and Vehicles for Land Transportation

Code	Classification	(1) No. of Factories	(2) Male Officers	(3) Female Officers	(4) Total No. of Officers	(5) Male Workers	(6) Female Workers	(7) Child Workers	(8) Total No. of Workers
5-1	Shipbuilding								
5-1-1	Construction of ships	1	202		202	1,378			1,378
5-1-2	Construction of ships and other instruments of transportation	5	75		75	561		153	714
5-1-3	Repairing of ships	7	33		33	365		122	487
5-2	Building of cars								
5-2-1	Railway workshops	1	10		10	956		42	998
5-2-2	Bicycles	1	5		5	26			26

Code	Classification	(1) No. of Factories	(2) Male Officers	(3) Female Officers	(4) Total No. of Officers	(5) Male Workers	(6) Female Workers	(7) Child Workers	(8) Total No. of Workers
5-2-3	Charcoal gas trucks	1	5		5	46		4	50
	Total for Group V.	16	330		330	3,332		321	3,653
Group VI. Manufacture of Bricks, Earthenware. Glass, etc.									
6-1	Bricks and tiles								
6-1-1	Bricks and tiles in general	2	55		55	430	130	22	582
6-1-2	Glazed tiles	2	25		25	134	118	3	255
6-2	Glass								
6-2-1	Glassware	21	157		157	1,032	3	755	1,790
6-2-2	Glass bevelling	3	13		13	102		7	109
6-3	Cement	1	58		58	215			215
6-4	Stone, stone powder, and lime								
6-4-1	Lime	1	5		5	70			70
6-4-2	Stone powder	3	37		37	84	8		92
6-4-3	Stone breaking	1	5		5	20			20
6-5	Crucibles								
6-5-1	Crucibles only	1	5		5	30			30
6-5-2	Crucibles and fire bricks	2	10		10	48		10	58
6-5-3	Crucibles, glassware, and fire bricks	1	40		40	300			300
6-6	Coal briquettes	6	84		84	386			386
	Total for Group VI.	44	494		494	2,851	259	797	3,907
Group VII. Building Material									
7-1	Building material	7	34		34	336		102	438
	Total for Group VII.	7	34		34	336		102	438

Code	Classification	(1) No. of Factories	(2) Male Officers	(3) Female Officers	(4) Total No. of Officers	(5) Male Workers	(6) Male Workers	(7) Child Workers	(8) Total No. of Workers
	Group VIII. Production and Transmission of Electricity and Supply of Water								
8-1	Electric and water works	3	321		321	1,020			1,020
	Total for Group VIII.	3	321		321	1,020			1,020
	Group IX. Manufacture of Chemicals and Allied Products								
9-1	Matches								
9-1-1	Matches	4	88		88	494	1,011	105	1,610
9-1-2	Shavings and splints	3	31		31	237	334	107	678
9-2	Soap								
9-2-1	Soap only	4	29		29	63	75	3	141
9-2-2	Soap, washing soda, and candles	1	15		15	24	12		36
9-3	Enamelled ware								
9-3-1	Enamelled were only	13	211	2	213	1,120	297	202	1,619
9-3-2	Enamelled ware and other products	4	58		58	594	88	48	730
9-3-3	Body of enamelled ware	2	5		5	70		6	76
9-4	Dyes, varnish, and printer's ink								
9-4-1	Varnish	3	53		53	364	16	16	396
9-4-2	Printer's ink	2	15		15	60		4	64
9-4-3	Dyes	1	18	1	19	34			34
9-5	Cosmetics	13	274	25	299	632	1,039	10	1,681
9-6	Medicine								
9-6-1	Medicine in general	6	159	2	161	187	195	6	388
9-6-2	Medicine and soap	1	84		84	280	166	5	451
9-7	Artificial resin								

Code	Classification	(1) No. of Factories	(2) Male Officers	(3) Female Officers	(4) Total No. of Officers	(5) Male Workers	(6) Female Workers	(7) Child Workers	(8) Total No. of Workers
9-7-1	Celluloid products	6	123		123	324	160	8	492
9-7-2	Beetle and bakelite	7	52		52	305	22	54	381
9-8	Acids								
9-8-1	Acids only	1	10		10	53			53
9-8-2	Acids, caustic soda, and bleaching powder	1	21		21	90		6	96
9-9	Calcium and magnesium carbonates	3	30		30	238	2		240
9-10	Oxygen and acetylene	1	1		1	22			22
9-11	Other chemical products	2	12		12	57		1	58
	Total for Group IX.	78	1,289	30	1,319	5,248	3,417	581	9,246
Group X. Textile Industries									
10-1	Cotton spinning and weaving								
10-1-1	Cotton ginning	5	73		73	129	130	42	301
10-1-2	Cotton fluffing								
10-1-2-1	Cotton fluffing only	7	43		43	363	112		475
10-1-2-2	Cotton fluffing and manufacture of other products	1	5		5	15			15
10-1-3	Cotton spinning								
10-1-3-1	Spinning only	12	384	316	700	4,705	16,918	650	23,177[1]
10-1-3-2	Spinning and weaving	16	481	437	918	6,226	26,335	458	36,579[2]
10-1-3-3	Spinning and making of cotton blankets	1	52	1	53	200	440	10	650
10-1-4	Cotton weaving								
10-1-4-1	Weaving only	69	1,278	9	1,287	3,002	5,484	241	8,727

Code	Classification	(1) No. of Factories	(2) Male Officers	(3) Female Officers	(4) Total No. of Officers	(5) Male Workers	(6) Female Workers	(7) Child Workers	(8) Total No. of Workers
10-1-4-2	Weaving and manufacture of machinery	1	54		54	247		56	303
10-1-5	Medicated gauze and cotton	3	26		26	91	36	16	143
10-2	Silk reeling and weaving								
10-2-1	Silk reeling								
10-2-1-1	Steam filature silk	49	1,167	116	1,283	953	22,606	6,169	29,728
10-2-1-2	Dupion silk	2	27		27	31	812	40	883
10-2-1-3	Silk waste	1	120		120				900(3)
10-2-2	Silk weaving	122	1,367	3	1,370	5,100	3,380	1,913	10,393
10-3	Wool spinning and weaving								
10-3-1	Wool weaving only	21	266		266	709	687	153	1,549
10-3-2	Wool spinning and weaving	2	143		143	310	400	30	740
10-3-3	Wool bowing	1	1		1	6	26		32
10-4	Spinning and weaving of waste cotton, wool, and silk	3	50		50	530	540	67	1,137
10-5	Dyeing								
10-5-1	Mercerized yarn and thread	16	80		80	679		2	681
10-5-2	Dyeing in general	30	328		328	1,241	5	125	1,371
10-5-3	Dyeing and printing of textiles	1	50		50	220	30	60	310
10-6	Printing of textiles	6	66		66	220	10	170	400
10-7	Thread making								
10-7-1	Warp and woof	4	48		48	46	318	4	368
10-7-2	Thread balls	3	31		31	63	150	6	219
10-7-3	Other kinds of thread	3	16		16	46	56		102
10-8	Making of trimmings and ribbons								

Code	Classification	(1) No. of Factories	(2) Male Officers	(3) Female Officers	(4) Total No. of Officers	(5) Male Workers	(6) Female Workers	(7) Child Workers	(8) Total No. of Workers
10-8-1	Ribbons	2	21		21	60	64		124
10-8-2	Elastic belts	3	50		50	88	51	6	145
10-8-3	Trimmings and ribbons	2	14		14	42	18		60
10-8-4	Trimmings, ribbons, and chopsticks	1	70		70	380	130		510
10-9	Cotton flannel finishing								
10-9-1	Cotton flannel finishing only	2	11		11	65			65
10-9-2	Cotton flannel finishing and dyeing and printing of textiles	2	8		8	78			78
	Total for Group X.	391	6,330	882	7,212	25,845	78,738	10,218	120,165[4]
Group XI.	Clothing Industries, Including Hosiery								
11-1	Knitted hosiery								
11-1-1	Knitted hosiery only	38	634	9	643	1,600	3,551	180	5,331
11-1-2	Knitted hosiery, underwear and sweaters, and other articles of apparel	14	313	3	316	488	1,195	44	1,727
11-2	Hats	7	57		57	272	116	76	464
11-3	Umbrellas	2	12		12	200	15	47	262
11-4	Handkerchiefs	7	77		77	115	346	5	466
11-5	Underwear and sweaters	16	310	2	312	684	1,381	107	2,172
11-6	Woollen and cotton blankets	1	10		10	3	3		6
11-7	Other articles of apparel								
11-7-1	Buttons	3	20		20	99	30	6	135
11-7-2	Scarfs, gloves, etc.	1	14		14		18	24	42
	Total for Group XI.	89	1,447	14	1,461	3,461	6,655	489	10,605

Code	Classification	(1) No. of Factories	(2) Male Officers	(3) Female Officers	(4) Total No. of Officers	(5) Male Workers	(6) Female Workers	(7) Child Workers	(8) Total No. of Workers
Group XII. Manufacture of Leather, Rubber Products, etc.									
12-1	Leather manufacturing								
12-1-1	Leather manufacturing only	9	58		58	393		21	414
12-1-2	Leather manufacturing and manufacture of glue	1	5		5	4	30	3	37
12-2	Manufacture of rubber goods	44	895	34	929	4,514*	6,638*	134*	11,286*
12-3	Manufacture of glue	1	11		11	80	15		95
Total for Group XII.		55	969	34	1,003	4,991*	6,683*	158*	11,832*
Group XIII. Preparation and Manufacture of Foods, Drinks and Tobacco									
13-1	Rice mills	1	20		20	32			32
13-2	Wheat flour mills	15	457		457	2,516			2,516
13-3	Sugar refineries	4	24		24	104	46		150
13-4	Manufactured foodstuffs								
13-4-1	Canned food	7	97		97	492	442	89	1,023
13-4-2	Bean curd products	1	2		2	39			39
13-4-3	Candies	2	14		14	41	30	11	82
13-5	Oil mills	10	212		212	2,020		6	2,026
13-6	Tea	44	126		126	1,010	1,776		2,786
13-7	Cigarettes	46	951	48	999	3,067*	14,052*	326	17,445*
13-8	Alcohol	1	6		6	31			31
13-9	Soda water and other soft drinks								
13-9-1	Soda water	1	10		10	30		2	32
13-9-2	Soda water and manufacture of ice	1	24		24	180		8	188

Code	Classification	(1) No. of Factories	(2) Male Officers	(3) Female Officers	(4) Total No. of Officers	(5) Male Workers	(6) Female Workers	(7) Child Workers	(8) Total No. of Workers
13-10	Condiments	5	96	3	99	288	144	3	435
13-11	Starch	1	6		6	60			60
13-12	Refined salt	1	9		9	100			100
13-13	Frozen egg products	1	56	2	58	150	200		350
13-14	Ice and cold storage	2	32		32	80			80
	Total for Group XIII.	143	2,142	53	2,195	10,240*	16,690*	445	27,375*

Group XIV. Manufacture of Paper, Book-Bindin and Printing

14-1	Paper manufacturing								
14-1-1	Paper	7	103		103	829	506		1,415[5]
14-1-2	Card-board	1	25		25	120	25	1	146
14-1-3	Tin foil	1	7		7	13	20		33
14-2	Printing								
14-2-1	Printing only	85	1,366	9	1,375	4,848	215	1,281	6,344
14-2-2	Printing and type casting	7	86	1	87	1,015	63	175	1,253
14-3	Paper manufactures								
14-3-1	Cartons	10	49		49	328	137	33	498
14-3-2	Cards, etc.	3	28		28	73	8	16	97
	Total for Group XIV.	114	1,664	10	1,674	7,226	974	1,506	9,786[6]

Group XV. Manufacture of Scientific and Musical Instruments Clocks and Watches, etc.

15-1	Musical instruments	2	32		32	51		10	61
15-2	Educational supplies	6	32		32	174	56	48	278
15-3	Scientific apparatus	5	52		52	227	19	72	318

Code	Classification	(1) No. of Factories	(2) Male Officers	(3) Female Officers	(4) Total No. of Officers	(5) Male Workers	(6) Female Workers	(7) Child Workers	(8) Total No. of Workers
15-4	Clocks and flash lights	1	15		15	160			160
15-5	Toys	4	30	1	31	125	78	42	245
	Total for Group XV.	18	161	1	162	737	153	172	1,062
Group XVI.	Other Manufacturing Industries								
16-1	Tooth brushes								
16-1-1	Tooth brushes only	5	79	1	80	219	349	7	575
16-1-2	Tooth brushes and tooth powder	1	6		6	40	20		60
16-2	Mirrors	4	23		23	164		73	237
16-3	Thermos bottles								
16-3-1	Whole bottle	2	50		50	142	22	98	262
16-3-2	Tin outside cover only	7	69		69	371	1	22	394
16-3-3	Vacuum bottles only	3	12		12	96		74	170
	Total for Group XVI.	22	239	1	240	1,032	392	274	1,698
	Grand Total for the Sixteen Groups	1,186	16,920	1,032	17,952	75,693*115,333*		18,266*214,736*(7)	

Notes:
(1) Including 904 persons whose sex is not known.
(2) Including 3,560 persons sex is not known.
(3) Separate figures for male, female and child workers included in this total are not available.
(4) Including 5,364 persons whose sex is not known.
(5) Including 80 persons whose sex is not known.
(6) Vide (5).
(7) Including 5,444 persons whose sex is not known.

TABLE B-IV. MOTIVE POWER

Code	Classification	(1) No. of Factories	(2) Power of Prime Movers (H.P.)	(3) Rented Electric Power (H.P.)	(4) Total (H.P.)
Group I. Woodworking Industries					
1-1	Saw mills	4	100.0	475.0	575.0
1-2	Manufacture of wooden articles				
1-2-1	Wooden boxes	1		7.0	7.0
1-2-2	Bobbins	5	105.0	55.5	160.5
	Total for Group I.	10	205.0	537.5	742.5
Group II. Furniture Manufacturing					
2-1	Steel furniture	6		205.0	205.0
2-2	Rugs and carpets	1		5.5	5.5
	Total for Group II.	7		210.5	210.5
Group III. Metal Industries					
3-1	Founding				
3-1-1	Machines and machine parts	17		92.5	92.5
3-1-2	Iron pipes	4		111.0	111.0
3-2	Steel refining	1		130.0	130.0
	Total for Group III.	22		333.5	333.5
Group IV. Manufacture of Machinery and Miscellaneous Metal Products					
4-1	Manufacture and repairing of machines				
4-1-1	Printing machines	6		64.5	64.5
4-1-2	Knitting machines	6		30.0	30.0
4-1-3	Spinning and weaving machines	13		249.5	249.5
4-1-4	Prime movers	13	100.0	151.0	251.0
4-1-5	Various kinds of machines	22		328.5	328.5
4-1-6	Machine parts				
4-1-6-1	Axes, etc.	1		5.0	5.0
4-1-6-2	Knitting needles	7	2.5	14.5	17.0
4-1-6-3	Faucets, valves, etc.	2		13.0	13.0
4-1-7	Repairing of machines and machine parts	11		77.0	77.0

Code	Classification	(1) No. of Factories	(2) Power of Prime Movers (H.P.)	(3) Rented Electric Power (H.P.)	(4) Total (H.P.)
4-2	Manufacture of metal products				
4-2-1	Boilers and water tanks	1		15.0	15.0
4-2-2	Tins				
4-2-2-1	Tins only	5		43.0	43.0
4-2-2-2	Tins and printing	4		65.0	65.0
4-2-2-3	Tins and other products	4		115.5	115.5
4-2-3	Aluminumware	4		338.5	338.5
4-2-4	Nails				
4-2-4-1	Nails only	4		95.0	95.0
4-2-4-2	Nails and other products	2		375.0	375.0
4-2-5	Lamps	3		38.0	38.0
4-2-6	Copper sheets	4		726.0	726.0
4-2-7	Iron bars	1		160.0	160.0
4-2-8	Other metal products	5		47.5	47.5
4-3	Manufacture of electric machines and apparatus				
4-3-1	Electric machines and apparatus	3		111.0	111.0
4-3-2	Electric machines and dry batteries	1		8.0	8.0
4-3-3	Electric fans, heaters, utensils, etc.	5	25.0	602.5	627.5
4-3-4	Electric supplies	4		41.5	41.5
4-3-5	Electric supplies and other products	2		36.0	36.0
4-3-6	Electric light bulbs	13		190.5	190.5
4-3-7	Neon light tubes	1		5.0	5.0
4-3-8	Dry batteries	3		35.0	35.0
4-3-9	Dry batteries and flash lights	1		10.0	10.0
4-3-10	Flash lights	8		109.5	109.5
4-3-11	Electric welding	1		20.0	20.0
4-4	Foundry works				
4-4-1	Spinning and weaving machines	3		40.0	40.0

Code	Classification	(1) No. of Factories	(2) Power of Prime Movers (H.P.)	(3) Rented Electric Power (H.P.)	(4) Total (H.P.)
4-4-2	Various kinds of machines	3		45.0	45.0
4-4-3	Metal products	1		5.0	5.0
	Total for Group IV.	167	127.5	4,210.5	4,338.0
Group V. Construction of Boats, Ships and Vehicles for Land Transportation					
5-1	Shipbuilding				
5-1-1	Construction of ships	1	900.0	1,230.0	2,130.0
5-1-2	Construction of ships and other instruments of transportation	5	69.0	211.0	280.0
5-1-3	Repairing of ships	7	135.0	111.0	246.0
5-2	Building of cars				
5-2-1	Railway workshops	1	400.0	*	400.0*
5-2-2	Bicycles	1		9.0	9.0
5-2-3	Charcoal gas trucks	1	10.0		10.0
	Total for Group V.	16	1,514.0	1,561.0*	3,075.0*
Group VI. Manufacture of Bricks, Earthenware, Glass, etc.					
6-1	Bricks and tiles				
6-1-1	Bricks and tiles in general	2	235.0		235.0
6-1-2	Glazed tiles	2		105.0	105.0
6-2	Glass				
6-2-1	Glassware	21	0.5	114.0*	114.5*
6-2-2	Glass bevelling	3		25.0	25.0
6-3	Cement	1	2,060.0		2,060.0
6-4	Stone, stone powder and lime				
6-4-1	Lime	1		5.0	5.0
6-4-2	Stone powder	3		340.0	340.0
6-4-3	Stone breaking	1		10.0	10.0
6-5	Crucibles				
6-5-1	Crucibles only	1		15.0	15.0
6-5-2	Crucibles and fire bricks	2		44.0	44.0
6-5-3	Crucibles, glassware, and fire bricks	1		150.0	150.0

Code	Classification	(1) No. of Factories	(2) Power of Prime Movers (H.P.)	(3) Rented Electric Power (H.P.)	(4) Total (H.P.)
6-6	Coal briquettes	6	256.0	234.5	490.5
	Total for Group VI.	44	2,551.5	1,042.5*	3,594.0*
Group VII. Building Material					
7-1	Building material	7		58.0*	58.0*
	Total for Group VII.	7		58.0*	58.0*
Group VIII. Production and Transmission of Electricity and Supply of Water					
8-1	Electric and water works	3	48,666.7	1,512.9	50,179.6
	Total for Group VIII.	3	48,666.7	1,512.9	50,179.6
Group IX. Manufacture of Chemicals and Allied Products					
9-1	Matches				
9-1-1	Matches	4	84.0	167.5	251.5
9-1-2	Shavings and splints	3	134.0	80.5	214.5
9-2	Soap				
9-2-1	Soap only	4	40.0	42.0	82.0
9-2-2	Soap, washing soda, and candles	1		5.0	5.0
9-3	Enamelled ware				
9-3-1	Enamelled ware only	13	70.0	404.0	474.0
9-3-2	Enamelled ware and other products	4	130.0	260.0	390.0
9-3-3	Body of enamelled ware	2		63.0	63.0
9-4	Dyes, varnish, and printer's ink				
9-4-1	Varnish	3		982.0	982.0
9-4-2	Printer's ink	2		115.0	115.0
9-4-3	Dyes	1		35.0	35.0
9-5	Cosmetics	13		615.0	615.0
9-6	Medicine				
9-6-1	Medicine in general	6	30.0	98.2	128.2
9-6-2	Medicine and soap	1	50.0	200.0	250.0
9-7	Artificial resin				

Code	Classification	(1) No. of Factories	(2) Power of Prime Movers (H.P.)	(3) Rented Electric Power (H.P.)	(4) Total (H.P.)
9-7-1	Celluloid products	6	300.0	303.0	603.0
9-7-2	Beetle and bakelite	7		61.5	61.5
9-8	Acids				
9-8-1	Acids only	1	24.0	57.0	81.0
9-8-2	Acids, caustic soda, and bleaching powder	1		*	*
9-9	Calcium and magnesium carbonates	3		267.0	267.0
9-10	Oxygen and acetylene	1		90.0	90.0
9-11	Other chemical products	2		30.0	30.0
	Total for Group IX.	78	862.0	3,875.7*	4,737.7*
Group X.	Textile Industries				
10-1	Cotton spinning and weaving				
10-1-1	Cotton ginning	5	275.0	40.0	315.0
10-1-2	Cotton fluffing				
10-1-2-1	Cotton fluffing only	7	60.0	600.0	660.0
10-1-2-2	Cotton fluffing and manufacture of other products	1		36.0	36.0
10-1-3	Cotton spinning				
10-1-3-1	Spinning only	12	7,270.0	21,193.5	28,463.5
10-1-3-2	Spinning and weaving	16	2,332.0	30,518.2	32,850.2
10-1-3-3	Spinning and making of cotton blankets	1		550.0	550.0
10-1-4	Cotton weaving				
10-1-4-1	Weaving only	69	165.0	4,157.8	4,322.8
10-1-4-2	Weaving and manufacture of machinery	1		70.0	70.0
10-1-5	Medicated gauze and cotton	3		50.5	50.5
10-2	Silk reeling and weaving				
10-2-1	Silk reeling				
10-2-1-1	Steam filature silk	49	983.5	165.5	1,149.0
10-2-1-2	Dupion silk	2	140.0		140.0
10-2-1-3	Silk waste	1	150.0		150.0

Code	Classification	(1) No. of Factories	(2) Power of Prime Movers (H.P.)	(3) Rented Electric Power (H.P.)	(4) Total (H.P.)
10-2-2	Silk weaving	122	290.0	2,641.5	2,931.5
10-3	Wool spinning and weaving				
10-3-1	Wool weaving only	21		491.5*	491.5*
10-3-2	Wool spinning and weaving	2	250.0	380.0	630.0
10-3-3	Wool bowing	1		15.0	15.0
10-4	Spinning and weaving of waste cotton, wool, and silk	3		670.0	670.0
10-5	Dyeing				
10-5-1	Mercerized yarn and thread	16		116.0	116.0
10-5-2	Dyeing in general	30		662.5	662.5
10-5-3	Dyeing and printing of textiles	1		300.0	300.0
10-6	Printing of textiles	6	140.0	18.5	158.5
10-7	Thread making				
10-7-1	Warp and woof	4		183.0	183.0
10-7-2	Thread balls	3		72.0	72.0
10-7-3	Other kinds of thread	3		53.0	53.0
10-8	Making of trimmings and ribbons				
10-8-1	Ribbons	2		48.0	48.0
10-8-2	Elastic belts	3		24.0	24.0
10-8-3	Trimmings and ribbons	2		16.0	16.0
10-8-4	Trimmings, ribbons, and chopsticks	1		200.0	200.0
10-9	Cotton flannel finishing				
10-9-1	Cotton flannel finishing only	2		85.0	85.0
10-9-2	Cotton flannel finishing and dyeing and printing of textiles	2		48.0	48.0
	Total for Group X.	391	12,055.5	63,405.5*	75,461.0*

Code	Classification	(1) No. of Factories	(2) Power of Prime Movers (H.P.)	(3) Rented Electric Power (H.P.)	(4) Total (H.P.)
Group XI. Clothing Industries, Including Hosiery					
11-1	Knitted hosiery				
11-1-1	Knitted hosiery only	38		714.0*	714.0*
11-1-2	Knitted hosiery, underwear and sweaters, and other articles of apparel	14		107.7*	107.7*
11-2	Hats	7		197.0	197.0
11-3	Umbrellas	2		52.5	52.5
11-4	Hankerchiefs	7		34.5	34.5
11-5	Underwear and sweaters	16	1.5	568.5	570.0
11-6	Woolen and cotton blankets	1		3.0	3.0
11-7	Other articles of apparel				
11-7-1	Buttons	3		26.0	26.0
11-7-2	Scarfs, gloves, etc.	1		7.5	7.5
	Total for Group XI.	89	1.5	1,710.7*	1,712.2*
Group XII. Manufacture of Leather, Rubber Products, etc.					
12-1	Leather manufacturing				
12-1-1	Leather manufacturing only	9	110.0	284.0	394.0
12-1-2	Leather manufacturing and manufacture of glue	1	47.0	23.0	70.0
12-2	Manufacture of rubber goods	44	415.0	6,498.2*	6,913.2*
12-3	Manufacture of glue	1	32.0	70.0	102.0
	Total for Group XII.	55	604.0	6,875.2*	7,479.2*
Group XIII. Preparation and Manufacture of Foods, Drinks, and Tobacco					
13-1	Rice mills	1		60.0	60.0
13-2	Wheat flour mills	15		12,235.0	12,235.0
13-3	Sugar refineries	4		326.5	326.5
13-4	Manufactured foodstuffs				

Code	Classification	(1) No. of Factories	(2) Power of Prime Movers (H.P.)	(3) Rented Electric Power (H.P.)	(4) Total (H.P.)
13-4-1	Canned food	7	60.0	262.0	322.0
13-4-2	Bean curd products	1		6.0	6.0
13-4-3	Candies	2		25.0	25.0
13-5	Oil mills	10	881.0	896.4	1,777.4
13-6	Tea	44		204.0	204.0
13-7	Cigarettes	46	25.0	2,898.5	2,923.5
13-8	Alcohol	1	7.0	23.0	30.0
13-9	Soda water and other soft drinks				
13-9-1	Soda water	1		8.0	8.0
13-9-2	Soda water and manufacture of ice	1	3.0	80.0	83.0
13-10	Condiments	5	30.0	155.0	185.0
13-11	Starch	1		90.0	90.0
13-12	Refined salt	1		15.0	15.0
13-13	Frozen egg products	1		200.0	200.0
13-14	Ice and cold storage	2		80.0*	80.0*
	Total for Group XIII.	143	1,006.0	17,564.4*	18,570.4*
Group XIV. Manufacture of Paper, Book-Binding and Printing					
14-1	Paper manufacturing				
14-1-1	Paper	7	2,677.0	1,757.0	4,434.0
14-1-2	Card-board	1		600.0	600.0
14-1-3	Tin foil	1		8.0	8.0
14-2	Printing				
14-2-1	Printing only	85		2,396.7*	2,396.7*
14-2-2	Printing and type casting	7		503.5	503.5
14-3	Paper manufactures				
14-3-1	Cartons	10		63.0	63.0
14-3-2	Cards, etc.	3		34.0	34.0
	Total for Group XIV.	114	2,677.0	5,362.2*	8,039.2*
Group XV. Manufacture of Scientific and Musical Instruments, Clocks and Watches, etc.					

Code	Classification	(1) No. of Factories	(2) Power of Prime Movers (H.P.)	(3) Rented Electric Power (H.P.)	(4) Total (H.P.)
15-1	Musical instruments	2		20.0	20.0
15-2	Educational supplies	6		53.0	53.0
15-3	Scientific apparatus	5		45.5	45.5
15-4	Clocks and flash lights	1		15.0	15.0
15-5	Toys	4		22.4	22.4
	Total for Group XV.	18		155.9	155.9
Group XVI. Other Manufacturing Industries					
16-1	Tooth brushes				
16-1-1	Tooth brushes only	5		113.5	113.5
16-1-2	Tooth brushes and tooth powder	1		35.0	35.0
16-2	Mirrors	4		73.0	73.0
16-3	Thermos bottles				
16-3-1	Whole bottle	2	24.0	55.0	79.0
16-3-2	Tin outside cover only	7		78.0	78.0
16-3-3	Vacuum bottles only	3		12.0	12.0
	Total for Group XVI.	22	24.0	366.5	390.5
	Grand Total for the Sixteen Groups	1,186	70,294.7	108,782.5*	179,077.2*

TABLE B-V. SALARIES AND WAGES

Code	Classification	(1) No. of Factories	(2) Maximum Rate of Salaries per Month $	(3) Minimum Rate of Salaries per Month $	(4) Maximum Rate of Wages per Month $	(5) Minimum Rate of Wages per Month $
Group I. Woodworking Industries						
1-1	Saw mills	4	45.00	8.00	51.00	0
1-2	Manufacture of wooden articles					
1-2-1	Wooden boxes	1	40.00	15.00	15.00	8.00
1-2-2	Bobbins	5	60.00	10.00	48.00	1.00
	Totals and Maxima and Minima for Group I.	10	60.00	8.00	51.00	0
Group II. Furniture Manufacturing						
2-1	Steel furniture	6	80.00	0.40	60.00	0
2-2	Rugs and carpets	1	26.00	5.00	26.00	2.00
	Totals and Maxima and Minima for Group II.	7	80.00	0.40	60.00	0
Group III. Metal Industries						
3-1	Founding					
3-1-1	Machines and machine parts	17	60.00	2.00	50.00	0.40
3-1-2	Iron pipes	4	60.00	10.00	36.00	0.40
3-2	Steel refining	1	80.00	50.00	50.00	15.00
	Totals and Maxima and Minima for Group III.	22	80.00	2.00	50.00	0.40
Group IV. Manufacture of Machinery and Miscellaneous Metal Products						
4-1	Manufacture and repairing of machines					
4-1-1	Printing machines	6	120.00	1.50	60.00	0
4-1-2	Knitting machines	6	50.00	0	80.00	0
4-1-3	Spinning and weaving machines	13	80.00	0	60.00	0
4-1-4	Prime movers	13	132.00	9.00	70.00	0
4-1-5	Various kinds of machines	22	140.00	7.00	70.00	0
4-1-6	Machine parts					

Code	Classification	(1) No. of Factories	(2) Maximum Rate of Salaries per Month $	(3) Minimum Rate of Salaries per Month $	(4) Maximum Rate of Wages per Month $	(5) Minimum Rate of Wages per Month $
4-1-6-1	Axes, etc.	1	45.00	10.00	45.00	0.50
4-1-6-2	Knitting needles	7	40.00	10.00	58.00	0.60
4-1-6-3	Faucets, valves, etc.	2	18.00	12.00	30.00	0.20
4-1-7	Repairing of machines and machine parts	11	130.00	10.00	60.00	0
4-2	Manufacture of metal products					
4-2-1	Boilers and water tanks	1	45.00	15.00	60.00	0
4-2-2	Tins					
4-2-2-1	Tins only	5	50.00	10.00	35.00	0
4-2-2-2	Tins and printing	4	60.00	2.00	80.00	0
4-2-2-3	Tins and other products	4	45.00	0	80.00	0.40
4-2-3	Aluminumware	4	60.00	0	65.00	1.00
4-2-4	Nails					
4-2-4-1	Nails only	4	90.00	0.40	70.00	0
4-2-4-2	Nails and other products	2	65.00	4.00	65.00	3.00
4-2-5	Lamps	3	20.00	0	50.00	0
4-2-6	Copper sheets	4	80.00	20.00	120.00	0.50
4-2-7	Iron bars	1	60.00	5.00	40.00	10.00
4-2-8	Other metal products	5	50.00	2.00	70.00	0.60
4-3	Manufacture of electric machines and apparatus					
4-3-1	Electric machines and apparatus	3	150.00	12.00	45.00	0
4-3-2	Electric machines and dry batteries	1	66.60	66.60	66.60	10.50
4-3-3	Electric fans, heaters, utensils, etc.	5	200.00	15.00	50.00	0.40
4-3-4	Electric supplies	4	100.00	1.00	60.00	1.00
4-3-5	Electric supplies and other products	2	50.00	1.00	45.00	0.40
4-3-6	Electric light bulbs	13	200.00	2.50	65.00	0
4-3-7	Neon light tubes	1	70.00	10.00	85.00	15.00
4-3-8	Dry batteries	3	40.00	8.00	30.00	1.00
4-3-9	Dry batteries and flash					

Code	Classification	(1) No. of Factories	(2) Maximum Rate of per Month $	(3) Minimum Rate of Salaries per Month $	(4) Maximum Rate of Wages per Month $	(5) Minimum Rate of Wages per Month $
	lights	1	60.00	20.00	40.00	6.00
4-3-10	Flash lights	8	80.00	10.00	80.00	0.50
4-3-11	Electric welding	1	70.00	15.00	90.00	9.00
4-4	Foundry works					
4-4-1	Spinning and weaving machines	3	100.00	1.00	40.00	0.40
4-4-2	Various kinds of machines	3	100.00	18.00	45.00	0
4-4-3	Metal products	1	10.00	0	8.00	0
	Totals and Maxima and Minima for Group IV.	167	200.00	0	120.00	0
Group V. Construction of Boats, Ships and Vehicles for Land Transportation						
5-1	Shipbuilding					
5-1-1	Construction of ships	1	*	20.00	100.00	9.00
5-1-2	Construction of ships and other instruments of transportation	5	100.00	1.00	60.00	1.00
5-1-3	Repairing of ships	7	150.00	5.00	70.00	0
5-2	Building of cars					
5-2-1	Railway workshops	1	124.00	62.00	100.00	6.00
5-2-2	Bicycles	1	50.00	8.00	40.00	6.00
5-2-3	Charcoal gas trucks	1	50.00	25.00	60.00	9.00
	Totals and Maxima and Minima for Group V.	16	150.00	1.00	100.00	0
Group VI. Manufacture of Bricks, Earthenware, Glass, etc.						
6-1	Bricks and tiles					
6-1-1	Bricks and tiles in general	2	80.00	10.00	18.00	2.00
6-1-2	Glazed tiles	2	40.00	3.00	40.00	6.00
6-2	Glass					
6-2-1	Glassware	21	120.00	0	80.00	1.00
6-2-2	Glass bevelling	3	60.00	10.00	50.00	1.00
6-3	Cement	1	*	18.00	65.00	15.00

Code	Classification	(1) No. of Factories	(2) Maximum Rate of Salaries per Month $	(3) Minimum Rate of Salaries per Month $	(4) Maximum Rate of Wages per Month $	(5) Minimum Rate of Wages per Month $
6-4	Stone, stone powder, and lime					
6-4-1	Lime	1	30.00	7.00	24.00	20.00
6-4-2	Stone powder	3	50.00	14.00	24.00	7.00
6-4-3	Stone breaking	1	15.00	1.00	8.00	3.00
6-5	Crucibles					
6-5-1	Crucibles only	1	40.00	15.00	40.00	15.00
6-5-2	Crucibles and fire bricks	2	80.00	2.00	45.00	1.00
6-5-3	Crucibles, glassware, and fire bricks	1	100.00	8.00	60.00	2.00
6-6	Coal briquettes	6	120.00	2.00	54.00	8.00
	Totals and Maxima and Minima for Group VI.	*44*	*120.00*	*0*	*80.00*	*1.00*
Group VII. Building Material						
7-1	Building material	7	60.00	0	60.00	0
	Totals and Maxima and Minima for Group VII.	*7*	*60.00*	*0*	*60.00*	*0*
Group VIII. Production and Transmission of Electricity and Supply of Water						
8-1	Electric and water works	3	210.00	14.00	107.00	11.00
	Totals and Maxima and Minima for Group VIII.	*3*	*210.00*	*14.00*	*107.00*	*11.00*
Group IX. Manufacture of Chemicals and Allied Products						
9-1	Matches					
9-1-1	Matches	4	150.00	3.00	45.00	0
9-1-2	Shavings and splints	3	60.00	10.00	60.00	4.00
9-2	Soap					
9-2-1	Soap only	4	100.00	0.50	30.00	0
9-2-2	Soap, washing soda, and candles	1	60.00	1.00	20.00	6.00
9-3	Enamelled ware					
9-3-1	Enamelled ware only	13	160.00	0	54.00	0
9-3-2	Enamelled ware and					

Code	Classification	(1) No. of Factories	(2) Maximum Rate of Salaries per Month $	(3) Minimum Rate of Salaries per Month $	(4) Maximum Rate of Wages per Month $	(5) Minimum Rate of Wages per Month $
	other products	4	100.00	2.00	60.00	1.00
9-3-3	Body of enamelled ware	2	45.00	12.00	40.00	0.70
9-4	Dyes, varnish, and printer's ink					
9-4-1	Varnish	3	180.00	5.00	50.00	0
9-4-2	Printer's ink	2	160.00	10.00	25.00	1.00
9-4-3	Dyes	1	45.00	2.00	33.00	16.50
9-5	Cosmetics	13	100.00	1.00	80.00	5.00
9-6	Medicine					
9-6-1	Medicine in general	6	55.00	1.00	30.00	6.00
9-6-2	Medicine and soap	1	*	15.00	45.00	6.00
9-7	Artificial resin					
9-7-1	Celluloid products	6	120.00	0	40.00	7.00
9-7-2	Beetle and bakelite	7	100.00	1.00	60.00	0.40
9-8	Acids					
9-8-1	Acids only	1	*	50.00	35.00	15.00
9-8-2	Acids, caustic soda, and bleaching powder	1	*	40.00	65.00	2.00
9-9	Calcium and magnesium carbonates	3	80.00	12.00	36.00	10.00
9-10	Oxygen and acetylene	1	450.00	450.00	70.00	60.00
9-11	Other chemical products	2	40.00	14.00	20.00	1.00
	Totals and Maxima and Minima for Group IX.	78	450.00	0	80.00	0
Group X. Textile Industries						
10-1	Cotton spinning and weaving					
10-1-1	Cotton ginning	5	24.00	1.00	36.00	5.00
10-1-2	Cotton fluffing					
10-1-2-1	Cotton fluffing only	7	60.00	0.40	24.00	4.50
10-1-2-2	Cotton fluffing and manufacture of other products	1	20.00	8.00	12.00	12.00
10-1-3	Cotton spinning					
10-1-3-1	Spinning only	12	280.00	4.00	70.00	2.24
10-1-3-2	Spinning and weaving	16	150.00	6.00	65.00	5.60
10-1-3-3	Spinning and mak-					

Code	Classification	(1) No. of Factories	(2) Maximum Rate of Salaries per Month $	(3) Minimum Rate of Salaries per Month $	(4) Maximum Rate of Wages per Month $	(5) Minimum Rate of Wages per Month $
	ing of cotton blankets	1	140.00	6.00	40.00	8.00
10-1-4	Cotton weaving					
10-1-4-1	Weaving only	69	200.00	0	70.00	0
10-1-4-2	Weaving and manufacture of machinery	1	200.00	0	60.00	2.00
10-1-5	Medicated gauze and cotton	3	50.00	1.00	30.00	4.00
10-2	Silk reeling and weaving					
10-2-1	Silk reeling					
10-2-1-1	Steam filature silk	49	52.00	4.00	32.00	4.00
10-2-1-2	Dupion silk	2	36.00	4.00	16.00	4.50
10-2-1-3	Silkwaste	1	200.00	20.00	60.00	9.00
10-2-2	Silk weaving	122	150.00	0	140.00	0
10-3	Wool spinning and weaving					
10-3-1	Wool weaving only	21	100.00	0	60.00	0
10-3-2	Wool spinning and weaving	2	50.00	5.00	60.00	9.00
10-3-3	Wool bowing	1	12.00	12.00	30.00	6.00
10-4	Spinning and weaving of waste cotton, wool, and silk	3	150.00	12.00	60.00	6.00
10-5	Dyeing					
10-5-1	Mercerized yarn and thread	16	65.00	1.00	30.00	0
10-5-2	Dyeing in general	30	120.00	2.00	60.00	0
10-5-3	Dyeing and printing of textiles	1	*	12.00	18.00	3.00
10-6	Printing of textiles	6	60.00	5.00	80.00	2.00
10-7	Thread making					
10-7-1	Warp and woof	4	100.00	2.00	25.00	1.00
10-7-2	Thread balls	3	30.00	1.00	30.00	1.00
10-7-3	Other kinds of thread	3	30.00	0.80	16.00	5.00
10-8	Making of trimmings and ribbons					
10-8-1	Ribbons	2	40.00	14.00	25.00	3.00

Code	Classification	(1) No. of Factories	(2) Maximum Rate of Salaries per Month $	(3) Minimum Rate of Salaries per Month $	(4) Maximum Rate of Wages per Month $	(5) Minimum Rate of Wages per Month $
10-8-2	Elastic belts	3	30.00	4.00	46.00	1.00
10-8-3	Trimmings and ribbons	2	30.00	8.00	16.00	3.00
10-8-4	Trimmings, ribbons, and chopsticks	1	130.00	12.00	60.00	10.00
10-9	Cotton flannel finishing					
10-9-1	Cotton flannel finishing only	2	40.00	1.00	24.00	10.00
10-9-2	Cotton flannel finishing and dyeing and printing of textiles	2	30.00	1.00	30.00	5.00
	Totals and Maxima and Minima for Group X.	*391*	*280.00*	*0*	*140.00*	*0*
Group XI. Clothing Industries Including Hosiery						
11-1	Knitted hosiery					
11-1-1	Knitted hosiery only	38	120.00	0.50	80.00	0
11-1-2	Knitted hosiery, underwear and sweaters, and other articles of apparel	14	100.00	0	60.00	0
11-2	Hats	7	60.00	1.00	40.00	0
11-3	Umbrellas	2	40.00	2.00	60.00	1.00
11-4	Handkerchiefs	7	80.00	3.00	40.00	1.00
11-5	Underwear and sweaters	16	150.00	1.00	60.00	0.40
11-6	Woollen and cotton blankets	1	45.00	2.00	35.00	6.00
11-7	Other articles of apparel					
11-7-1	Buttons	3	20.00	3.00	36.00	0
11-7-2	Scarfs, gloves, etc.	1	60.00	10.00	30.00	7.50
	Totals and Maxima and Minima for Group XI.	89	150.00	0	80.00	0
Group XII. Manufacture of Leather, Rubber Products, etc.						
12-1	Leather manufacturing					
12-1-1	Leather manufacturing only	9	150.00	6.00	60.00	0

Code	Classification	(1) No. of Factories	(2) Maximum Rate of Salaries per Month $	(3) Minimum Rate of Salaries per Month $	(4) Maximum Rate of Wages per Month $	(5) Minimum Rate of Wages per Month $
12-1-2	Leather manufacturing and manufacture of glue	1	50.00	20.00	55.00	4.00
12-2	Manufacture of rubber goods	44	150.00	0	60.00	1.00
12-3	Manufacture of glue	1	150.00	14.00	33.00	5.00
	Totals and Maxima and Minima for Group XII.	55	*150.00*	*0*	*60.00*	*0*
Group XIII.	Preparation and Manufacture of Foods, Drinks, and Tobacco					
13-1	Rice mills	1	30.00	1.00	16.00	10.00
13-2	Wheat flour mills	15	100.00	1.00	120.00	6.00
13-3	Sugar refineries	4	80.00	15.00	30.00	6.50
13-4	Manufactured foodstuffs					
13-4-1	Canned food	7	100.00	6.00	60.00	0
13-4-2	Bean curd products	1	16.00	14.00	9.00	7.50
13-4-3	Candies	2	40.00	1.00	30.00	1.00
13-5	Oil mills	10	130.00	1.00	100.00	0
13-6	Tea	44	34.50	4.00	37.50	2.81
13-7	Cigarettes	46	100.00	0	70.00	1.00
13-8	Alcohol	1	30.00	12.00	12.00	12.00
13-9	Soda water and other soft drinks					
13-9-1	Soda water	1	100.00	30.00	50.00	10.00
13-9-2	Soda water and manufacture of ice	1	*	18.00	50.00	10.00
13-10	Condiments	5	120.00	16.00	45.00	6.00
13-11	Starch	1	100.00	10.00	40.00	13.00
13-12	Refined salt	1	100.00	30.00	20.00	14.00
13-13	Frozen egg products	1	*	12.00	23.80	12.60
13-14	Ice and cold storage	2	80.00	14.00	64.00	10.00
	Totals and Maxima and Minima for Group XIII.	*143*	*120.00*	*0*	*120.00*	*0*
Group XIV.	Manufacture of Paper, Book-Binding and Printing					
14-1	Paper manufacturing					

Code	Classification	(1) No. of Factories	(2) Maximum Rate of Salaries per Month $	(3) Minimum Rate of Salaries per Month $	(4) Maximum Rate of Wages per Month $	(5) Minimum Rate of Wages per Month $
14-1-1	Paper	7	160.00	3.00	70.00	8.00
14-1-2	Card-board	1	120.00	18.00	60.00	9.00
14-1-3	Tin foil	1	20.00	6.00	30.00	5.00
14-2	Printing					
14-2-1	Printing only	85	200.00	0	180.00	0
14-2-2	Printing and type casting	7	170.00	10.00	100.00	0.50
14-3	Paper manufactures					
14-3-1	Cartons	10	50.00	5.00	42.00	0.40
14-3-2	Cards, etc.	3	100.00	6.00	40.00	1.00
	Totals and Maxima and Minima for Group XIV.	114	200.00	0	180.00	0
Group XV. Manufacture of Scientific and Musical Instruments, Clocks and Watches. etc.						
15-1	Musical instruments	2	25.00	10.00	63.00	0.40
15-2	Educational supplies	6	170.00	8.00	64.00	0
15-3	Scientific apparatus	5	120.00	8.00	50.00	0
15-4	Clocks and flash lights	1	120.00	10.00	80.00	10.00
15-5	Toys	4	80.00	0	40.00	0.60
	Totals and Maxima and Minima for Group XV.	18	170.00	0	80.00	0
Group XVI. Other Manufacturing Industries						
16-1	Tooth brushes					
16-1-1	Tooth brushes only	5	100.00	1.00	76.00	1.00
16-1-2	Tooth brushes and tooth powder	1	60.00	12.00	40.00	8.00
16-2	Mirrors	4	60.00	6.00	36.00	0
16-3	Thermos bottles					
16-3-1	Whole bottle	2	125.00	2.00	55.00	2.00
16-3-2	Tin outside cover only	7	80.00	0	45.00	0.40
16-3-3	Vacuum bottles only	3	50.00	5.00	130.00	1.00
	Totals and Maxima and Minima for Group XVI.	22	125.00	0	130.00	0
	Grand Totals and Maxima and Minima for the Sixteen Groups	1,186	450.00	0	180.00	0

TABLE B-VI. OPERATING TIME AND AVERAGE NUMBER OF YEARS AND MONTHS IN OPERATION

Code	Classification	(1) No. of Factories	(2) No. of Operating Hours per Day	(3) No. of Rest Days per Month (1)	(4) No. of Holidays per Year	(5) Average No. of Years & Months in Operation (2)
Group I. Woodworking Industries						
1-1	Saw mills	4	9.9	2.0	12.5	15/ 9
1-2	Manufacture of wooden articles					
1-2-1	Wooden boxes	1	10.0	0	9.0	6/
1-2-2	Bobbins	5	12.0	2.2	9.0	8/ 9
	Totals and Averages for Group I.	10	10.9	1.9	10.7	11/ 4
Group II. Furniture Manufacturing						
2-1	Steel furniture	6	10.3	0.6	15.0	8/10
2-2	Rugs and carpets	1	10.0	*	7.0	36/
	Totals and Averages for Group II.	7	10.3	0.6	11.0	12/ 9
Group III. Metal Industries						
3-1	Founding					
3-1-1	Machines and machine parts	17	10.6	0	10.1	10/ 4
3-1-2	Iron pipes	4	8.9	0	7.6	12/ 8
3-2	Steel refining	1	8.0	4.0	7.0	2/ 7
	Totals and Averages for Group III.	22	10.1	0.2	9.2	10/ 4
Group IV. Manufacture of Machinery and Miscellaneous Metal Products						
4-1	Manufacture and repairing of machines					
4-1-1	Printing machines	6	10.3	1.3	8.7	17/ 4
4-1-2	Knitting machines	6	10.2	0.3	9.0	20/ 3
4-1-3	Spinning and weaving machines	13	10.8	1.0	8.1	18/ 4
4-1-4	Prime movers	13	10.0	0.5	9.3	14/ 3

Code	Classification	(1) No. of Factories	(2) No. of Operating Hours per Day	(3) No. of Rest Days per Month	(4) No. of Holidays per Year	(5) Average No. of Years & Months in Operation
4-1-5	Various kinds of machines	22	10.3	0.4	9.9	11/ 5
4-1-6	Machine parts					
4-1-6-1	Axes, etc.	1	10.0	0	*	30/
4-1-6-2	Knitting needles	7	11.1	2.0	15.0	2/ 8
4-1-6-3	Faucets, valves, etc.	2	9.5	0	*	6/10
4-1-7	Repairing of machines and machine parts	11	10.9	0.6	9.0	15/ 5
4-2	Manufacture of metal products					
4-2-1	Boilers and water tanks	1	9.0	0	6.0	14/ 2
4-2-2	Tins					
4-2-2-1	Tins only	5	11.7	1.3	10.0	11/ 7
4-2-2-2	Tins and printing	4	10.6	2.0	9.7	7/ 9
4-2-2-3	Tins and other products	4	9.9	2.5	10.0	5/10
4-2-3	Aluminumware	4	9.5	1.0	10.0	5/11
4-2-4	Nails					
4-2-4-1	Nails only	4	12.2	1.5	6.2	5/ 5
4-2-4-2	Nails and other products	2	19.0	3.0	7.5	6/ 7
4-2-5	Lamps	3	11.0	1.3	10.0	14/
4-2-6	Copper sheets	4	9.5	2.0	11.6	2/ 3
4-2-7	Iron bars	1	12.0	0	30.0	1/ 4
4-2-8	Other metal products	5	9.9	1.5	15.0	1/11
4-3	Manufacture of electric machines and apparatus					
4-3-1	Electric machines and apparatus	3	9.5	1.3	8.0	9/ 4
4-3-2	Electric machines and dry batteries	1	8.0	4.0	7.0	7/
4-3-3	Electric fans, heaters, utensils, etc.	5	10.0	1.5	10.7	12/ 3
4-3-4	Electric supplies	4	10.2	1.5	7.5	3/ 9

Code	Classification	(1) No. of Factories	(2) No. of Operating Hours per Day	(3) No. of Rest Days per Month	(4) No. of Holidays per Year	(5) Average No. of Years & Months in Operation
4-3-5	Electric supplies and other products	2	9.5	0	12.5	6/
4-3-6	Electric light bulbs	13	10.1	2.2	8.2	2/ 1
4-3-7	Neon light tubes	1	8.0	4.0	7.0	3/ 6
4-3-8	Dry batteries	3	9.8	0.7	13.3	4/ 4
4-3-9	Dry batteries and flash lights	1	8.0	2.0	20.0	5/
4-3-10	Flash lights	8	10.8	0.6	16.7	4/ 2
4-3-11	Electric welding	1	*	*	*	15/ 3
4-4	Foundry works					
4-4-1	Spinning and weaving machines	3	9.8	0	12.0	22/ 5
4-4-2	Various kinds of machines	3	9.3	1.0	7.0	7/10
4-4-3	Metal products	1	10.0	0	10.0	5/
	Totals and Averages for Group IV.	*167*	*10.4*	*1.1*	*10.0*	*10/ 1*
Group V. Construction of Boats, Ships and Vehicles for Land Transportation						
5-1	Shipbuilding					
5-1-1	Construction of ships	1	13.0	4.0	*	69/
5-1-2	Construction of ships and other instruments of transportation	5	9.8	0	10.0	12/
5-1-3	Repairing of ships	7	10.2	0	5.5	19/ 6
5-2	Building of cars					
5-2-1	Railway workshops	1	10.0	4.0	7.0	27/
5-2-2	Bicycles	1	8.0	4.0	*	3/ 2
5-2-3	Charcoal gas trucks	1	10.0	2.0	15.0	/5
	Totals and Averages for Group V.	*16*	*10.1*	*0.9*	*8.4*	*18/ 5*
Group VI. Manufacture of Bricks, Earthenware, Glass, etc.						
6-1	Bricks and tiles					

Code	Classification	(1) No. of Factories	(2) No. of Operating Hours per Day	(3) No. of Rest Days per Month	(4) No. of Holidays per Year	(5) Average No. of Years & Months in Operation
6-1-1	Bricks and tiles in general	2	9.7	1.0	*	8/ 4
6-1-2	Glazed tiles	2	12.0	4.0	3.0	2/ 4
6-2	Glass					
6-2-1	Glassware	21	9.7	0.6	13.7	6/ 4
6-2-2	Glass bevelling	3	9.5	2.0	8.5	5/ 8
6-3	Cement	1	21.0	4.0	7.0	10/ 4
6-4	Stone, stone powder, and lime					
6-4-1	Lime	1	24.0	6.0	*	12/
6-4-2	Stone powder	3	11.5	2.3	8.0	7/ 5
6-4-3	Stone breaking	1	10.0	0	*	71/
6-5	Crucibles					
6-5-1	Crucibles only	1	10.0	2.0	10.0	/11
6-5-2	Crucibles and fire bricks	2	8.5	2.0	19.5	1/ 3
6-5-3	Crucibles, glassware, and fire bricks	1	10.0	0	8.0	1/ 3
6-6	Coal briquettes	6	14.3	1.5	7.5	5/ 9
	Totals and Averages for Group VI.	44	11.1	1.4	11.8	7/ 7
Group VII. Building Material						
7-1	Building material	7	9.6	0	8.2	12/ 2
	Totals and Averages for Group VII.	7	9.6	0	8.2	12/ 2
Group VIII. Production and Transmission of Electricity and Supply of Water						
8-1	Electric and water works	3	24.0	1.0	*	23/
	Totals and Averages for Group VIII.	3	24.0	1.0	*	23/
Group IX. Manufacture of Chemicals and Allied Products						
9-1	Matches					
9-1-1	Matches	4	9.7	1.0	15.0	3/11
9-1-2	Shavings and splints	3	9.3	0.7	8.3	12/ 4

Code	Classification	(1) No. of Factories	(2) No. of Operating Hours per Day	(3) No. of Rest Days per Month	(4) No. of Holidays per Year	(5) Average No. of Years & Months in Operation
9-2	Soap					
9-2-1	Soap only	4	8.7	1.3	10.0	11/
9-2-2	Soap, washing soda, and candles	1	10.0	0	7.0	20/ 8
9-3	Enamelled ware					
9-3-1	Enamelled ware only	13	11.7	1.9	13.1	4/ 8
9-3-2	Enamelled ware and other products	4	9.2	2.0	11.5	14/
9-3-3	Body of enamelled ware	2	9.0	1.0	26.5	10/ 9
9-4	Dyes, varnish, and printer's ink					
9-4-1	Varnish	3	9.3	2.0	20.0	14/ 4
9-4-2	Printer's ink	2	14.5	2.5	10.0	9/
9-4-3	Dyes	1	10.0	2.0	30.0	/10
9-5	Cosmetics	13	10.5	2.2	11.3	9/ 1
9-6	Medicine					
9-6-1	Medicine in general	6	9.3	2.5	10.0	9/11
9-6-2	Medicine and soap	1	9.0	4.0	*	12/ 6
9-7	Artificial resin					
9-7-1	Celluloid products	6	9.2	1.5	16.7	4/10
9-7-2	Beetle and bakelite	7	9.4	2.7	7.2	1/10
9-8	Acids					
9-8-1	Acids only	1	12.0	4.0	8.0	2/ 3
9-8-2	Acids, caustic soda, and bleaching powder	1	20.0	4.0	*	4/ 7
9-9	Calcium and magnesium carbonates	3	19.3	1.0	8.0	3/
9-10	Oxygen and acetylene	1	24.0	0	0	/ 2
9-11	Other chemical products	2	14.0	0	32.0	1/ 9
	Totals and Averages for Group IX.	78	*11.1*	*1.8*	*12.6*	*7/ 4*
Group X. Textile Industries						
10-1	Cotton spinning and weaving					

Code	Classification	(1) No. of Factories	(2) No. of Operating Hours per Day	(3) No. of Rest Days per Month	(4) No. of Holidays per Year	(5) Average No. of Years & Months in Operation
10-1-1	Cotton ginning	5	11.6	0	7.0	16/ 6
10-1-2	Cotton fluffing					
10-1-2-1	Cotton fluffing only	7	15.3	1.0	9.5	9/ 1
10-1-2-2	Cotton fluffing and manufacture of other products	1	12.0	*	*	3/
10-1-3	Cotton spinning					
10-1-3-1	Spinning only	12	22.5	3.7	5.0	14/ 2
10-1-3-2	Spinning and weaving	16	22.3	3.9	7.6	15/ 8
10-1-3-3	Spinning and making of cotton blankets	1	24.0	4.0	5.0	9/ 9
10-1-4	Cotton weaving					
10-1-4-1	Weaving only	69	12.2	1.3	12.3	6/ 7
10-1-4-2	Weaving and manufacture of machinery	1	10.0	2.0	21.0	14/ 5
10-1-5	Medicated gauze and cotton	3	9.0	1.0	9.5	6/ 6
10-2	Silk reeling and weaving					
10-2-1	Silk reeling					
10-2-1-1	Steam filature silk	49	10.7	2.6	8.0	8/ 4
10-2-1-2	Dupion silk	2	10.5	5.0	20.0	8/
10-2-1-3	Silk waste	1	22.0	4.0	2.0	11/
10-2-2	Silk weaving	122	15.8	1.9	17.1	4/
10-3	Wool spinning and weaving					
10-3-1	Wool weaving only	21	13.5	2.0	14.5	3/ 8
10-3-2	Wool spinning and weaving	2	9.0	*	7.0	3/11
10-3-3	Wool bowing	1	9.0	0	*	/ 1
10-4	Spinning and weaving of waste cotton, wool, and silk	3	19.3	3.3	7.3	1/ 9

Code	Classification	(1) No. of Factories	(2) No. of Operating Hours per Day	(3) No. of Rest Days per Month	(4) No. of Holidays per Year	(5) Average No. of Years & Months in Operation
10-5	Dyeing					
10-5-1	Mercerized yarn and thread	16	9.3	1.1	15.8	5/7
10-5-2	Dyeing in general	30	10.5	0.8	16.9	7/1
10-5-3	Dyeing and printing of textiles	1	20.0	4.0	*	*
10-6	Printing of textiles	6	9.7	1.5	7.0	9/4
10-7	Thread making					
10-7-1	Warp and woof	4	12.5	2.0	25.0	3/5
10-7-2	Thread balls	3	10.0	1.0	11.3	10/5
10-7-3	Other kinds of thread	3	8.8	1.3	18.0	10/4
10-8	Making of trimmings and ribbons					
10-8-1	Ribbons	2	15.0	3.0	9.0	14/4
10-8-2	Elastic belts	3	10.8	1.3	10.0	10/
10-8-3	Trimmings and ribbons	2	10.5	2.0	*	5/6
10-8-4	Trimmings, ribbons, and chopsticks	1	8.0	4.0	11.0	19/6
10-9	Cotton flannel finishing					
10-9-1	Cotton flannel finishing only	2	24.0	3.0	*	/9
10-9-2	Cotton flannel finishing and dyeing and printing of textiles	2	11.5	0	9.0	2/6
	Totals and Averages for Group X.	*391*	*13.7*	*1.9*	*14.2*	*6/8*
Group XI. Clothing Industries, Including Hosiery						
11-1	Knitted hosiery					
11-1-1	Knitted hosiery only	38	13.0	1.9	16.4	8/6
11-1-2	Knitted hosiery, underwear and sweaters, and other articles of apparel	14	11.3	1.4	12.8	9/5

Code	Classification	(1) No. of Factories	(2) No. of Operating Hours per Day	(3) No. of Rest Days per Month	(4) No. of Holidays per Year	(5) Average No. of Years & Months in Operation
11-2	Hats	7	9.5	1.7	21.7	10/ 7
11-3	Umbrellas	2	9.7	1.5	5.5	6/ 1
11-4	Handkerchiefs	7	11.3	1.7	12.3	7/ 7
11-5	Underwear and sweaters	16	10.2	1.8	18.6	8/ 1
11-6	Woollen and cotton blankets	1	9.0	2.0	30.0	15/
11-7	Other articles of apparel					
11-7-1	Buttons	3	9.3	0.7	6.0	5/ 7
11-7-2	Scarfs, gloves, etc.	1	10.0	3.0	*	2/ 8
	Totals and Averages for Group XI.	89	11.5	1.7	16.1	8/ 6
Group XII. Manufacture of Leather. Rubber Products. etc.						
12-1	Leather manufacturing					
12-1-1	Leather manufacturing only	9	9.2	1.5	11.8	11/ 4
12-1-2	Leather manufacturing and manufacture of glue	1	8.0	2.0	14.0	12/
12-2	Manufacture of rubber goods	44	11.6	2.4	9.3	3/ 6
12-3	Manufacture of glue	1	24.0	0	*	13/
	Totals and Averages for Group XII.	55	11.4	2.2	10.3	5/ 1
Group XIII. Preparation and Manufacture of Foods, Drinks, and Tobacco						
13-1	Rice mills	1	10.0	0	4.0	9/
13-2	Wheat flour mills	15	22.5	3.1	7.4	19/
13-3	Sugar refineries	4	9.4	2.3	4.0	3/ 2
13-4	Manufactured foodstuffs					
13-4-1	Canned food	7	10.7	0.7	11.0	10/ 1
13-4-2	Bean curd products	1	20.0	6.0	*	11/

Code	Classification	(1) No. of Factories	(2) No. of Operating Hours per Day	(3) No. of Rest Days per Month	(4) No. of Holidays per Year	(5) Average No. of Years & Months in Operation
13-4-3	Candies	2	11.0	0	8.0	5/ 6
13-5	Oil mills	10	12.9	1.4	17.5	17/11
13-6	Tea	44	10.3	0	10.2	5/ 2
13-7	Cigarettes	46	12.0	1.8	11.1	6/ 3
13-8	Alcohol	1	*	4.0	7.0	/ 5
13-9	Soda water and other soft drinks					
13-9-1	Soda water	1	8.0	4.0	*	*
13-9-2	Soda water and manufacture of ice	1	10.5	5.0	*	15/
13-10	Condiments	5	9.5	1.3	12.5	6/ 7
13-11	Starch	1	10.0	2.0	18.0	3/
13-12	Refined salt	1	24.0	0	5.0	5/
13-13	Frozen egg products	1	8.0	2.0	*	3/
13-14	Ice and cold storage	2	16.0	0	1.0	2/10
	Totals and Averages for Group XIII.	*143*	*12.2*	*1.4*	*10.1*	*7/11*
Group XIV. Manufacture of Paper, Book-Binding and Printing						
14-1	Paper manufacturing					
14-1-1	Paper	7	19.2	2.3	*	9/10
14-1-2	Card-board	1	24.0	2.0	12.0	11/ 7
14-1-3	Tin foil	1	*	*	*	9/ 6
14-2	Printing					
14-2-1	Printing only	85	11.0	2.9	10.6	11/ 8
14-2-2	Printing and type casting	7	8.6	2.6	10.0	16/ 6
14-3	Paper manufactures					
14-3-1	Cartons	10	10.8	2.4	5.7	7/ 2
14-3-2	Cards, etc.	3	10.0	2.7	9.0	15/ 6
	Totals and Averages for Group XIV.	*114*	*11.4*	*2.8*	*10.2*	*11/ 7*
Group XV. Manufacture of Scientific and Musical Instruments, Clocks and Watches,						

Code	Classification	(1) No. of Factories	(2) No. of Operating Hours per Day	(3) No. of Rest Days per Month	(4) No. of Holidays per Year	(5) Average No. of Years & Months in Operation
etc.						
15-1	Musical instruments	2	9.5	2.0	*	9/ 2
15-2	Educational supplies	6	9.8	1.8	8.4	5/10
15-3	Scientific apparatus	5	11.0	1.0	8.5	8/11
15-4	Clocks and flash lights	1	10.0	2.0	10.0	3/ 8
15-5	Toys	4	11.1	1.5	14.5	5/ 2
	Totals and Averages for Group XV.	18	10.4	1.6	9.8	6/10
Group XVI. Other Manufacturing Industries						
16-1	Tooth brushes					
16-1-1	Tooth brushes only	5	8.6	4.0	20.0	10/ 5
16-1-2	Tooth brushes and tooth powder	1	9.0	4.0	10.0	12/ 8
16-2	Mirrors	4	10.2	1.0	11.5	5/1
16-3	Thermos bottles					
16-3-1	Whole bottles	2	11.0	2.0	16.0	11/ 6
16-3-2	Tin outside cover only	7	9.8	0.7	11.7	1/ 7
16-3-3	Vacuum bottles only	3	9.7	1.5	14.5	1/
	Totals and Averages for Group XVI.	22	9.7	1.9	13.3	5/ 9
	Grand Totals and Averages for the Sixteen Groups	1186	12.0	1.7	12.1	8/ 4

Notes: (1) The "number of rest days per month" refers to the customary number of rest days per month of a factory or an industry, and workers who prefer to work on these rest days are usually given extra wages.

(2) The "average number of years and months in operation" means the average length of time from the first month of operation actual or calculated, until December, 1933.

TABLE B-VII. STATISTICS OF THE PRECEDING YEAR (1932)[1]

Code	Classification	(1) No. of Factories	(2) Salary Payments ($)	(3) Wage Payments ($)	(4) Value of Raw Materials ($)	(5) Value of Output ($)
	Group I. Woodworking Industries					
1-1	Saw mills	4	5,607.00	62,900.00	1,326,666.60*	1,529,200.00
1-2	Manufacture of wooden articles					
1-2-1	Wooden boxes	1	3,600.00	9,360.00	240,000.00	250,000.00
1-2-2	Bobbins	5	7,742.00*	79,085.00	302,420.00*	361,333.33*
	Total for Group I.	10	16,949.00*	151,346.00	1,869,086.60*	2,140,533.33*
	Group II. Furniture Manufacturing					
2-1	Steel furniture	6	25,274.00	90,759.00	367,441.60	760,350.00
2-2	Rugs and carpets	1	*	*	24,000.00	105,000.00
	Total for Group II	7	25,274.00*	90,759.00*	391,441.60	865,350.00
	Group III. Metal Industries					
3-1	Founding	17	12,228.00	78,504.00	240,040.60	575,000.00*
3-1-1	Machines and machine parts	4	5,424.00	34,022.40	196,560.00	375,000.00
3-1-2	Iron pipes					
3-2	Steel refining	1	7,200.00	15,000.00	14,000.00	36,000.00
	Total for Group III.	22	24,852.00	127,526.40	450,600.60	986,000.00*
	Group IV. Manufacture of Machinery and Miscellaneous Metal Products					
4-1	Manufacture and repairing of machines					
4-1-1	Printing machines	6	9,240.00	29,184.00	92,680.00*	225,000.00
4-1-2	Knitting machines	6	5,302.00	22,772.80	42,600.00	120,648.00
4-1-3	Spinning and weaving machines	13	49,901.00	158,285.00	512,795.96*	1,074,750.00

Code	Classification	(1) No. of Factories	(2) Salary Payments ($)	(3) Wage Payments ($)	(4) Value of Raw Materials ($)	(5) Value of Output ($)
4-1-4	Prime movers	13	59,304.00	143,888.00	343,193.20*	1,401,445.00
4-1-5	Various kinds of machines	22	91,896.00	298,086.00	712,300.80*	1,891,800.00*
4-1-6	Machine parts					
4-1-6-1	Axes, etc.	1	1,200,00	3,600.00	28,800.00	70,000.00
4-1-6-2	Knitting needles	7	2,018.00*	34,308.00	15,144.00	81,454.00
4-1-6-3	Faucets, valves, etc.	2	1,800.00*	8,474.40	429,600.00	610,000.00
4-1-7	Repairing of machines and machine parts	11	16,697.00	94,997.84	156,884.00*	505,750.00
4-2	Manufacture of metal products					
4-2-1	Boilers and water tanks	1	2,160.00	25,344.00	*	60,000.00
4-2-2	Tins					
4-2-2-1	Tins only	5	4,284.00	15,724.00*	81,000.00*	446,000.00
4-2-2-2	Tins and printing	4	13,128.00	57,500.00	350,160.00	660,000.00
4-2-2-3	Tins and other products	4	49,608.00	78,811.20	678,720.00	1,559,000.00
4-2-3	Aluminumware	4	6,240.00	41,832.00	674,400.00	626,000.00
4-2-4	Nails					
4-2-4-1	Nails only	4	3,010.00*	9,000.00*	275,356.80	428,800.00
4-2-4-2	Nails and other products	2	15,600.00	76,800.00	1,297,800.00	2,373,000.00
4-2-5	Lamps	3	4,080.00	15,480.00	129,996.00	164,000.00
4-2-6	Copper sheets	4	22,440.00	40,800.00	495,986.02	612,587.37
4-2-7	Iron bars	1	1,750.00	6,500.00	65,187.50	113,940.00
4-2-8	Other metal products	5	5,076.00	20,672.40	23,364.00	199,880.00
4-3	Manufacture of electric machines and apparatus					
4-3-1	Electric machines and apparatus	3	42,480.00	113,400.00	230,400.00	496,000.00

Code	Classification	(1) No. of Factories	(2) Salary Payments ($)	(3) Wage Payments ($)	(4) Value of Raw Materials ($)	(5) Value of Output ($)
4-3-2	Electric machines and dry batteries	1	36,000.00	20,000.00	100,000.00	180,000.00
4-3-3	Electric fans, heaters, utensils, etc.	5	32,100.00	160,023.00	638,400.00	2,648,000.00
4-3-4	Electric supplies	4	12,180.00	32,544.00	32,850.00*	141,400.00
4-3-5	Electric supplies and other products	2	3,360.00	14,400.00	50,042.52	154,980.00
4-3-6	Electric light bulbs	13	45,049.52	123,176.48	806,720.00	2,657,400.00
4-3-7	Neon light tubes	1	8,400.00	9,600.00	94,800.00	150,000.00
4-3-8	Dry batteries	3	1,570.00	9,088.00	99,240.00	213,466.67
4-3-9	Dry batteries and flash lights	1	2,880.00	9,840.00	72,000.00	101,000.00
4-3-10	Flash lights	8	21,110.00	73,116.00	454,673.36	1,161,920.00
4-3-11	Electric welding	1	1,800.00	7,800.00	24,000.00	60,000.00
4-4	Foundry works					
4-4-1	Spinning and weaving machines	3	10,200.00	15,900.00	26,497.50	306,553.20
4-4-2	Various kinds of machines	3	14,880.00	54,360.00	244,800.00	385,930.00
4-4-3	Metal products	1	600.00	3,000.00	15,096.00	18,000.00
	Total for Group IV.	167	597,343.52*	1,829,207.12*	9,295,487.66*	21,898,704.24*
Group V.	Construction of Boats, Ships and Vehicles for Land Transportation					
5-1	Shipbuilding					
5-1-1	Construction of ships	1	297,514.63	1,455,417.88	2,183,824.00	4,232,012.84
5-1-2	Construction of ships and other instruments of transportation	5	49,700.00	268,600.00	1,379,340.00	2,270,000.00
5-1-3	Repairing of ships	7	17,098.00	138,946.00	176,522.50	692,000.00

Code	Classification	(1) No. of Factories	(2) Salary Payments ($)	(3) Wage Payments ($)	(4) Value of Raw Materials ($)	(5) Value of Output ($)
5-2	Building of cars					
5-2-1	Railway workshops	1	51,903.31	567,785.81	401,903.51	1,089,396.74 [2]
5-2-2	Bicycles	1	2,000.00	6,500.00	33,600.00	*
5-2-3	Charcoal gas trucks	1	(3)	(3)	(3)	(3)
	Total for Group V.	16	418,215.94	2,437,249.69	4,175,190.01*	8,283,409.58*
Group VI. Manufacture of Bricks, Earthenware, Glass, etc.						
6-1	Bricks and tiles					
6-1-1	Bricks and tiles in general	2	27,000.00	63,600.00	33,600.00	553,000.00
6-1-2	Glazed tiles	2	5,784.00	62,766.00	67,921.20	352,049.96
6-2	Glass					
6-2-1	Glassware	21	46,737.00	223,826.60	406,000.75	1,258,764.00*
6-2-2	Glass bevelling	3	3,600.00	21,000.00	*	70,000.00
6-3	Cement	1	62,655.70	83,086.99	388,800.00	2,821,632.00
6-4	Stone, stone powder, and lime					
6-4-1	Lime	1	1,524.00	19,200.00	20,040.00	60,000.00
6-4-2	Stone powder	3	15,259.00	11,795.32	264,840.00	400,000.00
6-4-3	Stone breaking	1	960.00	1,680.00	1,920.00	10,000.00
6-5	Crucibles					
6-5-1	Crucibles only	1	(4)	(4)	(4)	(4)
6-5-2	Crucibles and fire bricks	2	4,800.00	20,000.00	13,250.00	80,000.00
6-5-3	Crucibles, glassware, and fire bricks	1	6,000.00	26,000.00	41,380.00	133,333.33
6-6	Coal briquettes	6	21,712.00	69,000.00	1,308,000.00	2,287,000.00
	Total for Group VI.	44	196,031.70	601,954.91	2,545,751.95*	8,025,779.29*

Code	Classification	(1) No. of Factories	(2) Salary Payments ($)	(3) Wage Payments ($)	(4) Value of Raw Materials ($)	(5) Value of Output ($)
	Group VII. Building Material					
7-1	Building material	7	11,124.00	110,120.00	171,320.00*	1,111,800.00*
	Total for Group VII.	7	11,124.00	110,120.00	171,320.00*	1,111,800.00*
	Group VIII. Production and Transmission of Electricity and Supply of Water					
8-1	Electric and water works	3	277,552.19	468,433.24		7,930,813.24
	Total for Group VIII	3	277,552.19	468,433.24		7,930,813.24
	Group IX. Manufacture of Chemicals and Allied Products					
9-1	Matches					
9-1-1	Matches	4	35,995.20	377,325.60	1,835,414.64	2,694,250.00
9-1-2	Shavings and Splints	3	17,678.14	78,119.03	658,652.19	878,677.50
9-2	Soap					
9-2-1	Soap only	4	7,464.00	14,304.00	300,496.00*	238,975.00
9-2-2	Soap, washing soda, and candles	1	4,800.00	4,080.00	11,940.00	57,800.00
9-3	Enamelled ware					
9-3-1	Enamelled ware only	13	138,500.16	209,545.68	2,050,977.00	3,698,000.00
9-3-2	Enamelled ware and other products	4	17,760.00	127,320.00	483,120.00	730,000.00
9-3-3	Body of enamelled ware	2	1,440.00	14,713.20	18,000.00	36,000.00
9-4	Dyes, varnish, and printer's ink					
9-4-1	Varnish	3	46,716.00	130,992.00	1,420,540.00	2,925,000.00
9-4-2	Printer's ink	2	15,900.00	12,468.00	341,683.20	1,135,000.00
9-4-3	Dyes	1	(5)	(5)	(5)	(5)

Code	Classification	(1) No. of Factories	(2) Salary Payments ($)	(3) Wage Payments ($)	(4) Value of Raw Materials ($)	(5) Value of Output ($)
9-5	Cosmetics	13	88,458.00*	371,290.00	3,015,886.07*	6,517,326.57
9-6	Medicine					
9-6-1	Medicine in general	6	25,120.00*	38,400.00*	708,000.00*	1,506,080.00*
9-6-2	Medicine and soap	1	51,936.00	41,160.00	2,001,140.00	2,800,000.00
9-7	Artificial resin					
9-7-1	Celluloid products	6	44,772.00	92,160.00	294,519.16	566,920.00
9-7-2	Beetle and bakelite	7	15,600.00*	48,000.00*	394,800.00*	620,000.00
9-8	Acids					
9-8-1	Acids only	1	(6)	(6)	(6)	(6)
9-8-2	Acids, caustic soda, and bleaching powder	1	26,000.00	16,800.00	41,280.00	599,400.00
9-9	Calcium and magnesium carbonates	3	7,830.00*	54,096.00	55,200.00	764,304.00
9-10	Oxygen and acetylene	1	(7)	(7)	(7)	(7)
9-11	Other chemical products	2	1,944.00	6,930.00	100,699.32	100,000.00
	Total for Group IX.	78	547,913.50*	1,627,703.51*	13,732,347.58*	25,867,733.07*
Group X	Textile Industries					
10-1	Cotton spinning and weaving					
10-1-1	Cotton ginning	5	18,000.00	23,431.00	5,532,200.00	5,745,812.00
10-1-2	Cotton fluffing					
10-1-2-1	Cotton fluffing only	7	13,564.00	73,900.00	963,706.68	1,266,933.33
10-1-2-2	Cotton fluffing and manufacture of other products	1	960.00	2,400.00	32,000.00	47,080.00
10-1-3	Cotton spinning					
10-1-3-1	Spinning only	12	279,939.00*	4,728,185.84*	34,790,455.00	41,283,840.00
10-1-3-2	Spinning and weaving	16	264,257.86	6,329,342.56	55,789,662.00	78,199,693.90

Code	Classification	(1) No. of Factories	(2) Salary Payments ($)	(3) Wage Payments ($)	(4) Value of Raw Materials ($)	(5) Value of Output ($)
10-1-3-3	Spinning and making of cotton blankets	1	24,000.00	72,000.00	384,000.00	2,000,000.00
10-1-4	Cotton weaving					
10-1-4-1	Weaving only	69	296,327.60*	1,245,840.50	17,659,782.93*	21,826,641.25*
10-1-4-2	Weaving and manufacture of machinery	1	14,400.00	24,000.00	123,114.00	645,044.10
10-1-5	Medicated gauze and cotton	3	6,912.00	20,004.00	93,888.00	121,000.00
10-2	Silk reeling and weaving					
10-2-1	Silk reeling					
10-2-1-1	Steam flature silk	49	234,918.00	1,427,400.00	5,732,224.00	7,017,108.008*
10-2-1-2	Dupion silk	2	6,072.00	52,577.50	301,770.00	348,600.00
10-2-1-3	Silk waste	1	28,660.00	72,700.00	300,000.00	705,600.00
10-2-2	Silk weaving	122	493,293.67*	2,990,564.78*	12,651,100.29*	20,211,577.25*
10-3	Wool spinning and weaving					
10-3-1	Wool weaving only	21	57,400.00	173,321.30	3,279,546.13	4,048,318.11*
10-3-2	Wool spinning and weaving	2	63,600.00	230,100.00	510,000.00	1,800,000.00
10-3-3	Wool bowing	1	(9)	(9)	(9)	(9)
10-4	Spinning and weaving of waste cotton, wool, and silk	3	9,700.00	77,100.00	315,000.00	675,000.00
10-5	Dyeing					
10-5-1	Mercerized yarn and thread	16	12,418.00	90,025.25	1,238,354.63	1,745,161.44
10-5-2	Dyeing in general	30	64,400.00	195,992.00	3,449,932.59*	5,173,100.00*
10-5-3	Dyeing and printing of textiles	1	60,000.00	38,500.00	1,210,000.00	1,666,666.67
10-6	Printing of textiles	6	22,650.00	49,116.00	111,090.00	318,000.00
10-7	Thread making					

Code	Classification	(1) No. of Factories	(2) Salary Payments ($)	(3) Wage Payments ($)	(4) Value of Raw Materials ($)	(5) Value of Output ($)
10-7-1	Warp and woof	4	15,360.00	77,552.00	1,160,189.28	1,065,555.55
10-7-2	Thread balls	3	5,736.00	24,774.00	263,989.32	455,910.00
10-7-3	Other kinds of thread	3	2,541.60	7,910.00	44,057.50	52,500.00
10-8	Making of trimmings and ribbons					
10-8-1	Ribbons	2	6,048.00	20,408.00	106,200.00	217,742.22
10-8-2	Elastic belts	3	9,388.00	45,400.00	210,285.84	330,000.04
10-8-3	Trimmings and ribbons	2	1,608.00	26,808.00	140,400.00*	194,944.00
10-8-4	Trimmings, ribbons, and chopsticks	1	60,480.00	199,260.00	33,029.40	1,000,000.00
10-9	Cotton flannel finishing					
10-9-1	Cotton flannel finishing only	2	(10)	(10)	(10)	(10)
10-9-2	Cotton flannel finishing and dyeing and printing of textiles	2	1,980.00	12,600.00	5,646.00	57,930.00
	Total for Group X	391	2,074,613.73*	18,331,212.73*	146,431,623.59*	198,219,757.86*

Group XI. Clothing Industries, Including

Hosiery

Code	Classification	(1)	(2)	(3)	(4)	(5)
11-1	Knitted hosiery					
11-1-1	Knitted hosiery only	38	147,598.44	1,176,595.61	6,934,565.24	9,040,588.96
11-1-2	Knitted hosiery, underwear and sweaters, and other articles of apparel	14	62,638.40	373,062.00	1,597,446.64*	1,796,841.33*
11-2	Hats	7	14,166.00*	108,790.00*	655,604.48	1,059,600.00
11-3	Umbrellas	2	3,000.00	77,460.00	94,320.00	422,000.00
11-4	Handkerchiefs	7	23,644.00*	63,221.00	613,780.00	1,530,400.00*

Code	Classification	(1) No. of Factories	(2) Salary Payments ($)	(3) Wage Payments ($)	(4) Value of Raw Materials ($)	(5) Value of Output ($)
11-5	Underwear and sweaters	16	94,034.00	456,416.00	3,059,753.90	5,338,383.33*
11-6	Woollen and cotton blankets	1	2,754.00	426.00	8,000.00	10,000.00
11-7	Other articles of apparel					
11-7-1	Buttons	3	2,890.00	16,110.00	74,100.00	93,300.00
11-7-2	Scarfs, gloves, etc.	1	10,800.00	6,912.00	171,000.00	178,200.00
	Total for Group XI.	89	361,524.84*	2,278,992.61*	13,208,570.26*	19,469,313.62*
Group XII. Manufacture of Leather, Rubber Products, etc.						
12-1	Leather manufacturing					
12-1-1	Leather manufacturing only	9	40,308.00	61,087.00	1,326,099.96	1,508,857.00
12-1-2	Leather manufacturing and manufacture of glue	1	(11)	(11)	(11)	(11)
12-2	Manufacture of rubber goods	44	374,138.00	2,143,374.00*	6,639,648.72*	19,349,394.13*
12-3	Manufacture of glue	1	9,942.00	15,307.00	100,699.32	130,400.00
	Total for Group XII.	55	424,388.00	2,219,768.00*	8,066,448.00*	20,988,651.13*
Group XIII. Preparation and Manufacture of Foods, Drinks, and Tobacco						
13-1	Rice mills	1	4,111.00	4,999.00	132,000.00	148,000.00
13-2	Wheat flour mills	15	158,354.00	654,000.00	60,374,762.00	72,683,247.00
13-3	Sugar refineries	4	17,682.00	31,445.50	4,228,728.40	4,329,920.00
13-4	Manufactured foodstuffs					
13-4-1	Canned food	7	28,260.00	172,016.00	1,330,447.48	3,690,000.00
13-4-2	Bean curd products	1	360.00	4,000.00	37,536.00	76,000.00
13-4-3	Candies	2	3,264.00	9,162.00	95,040.00	318,800.00

Code	Classification	(1) No. of Factories	(2) Salary Payments ($)	(3) Wage Payments ($)	(4) Value of Raw Materials ($)	(5) Value of Output ($)
13-5	Oil mills	10	59,836.67	253,196.67	14,293,373.30	13,114,083.33
13-6	Tea	44	19,111.50	114,810.50	620,122.50	1,026,723.66
13-7	Cigarettes	46	296,240.00	3,170,768.40	41,358,187.08	101,979,760.00*
13-8	Alcohol	1	(12)	(12)	(12)	(12)
13-9	Soda water and other soft drinks					
13-9-1	Soda water	1	5,000.00	10,000.00	25,800.00	90,000.00
13-9-2	Soda water and manufacture of ice	1	20,000.00	20,000.00	165,822.23	414,000.00
13-10	Condiments	5	53,088.00	118,512.00	1,978,920.00	3,970,000.00
13-11	Starch	1	2,640.00	12,000.00	240,000.00	393,600.00
13-12	Refined salt	1	6,000.00	7,500.00	55,000.00	504,000.00
13-13	Frozen egg products	1	30,000.00	72,000.00	1,902,666.12	2,660,000.00
13-14	Ice and cold storage	2	6,600.00	6,000.00	1,666.68	17,000.00*
	Total for Group XIII.	143	710,547.17*	4,660,410.07*	126,840,071.79*	205,415,133.99*
Group XIV. Manufacture of Paper, Book-Binding and Printing						
14-1	Paper manufacturing					
14-1-1	Paper	7	63,010.44	306,911.84	2,591,078.36	4,905,000.00
14-1-2	Card-board	1	12,000.00	48,000.00	172,800.00	600,000.00
14-1-3	Tin Foil	1	1,250.00	2,040.00	25,883.28	24,000.00
14-2	Printing					
14-2-1	Printing only	85	1,328,492.08	1,618,048.93	10,586,216.77*	16,880,995.75*
14-2-2	Printing and type casting	7	55,788.00	408,195.28	2,442,058.46	9,023,427.49
14-3	Paper manufactures					

Code	Classification	(1) No. of Factories	(2) Salary Payments ($)	(3) Wage Payments ($)	(4) Value of Raw Materials ($)	(5) Value of Ouput ($)
14-3-1	Cartons	10	11,828.00*	63,576.00	264,916.80*	482,600.00*
14-3-2	Cards, etc.	3	7,592.00	10,824.00	113,520.00	221,000.00
	Total for Group XIV.	114	1,479,960.52*	2,457,596.05	16,196,473.67*	32,137,023.24*
Group XV. Manufacture of Scientific and Musical Instruments, Clocks and Watches, etc						
15-1	Musical instruments	2	14,900.00	9,650.00	3,960.00*	125,000.00
15-2	Educational supplies	6	18,216.00	47,595.20	315,000.00	1,062,041.00
15-3	Scientific apparatus	5	12,384.00	46,820.00	87,400.00	165,000.00
15-4	Clocks and flash lights	1	11,700.00	79,200.00	68,400.00	200,000.00
15-5	Toys	4	7,390.00	23,351.40	66,733.32	167,111.11
	Total for Group XV.	18	64,590.00	206,616.60	541,493.32*	1,719,152.11
Group XVI. Other Manufacturing Industries						
16-1	Tooth brushes					
16-1-1	Tooth brushes only	5	26,916.00	76,620.00	327,640.00	1,050,499.84
16-1-2	Tooth brushes and tooth powder	1	2,592.00	15,840.00	125,040.00	300,000.00
16-2	Mirrors	4	4,940.00	26,380.00	182,635.80	240,800.00
16-3	Thermos bottles					
16-3-1	Whole bottle	2	6,025.15	31,754.20	143,484.40*	798,000.00
16-3-2	Tin outside cover only	7	4,220.00	26,720.00	43,894.00*	231,100.00
16-3-3	Vacuum bottles only	3	180.00	1,415.00	2,065.95	11,200.00
	Total for Group XVI.	22	44,873.15	178,729.20	824,760.15*	2,631,599.84
	Grand Total for the Sixteen Groups	1,186	7,275,753.26*	37,787,625.13*	344,740,666.78*	557,690,754.54*

Notes: (1) In our investigation schedules of this year, we elected to ask for the value of sales in 1932 instead of the value of output, as the latter would be difficult for the factories to determine, and inaccurate estimates would often be the result, while the value of sales could be reliably ascertained from their account books if they chose. Although there is always a difference between the value of sales and that of output as a factory usually has some unsold stock on hand at the beginning and end of a year, the difference is negligible in this country for the reason that most factories are operated on a small scale and the surplusage of goods in these cannot, therefore, be every large.

(2) Cost of production figure for 1932 only.

(3) No 1932 statistics for the factory concerned was established in July, 1933.

(4) No 1932 statistics for the factory concerned was established in January, 1933.

(5) No 1932 statistics for the factory concerned was established in 1933.

(6) The factory concerned did not have any output in 1932.

(7) No 1932 statistics for the factory concerned was established in October, 1933.

(8) Not including the value of by-products.

(9) No 1932 statistics for the factory concerned was established in November, 1933.

(10) No 1932 statistics for the factory concerned was established in March, 1933.

(11) The factory concerned suspended its operations in 1932 owing to the Sino-Japanese hostilities in Shanghai, hence the lack of statistics for this year.

(12) No 1932 statistics for the factory concerned was established in July, 1933.

APPENDIX C
STATISTICS OF SHANGHAI INDUSTRIES, 1928-1934.
TABLE C.I. CAPITALIZATION AND NUMBER OF WORKERS, 1928[1]

Classification	(1) No. of Foreign	(2) Chinese Capital ($)	(3) Factories Capital ($)	(4) Total Amount of Capital ($)	(5) Male Workers	(6) Female Workers	(7) Child Workers	(8) Total No. of Workers
Textile Industries								
Cotton spinning	55	37,230,000	152,350,800	189,580,800	28,760	62,584	2,998	94,342
Cotton weaving	99	2,243,650		2,243,650	4,323	4493	511	9,327
Silk reeling	90	2,425,900	76,000	2,501,900	2,148	39,484	10,831	52,463
Silk weaving	46	1,279,000		1,279,000	3,644	2,190	428	6,262
Wool weaving	7	213,700		213,700	417	255	156	828
Knitted goods	110	1,325,600	250,000	1,575,600	2,224	4,127	185	6,536
Others	13	369,400		369,400	312	417	45	774†
Total	*420*	*45,087,250*	*152,676,800*	*197,764,050†*	*41,828*	*113,550*	*15,154*	*170,532*
Chemical Industries								
Dyeing and printing of textiles	81[2]	601,450		601,450	2,675	421	94	3,190
Leather manufacturing	18	1,132,430	943,000	2,075,430	552	1	1	554
Cosmetics	20	615,600		615,600	212	381	37	630†
Soap and candles	23	633,900		633,900	372	174	9	555
Glassware	16	511,500	393,000	904,500	745	12	486	1,243
Medicine	14	313,100	640,900	954,000	121	96	2	219
Manufacture of paper	13	1,975,700		1,975,700	1,044	1,118	31	2,193
Match making	7	889,800		889,800	910	1,498	329	2,737

Classification	(1) No. of Factories	(2) Chinese Capital ($)	(3) Foreign Capital ($)	(4) Total Amount of Capital ($)	(5) Male Workers	(6) Female Workers	(7) Child Workers	(8) Total No. of Workers
Manufacture of enamelled ware	8	258,400		258,400	517	50	85	652
Manufacture of varnish	3	275,000		275,000	120	6	5	131
Others	9	187,800		187,800	160	88	6	254
Total	212	7,394,680	1,976,900	9,371,580	7,428	3,845	1,085	12,358
Preparation and Manufacture of Foods, Drinks and Tobacco								
Wheat flour mills	12	5,835,500		5,835,500	1,871			1,871
Rice mills	46	312,350		312,350	399			399
Oil mills	12	962,100	361,100	1,323,200	1,501			1,501
Soda water and other soft drinks	6	367,000		367,000	71			71
Frozen egg products	1		111,100	111,100	125	155	7	287
Condiments	5	252,000		252,000	106	43	2	151
Cigars and cigarettes	69	17,390,110	23,350,000	40,740,110	3,147	5,857	474	9,478
Candies and canned food	47	748,100		748,100	780	415	56	1,251
Others	4	25,600		25,600	46	5		51
Total	202	25,892,760	23,822,200	49,714,960†	8,046	6,475	539	15,060
Printing Industry								
Printing	210	10,457,100	615,791	11,072,891	6,542	596	1,110	8,248
Printer's ink	2	*		*	*		*	*
Total	212	10,457,100*	615,791	11,072,891*	6,542*	596	1,110*	8,248*
Foundries, Shipyards, Manu-								

Classification	(1) No. of Factories	(2) Chinese Capital ($)	(3) Foreign Capital ($)	(4) Total Amount of Capital ($)	(5) Male Workers	(6) Female Workers	(7) Child Workers	(8) Total No. of Workers
factories of Machinery, etc.								
Manufacture and repairing of machines	163	1,765,450		1,765,450	3,607	81	1,434	5,122
Manufacture of electrical instruments	21	517,300		517,300	941	418	86	1,445
Founding	47	120,700		120,700	653		277	930
Shipbuilding	2	38,000		38,000	65		72	137
Others	1	*		*	12			12
Total	234	2,441,450*		2,441,450*	5,278	499	1,869	7,646
Manufacture of Tools and Instruments								
Metal products	57	616,550	125,000	741,550	964	111	443	1,518
Wooden, rattan, and bamboo articles	13	57,350		57,350	279	100	12	391†
Musical instruments and toys	11	149,800	20,000	169,800	113	6	27	146
Scientific apparatus	3	80,300		80,300	73		11	84
Others	5	68,000		68,000	94	3	9	106
Total	89	972,000	145,000	1,117,000	1,523	220	502	2,245
Manufacture of Daily Necessities								
Hats	8	156,500	43,000	199,500	186	82	8	276
Umbrellas	9	62,200		62,200	90	53	21	164

Classification	(1) No. of Factories	(2) Chinese Capital ($)	(3) Foreign Capital ($)	(4) Total Amount of Capital ($)	(5) Male Workers	(6) Female Workers	(7) Child Workers	(8) Total No. of Workers
Brushes	6	80,500	700,000	780,500	116	292	23	431
Writing outfit	4	23,000		23,000	50	19	9	78
Spectacles	5	22,900		22,900	36		1	37
Clothing	3	40,000		40,000	550	400	100	1,050
Others	6	34,000		34,000	225	61	12	298
Total	41	419,100	743,000	1,162,100	1,253	907	174	2,334
Other Industries								
Building material (3)	21	1,532,000		1,532,000	872	70	26	968
Coal briquettes	8	197,300		197,300	162	2	9	173
Electric and water works	8	8,930,000	10,000,000	18,930,000	1,774		7	1,781
Trimmings and ribbons	23	26,300		26,300	148	222	70	440
Cartons	15	76,700		76,700	464	105	32	601†
Cotton ginning	5	150,160		150,160	416	300	23	739
Others	10	46,000		46,000	514	15	37	566
Total	90	10,958,460	10,000,000	20,958,460†	4,350	714	204	5,268
Grand Total	1,500	103,622,800*	189,979,691	293,602,491*	76,248*	126,806	20,637*	223,691*

Notes: (1) Data in this table as well as those in the one immediately following are taken from *Industries In Shanghai* published by the Bureau of Social Affairs of the Shanghai City Government.
(2) It is doubtful whether this figure does not include a certain number of small dye-houses.
(3) It may be worth mentioning that "Building material" here refers to factories manufacturing cement, bricks and tiles which regularly appear in Group VI (Manufacture of Bricks, Earthenware, Glass, etc.) in almost all other tables in this report.
(4) All totals marked† in the above table are worked out from their constituent figures by ourselves as the original totals do not tally with the constituent figures.

TABLE C-II. WORKING HOURS AND WAGE RATES, 1928

Classification	(1) No. of Factories	(2) Daily Wage Rates of Male Workers Highest ($)	(3) Daily Wage Rates of Male Workers Lowest ($)	(4) Daily Wage Rates of Female Workers Highest ($)	(5) Daily Wage Rates of Female Workers Lowest ($)	(6) Daily Wage Rates of Child Workers Highest ($)	(7) Daily Wage Rates of Child Workers Lowest ($)	(8) No. of Working Hours per Day Longest	(9) No. of Working Hours per Day Most Common	(10) No. of Working Hours per Day Shortest
Textile Industries										
Cotton spinning	55	2.88	0.32	1.86	0.18	0.65	0.22	12	12	10.5
Cotton weaving	99	2.04	0.13	2.00	0.10	0.60	0.06	12	10	8
Silk reeling	90	0.80	0.33	0.70	0.34	0.46	0.25	12	10	10
Silk weaving	46	3.00	0.30	3.00	0.17	1.00	0.23	12	10.5	8
Wool weaving	7	1.33	0.33	1.06	0.23	0.33	0.03	10	10	9
Knitted goods	110	2.00	0.17	1.50	0.10	*	0.10	12	10	8
Others	13	0.92	0.12	0.78	0.13	0.23	0.19	12	10	8
Chemical Industries										
Dyeing and printing of textiles	81	2.70	0.07	1.30	0.17	0.70	0.03	13	8,10	8
Leather manufacturing	18	2.00	0.13					10	9	7.5
Cosmetics	20	*	0.13	0.82	0.10	0.70	0.20	10	8,10	8
Soap and candles	23	1.50	0.10	0.74	0.20	0.33	0.13	10	10	8
Glassware	16	4.00	0.10	0.50	0.17	0.63	0.06	12	8,10,12	8
Medicine	14	1.00	0.10	0.57	0.32			10	8	8
Manufacture of paper	13	4.17	0.33	1.07	0.13	0.50	0.23	12	11,12	8
Match making	7	1.40	0.33	0.54	0.17	0.53	0.10	10	9,10	9
Manufacture of enamelled ware	8	3.00	0.17	0.67	0.20	*	0.07	10	9	8
Manufacture of varnish	3	2.00	0.33	0.47	0.33	0.47	0.33	9	9	8.5
Others	9	1.07	0.17	0.67	0.13			10	10	8
Preparation and Manufacture of Foods, Drinks and Tobacco										

Classification	(1) No. of Factories	(2) (3) Daily Wage Rates of Male Workers		(4) (5) Daily Wage Rates of Female Workers		(6) (7) Daily Wage Rates of Child Workers		(8) (9) (10) No. of Working Hours per Day		
		Highest ($)	Lowest ($)	Highest ($)	Lowest ($)	Highest ($)	Lowest ($)	Longest	Most Common	Shortest
Wheat flour mills	12	4.00	0.40					12	12	12
Rice mills	46	0.80	0.18					12	8	8
Oil mills	12	1.90	0.17					12	10	8
Soda water and other soft drinks	6	1.60	0.20					10	8	8
Eggs and egg products	1	*		0.60	0.40	0.40	0.40	9	*	9
Condiments	5	1.47	0.20	0.80	0.30	0.10	0.07	10	8,10	8
Cigars and cigarettes	69	2.67	0.07	1.50	0.13	1.00	0.07	12	10	8
Candies and canned food	47	2.80	0.07	0.67	0.10	0.27	0.07	14	10	7
Others	4	2.00	0.20					9	*	6
Printing Industry										
Printing	210	4.00	0.10	1.45	0.10	0.50	0.05	12	9,10	8
Printer's ink	2	*	*			*	*	*	*	*
Foundries, Shipyards. Manufactories of Machinery, etc.										
Manufacture and repairing of machines	163	2.40	0.10	0.57	0.30	0.60	0.06	12	9,10	8
Manufacture of electrical instruments	21	3.00	0.10	0.70	0.20	0.33	0.20	12	8	8
Founding	47	1.67	0.20			0.40	0.17	11	9,10	8
Shipbuilding	2	1.67	0.50					9	9	9
Others	1	*	*					*	*	*
Manufacture of Tools and Instruments										
Metal products	57	2.00	0.10	0.50	0.13	0.47	0.07	12	10	8
Wooden, rattan and bamboo articles	13	2.10	0.17	0.60	0.35	0.45	0.35	15	9,10	8
Musical instruments and toys	11	1.67	0.23	0.40	0.30			12	10	8

Classification	(1) No. of Factories	(2) Daily Wage Rates of Male Workers Highest ($)	(3) Daily Wage Rates of Male Workers Lowest ($)	(4) Daily Wage Rates of Female Workers Highest ($)	(5) Daily Wage Rates of Female Workers Lowest ($)	(6) Daily Wage Rates of Child Workers Highest ($)	(7) Daily Wage Rates of Child Workers Lowest ($)	(8) No. of Working Hours per Day Longest	(9) No. of Working Hours per Day Most Common	(10) No. of Working Hours per Day Shortest
Scientific apparatus	3	1.67	0.13					9	8	8
Others	5	1.00	0.20	0.43	0.40			10	9	8
Manufacture of Daily Necessities										
Hats	8	1.67	0.20	0.70	0.20			11	9	8
Umbrellas	9	1.00	0.10	0.84	0.40			12	10	8
Brushes	6	1.50	0.40	0.60	0.10			10	9	9
Writing outfit	4	1.00	0.27	0.50	0.24	0.40	0.30	10	10	9
Spectacles	5	2.67	0.10					10	10	9
Clothing	3	1.00	0.80	0.50	0.30			10	10	8
Others	6	1.00	0.17	0.67	0.50			9	*	8
Other Industries										
Building material	21	3.33	0.20	0.28	0.20	0.30	0.22	10	9,10	8
Coal briquettes	8	2.00	0.20			0.50	0.27	11	10	7
Electric and water works	8	3.47	0.48					12	8	6
Trimmings and ribbons	23	0.83	0.10	0.40	0.17	0.40	0.27	12	10	6
Cartons	15	1.67	0.10	1.10	0.10	0.33	0.23	12	9,10	8
Cotton ginning	5	0.73	0.20	*	0.25	0.40	0.07	11	11	9
Others	10	2.40	0.10	1.00	0.60	0.50	*	10	9	7.5

Notes: (1) In *Industries In Shanghai* wherefrom figures in this table are taken there are given four kinds of wage rates, namely; (a) highest, (b) average highest per industry, (c) lowest, and (d) average lowest per industry, but what are reproduced here are limited to the first and third kinds only.

(2) By "Most Common" under the heading of "No of Working Hours per Day" is meant here the *modal* number of working hours per day per industry. As it is possible to have two or three modes in a frequency distribution, so there are in some cases two or three figures for one industry in this column.

TABLE C-III. NUMBER OF WORKERS, 1929[1,2]

Classification	(1) No. of Factories	(2) Male Workers	(3) Female Workers	(4) Child Workers	(5) Total
Woodworking Industry					
Saw mills	23[3]	1,886[4]			1,886[4]
Total	*23*	*1,886*			*1,886*
Metal Industry					
Foundries	100	997		452	1,449
Total	*100*	*997*		*452*	*1,449*
Manufacture of Machinery and Miscellaneous Metal Products					
Machine workshops	418	5,834		2,978	8,812
Total	*418*	*5,834*		*2,978*	*8,812*
Construction of Boats, Ships, and Vehicles for Land Transportation					
Shipbuilding	13	5,994[5]		254[5]	6,248[5]
Total	*13*	*5,994*		*254*	*6,248*
Manufacture of Bricks, Earthenware, Glass, etc.					
Manufacture of glassware	30	1,588		1,455	3,043
Total	*30*	*1,588*		*1,455*	*3,043*
Manufacture of Chemicals and Allied Products					
Soap making	36	800	305		1,105
Manufacture of matches	7	911	1,232	553	2,696
Manufacture of enamelled ware	16	1,857	353	90	2,300
Total	*59*	*3,568*	*1,890*	*643*	*6,101*
Textile Industries					
Silk reeling	107	1,712[6]	37,211[6]	12,453[6]	51,376[6]
Cotton spinning	61 (33)	*	*	*	127,604 (71,029)
Silk weaving	48	2,283	1,109		3,392
Cotton weaving	105	3,547	4,172	303	8,022
Knitted goods	102	2,236	6,261	128	8,625
Dyeing	48	2,914			2,914
Total	*471 (33)*	*12,692*	*48,753*	*12,884*	*201,933[7] (71,029)*
Manufacture of Leather, Rubber					

Classification	(1) No. of Factories	(2) Male Workers	(3) Female Workers	(4) Child Workers	(5) Total
Products, etc.					
Manufacture of leather	150 [8]	1,552	2	296	1,850
Total	*150*	*1,552*	*2*	*296*	*1,850*
Preparation and Manufacture of Foods, Drinks and Tobacco					
Wheat flour mills	13	2,112			2,112
Oil mills	11	1,951			1,951
Frozen egg products	7	1,399	2,186		3,585
	(7)	(1,399)	(2,186)		(3,585)
Cigars and cigarettes	72	7,296	15,612	1,259	24,167
	(2)	(4,487)	(4,411)	(1,259)	(10,157)
Total	*103*	*12,758*	*17,798*	*1,259*	*31,815*
	(9)	(5,886)	(6,597)	(1,259)	(13,742)
Manufacture of Paper, Book-Binding and Printing					
Manufacture of paper	7	872	681		1,553
Printing	219	7,455	430	2,452	10,337
	(6)	(467)	(19)	(146)	(632)
Total	*226*	*8,327*	*1,111*	*2,452*	*11,890*
	(6)	(467)	(19)	(146)	(632)
Grand Total	*1,593*	*55,196*	*69,554*	*22,673*	*275,027* [7]
	(48)	(6,353)	(6,616)	(1,405)	(85,403)

Notes: (1) Data in this table together with Notes (4) and (5) are taken from *Wages And Hours Of Labour* published by the Bureau of Social Affairs of the Shanghai City Government, all estimated figures excepting those for the silk reeling industry being excluded.

(2) Subscripts in brackets in this table refer to either the number of foreign factories or the number of workers in foreign factories, as the case may be and as far as can be ascertained.

(3) Including a factory which judging from its name, Yeh Chun, is probably a Japanese concern.

(4) Refering to workers sawing wood by machine process only.

(5) Refering to regular day-workers only, those workers under the "contract" system being excluded.

(6) Partly Estimated from the number of reels in different filatures.

(7) Including 127,604 persons whose sex is not known.
(8) Mostly old-fashioned tanneries.

TABLE CVI. STATISTICS OF SHANGHAI INDUSTRIES, 1934*

Classification	No. of Factories				No. of Workers				
	Using Motive Power	Using Man-Power	Unknown	Total	Males	Females	Child Workers	Apprentices	Total
Group I. Power Plants									
Electric works	5			5	3,808			20	3,828[1]
Water works	4			4	1,146				1,146[2]
Gas works	4			4	281			3	284[3]
Total for Group I.	13			13	5,235			23	5,258
Group II. Manufacture of Machinery									
Petrol engines	6			6	749			136	885
Boilers	4	10		14[4]	168			77	245
Spinning machines	14	1		15	412			361	773
Weaving Looms	12	5	1	18	270			125	395
Dyeing and bleaching machines	6			6	101			116	217
Cotton gins	6			6	82			91	173
Napping machines	1		1	2	32			23	55
Other Weaving equipments	13	9	9	31	431	233		64	728
Knitting machines	35		5	40	406	6		261	673
Knitting needles	14			14	264	61	20	80	425
Silk reeling and weaving machines	6	2	1	9	37			50	87
Printing machines	22			22	206			183	389
Rice milling machines	7			7	21			80	101
Flour milling machines	6			6	105			100	205
Cigarette making machines	6			6	44			46	90
Lathes	8		1	9	22			74	96
Other kinds of machines	15	1	1	17	149			138	287

Classification	No. of Factories				No. of Workers				
	Using Motive Power	Using Man-Power	Unknown	Total	Males	Females	Child Workers	Apprentices	Total
Machine parts	44	16		60	345			299	644
Machine repairing	43	9		52	286			340	626
Electro-plating	66	1		67	676			404	1,080
Others	125	14	6	145	1,823			1,328	3,151
Total for Group II.	459	68	25	552	6,629	300	20	4,376	11,325
Group III. Manufacture of Electrical Machinery and Apparatus									
Electrical generators and motors	8			8	552	89	30	97	768
Electric bulbs	14		1	15	1,023	963	29	144	2,159
Flash lights	10		1	11	295			72	367
Electric batteries	5	11		16	281	103	21	55	460
Electrical instruments	10		2	12	596	2		127	725
Electric supplies	15	1	6	22	98	25		110	233
Wireless sets	3			3	82			18	100
Neon light tubes	3	1	2	6	101			101	202
Other electrical industries	1	2		3	15			2	17
Electric welding	5	16	22	43	150			144	294
Total for Group III.	74	31	34	139	3,193	1,182	80	870	5,325
Group IV. Metal Industries									
Foundries	65	1	45	111	2,366		8	944	3,318
Iron forging	9	191	6	206	1,457			390	1,847
Copper sheets, &c.	6	1		7	391				391
Manufacture of tin foil	2	3		5	118	25		6	149

Classification	No. of Factories				No. of Workers				
	Using Motive Power	Using Man-Power	Unknown	Total	Males	Females	Child Workers	Apprentices	Total
Total for Group IV.	82	196	51	329	4,332	25	8	1,340	5,705
Group V. Chemical Industries									
Acids	4			4[5]	206			6	212
Caustic soda		4	1	5[6]	18		1	19	38
Soap and candles	10	17	5	32	852	305		16	1,173
Cosmetics	11	21		32	756	884	2	44	1,686
Dyes	1		1	2[7]	28			28	56
Varnish	10	1		11	318	17	4	5	344
Printers' ink	7	3	1	11	219			24	243
Medicine	8	3	1	12	208	201	7	3	419
Peppermint	4		1	5[8]	37	3		2	42
Alcohol	1			1	24				24
Various kinds of chemical raw materials	8	4	1	13	291	32		7	330 (9)
Sensitised paper			1	1					
Enamelled ware	16	6	2	24	1,569	272		392	2,233
Matches	6			6	932	1,095	124	52	2,203
Celluloid products	5			5[10]	196	100		16	312
Bakelite products	8		1	9	364	30	30	25	449
Total for Group V.	99	59	15	173	6,018	2,939	168	639	9,764
Group VI. Manufacture of Metal Products									
Metallic furniture	4	2	4	10	546		20	8	574
Brass and iron bedsteads	7	14	1	22	104			153	257

Classification	No. of Factories					No. of Workers				
	Using Motive Power	Using Man-Power	Unknown	Total		Males	Females	Child Workers	Apprentices	Total
Safes	1	3		4		133			82	215
Tins	27	3	1	31		669	102	35	358	1,164
Lamps	11	13	1	25[11]		300	82	3	119	504
Nails	15	1	7	23		518	15	15	75	623
Aluminum and lead wires	4			4		57	4	6	3	70
Faucets	4	7	3	14		36			96	132
Weighing scales	3	15	2	20		91			25	116
Aluminumware	8	5	1	14		399	35	10	113	557
Iron and brass pipes	9	3		12		414			112	526
Hardware	12	23	17	52		231			290	521
Padlocks	5	4	1	10		145	101			246
Steel window frames	7	9		16		506			74	580
Knives	9	7	1	17		128	14	10	95	247
Others	17	19	9	45		660	120		133	913
Total for Group VI.	*143*	*128*	*48*	*319*		*4,937*	*473*	*99*	*1,736*	*7,245*
Group VII. Woodworking Industries										
Saw mills	14	1	3	18		379			1	380
Match splints	5			5		762	377	231		1,370
Cork stoppers		9	1	10		63			23	86
Wooden boxes	1	12		13		208	6		73	287
Toothpicks	1	1		2		15	26			41
Wooden furniture	1	6		7		715		10	52	777
Total for Group VII.	*22*	*29*	*4*	*55*		*2,142*	*409*	*241*	*149*	*2,941*

	No. of Factories				No. of Workers				
Classification	Using Motive Power	Using Man-Power	Unknown	Total	Males	Females	Child Workers	Apprentices	Total

Classification	Using Motive Power	Using Man-Power	Unknown	Total	Males	Females	Child Workers	Apprentices	Total
Group VIII. Manufacture of Bricks, Earthenware, Glass, etc.									
Glass	28	21	4	53	2,697	4	353	727	3,781
Stone powder	10	1	1	12	152	8			160
Pottery	3	1	2	6	135	82	3		220
Crucibles	4			4	105		9		114
Stone articles		2		2	9		2		11
Bricks	5	3	2	10	769	153	7	10	939
Stone breaking	4	5		9	101	25	2	8	136
Tiles	1	3	1	5	320				320
Cement	1			1	224				224
Lime	1	7		8	102			1	103
Slate	4	2	2	8	185			47	232
Total for Group VIII.	61	45	12	118	4,799	272	376	793	6,240
Group IX. Manufacture of Paper, Book-Binding and Printing									
Manufacture of paper	8			8	1,518	165		2	1,685
Manufacture of card-board	3			3	66	9		19	94
Other kinds of paper	1	4	1	6	37	14		18	69
Printing with letter press	111	76	25	212	3,220	37	18	1,232	4,507
Lithographic and offset printing	77	4		81	2,392	152		771	3,315
Book and newspaper printing and publishing	20		8	28	2,955	754	10	296	4,015
Engraving	4	9	1	14	191	20		72	283

Classification	No. of Factories					No. of Workers				
	Using Motive Power	Using Man-Power	Unknown	Total	Males	Females	Child Workers	Apprentices	Total
Type casting	8		1	9	546	18		111	675
Book-binding	7	27	1	35	554	222	16	301	1,093
Others	3	3	1	7	127			26	153
Total for Group IX.	242	123	38	403	11,606	1,391	44	2,848	15,889
Group X. Construction of Boats, Ships, and Vehicles for Land Transportation									
Shipbuilding	7	3	33	43	6,296			106	6,402[13]
Manufacture and repairing of steam-ship engines	5	2	1	8	69			96	165
Manufacture of railway cars, &c.	4		1	5	1,219			39	1,258[14]
Manufacture of automobile accessories	6	1		7	31			21	52
Repairing of automobiles	6	3	1	10	99			41	140[15]
Manufacture of other instruments of transportation	5	1	1	7	42		1	13	56[16]
Total for Group X.	33	10	37	80	7,756		1	316	8,073
Group XI. Textile Industries									
(1) Cotton spinning and weaving									
Cotton spinning and weaving	43		6	49	43,252	57,802	4,914		105,968
Cotton spinning only	15			15	5,910	18,189	979	4,927	30,005
Cotton weaving only	53	57	13	123	3,528	2,429	32	255	6,244
Cotton weaving and dyeing	47	24	3	74	2,802	2,941	16	143	5,902
Weaving of canvas	4	2		6	176	270		4	450
Weaving of towels and bed sheets	12	7	1	20	1,571	298	60	209	2,138
Making of warp and woof	6		2	8	98	91		3	192

Classification	No. of Factories				No. of Workers				
	Using Motive Power	Using Man-Power	Unknown	Total	Males	Females	Child Workers	Apprentices	Total
Cotton flannel finishing	9	5	3	17	192	3	2	9	206
Pattern cards	2	2	2	6	25	5		8	38
Mercerized thread	8	1		9	404				404
Cotton fluffing	15		6	21	672	686		2	1,360
Weaving of cotton flannel	6		3	9	146	68		22	236
Medicated gauze and cotton	4	1		5	126	45	11	7	189
(2) Silk, wool and flax manufactures									
Silk reeling and weaving									
Steam filatures	33		11	44	2,340	12,651	2,697	384	18,072
Reeling of silk waste	2		2	4	2,514	5,797	50		8,361
Silk weaving	304	4	4	312	8,799	3,815	221	1,297	14,132
Wool spinning and weaving	3			3	348	185		12	545
Wool spinning and weaving		27		27	904			10	914
Manufacture of rugs and carpets	17		6	23	579	644	46	57	1,326
Manufacture of woollen lining	1	1	1	3	70	32		102	204
Linen fabrics									
(3) Affiliated industries									
Dyeing	36	29	22	87	1,377			103	1,480
Printing of textiles	11	18	8	37	918	57	15	433	1,423
Dyeing and finishing	12	4	2	18	791	13		51	855
Total for Group XI.	643	182	95	920	77,542	106,021	9,043	8,038	200,644
Group XII. Manufacture of Leather, Rubber Products, etc.									
Tanning	18	28	4	50	941			66	1,007

Classification	No. of Factories					No. of Workers				
	Using Motive Power	Using Man-Power	Unknown	Total	Males	Females	Child Workers	Apprentices	Total
Manufacture of leather articles	4	21		25	267			83	350
Manufacture of rubber shoes	45		2	47[17]	4,658	6,782	18	53	11,511
Manufacture of tires	3			3[18]	302	141	10	12	465
Others	3		2	5	42				42
Total for Group XII.	73	49	8	130	6,210	6,923	28	214	13,375
Group XIII. Preparation and Manufacture of Foods, Drinks and Tobacco									
Liquor	1	4	3	8	366				366
Chinese sauce	1	5		6	53			3	56
Condiments	10	2		12	338	134	4	3	479
Soft drinks	5	1	5	11	276	4	6		286[19]
Ice and cold storage	9		4	13	462	550			1,012
Tea	12			12	206	254		1	461
Sugar	5	2	2	9	234	30			264
Canned food	8	2		10	525	238		70	833
Candies	7	7		14	118	133	2	18	271
Bread and biscuits	6	10	1	17	356	81	2	469	908
Cigars and cigarettes	49	5	7	61	10,836	14,744	243	89	25,912
Wheat flour	15		1	16	3,184			110	3,294
Oil	12		4	16	2,201				2,201
Rice	38			38	232			18	250
Egg flour	3			3	1,370				1,370
Starch	4	3		7	137				137
Others	6	9	3	18	316	15		3	334

Classification	No. of Factories					No. of Workers				
	Using Motive Power	Using Man-Power	Unknown	Total	Males	Females	Child Workers	Apprentices	Total
Total for Group XIII. Manufacture of Clothing and Allied products	191	50	30	271	21,210	16,183	257	784	38,434
Group XIV.									
Hats	14	11	1	26	455	184	13	113	765
Woollen and cotton knitted goods	32	22	4	58	1,508	1,600	50	202	3,360
Knitted hosiery	55	65	6	126	3,104	4,206	59	236	7,605
Sewing of knitted hosiery	3	4		7	40	25		10	50
Leather shoes	2	14		16	178	482		41	244
Military uniforms	49	13	1	63	770	482		2	1,254
Handkerchiefs	13	1	1	15	151	630		14	795
Thread for embroidery	1	7		8	59	2			61
Thread and yarn	4	3		7	54	62		4	120
Waxed thread	8	1	2	11	197	178		4	379
Thread on spools	6		1	7	36	109	10	4	159
Elastic belts	5		1	6	86	31		6	123
Silk trimmings	24	2		26	1,259	326	7	25	1,617
Cotton ribbons	12	21		33	254	42	3	61	360
Leather belts used by the military		1		1	5			1	6
Buttons	7	2	1	10	86	7		21	114
Others	5	2	7	14	121	30		14	165
Total for Group XIV.	240	169	25	434	8,363	7,914	142	758	17,177
Group XV. Making of Scientific and Musical Instruments, Clocks and Watches, etc.	1	1	1	3	24	2		10	36
Ornaments	1			1					

Classification	No. of Factories				No. of Workers				
	Using Motive Power	Using Man-Power	Unknown	Total	Males	Females	Child Workers	Apprentices	Total
Wooden frames of mirrors	2	12		14	197	14		34	245
Organs		9	3	12	138	3		20	161
Gramaphones and gramaphone records	5	2	1	8	228	8		10	246
Scientific apparatus	6	4	1	11	95	9		54	158
Clocks	4	2	2	8	233			12	245
Educational supplies	4	15	4	23	180	110		49	339
Stencil paper	1	2	1	4	79	6		4	89
Typewriters	2	1	2	5²⁰	30			21	51
Fountain pens	5			5²¹	98	13		41	152
Athletic goods	2	4	2	8	110	4		17	131
Toys	9	12		21	234	61		77	372
Total for Group XV.	41	64	17	122	1,646	230		349	2,225
Group XVI. Other Manufacturing Industries									
Thermos bottles	28	1	1	30	739	119	10	267	1,135
Coal briquettes	10		5	15	407	7		6	420
Machine-made ropes	1	4		5	168	60		5	233
Umbrellas	5	14	4	23	223	74	12	102	411
Spectacles	4	2		6	285			122	407
Mirrors	7	2	2	11	227		30	87	344
Tooth brushes	9	1		10	236	201	6	81	524
Cartons	27	25	24	76	946	217		209	1,372
Total for Group XVI.	91	49	36	176	3,231	678	58	879	4,846
Grand Total for the Sixteen Groups	2,507	1,252	475	4,234	174,849	144,940	10,565	24,112	354,466

*Figures in this table together with Notes 1 to 21 are taken from Chapter XVI of *the Shanghai Year Book, 1935* published by the History Compilation Bureau of Greater Shanghai. According to the same chapter all of the figures are compiled from data contained in *the Directory of Shanghai Factories, 1934* published by the Bureau of Social Affairs of the Shanghai City Government, with the only exception of the section on power plants where reference is made to *Industries in Shanghai*, also a publication of the latter organization in 1930. Upon checking we find the figures do not tally with those of *the Directory* which we have incorporated in Table III, Appendix D. *The Directory*, however, gives no separate figures for the minor divisions as are given here.

Notes:

(1) Number of workers of four plants only, the number of extemporary workers of one of the four plants being also lacking.
(2) Number of workers of three plants only.
(3) Number of workers of two plants only.
(4) Including one "cold works" factory.
(5) Including Tien Lee Synthetic Nitrogen Products Co., Ltd., whose goods have not been marketed.
(6) Including Tien Yuan Electro & Chemical Works which manufactures acids as well as caustic soda.
(7) Including Chung Foo Factory which has not started operations.
(8) Including manufactories of camphor.
(9) Number of workers not reported.
(10) Including manufactories of artificial ivory.
(11) Including manufactories of silk lamp shades.
(12) Including lithographic and rubber offset printing.
(13) Number of workers of fifteen factories only.
(14) Number of workers of four factories only.
(15) Number of workers of nine factories only.
(16) Number of workers of four factories only.
(17) All of these factories use both man-labour and motive power.
(18) Vide (17).
(19) Not including workers extemporarily employed in the summer season.
(20) Including manufactories of other kinds of educational equipment.
(21) Including manufactories of pencils.

APPENRIX D
COMPARATIVE STATISTICS
TABLE D-I. COMPARISON OF CAPITALIZATION AND NUMBER OF WORKERS OF INDIVIDUAL INDUSTRIES

Classification	(1) Kinds of Data	(2) No. of Factories	(3) Amount of Capital ($)	(4) No. of Workers Male	(5) Female	(6) Child	(7) Total
Woodworking Industries							
Saw mills	a						
	b	23		1,886			1,886
	c	8	79,333*	390		2	392
	d	4	345,944	376		2	378
Manufacture of wooden, ratten and bamboo articles	a	13	57,350	279	100	12	391
	b						
	c	14	327,809	444	65	84	593
	d	6	266,531	366	17	28	411
Metal Industry							
Founding	a	47	120,700	653		277	930
	b	100		997		452	1,449
	c	35	175,200	498		275	773
	d	21	161,000	484		268	752
Manufacture of Machinery and Miscellaneous Metal Products							
Manufacture and repairing of machines	a	163	1,765,450	3,607	81	1,434	5,122
	b	418		5,834		2,978	8,812
	c	173	1,979,119*	3,580	150	2,175	5,905
	d	85	2,181,489*	3,171	76	1,625	4,872
Manufacture of metal products	a	57	741,550 (125,000)	964	111	443	1,518
	b						
	c	61	603,133*	1,202	142	631	1,975
	d	46	1,943,860	2,406	336	485	3,227

Classification	(1) Kinds of Data	(2) No. of Factories	(3) Amount of Capital ($)	(4) No. of Workers Male	(5) Female	(6) Child	(7) Total
Manufacture of electric machines and apparatus	a	21	517,300	941	418	86	1,445
	b						
	c	54	1,055,072	1,483	360	448	2,291
	d	42	3,655,020*	2,406	644	573	3,623
Construction of Boats, Ships, and Vehicles for Land Transportation							
Shipbuilding	a	2	38,000	65		72	137
	b	13		5,994		254	6,248
	c	9	384,500*	2,126		132	2,258
	d	14	463,000*	2,329		301	2,630
Manufacture of Bricks, Earthenware, Glass, etc.							
Bricks and cement	a	21	1,532,000	872	70	26	968
	b						
	c	5	2,755,600	842	192	20	1,054
	d	5	2,858,600	779	248	25	1,052
Glassware	a	16	904,500 (393,000)	745	12	486	1,243
	b	30		1,588		1,455	3,043
	c	24	417,039	815	11	668	1,494
	d	27	603,500*	1,230	3	836	2,069
Coal briquettes	a	8	197,300	162	2	9	173
	b						
	c	12	422,000*	317			317
	d	6	390,000*	386			386
Production and Transmission of Electricity and Supply of Water							
Electric and water works	a	8	18,930,000 (10,000,000)	1,774		7	1,781
	b						

Classification	(1) Kinds of Data	(2) No. of Factories	(3) Amount of Capital ($)	(4)	(5)	(6)	(7)
				\multicolumn{4}{c}{No. of Workers}			
				Male	Female	Child	Total
	c	5	11,260,000	1,079			1,079
	d	3	11,290,000	1,020			1,020
Manufacture of Chemicals and Allied Products							
Matches	a	7	889,800	910	1,498	329	2,737
	b	7		911	1,232	553	2,696
	c	4	2,240,080	754	1,101	149	2,004
	d	7	3,536,900	731	1,345	212	2,288
Soap and candles	a	23	633,900	372	174	9	555
	b	36		800	305		1,105
	c	13	962,222	389	235	14	638
	d	6	655,000	367	253	8	628
Enamelled ware	a	8	258,400	517	50	85	652
	b	16		1,857	353	90	2,300
	c	10	814,000	1,348	234	235	1,817
	d	19	1,327,500	1,784	385	256	2,425
Varnish	a	3	275,000	120	6	5	131
	b						
	c	4	571,000	183	16		199
	d	3	570,000	364	16	16	396
Printer's ink	a	2					
	b						
	c	5	88,000	48*			48*
	d	2	150,000	60		4	64
Cosmetics	a	20	615,600	212	381	37	630
	b						
	c	13	3,291,000	432	967	6	1,405
	d	11	5,125,000	376	817	10	1,203
Medicine	a	14	954,000 (640,900)	121	96	2	219
	b						
	c	2	700,000	90	120	6	216
	d	6	1,070,000	187	195	6	388
Textile Industries							
Cotton ginning	a	5	150,160	416	300	23	739
	b						
	c	8	87,000*	181	331	10	522
	d	5	43,000*	129	130	42	301

Classification	(1) Kinds of Data	(2) No. of Factories	(3) Amount of Capital ($)	(4) Male	(5) Female	(6) Child	(7) Total
				\multicolumn{4}{c}{No. of Workers}			
Cotton spinning	a	55	189,580,800 (152,350,800)	28,760	62,584	2,998	94,342
	b	61 (33)					127,604 (71,029)
	c	29	37,952,220*	12,957*	47,353*	2,414*	62,724*
	d	29	49,117,474	11,131	43,693	1,118	60,406
Cotton weaving	a	99	2,243,650	4,323	4,493	511	9,327
	b	105		3,547	4,172	303	8,022
	c	73	5,253,073*	3,879	3,596	414	7,889
	d	70	4,276,898*	3,249	5,484	297	9,030
Silk reeling	a	90	2,501,900 (76,000)	2,148	39,484	10,831	52,463
	b	107		1,712	37,211	12,453	51,376
	c	66	2,778,611	1,487	29,709	9,161	40,357
	d	49	214,930*	953	22,606	6,169	29,728
Silk weaving	a	46	1,279,000	3,644	2,190	428	6,262
	b	48		2,283	1,109		3,392
	c	250	4,549,383*	5,302	2,974*	1,191	9,467*
	d	122	4,206,855*	5,100	3,380	1,913	10,393
Wool weaving	a	7	213,700	417	255	156	828
	b						
	c	14	1,586,443	534	641	112	1,287
	d	26	3,436,675*	1,549	1,627	250	3,426
Dyeing and printing of textiles	a	81	601,450	2,675	421	94	3,190
	b	48		2,914			2,914
	c	50	1,310,734*	1,860*	41*	402*	2,303*
	d	53	1,393,000	2,360	45	357	2,762
Manufacture of trimmings and ribbons	a	23	26,300	148	222	70	440
	b						
	c	29	289,344*	464	357	71	892
	d	8	314,000	570	263	6	839
Clothing Industries Including Hosiery Knitted goods	a	110	1,575,600 (250,000)	2,224	4,127	185	6,536
	b	102		2,236	6,261	128	8,625

Classification	(1) Kinds of Data	(2) No. of Factories	(3) Amount of Capital ($)	(4) No. of Workers Male	(5) No. of Workers Female	(6) No. of Workers Child	(7) No. of Workers Total
Hats	c	124	3,826,643*	2,871	6,097	621	9,589
	d	69	4,445,626	2,775	6,130	331	9,236
	a	8	199,500 (43,000)	186	82	8	276
	b						
Umbrellas	c	12	323,778	258	127	74	459
	d	7	238,000	272	116	76	464
	a	9	62,200	90	53	21	164
	b						
Clothes	c	14	33,000*	127	151	52	330
	d	2	61,500	200	15	47	262
	a	3	40,000	550	400	100	1,050
	b						
Manufacture of Leather, Rubber Products. etc.	c						
	d						
Manufacture of leather	a	18	2,075,430 (943,000)	552	1	1	554
	b	150		1,552	2	296	1,850
	c	18	703,128	463		43	506
	d	10	980,000	397	30	24	451
Preparation and Manufacture of Foods, Drinks and Tobacco							
Rice mills	a	46	312,350	399			399
	b						
	c	12	116,722*	166		16	182
	d	1	10,000	32			32
Wheat flour mills	a	12	5,835,500	1,871			1,871
	b	13		2,112			2,112
	c	15	6,463,889	2,403			2,403
	d	15	6,249,650	2,516			2,516
Candies and canned food	a	47	748,100	780	415	56	1,251
	b						

Classification	(1) Kinds of Data	(2) No. of Factories	(3) Amount of Capital ($)	(4) Male	(5) Female	(6) Child	(7) Total
				\multicolumn{4}{c}{No. of Workers}

Classification	Kinds of Data	No. of Factories	Amount of Capital ($)	Male	Female	Child	Total
	c	18	542,072	435	380	111	926
	d	9	1,497,600	533	472	100	1,105
Oil mills	a	12	1,323,200 (361,100)	1,501			1,501
	b	11		1,951			1,951
	c	14	1,350,778	2,814		11	2,825
	d	10	1,271,056	2,020		6	2,026
Cigars and cigarettes	a	69	40,740,110 (23,850,000)	3,147	5,857	474	9,478
	b	72 (2)		7,296 (4,487)	15,612 (4,411)	1,259 (1,259)	24,167 (10,157)
	c	51	21,230,872*	2,539*	11,207*	395	14,141*
	d	46	19,002,667*	3,067	14,052	326	17,445
Soda water and other soft drinks	a	6	367,000	71			71
	b						
	c	2	310,000	188		8	196
	d	2	350,000	210		10	220
Condiments	a	5	252,000	106	43	2	151
	b						
	c	8	541,000	337	123	6	466
	d	5	870,000	288	144	3	435
Frozen egg products	a	1	111,100 (111,100)	125	155	7	287
	b	7 (7)		1,399 (1,399)	2,186 (2,186)		3,585 (3,585)
	c	1	500,000	150	200		350
	d	1	500,000	150	200		350
Manufacture of Paper, Book-Binding and Printing							
Manufacture of paper	a	13	1,975,700	1,044	1,118	31	2,193
	b	7		872	681		1,553
	c	7	2,072,222	768	482	4	1,254
	d	7	2,306,389	829	506		1,415
Printing	a	210	11,072,891 (615,791)	6,542	596	1,110	8,248
	b	219 (6)		7,455 (467)	430 (19)	2,452 (146)	10,337 ((632))
	c	106	14,596,189*	5,920	811	1,479	8,210

Classification	(1) Kinds of Data	(2) No. of Factories	(3) Amount of Capital ($)	(4) Male	(5) Female	(6) Child	(7) Total
				\multicolumn{3}{c}{No. of Workers}	
Cartons	d	92	13,149,000*	5,863	278	1,456	7,597
	a	15	76,700	464	105	32	601
	b						
	c	20	120,000	314	143	68	525
	d	10	134,000	328	137	33	498
Manufacture of Scientific and Musical Instruments, Clocks and Watches, etc.							
Musical instruments and toys	a	11	169,800 (20,000)	113	6	27	146
	b						
	c	24	220,467	568		159	727
	d	6	165,000	176	78	52	306
Writing outfit	a	4	23,000	50	19	9	78
	b						
	c	9	190,300	116	58	13	187
	d	5	241,000	134	50	44	228
Scientific apparatus	a	3	80,300	73		11	84
	b						
	c	5	35,500	60	10	46	116
	d	5	148,500	227	19	72	318
Other Manufacturing Industries							
Tooth brushes	a	6	780,500 (700,000)	116	292	23	431
	b						
	c	6	212,300	197	151	84	432
	d	6	260,000	259	369	7	635
Spectacles	a	5	22,900	36		1	37
	b						
	c						
	d						

Notes: (1) In the "Kinds of Data" column of the above table, "a" stands for data taken from *Industries in Shanghai* covering 1928, "b" for these of 1929 from *Wages and Hour of Labour* while "c" and "d" stands corresponding statistical result of our 1931 and 1933 survey.

(2) As a detailed comparision of the statistics for 1931 and 1933 is shown in Table D-III of this Appenclit and industries which have figures for one or both of the years only and none for 1928 or 1929 purposely excluded from this table to avoid duplication.

(3) There being a slight difference in classification methods, the figures for "Others" of the various major industrial groups appearing in *Industries in Shanghai* cannot be made use of in the table above.

(4) The incompleteness of the statistics given makes the calculation of group and grand totals meaningless.

(5) The absence of capitalization figures after "b" in the table is due to the lack of same in the original source, *Wages and Hours of Labour*.

(6) Figures in brackets refer to the number of foreign factories included, their number of workers, or the amount of capital involved as the case may be.

(7) Figures after "b" under "Manufacture and repairing of machines" represent not only those for this sub-division, but also the next two subdivisions for which separate figures are not availble.

TABLE D.II. COMPARISON OF CAPITALIZATION AND NUMBER OF WORKERS OF THE SIXTEEN INDUSTRIAL GROUPS

	(1)	(2)	(3)	(4)	(5)	(6)	(7)	(8)
Classification	Kinds of Data	No. of Factories	Amount of Capital ($)	Male	Female	Child	Unclassified	Total
						No. of Workers		
I. Woodworking Industry	a	23		1,886				1,886
	b	22	407,142*	834	65	86		985
	c	10	612,475	742	17	30		789
	d	68	9,149,900 (89)	2,488	409	390	724	4,011 (52)
II. Furniture Manufacturing	a							
	b	17	835,500	1,279		309		1,588
	c	7	378,500	478	300	216		994
	d							
III. Metal Industry	a	100		997		452		1,449
	b	36	375,200	527		276		803
	c	22	361,000	517		270		787
	d	489	1,088,500 (120)	3,008	25	1,349	1,116	5,498 (365)
IV. Manufacture of Machinery and Miscellaneous Metal Products	a	418		5,834		2,978		8,812
	b	288	3,637,324*	6,265	652	3,254		10,171
	c	173	7,780,369*	7,083	1,056	2,683		11,722
	d	1,519	9,377,850 (588)	13,927	1,861	7,050	852	23,690 (846)

V. Construction of Boats, Ships, and

Classification	(1) Kinds of Data	(2) No. of Factories	(3) Amount of Capital ($)	(4) Male	(5) Female	(6) Child	(7) Unclassified	(8) Total
Vehicles for Land Transportation	a	13		5,994		254		6,248
	b	21	459,300*	2,260		198	1,037	3,495
	c	17	533,000*	3,357		347		3,704
	d	88	8,978,250 (26)	1,413		317	6,306	8,036 (47)
VI. Manufacture of Bricks, Earthenware, Glass, etc.	a	30		1,588		1,455		3,043
	b	44	3,405,855*	1,972	247	691		2,910
	c	41	4,038,100*	2,561	259	871		3,691
	d	135	3,415,200 (64)	3,562	272	1,120	1,207	6,161 (108)
VII. Building Material	a							
	b	5	69,555*	169		26		195
	c	7	165,000*	336		102		438
	d							
VIII. Production and Transmission of Electricity and Supply of Water	a							
	b	5	11,260,000	1,079				1,079
	c	3	11,290,000	1,020				1,020
	d	13	88,010,000 (9)	5,235		23		5,258 (9)
IX. Manufacture of Chemicals and								

Classification	(1) Kinds of Data	(2) No. of Factories	(3) Amount of Capital ($)	(4) Male	(5) Female	(6) Child	(7) Unclassified	(8) Total
Allied Products	a	59	9,394,246	3,568	1,890	643		6,101
	b	60		3,812*	3,271	481		7,564*
	c	78	15,200,094*	5,248	3,417	581		9,246
	d	209	15,890,700	5,598	3,011	773	715	10,097
			(144)					(176)
X. Textile Industry	a	471		12,692	48,753	12,884	127,604	201,933
	b	546	54,743,285*	27,504*	87,540*	14,198*	10	129,252*
	c	391	63,623,946*	25,845	78,738	10,218	5,364	120,165
	d	1,006	269,271,200	45,978	83,935	15,883	1,297	147,093
			(542)					(828)
XI. Clothing Industry Including Hosiery	a							
	b	170	4,455,387*	3,371	7,015	791		11,177
	c	89	4,974,459	3,461	6,655	489		10,605
	d	473	6,670,400	7,109	7,972	673	1,510	17,264
			(275)					(369)
XII. Manufacture of Leather, Rubber Products, etc.	a	150		1,552	2	296		1,850
	b	57	3,226,840*	4,054	4,294	208		8,556
	c	55	5,063,888*	4,991	6,683	158		11,832
	d	132	350,750	6,180	6,923	242		13,345
			(83)					(117)
XIII. Preparation and Manufacture of Foods, Drinks and Tobacco	a	103		12,758	17,798	1,259		31,815
	b	175	32,000,832*	9,987*	12,793*	556		23,336*

Classification	(1) Kinds of Data	(2) No. of Factories	(3) Amount of Capital ($)	(4) Male	(5) Female	(6) Child	(7) Unclassified	(8) Total
	c	143	31,093,173*	10,240	16,600	445		27,375
	d	323	39,248,091 (221)	17,175	16,486	611	1,600	35,872 (255)
XIV. Manufacture of Paper, Book-Binding and Printing	a	226		8,327	1,111	2,452		11,890
	b	155	16,898,611*	7,405	1,663	1,624		10,692
	c	114	16,073,389*	7,226	974	1,506	80	9,786
	d	577	22,508,700 (293)	11,030	718	2,672	1,419	15,839 (385)
XV. Manufacture of Scientific and Musical Instruments, Clocks and Watches, etc.	a							
	b	39	453,267	771	68	232		1,071
	c	18	624,500	737	153	172		1,062
	d	124	2,233,400 (69)	1,586	230	347	191	2,354 (104)
XVI. Other Manufacturing Industries	a							
	b	32	707,150*	708	452	118		1,278
	c	18	874,000*	951	391	178		1,520
	d	262	2,100,400 (117)	2,943	656	960	508	5,067 (148)
All Industries	a	1,593		55,196	69,554	22,673	127,604	275,027
	b	1,672	142,329,494*	71,997*	118,060*	23,048*	1,047	214,152*
	c	1,186	162,685,893*	75,693	115,333	18,266	5,444	214,736
	d	5,418	478,293,341 (2540)	127,232	122,498	32,410	17,445	299,585 (3893)

Notes: (1) In the above table under the heading of "Kinds of Data", "a" stands for data of 1929 from *Wages and Hours of Labour*, "b" and "c" our own figures for 1931 and 1933, and "d" those taken from the *Directory of Shanghai Factories, 1934*.
(2) In the *Directory of Shanghai Factories*, three main divisions Correspond to Group IV, namely, "Manufacture of Machinery", "Manufacture of Electrical Apparatus" and "Manufacture of Metal Products". In order to make comparison possible, only the totals of these three divisions are shown in the table above. Likewise, the separate figures for child workers and apprentices given by *the Directory* are added together and only the sum is incorporated into the table under "Child Workers" to facilitate comparison.
(3) The figures in brackets in the table denote the number of factories, of which the capitalization or number of workers is known and represented by the figures immediately preceding them.
(4) No data from *Industries in Shanghai* are included in this table because the groups of industries are classified differently in that publication, and its figures are, therefore, not comparable with those from other sources.

TABLE D-III. COMPARISON OF MAJOR STATISTICAL DATA OF THE 1931 AND 1933 SURVEYS

Code	Classification	Kinds of Data (1)	(2) No. of Factories	(3) Amount of Capital ($)	(4) Male Workers	(5) Female Workers	(6) Child Workers	(7) Total No. of Workers	(8) Rented Electric Power (H.P.)	(9) Power of Prime Movers (H.P.)	(10) Value of Output of the Preceding Year ($)
Group I. Woodworking Industries											
1-1	Saw mills	a	8	79,333*	390		2	392	578.0	35.0	1,605,555.55*
		b	2	40,000	296		2	298	305.0		350,000.00
		c	4	345,944	376		2	378	475.0	100.0	1,529,200.00
1-2	Manufacture of wooden articles	a	13	323,809	422	50	77	549	141.0	130.0	577,891.77*
		b	6	206,309	347	36	52	435	80.5	130.0	404,277.77*
		c	6	266,531	366	17	28	411	62.5	105.0	611,333.33*
1-3	Manufacture of bamboo articles	a	1	4,000	22	15	7	44	10.0		20,000.00
		b	1	4,000	22	15	7	44	10.0		20,000.00
		c									
Total for Group I.		a	22	407,142*	834	65	86	985	729.0	165.0	2,203,447.32*
		b	9	340,309	665	51	61	777	395.5	130.0	774,277.77*
		c	10	612,475	742	17	30	789	537.5	205.0	2,140,533.33*
Group II. Furniture Manufacturing											
2-1	Wooden furniture	a	3	420,000	689			689			1,150,000.00
		b									
		c									
2-2	Steel furniture	a	9	371,800	427		164	591	270.0		535,800.00*
		b	3	360,000	394		120	514	240.0		460,000.00*
		c	6	368,500	403		141	544	205.0		760,350.00
2-3	Rugs and carpets	a	5	43,700	163		145	308			151,343.95*
		b									
		c	1	10,000	75		75	450	5.5		105,000.00
Total for Group II.		a	17	835,500	1,279	300	309	1,588	270.0		1,837,143.95*
		b	3	360,000	394		120	514	240.0		460,000.00*
		c	7	378,500	478	300	216	994	210.5		865,350.00
Group III. Metal Industries											
3-1	Founding	a	35	175,200	498		275	773	162.0		789,530.00*
		b	8	106,000	213		89	302	54.0		383,200.00
		c	21	161,000	484		268	752	203.5		950,000.00*
3-2	Steel refining	a	1	200,000	29		1	30	130.0		(2)
		b	1	200,000	29		1	30	130.0		(2)
		c	1	200,000	33		2	35	130.0		36,000.00
total for Group III.		a	36	375,200	527		276	803	292.0		789,530.00*
		b	9	306,000	242		90	332	184.0		383,200.00
		c	22	361,000	517		270	787	333.5		986,000.00*
Group IV. Manufacture of Machinery and Miscellaneous Metal Products											

Code	Classification	(1) Kinds of Data	(2) No. of Factories	(3) Amount of Capital ($)	(4) Male Workers	(5) Female Workers	(6) Child Workers	(7) Total No. of Workers	(8) Rented Electric Power (H.P.)	(9) Power of Prime Movers (H.P.)	(10) Value of Output of the Preceding Year ($)
4-1	Manufacture and repairing of machines	a	173	1,979,119*	3,580	150	2,175	5,905	2,414.0	382.5	4,937,146.64*
		b	48	1,546,768*	2,671	150	1,178	3,999	1,862.5	382.5	2,276,045.48*
		c	85	2,181,489*	3,171	76	1,625	4,872	1,004.0	102.5	6,021,330.20*
4-2	Manufacture of metal products	a	61	603,133*	1,202	142	631	1,975	579.5		2,878,914.44*
		b	14	372,000	668	139	439	1,246	334.0		2,056,400.00
		c	46	1,943,860	2,406	336	485	3,227	2,109.5		8,084,307.37
4-3	Manufacture of electric machines and apparatus	a	54	1,055,072	1,483	360	448	2,291	567.3	25.0	3,173,430.85*
		b	20	922,522	1,130	317	297	1,744	392.5	25.0	2,427,444.41*
		c	42	3,655,020*	2,406	644	573	3,623	1,169.0	25.0	7,964,166.67
Total for Group IV.		a	288	3,637,324*	6,265	652	3,254	10,171	3,560.8	407.5	10,989,491.93*
		b	82	2,841,290*	4,469	606	1,914	6,989	2,589.0	407.5	6,759,889.59*
		c	173	7,780,369*	7,983	1,056	2,683	11,722	4,282.5	127.5	22,069,804.24*
Group V. Construction of Boats, Ships, and Vehicle for Land Transportation
5-1	Construction of ships and cars	a	21	459,300*	2,260		198	3,495[3]	2,936.8	515.0	7,390,466.80*
		b	10	401,500*	2,194		145	3,376[3]	2,893.3	500.0	7,297,429.02*
		c	17	533,000*	3,357		347	3,704	1,567.0*	1,514.0	8,343,409.58*
Total for Group V.		a	21	459,300*	2,260		198	3,495[3]	2,936.8	515.0	7,390,466.80*
		b	10	401,500*	2,194		145	3,376[3]	2,893.3	500.0	7,297,429.02*
		c	17	533,000*	3,357		347	3,704	1,567.0*	1,514.0	8,343,409.58*
Group VI. Manufacture of Bricks, Earthenware, Glass, etc.
6-1	Bricks and crucibles	a	5	1,137,000	649	192	23	864	55.0	205.0	631,411.10
		b	3	1,120,000	619	192	19	830	55.0	205.0	591,133.33
		c	8	1,570,000	942	248	35	1,225	314.0	235.0	1,118,383.29*
6-2	Glassware	a	24	417,039	815	11	668	1,494	87.5	24.0	886,658.00*
		b	9	347,000	512	11	348	871	66.0	24.0	656,014.00
		c	27	603,500*	1,230	3	836	2,069	151.0*	0.5	1,339,964.00*
6-3	Cement	a	1	1,658,600	220			220		2,060.0	1,804,320.42
		b	1	1,658,600	220			220		2,060.0	1,804,320.42
		c	1	1,658,600	215			215		2,060.0	2,821,632.00
6-4	Lime and stone breaking	a	14	213,216*	288	44		332	333.0		693,306.40*
		b	2	23,000	101			101	25.0		85,000.00
		c	5	226,000	174	8		182	355.0		470,000.00
Total for Group VI.		a	44	3,405,855*	1,972	247	691	2,910	475.5	2,289.0	4,015,695.92*
		b	15	3,128,600	1,452	203	367	2,022	146.0	2,289.0	3,136,467.75
		c	41	4,038,100*	2,561	259	871	3,691	820.0*	2,295.5	5,749,979.29

Code	Classification	(1) Kinds of Data	(2) No. of Factories	(3) Amount of Capital ($)	(4) Male Workers	(5) Female Workers	(6) Child Workers	(7) Total No. of Workers	(8) Rented Electric Power (H. P.)	(9) Power of Prime Movers (H. P.)	(10) Value of Output of the Preceding Year ($)
Group VII. Building Material											
7-1	Building material	a	5	69,555*	169		26	195	6.0	50.0	425,555.55*
		b	2	55,555*	111		20	131	6.0	50.0	305,555.55*
		c	7	165,000*	336		102	438	58.0*		1,111,800.00*
	Total for Group VII.	a	5	69,555*	169		26	195	6.0	50.0	425,555.55*
		b	2	55,555*	111		20	131	6.0	50.0	305,555.55*
		c	7	165,000*	336		102	438	58.0*		1,111,800.00*
Group VIII. Production and Transmission of Electricity and Supply of Water											
8-1	Electric and water works	a	5	11,260,000	1,079			1,079	1,512.9	51,581.3	6,778,300.24
		b	4	11,110,000	1,060			1,060	1,512.9	51,133.3	6,668,300.24
		c	3	11,290,000	1,020			1,020	1,512.9	48,666.7	7,930,813.24
	Total for Group VIII.	a	5	11,260,000	1,079			1,079	1,512.9	51,581.3	6,778,300.24
		b	4	11,110,000	1,060			1,060	1,512.9	51,133.3	6,668,300.24
		c	3	11,290,000	1,020			1,020	1,512.9	48,666.7	7,930,813.24
Group IX. Chemicals and Allied Products											
9-1	Matches	a	4	2,240,080	754	1,101	149	2,004	58.0	144.0	2,589,861.11
		b	3	2,140,080	683	999	141	1,823	58.0	144.0	2,449,861.11
		c	7	3,536,900	731	1,345	212	2,288	248.0	218.0	3,572,927.50
9-2	Soap, washing soda and candles	a	14	1,002,222	409	235	14	658	98.0	81.0	4,217,999.88
		b	3	600,000	208	207	6	421	67.0	62.0	2,749,122.11
		c	6	655,000	367	253	8	628	247.0	90.0	3,096,775.00
9-3	Enamelled ware	a	10	814,500	1,348	234	235	1,817	460.3	244.0	2,776,666.67
		b	6	770,000	1,277	229	206	1,712	426.3	244.0	2,646,666.67
		c	19	1,327,500	1,784	385	256	2,425	727.0	200.0	4,464,000.00
9-4	Varnish and printer's ink	a	9	659,000	231*	16		247*	471.0		1,296,180.00*
		b	3	545,000	171	16		187	352.0		1,010,000.00*
		c	5	720,000	424	16	20	460	1,097.0		4,060,000.00
9-5	Dyes	a									
		b									(4)
		c	1	100,000	34			34	35.0		3,103,154.97
9-6	Cosmetics	a	13	3,291,000	432	967	6	1,405	63.5		2,900,316.97
		b	5	3,200,000	385	788		1,173	62.5		5,457,326.57
		c	11	5,125,000	376	817	10	1,203	263.0		942,080.00
9-7	Medicine	a	2	700,000	90	120	6	216	52.4		942,080.00
		b	2	700,000	187	120	6				
		c	6	1,070,000		195	6	388	98.2	30.0	1,506,080.00*
9-8	Celluloid products	a	6	167,944	208	98	10	316	179.5		425,555.56

Code	Classification	(1) Kinds of Data	(2) No. of Factories	(3) Amount of Capital ($)	(4) Male Workers	(5) Female Workers	(6) Child Workers	(7) Total No. of Workers	(8) Rented Electric Power (H. P.)	(9) Power of Prime Movers (H. P.)	(10) Value of Output of the Preceding Year ($)
9-9	Beetle and bakelite	b	4	160,000	169	93	5	267	171.5		425,555.56
		c	6	260,000	324	160	8	492	303.0	300.0	566,920.00
9-10	Caustic soda	a									
		b									
		c	7	229,000*	305	22	54	381	61.5		620,000.00
9-11	Calcium and magnesium carbonates	a									
		b	1	750,000	53			53	57.0	24.0	(5)
		c									
9-12	Oxygen and acetylene	a									
		b									
		c	3	650,000	238	2		240	267.0		764,304.00
9-13	Other chemical products	a	1	250,000	22			22	90.0		
		b	2	520,000	340	500	61	901	700.0	50.0	1,000,000.00
		c	2	520,000	340	500	61	901	700.0	50.0	1,000,000.00
	Total for Group IX.	a	5	526,694	403	222	7	632	382.0*		1,759,400.00
		b	60	9,394,246	3,812*	3,271	481	7,564*	2,082.7	519.0	16,351,498.19*
		c	28	8,635,680	3,323	2,952	425	6,700	1,889.7	500.0	14,114,602.42*
			78	15,200,094*	5,248	3,417	581	9,246	3,875.7*	862.0	25,867,733.07*
Group X. Textile Industries											
10-1	Cotton ginning	a	8	87,000*	181	331	10	522	40.0	275.0	5,543,585.00
		b	4	66,000	144	270		414	40.0	195.0	4,197,860.00
		c	5	43,000*	129	130	42	301	40.0	275.0	5,745,812.00
10-2	Cotton fluffing	a	3	83,333	130	130		260	468.3	60.0	814,868.89
		b	3	83,333	130	130		260	468.3		814,868.89
		c	8	88,889	378	112		490	636.0		1,314,013.33
10-3	Cotton spinning	a	29	37,952,220*	12,957*	47,353*	2,414*	62,724*	39,471.9	5,485.0	117,121,331.06*
		b	29	37,952,220*	12,957*	47,353*	2,414*	62,724*	39,471.9	5,485.0	117,121,331.06*
		c	29	49,117,474	11,131	43,693	1,118	60,4067	52,261.7	9,602.0	121,483,533.90
10-4	Cotton weaving	a	73	5,253,073	3,879	3,596	414	7,889	2,589.2	140.0	14,349,177.54*
		b	34	5,161,278	3,432	3,009	278	6,719	2,561.7	140.0	13,275,881.75*
		c	70	4,276,898*	3,249	5,484	297	9,030	4,227.8*	165.0	22,471,685.35*
10-5	Medicicated gauze and cotton	a	2	15,000	66	16	10	92	11.5		42,480.00
		b	2	15,000	66	16	10	92	11.5		42,480.00
		c	3	68,000	91	36	16	143	50.5		121,000.00
10-6	Steam filature silk	a	66	2,778,611	1,487	29,709	9,161	40,357		1,331.0	29,129,307.78*
		b	66	2,778,611	1,487	29,709	9,161	40,357		1,331.0	29,129,307.78*
		c	49	214,930*	953	22,606	6,169	29,728	165.5	983.5	7,017,108.00*
10-7	Dupion silk and silk waste	a	7	445,366	300	2,061	147	2,508		306.0	2,034,701.37

Code	Classification	(1) Kinds of Data	(2) No. of Factories	(3) Amount of Capital ($)	(4) Male Workers	(5) Female Workers	(6) Child Workers	(7) Total No. of Workers	(8) Rented Electric Power (H.P.)	(9) Power of Prime Movers (H.P.)	(10) Value of the Output of the Preceding Year ($)
10-8	Silk weaving	b	5	430,277	272	1,996	147	2,415		306.0	1,904,020.58
		c	3	384,225	31	812	40	1,783[8]		290.0	1,054,200.00
		a	250	4,549,383*	5,302*	2,974*	1,191	9,467*	2,646.8	140.0	18,759,373.53*
		b	77	3,911,166*	3,552	2,433	869	6,854	1,905.2	140.0	15,689,322.31*
		c	122	4,026,855*	5,100	3,380	1,913	10,393	2,641.5	290.0	20,211,577.25*
10-9	Wool bowing	a									
		b									(9)
		c	1	2,000	6	26		32			
10-10	Wool spinning and weaving	a	15	1,864,221	534	641	112	1,297[10]	454.5	364.0	2,370,833.32
		b	12	1,549,443	522	609	105	1,236	254.5	364.0	2,322,222.21
10-11	Other animal tissue textiles	c	26	3,436,675*	1,549	1,627	250	3,426	1,541.5*	250.0	6,523,318.11*
		a	1	3,000	5	*		5*	5.0		8,333.33
		b									
		c									
10-12	Mercerized yarn	a	11	89,778*	499		1	500	79.0		829,305.55*
		b	8	60,778*	424			424	75.0		643,055.55
		c	16	128,000	679		2	681	116.0		1,745,161.44*
10-13	Dyeing	a	20	1,146,556	1,064	30	167	1,261	845.0	100.0	4,606,877.78*
		b	12	1,073,889	926	30	143	1,099	789.0	100.0	4,289,266.67*
		c	31	1,223,000*	1,461	35	185	1,681	962.5		6,839,766.67*
10-14	Printing of textiles	a	19	74,400	297*	11*	234*	542*	36.0		229,210.00*
		b	4	30,000	128	10	135	273	19.5		170,000.00
		c	6	42,000	220	10	170	400	18.5		318,000.00
10-15	Thread making	a	11	107,000	307	331	264	902	129.0	140.0	915,695.55*
		b	4	72,000	272	214	262	748	95.0	150.0	656,035.55
		c	10	167,000	155	524	10	689	308.0	150.0	1,573,965.55
10-16	Making of trimmings and ribbons	a	29	289,344*	464	357	71	892	407.5		1,548,224.90*
		b	4	224,000	268	329	8	605	317.0		1,072,166.22*
		c	8	314,000	570	263	6	839	288.0		1,742,686.26
10-17	Cotton flannel finishing	a	2	5,000	32		2	34	23.0		
		b									(11)
		c	4	91,000	143			143	133.0		57,930.00
	Total for Group X.	a	546	54,743,285*	27,504*	87,540*	14,198*	129,252[12]*	47,206.7	8,291.0	198,303,305.60*
		b	264	53,416,995*	24,580*	86,108*	13,532*	124,220*	46,008.6	8,211.0	191,327,818.55*
		c	391	63,623,946*	25,845	78,738	10,218	120,165[18]	63,405.5*	12,055.5	198,219,757.86*
Group XI. Clothing Industries Including Hosiery											
11-1	Knitted hosiery	a	74	2,788,472*	1,769	4,291	442	6,502	670.5*	25.0	7,569,446.36*
		b	30	2,628,111	1,405	3,266	381	5,052	628.6*	25.0	6,361,117.78*
11-2	Knitted hosiery and other articles	c	38	1,960,749	1,600	3,551	180	5,331	714.0*		9,040,588.96

Code	Classification	(1) Kinds of Data	(2) No. of Factories	(3) Amount of Capital ($)	(4) Male Workers	(5) Female Workers	(6) Child Workers	(7) Total No. of Workers	(8) Rented Electric Power (H. P.)	(9) Power of Prime Movers (H. P.)	(10) Value of Output of the Preceding Year ($)
	of apparel	a	27	300,255	482	771	85	1,338	47.9		1,466,994.75*
		b	7	220,000	304	328	65	697	40.7		771,645.87*
		c	15	1,471,710	491	1,198	44	1,733	110.7*		1,806,841.33*
11-3	Straw, felt and Chinese hats	a	12	323,778	258	127	74	459	152.0	*	1,066,983.33
		b	3	162,000	130	70	28	228	140.0	*	647,055.56
		c	7	238,000	272	116	76	464	197.0		1,059,600.00
11-4	Umbrellas	a	14	33,000*	127	151	52	330	30.0		531,908.00*
		b	1	4,000	12	27	18	57	30.0		180,000.00
		c	2	61,500	200	15	47	262	52.5		422,000.00
11-5	Handkerchiefs	a	10	146,444	41	512	9	562	37.0		1,697,933.32
		b	5	111,944	16	480		496	28.0		1,033,333.32
		c	7	113,000	115	346	5	466	34.5		1,530,400.00*
11-6	Underwear and sweaters	a	23	737,916	620	1,035	94	1,749	480.5		3,104,919.99
		b	9	649,722	487	923	78	1,488	462.5		2,795,424.43
		c	16	1,013,167	684	1,381	107	2,172	568.5	1.5	5,338,583.33*
11-7	Buttons	a	3	13,500	39	31		70	8.0		31,520.00
		b	1	10,000	5	30		35	3.0		16,880.00
		c	3	33,000	99	30	6	135	26.0		93,300.00
11-8	Other articles of apparel	a	7	112,022	35	97	35	167	19.0		167,500.00
		b	2	87,500		49	24	73	10.5		17,500.00
		c	1	83,333		18	24	42	7.5		178,200.00
	Total for Group XI.	a	170	4,455,387*	3,371	7,015	791	11,177	1,444.9*	25.0*	15,637,205.75*
		b	58	3,883,277	2,339	5,173	594	8,126	1,343.3*	25.0*	11,822,876.96*
		c	89	4,974,459	3,461	6,655	489	10,605	1,710.7*	1.5	19,469,313.62*
Group XII. Manufacture of Leather, Rubber Products, etc.											
12-1	Leather manufacturing	a	18	703,128	463		43	506	368.5	177.5	2,350,623.67*
		b	7	630,000	332		25	357	237.0	110.0	1,620,857.00
		c	10	980,000	397	30	24	451	307.0	157.0	1,508,857.00
12-2	Leather goods	a	9	115,600*	1,044	63	94	1,201			2,405,100.00
		b										
		c										
12-3	Rubber goods	a	29	2,348,112	2,469	4,216	71	6,756	3,241.7	976.7	4,668,149.99*
		b	25	2,292,112	2,423	4,208	66	6,697	3,168.7	976.7	4,566,149.99*
		c	44	4,923,888*	4,514*	6,658*	134*	11,286*	6,498.2*	415.0	19,349,394.13*
12-4	Glue	a	1	60,000	78	15		93	70.0	32.0	120,000.00
		b	1	60,000	78	15		93	70.0	32.0	120,000.00
		c	1	60,000	80	15		95	70.0	32.0	130,400.00
	Total for Group XII.	a	57	3,226,840*	4,054	4,294	208	8,556	3,686.2	1,186.2	9,543,873.66*
		b	33	2,982,112	2,833	4,223	91	7,147	3,475.7	1,118.7	6,307,006.99*

(1) Code	Classification	(1) Kinds of Data	(2) No. of Factories	(3) Amount of Capital ($)	(4) Male Workers	(5) Female Workers	(6) Child Workers	(7) Total No. of Workers	(8) Rented Electric Power (H. P.)	(9) Power of Prime Movers (H. P.)	(10) Value of Output of the Preceding Year ($)
	Group XIII. Preparation and Manufacture of Foods, Drinks, Tobacco, etc.	c	55	5,063,888*	4,991*	6,683*	158*	11,832*	6,875.2*	604.0	20,988,651.13*
13-1	Rice mills	a	12	116,722*	166		16	182	527.0*		977,400.00*
		b	1	27,778	24		8	32	80.0		7,000.00
		c	1	10,000	32			32	60.0		148,000.00
13-2	Wheat flour mills	a	15	6,463,889	2,403			2,403	11,365.8	325.0	62,728,355.33*
		b	14	6,313,889	2,381			2,381	11,365.8	200.0	62,626,445.61*
		c	15	6,249,650	2,516			2,516	12,235.0		72,683,247.00
13-3	Rice and other flour mills	a	4	7,700	19		1	20	25.0*		12,060.00
		b									
		c									
13-4	Sugar refineries	a	4	86,778	138	4	2	144	6.0		838,888.88
		b	1	20,000	40	4		44	6.0		555,555.55
		c	4	256,000	104	46		150	326.5		4,339,920.00
13-5	Manufactured foodstuffs	a	22	551,272	495	380	115	990	112.0		1,427,466.67*
		b	4	494,000	337	269	70	676	59.5		1,046,000.00*
		c	10	1,501,600	572	472	100	1,144	293.0	60.0	4,084,800.00
13-6	Oils mills	a	14	1,350,778	2,814		11	2,825	924.0	957.0	13,940,913.87
		b	11	1,208,056	2,167		6	2,173	924.0	945.0	12,594,247.21
		c	10	1,271,056	2,020		6	2,026	896.4	881.0	13,114,083.33
13-7	Tea	a	31	138,821	505*	866*		1,371*	163.0		848,853.66*
		b	22	99,211	441	757		1,198	104.5		739,253.66*
		c	44	248,200	1,010	1,776		2,786	204.0		1,026,723.66
13-8	Cigars and cigarettes	a	51	21,230,872*	2,539*	11,207*	395	14,141*	2,726.5*		46,844,969.00*
		b	47	21,153,372*	2,513*	11,032*	395	13,940*	2,726.5*		46,675,769.00*
		c	46	19,002,667*	3,067*	14,952*	326	17,445*	2,898.5	25.0	101,979,760.00*
13-9	Wine and spirits	a	1	150,000	20			20			50,000.00
		b									
		c									
13-10	Alcohol	a									
		b									
		c									(14)
13-11	Soda water and other soft drinks	a	1	70,000	31		8	31	23.0	7.0	421,000.00
		b	2	310,000	188		8	196	83.0	3.0	414,000.00
		c	1	300,000	180			188	80.0	3.0	504,000.00*
13-12	Condiments	a	2	350,000	210	123	10	220	88.0	3.0	3,811,840.00
		b	8	541,000	337	115	6	466	95.5	68.0	3,550,000.00
			3	350,000	270		5	390	72.0	68.0	
		c	5	870,000	288	144	3	435	155.0	30.0	3,970,000.00

Code	Classification	(1) Kinds of Data	(2) No. of Factories	(3) Amount of Capital ($)	(4) Male Workers	(5) Female Workers	(6) Child Workers	(7) Total No. of Workers	(8) Rented Electric Power (H. P.)	(9) Power of Prime Movers (H. P.)	(10) Value of Output of the Preceding Year ($)
13-13	Casings	a	3	12,000	52	13		65			118,756.00
		b									
		c									
13-14	Refined salt	a	1	240,000	40		2	42	*		300,000.00
		b	1	240,000	40		2	42	*		300,000.00
		c	1	240,000	100			100	15.0		504,000.00
13-15	Frozen egg products	a	1	500,000	150	200		350	200.0		(15)
		b	1	500,000	150	200		350	200.0		2,660,000.00
		c	1	500,000	150	200		350	200.0		64,180.00
13-16	Starch	a	2	15,000	35			35	10.5		
		b									
		c									
13-17	Ice and cold storage	a	1	100,000	60			60	90.0		393,600.00
		b	4	286,000	86			86	190.0	200.0	72,200.00*
		c	1	100,000	30			30	80.0		17,000.00
			2	424,000	80			80	80.0*		17,000.00*
Total for Group XIII.		a	175	32,000,832*	9,987*	12,793*	556	23,336*	16,528.3*	1,553.0	132,456,883.35*
		b	107	30,896,306*	8,573*	12,377*	494	21,444*	15,698.3*	1,216.0	128,525,270.97*
		c	143	31,093,473*	10,240*	16,690*	445	27,375*	17,564.4*	1,006.0	205,415,133.99*

Group XIV. Manufacture of Paper. Book-Binding and Printing

Code	Classification	(1) Kinds of Data	(2) No. of Factories	(3) Amount of Capital ($)	(4) Male Workers	(5) Female Workers	(6) Child Workers	(7) Total No. of Workers	(8) Rented Electric Power (H. P.)	(9) Power of Prime Movers (H. P.)	(10) Value of Output of the Preceding Year ($)
14-1	Paper	a	7	2,072,222	768	482	4	1,254	2,641.0	1,337.0	3,509,583.34
		b	7	2,072,222	768	482	4	1,254	2,641.0	1,337.0	3,509,583.34
		c	7	2,306,389	829	506	141516	1,4415	1,757.0	2,677.0	4,905,000.00
14-2	Card board and tin foil	a	2	7,600*	150	48	4	202	2,508.0		675,388.89
		b	2	7,600*	150	48	4	202	2,508.0		675,388.89
		c	2	407,600	133	45	1	179	608.0		624,000.00
14-3	Printing	a	106	14,596,189*	5,920	811	1,479	8,210	3,612.5		23,612,707.32*
		b	52	14,124,889*	5,251*	811	1,148	7,212	3,336.5		22,287,127.32*
		c	92	13,149,000*	5,863	278	1,456	7,597	2,900.2*		25,904,423.24*
14-4	Book-binding	a	14	11,700	170	148	49	367			56,909.00
		b									
		c									
14-5	Paper manufactures	a	25	210,900	385	174	88	647	112.0		601,815.00
		b	8	167,400	222	84	23	329	78.5		300,400.00
		c	13	210,400	401	145	49	595	97.0		703,600.00*
14-6	Engraving	a	1	*	12			12			5,000.00
		b									
		c									
Total for Group XIV.		a	155	16,898,611*	7,405	1,663	1,624	10,692	8,873.5	1,337.0	28,461,403.55*
		b	69	16,372,111*	6,393	1,425	1,179	8,997	8,564.0	1,337.0	26,862,499.55*

Code	Classification	(1) Kinds of Data	(2) No. of Factories	(3) Amount of Capital ($)	(4) Male Workers	(5) Female Workers	(6) Child Workers	(7) Total No. of Workers	(8) Rented Electric Power (H.P.)	(9) Power of Prime Movers (H.P.)	(10) Value of Output of the Preceding Year ($)
Group XV. Manufacture of Scientific and Musical Instruments, Clocks and Watches, etc.		c	114	16,073,389*	7,226	974	1,506	9,786[17]	5,362.2*	2,677.0	32,137,023.24*
15-1	Musical instruments	a	18	179,167	382		109	491	38.0		704,725.00
		b	1	3,000	21		10	31	10.0		25,000.00
		c	2	105,000	51		10	61	20.0		125,000.00
15-2	Educational supplies and toys	a	15	231,600	302	58	63	423	33.4		541,220.00*
		b	3	31,000	88	48	22	158	20.9		779,500.00
		c	10	321,000	299	134	90	523	75.4		1,229,152.11
15-3	Scientific apparatus	a	5	35,500	60	10	46	116	22.0		84,000.00
		b	2	23,500	34	9	26	69	12.5		59,000.00
		c	5	148,500	227	19	72	318	45.5		165,000.00
15-4	Clocks	a	1	7,000	27		14	41	8.0		*
		b	1	7,000	27		14	41	8.0		*
		c	1	50,000	160			160	15.0		200,000.00
Total for Group XV.		a	39	453,267	771	68	232	1,071	101.4		1,389,945.00*
		b	7	64,500	170	57	72	299	51.4		163,500.00*
		c	18	624,500	737	153	172	1,062	155.9		1,719,152.11
Group XVI. Other Manufacturing Industries											
16-1	Tooth brushes	a	6	212,300	197	151	84	432	105.0		308,800.00
		b	3	208,500	161	150	76	387	95.0		364,800.00
		c	6	260,000	259	369	7	635	148.5		1,350,409.84
16-2	Mirrors	a	4	60,000	187		34	221	70.0		281,500.00
		b	3	50,000	171		31	202	66.0		244,500.00
		c	4	54,000	164		73	237	73.0		240,800.00
16-3	Boal briquettes	a	12	422,000*	317			317	338.0	256.0	2,023,800.00*
		b	4	300,000	220			220	119.0	256.0	1,566,300.00
		c	6	390,000*	386			386	234.5	256.0	2,287,000.00
16-4	Thermos bottles (whole bottle)	a									
		b									
		c									
16-5	Straw ropes	a	2	170,000	142	22	98	262	55.0	24.0	798,000.00*
		b									
		c	10	12,850	7	301		308			50,980.00*
Total for Group XVI.		a	32	707,150*	708	452	118	1,278	513.0	256.0	2,755,080.00*
		b	10	558,500	552	150	107	809	280.0	256.0	2,175,600.00
		c	18	874,000*	951	391	178	1,520	511.0	280.0	4,676,299.84
Grand Total for the Sixteen Groups		a	1,672	142,329,494*	71,997*	118,060*	23,048*	214,152[18]*	90,213.7*	68,175.0*	439,328,826.81*
		b	710	135,352,135*	59,370*	113,325*	19,211*	192,043[19]*	85,277.7*	67,173.5*	407,084,295.68*
		c	1,186	163,683,893*	75,693*	115,333*	18,266*	214,736[20]*	108,782.5*	70,294.7	557,690,754.54*

Notes: (1) Under "Kinds of Data" above, "a" denotes figures for all factories covered by our investigations in 1931, "b" those for factories that came up to the standard of the Factory Law, and "c" data concerning factories investigated by us in 1933, all of which came up to the legal standard.
(2) The factory referred to was established in May, 1931, and had, therefore, no output in the previous year.
(3) Including 1,037 persons whose sex is not known.
(4) As the one factory in this division came into being in February, 1933, there had been no output in 1932.
(5) No output was turned out in 1932.
(6) The one factory in this division was established in October, 1933, and had, therefore, no output in 1932.
(7) Including 4,464 persons whose sex is not known.
(8) Including 900 persons whose sex is not known.
(9) The said factory was not established until November, 1933, and consequently had no output in 1932.
(10) Including 10 persons whose sex is not known.
(11) Both factories, being established in 1933, were not yet in existence in 1932.
(12) Vide (10).
(13) Including 5,364 persons whose sex is not known.
(14) The factory started operations in July, 1933, and had, therefore, no output in the previous year.
(15) Established in 1931, this factory had no output in 1930.
(16) Including 80 persons whose sex is not known.
(17) Vide (16).
(18) Including 1,047 persons whose sex is not known.
(19) Including 1,037 persons whose sex is not known.
(20) Including 5,444 persons whose sex is not known.

TABLE D-IV. CAPITALIZATION OF TWELVE LEADING INDUSTRIES

Classification	Number of Factories		Average Capitalization Per Factory ($)		Value of Raw Materials as Percentages of Total Capital (1933)	Value of Output as Percentages of Total Capital	
	1931	1933	1931	1933		1931	1933
Foundries	35	20	5,006	8,050	219%	503	481
Machinery Industry	289	162	13,632	47,681	129	307	298
Chemical Industry	60	78	156,571	194,873	112	190	187
Matches	3	4	720,027	830,000	55	100	81
Cotton Spinning	27	29	1,405,638	1,693,706	185	378	247
Cotton Weaving	61	69	73,329	61,984	447	287	543
Steam Filatures	66	9	42,100	23,881	637	1,118	941
Silk Weaving	251	115	19,101	35,016	325	455	517
Knitted Goods	96	52	32,127	65,913	250	325	350
Rubber Goods	29	41	80,969	98,144	239	565	590
Wheat Flour	14	15	461,706	416,643	966	1,167	1,163
Cigarettes	44	45	479,811	422,281	219	1,149	540

Average and percentage figures in the above table as well as those in Tables D-V, D-VI and E-I are calculated from our unpublished data with the following limitations: (1) in case of average figures per factory, only factories reporting their capitalization, number of workers, number of horsepower, or value of output are included; (2) in case of average figures per worker, only factories reporting both sets of figures needed for calculating these averages are included; and (3) in case of percentage figures, only factories reporting both sets of figures needed for calculating these percentages are included. Hence the same figures may not agree with results that may be obtained from our data published elsewhere in this report.

TABLE D-V. POWER STATISTICS OF TWELVE LEADING INDUSTRIES

Classification	Number of Factories		Average No. of Horsepower Per Factory		Average No. of Horsepower Per Worker	
	1931	1933	1931	1933	1931	1933
Foundries	34	21	4.8 H.P.	9.7 H.P.	0.21 H.P.	0.27 H.P.
Machinery Industry	280	167	14.9	26.0	0.40	0.38
Chemical Industry	47	77	55.3	61.5	0.37	0.52
Matches	2	4	71.0	53.9	0.11	0.13
Cotton Spinning	29	29	1,550.2	2,133.2	0.67	1.02
Cotton Weaving	34	70	61.9	61.7	0.38	0.48
Steam Filatures	66	49	20.2	23.4	0.03	0.04
Silk Weaving	249	122	11.7	24.0	0.29	0.28
Knitted Goods	43	50	17.2	16.4	0.13	0.12
Rubber Goods	29	41	145.5	168.6	0.62	0.67
Wheat Flour	15	15	779.4	815.7	4.86	4.86
Cigarettes	45	46	60.5	63.5	0.20	0.17

TABLE D-VI. RAW MATERIALS AND OUTPUT OF TWELVE LEADING INDUSTRIES.

	Number of Factories		Average Value of Output Per Factory ($)		Value of Raw Materials as Percentages of Value of Output
	1931	1933	1931	1933	(1933)
Foundries	28	20	28,197.50	47,500.00	44
Machinery Industry	260	154	43,921.42	142,199.38	44
Chemical Industry	50	69	327,029.96	374,894.68	55
Matches	3	4	720,000.00	673,562.50	68
Cotton Spinning	21	29	5,577,206.24	4,189,087.37	75
Cotton Weaving	53	61	238,310.12	368,388.28	88
Steam Filatures	62	48	469,827.54	146,189.75	82
Silk Weaving	149	103	130,837.52	195,427.67	63
Knitted Goods	81	49	111,476.31	228,600.62	70
Rubber Goods	19	33	245,692.10	586,345.28	38
Wheat Flour	14	15	4,480,596.81	4,845,549.80	83
Cigarettes	36	40	1,291,554.69	2,546,669.00	40

APPENDIX E
LABOUR STATISTICS

TABLE E.I. LABOR STATISTICS OF TWELVE LEADING INDUSTRIES.

Classification	Number of Factories		Average No. of Workers Per Factory		Average Value of Output Per Worker		Wage Payments as Percentages of Value of Output	
	1931	1933	1931	1933	1931	1933	1931	1933
Foundries	35	21	22	36	1,203	1,316	14.0%	11.1%
Machinery Industry	295	167	36	68	1,177	2,077	13.8	8.5
Chemical Industry	59	78	128	118	2,253	2,894	6.6	6.4
Matches	3	4	473	402	1,523	1,673	14.6	14.0
Cotton Spinning	28	29	2,240	2,083	2,502	2,011	5.5	9.3
Cotton Weaving	63	70	102	129	2,050	2,652	7.5	5.7
Steam Filatures	66	49	611	607	762	241	5.5	19.9†
Silk Weaving	257	122	40	85	2,452	2,131	8.5	14.2
Knitted Goods	97	52	80	136	1,529	1,741	8.6	12.5
Rubber Goods	29	42	233	269	1,388	2,119	9.7	8.6
Wheat Flour	15	15	160	168	28,539	28,888	0.7	0.9
Cigarettes	44	45	312	388	4,484	6,282	3.6	3.0

† In this year the filatures lost many, as may be seen from the high percentages which raw material cost and wage payments constituted of the value of output. In fact, these two items alone already exceeded 100%.

TABLE E-II. WAGE EARNINGS IN DIFFERENT INDUSTRIES
Unit, Standard Dollar

Classification	Male Workers		Female Workers		Child Workers	
	Per Hour	Per Day	Per Hour	Per Day	Per Hour	Per Day
Saw Mills	0.069	0.621	—	—	—	—
Foundries	0.086	0.774	—	—	—	—
Manufactories of Machinery	0.087	0.783	—	—	—	—
Shipbuilding	0.113	1.017	—	—	—	—
Manufacture of Glass	0.084	0.672	—	—	0.040	0.320
Manufacture of Soap	0.059	0.543	0.035	0.322	—	—
Manufacture of Matches	0.086	0.803	0.027	0.240	0.025	0.203
Manufacture of Enamelled Ware	0.059	0.555	0.047	0.423	0.036	0.324
Silk Reeling	0.061	0.732	0.049	0.539	0.030	0.330
Cotton Spinning	0.047	0.552	0.038	0.452	0.025	0.300
Silk Weaving	0.120	1.260	0.086	0.894	—	—
Cotton Weaving	0.065	0.722	0.047	0.545	0.031	0.357
Knitted Goods	0.081	0.818	0.066	0.634	—	—
Dyeing	0.060	0.468	—	—	—	—
Manufacture of Leather	0.069	0.621	—	—	—	—
Wheat Flour Mills	0.051	0.561	—	—	—	—
Oil Mills	0.069	0.600	—	—	—	—
Eggs Products	0.067	0.623	0.051	0.459	—	—
Cigar & Cigarettes	0.079	0.822	0.070	0.581	0.042	0.416
Manufacture of Paper	0.060	0.660	0.032	0.352	—	—
Printing	0.146	1.226	0.102	0.826	0.041	0.418

Data in the above table and the one immediately following are taken from *Wages And Hours Of Labour* published by Bureau of Social Affairs of the City Government of Greater Shanghai.

TABLE E-III. WORKING HOURS PER DAY IN DIFFERENT INDUSTRIES

Classification	Male Workers	Female Workers	Child Workers
Saw Mills	9	—	—
Foundries	9	—	—
Manufacture of Machinery	9	—	—
Shipbuilding	9	—	—
Manufacture of Glass	8	—	8
Manufacture of Soap	9 1/5	9 1/5	—
Manufacture of Matches	9 1/3	8 9/10	8 1/10
Manufacture of Enamelled Ware	9 2/5	9	9
Silk Reeling	12	11	11
Cotton Spinning	11 3/4	11 9/10	12
Silk Weaving	10 1/2	10 2/5	—
Cotton Weaving	11 1/10	11 3/5	11 1/2
Knitted Goods	10 1/10	9 3/5	—
Dyeing	7 4/5	—	—
Manufacture of Leather	9	—	—
Wheat Flour Mills	11	—	—
Oil Mills	8 7/10	—	—
Eggs Products	9 3/10	9	—
Cigars & Cigarettes	10 2/5	8 3/10	9 9/10
Manufacture of Paper	11	11	—
Printing	8 2/5	8 1/10	10 1/5

TABLE E-IV. STRIKES AND LOCKOUTS—INDUSTRIES AND SERVICES AFFECTED, 1918-1932

Classification	Number of Cases	Percentage of Total
A. Primary Production		
I. Agriculture		
II. Mining & quarrying		
B. Secondary Production		
III. Manufacturing industries		
1. Woodworking	29	2.59
2. Furniture Manufacture	20	1.78
3. Metal industry	3	0.27
4. Machinery, etc.	36	3.21
5. Vehicles for transportation	38	3.39
6. Bricks, glass, etc.	4	.36
7. House & road building	13	1.16
8. Gas, water & electricity	26	2.32
9. Chemicals, etc.	26	2.32
10. Textile industry	399	35.59
11. Wearing apparels	53	4.73
12. Leather, rubber, etc.	11	.98
13. Foods & drinks	81	7.23
14. Paper & Printing	107	9.54
15. Clocks, scientific instruments, etc.	20	1.78
16. Others	31	2.76
C. Service		
IV. Transport & communication	113	10.08
V. Commerce & finance		
1. General traders	75	6.69
2. Brokers, exchanges, etc.	1	.09
3. Real estate, renting agencies, etc.		
4. Money & banking	4	.36
5. Hotels, resorts, etc.	14	1.25
VI. Public service & defence	1	.09
VII. Professional service		
VIII. Domestic & personal service	16	1.43
Total	1,121	100.00

Data in the above table as well as those in Tables E-V to E-VIII are taken from *Strikes And Lockouts In Shanghai Since 1918* published by the Bureau of Social Affairs of the City Government of Greater Shanghai.

TABLE E-V. STRIKES AND LOCKOUTS—MATTERS IN DISPUTE, 1918-1932

Classification	Number of Cases	Percentage of Total
A. Related to Collective Bargaining		
I. Trade unionism or collective agreement		
1. Trade unionism	9	0.80
2. Collective agreement	128	11.42
II. Conditions of employment		
1. Wages	488	43.53
2. Hours of labor	25	2.23
3. Engagement or dismissal of workers	216	19.27
4. Treatment	67	5.98
5. Regulations or system of work	21	1.87
6. Others	70	6.25
B. Not Related to Collective Bargaining		
I. Sympathetic	23	2.05
II. Political	12	1.07
III. Others	62	5.53
Total	*1,121*	*100.00*

Table E-VI. STRIKES AND LOCKOUTS—RESULTS OF DISPUTES, 1918-1932

Classification	Number of Cases	Percentage of Total
A. Workers' demands entirely accepted	261	23.28
B. Workers' demands partially accepted	406	36.22
C. Workers' demands rejected	281	25.07
D. Employers' demands entirely accepted	6	0.53
E. Employers' demands partially accepted	10	0.89
F. Employers' demands rejected	5	0.45
G. Results indeterminate or unknown	150	13.38
H. Settlement pending	2	0.18
Total	*1,121*	*100.00*

TABLE E-VII. STRIKES AND LOCKOUTS—NATIONALITY OF MANAGEMENT, 1918-1932

Classification	Number of Cases	Percentage of Total
A. Chinese	720	64.23
B. Foreign		
Japanese	159	14.18
British	136	12.13
American	36	3.21
German	2	0.18
French	28	2.50
Italian	1	0.09
Others	22	1.96
C. Unknown	17	1.52
Total	1,121	100.00

TABLE E-VIII. STRIKES AND LOCKOUTS—NUMBER OF CASES, NUMBER OF ESTABLISHMENTS AND OF WORKERS INVOLVED, AND INDUSTRIAL LOSS IN THE FORM OF MAN-DAYS AND WAGES, 1927-1932[1]

Year	Number of Cases	No. of Establishments Involved	No. of Workers Involved	Man-Days Lost	Wages Lost ($)
1927	117	11,698	881,289	7,622,029.0	3,710,116.26
1928	118	5,433	204,563	2,049,826.0	835,962.73
1929	108	1,011	65,557	711,921.2	344,568.21
1930	87	672	64,130	801,531.0	358,602.28
1931	122	1,825	74,188	685,941.5	316,559.53
1932	82	450	71,395	710,605.1[2]	296,846.86[2]
Total	634	21,089	1,361,122	12,581,853.8	5,862,655.87
Average	106	3,515	226,854	2,096,975.6	977,109.31

Notes: (1) According to unpublished data of the Bureau of Social Affairs of the City Government of Greater Shanghai, the number of cases and the number of establishments and workers involved in 1933 and 1934 were respectively 88 and 63 cases, 574 and 441 establishments, and 74,727 and 28,923 workers, while comparative statistics of the number of cases between the Bureau and Dr. Ta Chen prior to 1927 are as follows:

	1918	1919	1920	1921	1922	1923	1924	1925	1926
Bureau of Social Affairs	21	23	33	19	29	14	16	75	257
Dr. Ta Chen	22	57	35	21	31	16	16	72	264

(2) Two cases not settled at the end of the year not included.

TABLE E-IX. INDUSTRIAL DISPUTES—NUMBER OF CASES AND NUMBER OF ESTABLISHMENTS AND OF WORKERS INVOLVED, 1928-1932

Year	Number of Cases	Number of Establishments	Number of Workers			
			Males	Females	Child Workers	Total
1928	237	3,477	48,465	57,291	16,227	121,983
1929	338	4,237	40,068	14,798	2,080	56,946
1930	339	2,017	39,269	62,578	16,470	118,317
1931	324	616	35,158	74,387	22,168	131,713
1932	253	1,452	33,950	19,880	1,992	55,822
Total	*1,491*	*11,799*	*196,910*	*228,934*	*58,937*	*484,781*
Average	*298*	*2,360*	*39,382*	*45,787*	*11,787*	*96,956*

Notes: (1) Data in the above table as well as those in Tables E-X to E-XIV are taken from *Industrial Disputes In Shanghai Since 1928* publisheded by Bureau of Social Affairs of the City Government of Greater Shanghai.

(2) According to unpublished data of the Bureau of Social Affairs of the City Government of Greater Shanghai, the number of cases and the number of establishments and workers involved in 1933, 1934 and 1935 were: 301, 232 and 205 cases; 730, 912 and 395 establishments; and 94,915, 34,891 and 48,065 workers respectively.

TABLE E-X. INDUSTRIAL DISPUTES—MATTERS IN DISPUTE, 1928-1932

Classification	Number of Cases	Percentage of Total
A. Related to Collective Bargaining		
I. Trade unionism or collective agreement		
1. Trade unionism	13	0.87
2. Collective agreement	138	9.25
II. Conditions of employment		
1. Wages	163	10.93
2. Hours of labor	8	0.54
3. Engagement or dismissal of workers	1,018	68.28
4. Treatment	103	6.91
5. Regulations or system of work	15	1.01
6. Others	30	2.01
B. Not Related to Collective Bargaining		
I. Sympathetic		
II. Political	1	0.07
III. Others	2	0.13
Total	*1,491*	*100.00*

TABLE E-XI. INDUSTRIAL DISPUTES—INDUSTRIES AND SERVICES AFFECTED, 1928-1932

Classification	Number of Cases	Percentage of Total
A. Primary Production		
I. Agriculture		
II. Mining and quarrying		
B. Secondary Production		
III. Manufacturing industries		
1. Woodworking	16	1.07
2. Furniture Manufacture	23	1.54
3. Metal industry	2	0.13
4. Machinery, etc.	29	1.95
5. Vehicles for transportation	33	2.21
6. Bricks, glass, etc.	12	0.80
7. House and road building	5	0.34
8. Gas, water and electricity	12	0.80
9. Chemicals, etc.	49	3.29
10. Textile industry	490	32.86
11. Wearing apparels	120	8.05
12. Leather, rubber, etc.	28	1.88
13. Foods and drinks	132	8.85
14. Paper and printing	133	8.92
15. Clocks, scientific instruments, etc.	16	1.07
16. Others	54	3.62
C. Service		
IV. Transport and communication	42	2.82
V. Commerce and finance		
1. General traders	250	16.77
2. Brokers, exchanges, etc.		
3. Real estate, renting agencies, etc.		
4. Money and banking	5	0.34
5. Hotels, resorts, etc.	32	2.15
VI. Public service and defence		
VII. Professional service		
VIII. Domestic and personal service	8	0.54
Total	1,491	100.00

TABLE E-XII. INDUSTRIAL DISPUTES—METHODS OF MEDIATION, 1928-1932

Classification	Number of Cases	Percentage of Total
A. Settled by direct negotiation	133	8.92
B. Settled by the mediation of a third party		
1. The Concilation Board	394	26.41
2. The Arbitration Board	61	4.09
3. The Bureau of Social Affairs	849	56.96
4. Other agencies	52	3.49
C. Terminated without negotiation	2	0.13
Total	*1,491*	*100.00*

TABLE E-XIII. INDUSTRIAL DISPUTES—RESULTS OF DISPUTES, 1928-1932

Classification	Number of Cases	Percentage of Total
A. Completely favourable for workers	335	22.47
B. Partially favourable for workers	911	61.10
C. Unfavourable for workers	195	13.08
D. Results indeterminate or unknown	37	2.48
E. Settlement pending	13	0.87
Total	*1,491*	*100.00*

TABLE E-XIV. INDUSTRIAL DISPUTES—NATIONALITY OF MANAGEMENT, 1928-1932

Classification	Number of Cases	Percentage of Total
A. Chinese	1,401	93.97
B. Foreign		
Japanese	25	1.68
British	40	2.68
American	7	0.47
French	14	0.93
German	1	0.07
Italian		
Others	3	0.20
C. Unknown		
Total	1,491	100.00

TABLE E-XV. COST OF LIVING AND WAGE INDICES IN SHANGHAI

Year	Cost of Living 1926=100 (1)	Wage Rates 1930=100 (2)
1926	100.0	—
1927	106.7	—
1928	102.5	—
1929	107.9	—
1930	121.8	100.00
1931	125.9	96.61
1932	119.1	96.61
1933	107.2	98.31
1934	106.2	94.92
1935	106.6	—

Notes: (1) Taken from *Prices And Price Indexes In Shanghai*.

(2) Based upon figures in *Wage Rates in Shanghai* by T. Y. Tsha and material especially supplied by The Bureau of Social Affairs of the Shanghai City Government.

APPENDIX F
ECONOMIC AND RELATED STATISTICS
TABLE F-I. POPULATION OF SHANGHAI

Year	Chinese Territory (1)	International Settlement (2) (4)	French Concession (3)	Total
1925	—	808,368	297,072	—
1926	—	825,800	—	—
1927	—	835,965	—	—
1928	—	845,835	358,453	—
1929	—	855,260	—	—
1930	1,702,130	998,362	434,807	3,135,299
1031	1,836,189	1,015,394	456,012	3,307,595
1932	1,580,436	1,062,789	478,552	3,121,777
1933	1,795,953	1,099,420	496,536	3,391,909
1934	1,925,778	1,135,773	498,193	3,559,744
1935	2,044,014	1,149,443	—	—

(1) Figures based upon *Monthly Population Statistical Tables* issued by the Bureau of Public Safety of the Shanghai City Government.

(2) Based upon data in *Shanghai Municipal Reports*.

(3) Based upon data in *Annual Reports* of Conseil d'Administration Municipal de la Concession Francaise de Changhai.

(4) Not including foreign residents in Pootung and External Roads Areas as well as Chinese residents in shipping and boats and villages and huts within Settlement limits whose numbers are given below:

	Foreign Residents in Pootung	Foreign Residents in External Roads Areas	Chinese Residents in Villages and Huts	Chinese Residents in Shipping and Boats
1925	298	7,097	10,381	14,082
1926	—	7,465	—	15,000
1927	—	7,720	—	15,000
1928	—	7,895	—	14,530
1929	—	8,385	—	—
1930	—	9,506	—	—
1931	—	9,837	—	—
1932	—	12,005	—	—
1933	—	12,526	—	—
1934	—	13,048	—	—
1935	—	10,332	—	—

TABLE F-II. POPULATION MOVEMENTS IN SHANGHAI CHINESE TERRITORY

Year	Incoming			Outgoing		
	Male	Female	Total	Male	Female	Total
1929	109,341	80,765	190,106	36,793	29,506	66,299
1930	145,670	108,860	254,530	85,562	63,207	148,769
1931	178,963	127,749	306,712	121,874	86,832	208,706
1932	272,733	200,495	473,228	117,697	81,345	199,042
1933	268,161	190,104	458,265	178,830	123,270	302,100
1934	248,790	167,287	416,077	188,202	128,403	316,605

Based upon data in *the Shanghai Year Book, 1935* published by the History Compilation Bureau of Greater Shanghai, and *Statistics In Shanghai* published by the Shanghai Civic Association.

TABLE F-III. POPULATION DENSITY IN SHANGHAI

Year	Chinese Territory (1)	International Settlement (2)	French Concession (3)
1925	—	35,772	29,068
1926	—	36,543	—
1927	—	36,993	—
1928	—	37,430	35,074
1929	—	37,847	—
1930	3,441	44,180	42,545
1931	3,712	44,933	44,619
1932	3,195	45,888	46,825
1933	3,630	47,470	48,585
1934	3,893	49,040	48,747
1935	4,132	49,630	—

Notes: (1) Data from *the Shanghai Year Book, 1935*.

(2) Calculated from population data in Table F-I and area of the International Settlement in *Shanghai Municipal Reports* of the various years.

(3) Data specially supplied by Conseil d'Administration Municipale de la Concession Francaise de Changhai.

TABLE F-IV. LAND VALUES IN THE INTERNATIONAL
SETTLEMENT OF SHANGHAI

Unit, Shanghai Tael

Year	Eastern District	Western District	Northern District	Central District	Whole Settlement
1924	8,428.71	8,452.77	23,241.56	66,729.42	16,206.80
1927	8,808.60	11,547.70	26,623.26	77,543.17	18,651.93
1930	11,864.45	20,457.35	37,857.37	107,878.16	26,986.26
1933	15,384.93	28,194.08	41,801.60	132,451.23	33,877.31

Based upon the *Assessment Schedules* of the Shanghai Municipal Council.

TABLE F-V. HOUSING STATISTICS OF THE INTERNATIONAL SETTLEMENT OF SHANGHAI[1]

Year	Foreign Styled Buildings					Chinese Buildings					Total				
	Unoccupied	Occupied	Total No. of Buildings	Unoccupied Buildings as Percentage of Total	Assessed Value of Total No. of Buildings[2] ($)	Unoccupied	Occupied	Total No. of Buildings	Unoccupied Buildings as Percentage of Total	Assessed Value of Total No. of Buildings ($)	Unoccupied	Occupied	Total No. of Buildings	Unoccupied Buildings as Percentage of Total	Assessed Value of Total No. of Buildings ($)
1925	5,597	623	6,220	10.0	21,908,030	67,998	2,439	70,437	3.5	22,192,916	73,595	3,062	76,657	4.0	44,100,946
1926	5,981	532	6,513	8.2	23,043,683	71,852	2,125	73,977	2.9	24,314,028	77,833	2,657	80,490	3.3	47,357,711
1927	6,346	432	6,778	6.4	24,474,404	73,380	3,149	76,529	4.1	25,947,080	79,726	3,581	83,307	4.3	50,421,484
1928	6,582	393	6,975	5.6	25,852,197	75,508	2,051	77,559	2.6	27,370,248	82,090	2,444	84,534	2.9	53,222,445
1929	7,154	522	7,676	6.8	28,186,621	76,327	1,325	77,652	1.7	29,092,248	83,481	1,847	85,328	2.2	57,278,869
1930	8,170	799	8,969	8.9	32,054,606	76,362	1,545	77,907	2.0	30,628,852	84,532	2,344	86,876	2.7	62,683,458
1931	8,989	1,112	10,101	11.0	36,403,053	78,812	1,796	80,608	2.2	33,412,876	87,861	2,908	90,709	3.2	69,815,929
1932	9,929	1,436	11,365	12.6	46,330,209	80,025	3,347	83,372	4.0	35,538,176	89,954	4,783	94,737	5.0	81,868,385
1933	10,725	1,384	12,109	11.4	51,470,858	80,520	4,364	84,884	5.1	37,450,746	91,245	5,748	96,993	5.9	88,921,604
1934	11,454	1,813	13,267	13.7	57,110,295	81,478	5,238	86,716	6.0	39,071,210	92,932	7,051	99,983	7.0	96,181,505

Notes: (1) Based upon data in *Shanghai Municipal Reports*.
(2) Figures for 1925-1932 in this column are converted from figures in taels at average annual dollar rates as published in *The Shanghai Market Prices Report*.

TABLE F-VI. NUMBER OF HOUSES IN THE FRENCH CONCESSION OF SHANGHAI

Year	Foreign Style	Chinese Style	Total
1925	2,429	23,549	25,978
1926	2,627	25,982	28,609
1927	3,031	27,099	30,130
1928	3,603	29,000	32,603
1929	4,469	31,596	36,065
1930	5,559	34,679	40,238
1931	6,184	37,026	43,210
1932	6,366	38,540	44,906
1933	6,805	40,360	47,165
1934	7,329	41,021	48,350

Based upon data in *Annual Reports* of Conseil d'Administration Municipale de la Concession Francaise de Changhai.

TABLE F-VII. STATISTICS OF NEW BUILDINGS IN CHINESE TERRITORY OF SHANGHAI

Year	Number				Area in Square Meters				Assessed Value ($)		
	Factories	Godowns	Others	Total	Factories	Others	Total		Factories	Others	Total
1928	102	47	892	1,041	67,890	154,050	221,940		1,211,220	3,545,900	4,757,120
1929	154	34	1,207	1,395	116,050	253,150	369,200		2,842,100	7,955,800	10,797,900
1930	198	56	1,533	1,787	116,040	398,830	514,870		3,301,310	13,954,970	17,256,280
1931	221	73	2,286	2,580	103,550	429,780	533,330		3,239,280	14,572,970	17,812,250
1932	118	47	2,003	2,168	125,260	434,110	559,370		2,037,720	14,951,030	16,988,750
1933	151	37	2,837	3,025	101,020	554,360	655,380		3,422,690	19,384,810	22,807,500
1934	137	40	2,509	2,686	76,660	570,970	647,630		2,290,070	21,444,210	23,734,280

Based upon data specially supplied by the Bureau of Public Works of the Shanghai City Government.

TABLE F-VIII. STATISTICS OF NEW BUILDINGS IN THE
INTERNATIONAL SETTLEMENT OF SHANGHAI[1]

Year	Factories	Godowns	Other Kinds of Buildings	Total No. of Buildings	Assessed Value of Total No. of Buildings[2]
1925	13	19	8,934	8,966	$20,488,878
1926	22	21	6,204	6,247	29,361,379
1927	19	14	3,587	3,620	12,653,955
1928	90	53	4,568	4,711	27,916,240
1929	77	52	7,457	7,586	34,974,564
1930	65	64	8,707	8,836	64,466,532
1931	105	27	8,567	8,699	51,470,266
1932	57	27	3,355	3,439	25,762,522
1933	90	20	5,020	5,130	35,418,321
1934	145	18	4,408	4,571	27,600,350

Notes: (1) Based upon data in *Shanghai Municipal Reports*.

(2) Figures for 1925-1932 in this column are converted from figures in terms of taels at average annual dollar rates as published in *The Shanghai Market Prices Report*.

TABLE F-IX. STATISTICS OF NEW BUILDINGS IN THE FRENCH
CONCESSION OF SHANGHAI

Year	Chinese Buildings	Foreign Style Buildings	Total No. of Buildings	Assessed Value of Total No. of Buildings
1925	2,947	498	3,445	$10,224,000
1926	2,433	198	2,631	6,831,000
1927	1,117	404	1,521	4,140,000
1928	1,901	527	2,428	12,617,000
1929	2,596	911	3,507	17,467,000
1930	3,083	1,090	4,173	18,589,000
1931	2,347	625	2,972	16,014,000
1932	1,514	182	1,696	11,274,000
1933	1,820	439	2,259	13,951,800
1934	661	524	1,185	12,776,000

Based upon data in *Annual Reports* of Conseil d'Administration Municipale de la Concession Française de Changhai.

TABLE F-X. MILEAGE OF ROADS IN SHANGHAI

Year	Chinese Territory (1)	International Settlement (2)	French Concession (3)	Total
1925	——	166.502	53.050	——
1926	93.786	170.516	55.915	320.217
1927	112.414	170.981	57.175	340.570
1928	126.177	173.570	57.740	357.487
1929	146.092	174.870	58.542	379.504
1930	155.578	175.964	62.238	393.780
1931	164.147	178.643	63.249	406.039
1932	166.726	179.934	63.519	410.179
1933	190.068	182.009	64.194	436.271
1934	213.487	183.028	64.617	461.132

Notes: (1) Computed from data specially supplied by the Bureau of Public Works of the Shanghai City Government.
(2) Based upon data in *Shanghai Municipal Reports*.
(3) Based upon data in *Annual Reports* of Conseil d'Administration Municipale de la Concession Francaise de Changhai.

TABLE F-XI. NUMBER OF VEHICLES IN THE INTERNATIONAL SETTLEMENT OF SHANGHAI

Year	Rickshas Public	Rickshas Private	Carriages Public	Carriages Private	Motor Cars	Motor Cycles	Bicycles	Wheel-Barrows	Carts
1925	10,000	10,126	306	299	4,010	—	9,817	11,688	4,366
1926	9,953	10,294	295	252	4,792	—	15,053	11,699	6,390
1927	9,996	9,540	267	198	5,328	—	15,436	10,240	6,262
1928	9,995	9,612	251	156	5,649	—	17,739	10,865	7,410
1929	9,995	9,873	227	113	6,472	—	20,327	11,113	8,775
1930	9,995	10,390	189	83	6,896	733	21,530	10,530	9,608
1931	9,995	11,446	165	76	7,539	747	23,547	10,819	11,011
1932	9,994	11,202	118	68	8,073	815	25,273	8,562	11,320
1933	9,990	12,538	100	61	8,450	717	29,242	8,841	13,242
1934	9,990	12,232	95	51	9,337	706	32,916	7,739	14,967

Based upon data in *Shanghai Municipal Reports*.

TABLE F-XII. INDICES OF WHOLESALE PRICES IN SHANGHAI

Year	Textile Fibres & Manufactures Thereof	Building Materials	Chemicals & Preparations Thereof	General Index
1925	106.8	96.4	101.9	99.3
1926	100.0	100.0	100.0	100.0
1927	100.9	105.4	102.6	104.4
1928	102.1	103.0	101.2	101.7
1929	101.9	108.1	105.8	104.5
1930	105.6	118.2	120.1	114.8
1931	118.8	135.4	150.7	126.7
1932	98.4	124.4	151.6	112.4
1933	89.9	113.1	153.4	103.8
1934	82.2	106.9	139.2	97.1

Taken from *Prices And Price Indexes In Shanghai*. The general index is constructed from wholesale prices of eight commodity groups, only indices of three of which are given above.

TABLE F-XIII. VOLUME OF TRADE OF SHANGHAI[1]

Unit, Standard Dollar

Year	Imports From			Exports to			Re-exports to Chinese Ports	Total of Foreign Trade	Total of Domestic Trade	Total of All Trade
	Foreign Countries and Hongkong	Chinese Ports	Total	Foreign Countries and Hongkong[2]	Chinese Ports	Total				
1925	672,881,248	563,667,868	1,236,549,116	477,036,920	397,687,393	874,724,313	108,951,554	1,149,918,168	1,070,306,815	2,220,224,983
1926	929,433,321	620,747,887	1,550,181,208	563,840,106	494,419,004	1,058,259,110	114,309,712	1,493,273,427	1,229,476,603	2,722,750,030
1927	709,384,110	530,889,386	1,240,273,496	514,928,421	453,099,668	968,028,089	97,430,614	1,224,312,531	1,081,419,668	2,305,732,199
1928	854,731,091	612,345,411	1,467,076,502	564,338,990	524,525,117	1,088,864,107	116,860,602	1,419,070,081	1,253,731,130	2,672,801,211
1929	973,198,192	536,967,790	1,510,165,982	567,175,708	489,806,224	1,056,981,932	72,040,879	1,540,373,900	1,098,814,893	2,639,188,793
1930	1,059,037,584	516,677,988	1,575,715,572	487,136,192	578,152,652	1,065,288,844	63,104,733	1,546,173,776	1,157,935,373	2,704,109,149
1931	1,298,698,318	524,215,273	1,822,913,591	432,308,293	608,364,729	1,040,673,022	60,887,378	1,731,006,611	1,193,467,380	2,924,473,991
1932	795,161,405	272,332,790	1,067,494,195	246,669,142	464,437,754	711,106,896	36,851,058	1,041,830,547	773,621,602	1,815,452,149
1933	736,219,840	220,368,744	956,588,584	315,758,208	458,734,862	774,493,070	29,051,420	1,051,978,048	708,155,026	1,760,133,074
1934	600,483,211	314,470,199	914,953,410	272,304,703	452,034,823	724,339,526	23,080,765	872,787,914	789,585,787	1,662,373,701

Notes: (1) Based upon the reports of Chinese Maritime Customs.
(2) Figures in this column include Chinese produce from other Chinese ports re-exported to foreign countries and Hongkong as well as Chinese produce of local origin exported to foreign countries and Hongkong.

F-XIV. NET VALUE AND INDICES OF THE FOREIGN TRADE OF SHANGHAI

1926=100

Period	Exports		Imports		Total		Percentage of Foreign Trade of All China
	Value	Index	Value	Index	Value	Index	
1926	$563,840,106	100.0	$603,595,536	100.0	$1,167,435,642	100.0	37.7
1927	514,928,421	91.3	458,220,075	75.9	973,148,496	83.3	32.3
1928	564,338,990	100.1	578,543,831	95.8	1,142,882,821	97.9	33.5
1929	567,175,708	100.6	649,359,139	107.6	1,216,534,847	104.2	34.2
1930	487,136,192	86.4	732,620,870	121.4	1,219,757,062	104.5	35.5
1931	432,308,293	76.7	996,202,357	165.0	1,428,510,650	122.4	39.1
1932	246,404,886	43.7	781,123,795	129.4	1,027,528,681	88.0	42.8
1933	315,485,016	55.9	728,333,916	120.7	1,043,818,932	89.4	53.3
1934	271,945,103	48.2	596,440,161	98.8	868,385,264	74.4	55.5
1935	288,721,137	51.2	505,194,859	83.7	793,915,996	68.0	53.1

Notes (1) Value figures in the above table are based upon the reports of Chinese Maritime Customs.
(2) Beginning with August, 1932 the imports into and exports from Manchuria have been excluded from the figures for all China, and hence the percentage which Shanghai constitutes of the total has become considerably larger.

F.XV. NET VALUE AND INDICES OF FOREIGN TRADE OF CHINA
1926 = 100

Year	Exports Value	Exports Index	Imports Value	Imports Index	Total Value	Total Index
1926	$1,346,571,253	100.0	$1,751,536,712	100.0	$3,098,107,965	100.0
1927	1,431,209,433	106.3	1,578,147,470	90.1	3,009,356,903	97.1
1928	1,544,531,071	114.7	1,863,320,124	106.4	3,407,851,195	110.0
1929	1,582,440,841	117.5	1,972,083,403	112.6	3,554,524,244	114.7
1930	1,394,166,319	103.5	2,040,599,446	116.5	3,434,765,765	110.9
1931	1,416,962,868	105.2	2,233,376,164	127.5	3,650,339,032	117.8
1932	767,535,334	57.0	1,634,726,298	93.3	2,402,261,632	77.5
1933	611,827,990	45.4	1,345,567,188	76.8	1,957,395,178	63.2
1934	535,214,279	39.7	1,029,665,224	58.8	1,564,879,503	50.5
1935	575,809,060	42.8	919,211,322	52.5	1,495,020,382	48.2

Based upon the reports of Chinese Maritime Customs.

TABLE F-XVI. NET VALUE OF IMPORTS OF CERTAIN MANUFACTURED PRODUCTS INTO SHANGHAI AND ALL CHINA[1]

Unit, Staridard Dollar

Year	Cotton Yarn (a)	(b)	Wheat Flour (a)	(b)	Cigarettes (a)	(b)	Soap[2] (a)	(b)	Matches (a)	(b)	Knitted Goods (a)	(b)	Total (a)	(b)
1925	61,071,439	8,939,030	23,221,730	337,195	27,682,859	7,562,442	3,477,115	559,127	1,833,944	38,937	3,058,069	444,711	120,345,156	17,880,542
1926	44,013,375	5,789,651	36,944,080	1,376,627	32,351,681	11,008,811	3,424,766	934,625	2,283,168	137,831	3,747,526	597,521	122,764,596	19,845,066
1927	27,629,912	1,776,565	33,195,275	1,483,219	19,887,300	4,994,431	3,268,436	565,978	3,825,131	234,647	2,954,470	422,241	90,760,524	9,477,081
1928	25,977,820	2,404,552	49,021,538	1,850,454	39,147,001	20,181,544	5,122,372	1,094,426	4,022,137	387,415	3,446,852	723,703	126,732,720	26,642,094
1929	22,352,236	3,000,522	98,004,218	2,044,746	32,321,674	12,904,990	4,291,266	722,429	5,179,189	1,230,745	3,984,847	818,603	166,133,430	20,722,035
1930	15,636,314	1,349,000	47,292,647	2,407,361	40,143,797	13,876,762	3,588,803	893,374	5,729,640	720,657	5,308,922	1,132,898	117,700,123	20,380,052
1931	6,375,102	1,982,845	44,577,828	587,442	20,407,715	9,959,040	2,438,969	545,574	1,810,464		5,207,144	950,180	80,817,222	14,025,081
1932 [3] [4]	14,846,037	5,097,517	55,229,026	8,836,255	5,364,208	1,524,946	1,331,521	377,636	362,601	46,168	3,771,441	289,166	80,904,834	16,171,688
1933 [5]	3,915,644	1,279,807	27,868,396	1,474,014	2,719,091	2,059,091	1,124,973	769,221	927,709	5,206	2,822,642	623,877	38,483,455	6,211,216
1934	2,938,966	1,206,772	7,075,112	2,631,757	2,034,701	1,598,811	1,045,589	595,525	96,175	5,106	1,018,260	519,768	14,208,803	6,557,739
1935	2,260,198	778,348	6,006,607	987,605	1,689,724	1,234,256	998,291	484,223	92,971	6,135	589,981	293,051	11,637,772	3,783,618

Nootes: (1) Figures in columns (a) of this table stand for imports into all China while those in columns (b) for imports into Shanghai. Both kinds of figures are based upon data in the reports of Chinese Maritime Customs.

(2) Not including the combined figures for "candles, and soap, n.o.r." which appear in Customs Reports since 1932.

(3) Beginning from August of this year figures for Manchurian ports have failed to be included in those in columns (a).

(4) Figures in columns (b) for this and the following three years are not very exact as they are computed from annual figures in Customs Gold Units multiplied by average annual conversion rates instead of from the sum totals of separate monthly figures in Customs Gold Units multiplied by monthly conversion rates.

(5) The smaller figures in columns (b) for this and the following two years may be partly accounted for by the fact that beginning from this year importers in various Chinese ports who formerly paid duty on their cargoes in Shanghai as a port of transshipment have elected to pay the same at their own ports, so as to avoid payment of wharfage and conservancy dues at Shanghai as was required in the old procedure.

TABLE F-XVII. NET VALUE OF IMPORTS OF CERTAIN INDUSTRIAL RAW MATERIALS INTO SHANGHAI AND ALL CHINA[1]

Unit, Standard Dollar

Year	Cotton (a)	Cotton (b)	Wheat (a)	Wheat (b)	Tobacco Leaves and Prepared Tobacco (a)	Tobacco Leaves and Prepared Tobacco (b)	Soda Ash and Caustic Soda (a)	Soda Ash and Caustic Soda (b)	Acids (a)	Acids (b)	Match Making Materials (a)	Match Making Materials (b)	Wood Shavings & Splints for Match Making (a)	Wood Shavings & Splints for Match Making (b)	Total (a)	Total (b)
1925	109,005,745	90,007,050	4,136,096	3,443,590	31,012,957	16,718,008	4,622,048	1,521,764	1,274,578	323,807	2,864,180	254,901	1,236,902*		152,915,604	112,269,120
1926	146,063,341	117,093,423	27,989,772	27,429,096	40,217,386	26,094,908	5,013,708	1,047,693	1,667,367	536,905	3,056,631	443,715	1,162,858*		224,008,205	172,645,740
1927	124,348,113	93,593,472	10,992,729	10,743,391	34,844,900	22,214,511	5,568,967	1,462,870	2,494,668	715,937	3,518,240	845,031	1,456,202*		181,767,617	129,575,212
1928	105,915,048	84,634,248	5,201,984	4,532,649	54,035,338	37,285,495	5,828,643	1,462,100	2,751,838	1,171,149	3,622,394	814,842	1,451,627*		177,355,245	130,280,483
1929	141,970,969	109,659,582	33,389,163	32,135,172	41,753,152	22,772,929	6,458,773	1,439,492	2,046,787	1,025,451	3,275,807	672,933	1,122,886*		228,894,651	167,705,559
1930	206,069,912	165,354,753	19,990,215	17,509,322	48,453,370	29,840,537	9,715,319	3,178,521	2,822,600	1,751,943	3,868,131	771,771	1,356,928*		290,919,547	218,406,847
1931	279,010,139	226,129,852	136,542,031	115,500,013	75,888,310	53,662,597	10,127,569	3,809,835	3,791,720	1,869,958	5,585,259	1,448,088	1,773,594*		510,945,028	402,420,343
1932[2][3]	186,782,997	107,538,694	80,643,001	36,687,701	37,665,647	22,812,347	4,985,658	1,363,684	2,346,854	589,787			844,730	65,002	313,268,887	169,057,215
1933	98,206,071	90,279,557	88,043,295	70,263,360	26,269,818	25,009,410	4,955,810	3,137,969	3,063,011	1,255,437			737,296	101,834	221,275,301	190,047,567
1934	90,246,597	85,433,749	31,869,171	28,019,114	31,517,810	29,145,662	5,181,391	3,060,491	2,841,984	1,164,578			485,859	26,625	162,142,812	146,848,219
1935	42,523,725	38,306,287	36,986,186	31,927,691	8,889,475	8,315,032	4,191,493	2,821,890	1,976,971	1,067,079			288,778	38,846	94,856,628	82,476,825

Notes: (1) a. All China: b. Shanghai.

(2) See Note (3) under Table F-XXVI

(3) See Note (4) under Table F-XXVI

(4) Figures marked with asterisks in column (a) of "Wood Shavings & Splints for Match Making" and already included in figures in column (a) of "Match Making Materials."

TABLE F-XVIII. NET VALUE OF IMPORTS OF AGRICULTURAL AND INDUSTRIAL MACHINERY INTO SHANGHAI AND ALL CHINA[1][2]

Unit, Standard Dollar

Year	Sewing & Knitting Machinery		Sewing, Knitting & Embroidery Machinery & Parts Thereof		Agricultural Machinery		Agricultural Machinery & Parts Thereof		Machinery for Electric Power Stations		Electrical Machinery		Printing, Book-Binding & Paper-cutting Machinery	
	(a)	(b)	(a)	(b)	(a)	(b)	(a)	(b)	(a)	(b)	(a)	(b)	(a)	(b)
1925	629,927	85,805			251,287	33,243			1,336,999	643,203			1,015,017	766,743
1926	1,013,834	158,774			796,979	156,392			1,295,642	505,937			903,143	636,846
1927	1,194,991	184,059			1,037,591	231,785			2,012,205	1,196,679			676,995	380,846
1928	1,630,779	417,901			1,158,161	234,026			2,050,191	1,172,088			1,198,247	1,048,137
1929	2,361,451	776,708			2,192,458	359,018			3,945,135	2,396,343			2,056,487	1,378,713
1930	1,240,673	399,406			2,321,041	543,486			5,582,696	3,096,743			1,738,521	1,298,657
1931	1,004,703	601,908			1,062,864	589,566			5,728,270	3,327,692			1,139,879	983,341
1932 [3] [4]			914,409	263,528			91,687	4,307			6,615,958	2,151,519		
1933			1,077,155	586,599			29,764	−1,138[5]			4,995,599	2,732,044		
1934			1,397,586	1,006,616			14,712	2,425			5,762,160	3,296,440		
1935			900,817	529,793			50,057	14,070			5,924,959	2,903,800		

Notes: (1) a. All China; b. Shanghai.
(2) Due to revision of classification of returns by the Chinese Maritime Customs in 1932, the names of some articles in the Customs Reports of that year have no counterpart in the Reports issued previously. This explains why we have to use so many headings in this table.
(3) See Note (3) under Table F-XVI.
(4) See Note (4) under Table F-XVI.
(5) This negative figure only shows that there were more re-exports of agricultural machinery from than imports into Shanghai in 1933 within the cognizance of the Maritime Customs. It is probable that Shanghai re-exported her agricultural machinery in other years by railway since she is not an agricultural center.

TABLE F-XVIII. Continued (1)

Year	Printing, Book-Binding and Paper-Cutting Machinery & Parts Thereof		Propelling Machinery		Prime Movers & Parts Thereof		Pumps & Pumping Machinery		Textile Machinery		Bobbins		Textile Machinery & Parts Thereof	
	(a)	(b)	(a)	(b)	(a)	(b)	(a)	(b)	(a)	(b)	(a)	(b)	(a)	(b)
1925			2,991,023	1,284,574			1,001,767	481,646	5,307,836	3,932,591	317,489	221,574		
1926			2,962,392	1,529,521			831,339	320,825	6,322,046	4,875,015	637,513	497,815		
1927			4,642,779	2,295,423			831,855	380,062	5,779,018	4,707,966	668,407	447,774		
1928			3,997,809	2,177,958			1,218,515	563,546	6,395,835	4,928,752	384,491	274,582		
1929			5,360,615	2,980,906			1,219,810	567,568	13,915,668	10,199,575	478,639	347,975		
1930			5,852,727	4,059,205			1,734,436	955,115	21,803,685	16,370,180	715,634	508,234		
1931			8,834,670	5,713,753			1,446,011	641,631	21,501,360	17,184,808	828,343	596,388		
1932 (3) (4)	1,137,472	492,671			6,955,605	1,996,288	748,109	210,899					16,105,186	7,791,686
1933	770,502	576,710			3,923,896	2,530,653	1,360,062	840,931					9,081,377	7,588,193
1934	1,379,305	1,048,958			8,216,571	5,363,769	1,331,608	629,806					14,206,097	8,973,328
1935	2,888,288	1,003,841			5,395,050	2,431,155	1,516,935	672,822					14,390,989	8,978,175

TABLE F-XVIII. Continued (2)

Year	Brewing, Distilling & Sugar Refining Machinery, etc.		Other Kinds of Machinery & Parts Thereof		Lathes		Cigar & Cigarette Manufacturing Machinery & Parts Thereof		Machinery & Machine Parts Not Otherwise Recorded		Total	
	(a)	(b)	(a)	(b)	(a)	(b)	(a)	(b)	(a)	(b)	(a)	(b)
1925	9,558	5,113	12,355,613	3,382,242	354,420	15,639					25,570,936	9,952,373
1926	6,857	151	12,958,673	4,421,668	544,719	148,148					28,273,137	13,241,092
1927	14,728	8,000	13,170,109	3,637,709	582,648	86,989					30,611,326	13,557,230
1928	156,493	126,796	14,161,963	3,931,172	582,134	203,852					32,934,618	15,078,810
1929	97,397	4,140	17,775,602	5,324,657	424,887	152,824					49,828,149	24,488,427
1930	111,305	37,604	29,848,826	8,354,230	334,242	157,732					71,283,786	35,780,592
1931	96,602	37,845	28,126,267	12,870,950	398,686	245,608					70,167,655	42,793,490
1932 (3) (4)							930,604	499,501	13,892,242	5,117,261	47,391,272	18,527,660
1933							255,417	210,917	16,804,785	11,328,725	38,298,557	26,402,634
1934							144,351	121,452	21,739,598	10,237,607	54,191,988	30,680,401
1935							141,413	39,902	29,409,246	9,659,681	60,617,754	26,233,239

TABLE F-XIX GROSS VALUE OF EXPORTS OF CERTAIN FACTORY PRODUCTS FROM SHANGHAI AND ALL CHINA[1][2]

Unit, Standard Dollar

Year	Cotton Yarn		Steam Filature Silk		Cigarettes		Matches in General		Safety Matches		Wheat Flour		Machine-milled Wheat Flour & Samolina	
	(a)	(b)	(a)	(b)	(a)	(b)	(a)	(b)	(a)	(b)	(a)	(b)	(a)	(b)
1925 [3]	5,867,133	5,016,905	189,426,825	68,048,663	23,751,755	17,418,004	260,438	40,558			2,030,371	1,777,404		
1926	16,845,024	14,994,983	197,242,848	68,067,594	24,017,818	19,432,878	23,367	—			831,001	803,446		
1927	30,800,406	24,194,187	171,086,356	67,055,510	27,686,835	23,696,303	21,827	—			869,876	824,112		
1928	33,637,281	27,974,630	201,675,447	87,196,355	31,504,231	26,678,025	866,320	100,530			658,923	516,031		
1929 [4]	28,582,773	22,475,111	200,292,007	87,792,607	19,209,602	13,399,503	189,397	7,000			196,009	167,569		
1930	29,548,395	21,433,822	150,597,388	62,705,013	12,644,074	8,098,355	180,295	922			44,118	34,141		
1931	53,321,631	38,104,293	109,207,014	38,749,911	7,696,283	7,003,016	288,306	11,105			225,676	217,525		
1932 [5]	20,821,597	25,585,537	39,478,844	18,374,472	2,404,370	1,855,184			221,671	8,863			3,802,321	2,651,381
1933 [6]	40,021,859	36,502,907	39,426,619	22,963,808	1,244,815	848,377			364,824	34,007			4,124,657	4,123,676
1934	31,400,412	30,561,036	17,912,246	8,833,353	1,675,344	945,837			245,525	22,752			634,348	633,489
1935	19,234,489	17,337,904	29,217,192	22,547,370	1,359,652	846,950			140,997	9,576			40,908	38,716

TABLE F-XIX. Continued

Year	Toilet Soap		Household & Laundry Soap		Cotton Socks & Stockings		Knitted Goods		Total	
	(a)	(b)	(a)	(b)	(a)	(b)	(a)	(b)	(a)	(b)
1925 [3]	22,273	22,929	124,218	116,273	362,932			504,759	221,845,045	92,945,495
1926	58,649	56,253	194,222	189,640	407,378			393,678	239,620,307	103,938,472
1927	82,801	79,073	320,181	306,292	408,233			551,580	231,276,515	116,707,057
1928	49,004	47,386	394,753	384,910	277,598			720,913	269,063,557	143,618,780
1929 [4]	36,946	36,261	424,885	420,353	250,017			1,038,475	249,181,636	125,336,879
1930	78,693	76,295	1,144,979	1,087,194	326,340			1,407,221	194,564,282	95,740,963
1931	215,529	206,709	806,788	800,056	354,387*		1,976,625	1,664,682	173,737,852	86,756,297
1932 [5]			428,112	416,207	212,877*		791,307	661,547	76,946,222	49,553,221
1933 [6]			314,818	305,335	819,317*		1,054,891	939,059	86,552,483	65,717,159
1934			279,213	275,577	454,211*		598,820	496,122	52,745,908	41,768,166
1935			184,768	183,705	409,310*		433,629	364,709	50,600,635	41,328,030

Notes: (1) a, All China; b, Shanghai.
(2) See Note 2 under Table F-XVIII.
(3) In the earlier years Shanghai exports to foreign countries were given in the Customs Reports in quantities, and only the totals of "exports" to both foreign countries and Chinese ports were in value. We are therefore obliged to compute, for the first seven years, the value from the quantities.
(4) In this year it is provisionally granted that Chinese cargoes shipped from one treaty port and transshipped at a foreign port (e. g. Hongkong) no longer loses its native status on re-entering China. This explains, perhaps, some of the decreased figures in 1930 and later years.
(5) See Note 3 under Table F-XVI.
(6) According to the introduction in Volume I of The Trade of China, 1933, this is the first complete year during which produce sent to an ocean port like Shanghai for subsequent transshipment abroad has been treated statistically as a domestic movement of cargo at the port of first shipment and as a direct export abroad at the ocean port concerned, so that increases in columns (b) for this year may not appear as they actually are.
(7) Figures marked with asterisks in column (a) of "Cotton Socks & Stockings" are already included in figures in column (a) of "Knitted Goods."

TABLE F-XX. VESSELS ENTERED AND CLEARED AT THE PORT OF SHANGHAI

Year	To and From Abroad		To and From Chinese Ports		Total	
	No.	Tonnage	No.	Tonnage	No.	Tonnage
1925	—	—	—	—	19,861	30,284,855
1926	—	—	—	—	22,686	33,323,429
1927	—	—	—	—	21,514	30,151,653
1928	—	—	—	—	22,268	34,586,406
1929	—	—	—	—	22,289	35,869,560
1930	—	—	—	—	23,739	37,110,641
1931	—	—	—	—	20,795	37,972,893
1932	—	17,612,844	—	16,404,623	—	34,017,467
1933	4,136	17,881,928	13,979	17,340,415	18,115	35,222,343
1934	3,726	16,854,481	14,071	18,644,193	17,797	35,498,674

Based upon the reports of Chinese Maritime Customs.

TABLE F-XXI. INLAND WATER NAVIGATION VESSELS ENTERED AND CLEARED AT THE PORT OF SHANGHAI

Year	No.	Tonnage
1925	15,905	2,362,270
1926	18,857	2,652,908
1927	15,908	2,311,670
1928	18,690	3,051,365
1929	20,640	3,449,834
1930	23,790	3,858,163
1931	22,838	3,965,810
1932	—	—
1933	28,270	4,103,598
1934	27,858	4,381,162

Based upon the reports of Chinese Maritime Customs.

TABLE F-XXII. FREIGHT STATISTICS OF THE NANKING-SHANGHAI AND SHANGHAI-HANGCHOW-NINGPO RAILWAYS

Year	Nanking-Shanghai Railway		Shanghai-Hangchow-Ningpo Railway	
	Tons	Ton-kilometers	Tons	Ton-kilometers
1925	1,046,004	207,027,418	823,403	107,443,052
1926	1,532,315	321,133,658	879,966	118,219,635
1927	748,600	158,970,840	543,598	72,201,834
1928	1,296,223	272,450,274	889,656	116,743,786
1929	1,447,680	296,024,720	901,845	118,517,563
1930	1,383,414	290,411,387	981,008	136,624,808
1931	1,396,987	277,071,434	950,528	134,609,468
1932	841,749	168,551,342	776,734	102,416,065
1933	1,422,360	288,170,427	902,758	123,649,684
1934	1,587,474	306,980,899	1,030,551	143,370,568

Based upon data especially supplied by the Statistical Division of the Ministry of Railways.

TABLE F-XXIII. PASSENGER STATISTICS OF THE NANKING-SHANGHAI AND SHANGHAI-HANGCHOW-NINGPO RAILWAYS

Year	Nanking-Shanghai Railway		Shanghai-Hangchow-Ningpo Railway	
	Passengers	Passenger-kilometers	Passengers	Passenger-kilometers
1925	8,863,989	609,655,396	5,173,625	252,610,953
1926	11,313,102	794,195,568	5,450,612	284,785,526
1927	8,657,304	660,240,092	3,885,704	231,713,033
1928	10,861,405	820,473,826	5,207,158	304,114,703
1929	11,708,039	901,712,472	5,341,510	331,655,700
1930	12,813,362	937,513,543	5,675,659	376,698,714
1931	13,181,044	984,235,345	5,778,112	382,689,096
1932	7,903,520	689,049,807	5,197,952	320,315,583
1933	10,277,242	908,485,806	5,240,770	340,115,332
1934	10,750,306	970,902,302	5,223,470	348,622,314

Based upon data especially supplied by the Statistical Division of the Ministry of Railways.

TABLE F-XXIV. REVENUE OF THE NANKING-SHANGHAI AND SHANGHAI-HANGCHOW-NINGPO RAILWAYS

Unit, Standard Dollar

Year	Nanking-Shanghai Railway							Shanghai-Hangchow-Ningpo Railway						
	Revenue from Passenger Traffic		Revenue from Freight Traffic		Miscellaneous Revenue	Total	Revenue from Passenger Traffic		Revenue from Freight Traffic		Miscellaneous Revenue	Total
	Passengers	Others	Freight	Others			Passengers	Others	Freight	Others		
1925	4,741,006	1,048,934	1,523,722	1,282,042	247,989	8,843,693	2,632,327	421,254	1,191,899	74,709	109,143	4,429,232
1926	5,909,342	488,229	2,213,546	403,051	143,084	9,157,252	3,111,399	438,444	1,305,225	66,722	56,836	4,978,626
1927	5,381,280	1,250,974	1,125,953	231,060	144,932	8,134,199	2,590,525	1,004,657	958,836	46,045	46,363	4,646,426
1928	7,687,317	450,136	2,115,667	473,860	149,103	10,876,083	3,526,701	378,257	1,567,028	80,353	69,736	5,622,075
1929	8,665,975	507,726	2,316,898	409,164	140,118	12,039,882	3,832,925	284,110	1,606,267	103,999	100,014	5,927,315
1930	8,976,198	609,868	2,186,078	404,515	254,412	12,431,071	4,102,107	306,767	1,777,674	121,966	87,718	6,396,232
1931	10,901,142	822,917	2,543,856	393,361	379,834	15,041,110	4,748,274	347,435	2,044,180	141,846	105,109	7,386,844
1932	7,388,160	631,989	1,651,307	234,078	163,255	10,068,789	4,217,101	297,601	1,568,696	98,120	53,137	6,234,655
1933	9,739,422	782,434	2,625,899	406,640	318,400	13,872,795	4,351,284	168,158	1,901,732	143,128	108,398	6,672,700
1934	10,100,228	677,403	3,653,889	617,192	168,378	15,217,090	4,407,548	113,154	2,001,337	107,877	135,272	6,765,188

Based upon data especially supplied by the Statistical Division of the Ministry of Railways.

TABLE F-XXV. INTEREST AND DISCOUNT RATES IN SHANGHAI

Unit, Cent

Period	Native Rate of Interest (1)	Call Loan Rate (2)	Discount Rate on Joint Reserve Notes (3)
1926	15	—	—
1927	8	—	—
1928	14	—	—
1929	14	—	—
1930	7	—	—
1931	13	—	—
1932	10	—	—
1933	5	—	—
1934	9	10.50	13.50
1935	14	14.31	19.40

(1) Official interest rate per one thousand dollars per day of the Native Bankers Association, based upon *Prices And Price Indexes In Shanghai*.
(2) Official interest rate per one thousand dollars per day of the Joint Reserve Board of the Shanghai Bankers Association, on loans to member banks, based upon the former's reports and unpublished data.
(3) Official discount rate per one thousand dollars per day of the Joint Reserve Board of the Shanghai Bankers Association, for business firms, based upon the former's reports and unpublished data.

TABLE F-XXVI. BUSINESS STATISTICS OF TWENTY-EIGHT CHINESE BANKS IN SHANGHAI(1)

Unit, Standard Dollar

Year	Loans, Discounts & Overdrafts	Current Accounts & Fixed Deposits	Notes in Circulation(2)	Investment in Securities	Cash on Hand	Paid-up Capital
1925	763,738,118	783,297,475	221,806,026	64,730,228	115,651,786	114,065,434
1926	887,344,434	934,821,402	246,525,163	90,058,145	124,302,111	114,996,890
1927	908,019,930	976,122,496	278,730,410	104,324,217	123,153,055	117,049,543
1928	1,056,358,175	1,123,470,646	330,858,375	126,221,773	122,657,074	144,160,093
1929	1,221,940,222	1,320,151,727	376,053,697	141,893,322	139,531,805	149,025,268
1930	1,420,540,837	1,620,261,033	448,620,188	222,311,189	156,480,337	150,197,868
1931	1,603,995,114	1,866,656,525	437,139,770	239,236,974	194,280,724	155,784,785
1932	1,661,910,732	1,974,097,476	477,080,354	239,239,735	253,351,671	156,777,676
1933	2,023,179,920	2,418,580,782	548,480,924	274,973,672	305,137,855	173,885,326
1934	2,253,966,384	2,751,364,925	657,288,292	475,563,949	281,110,201	254,439,976

Notes: (1) Taken from *An Analysis of the Accounts of the Principal Chinese Banks* published by the Research Department of the Bank of China.
(2) Including notes issued for account of other banks.

TABLE F-XXVII. PERCENTAGE INCREASES IN THE BUSINESS OF TWENTY-EIGHT CHINESE BANKS IN SHANGHAI[1]

Item	1925-1934	Average Increase Every Two Years	Actual Increase, 1931-1933
Paid-up Capital	123	25	12
Reserve Fund & Surplus	61	12	28
Net Profit	85	17	27
Current Accounts & Fixed Deposits	251	50	30
Loans, Discounts & Overdrafts	195	39	26
Cash on Hand	143	29	57
Notes in Circulation[2]	196	39	25
Investment in Securities	635	127	15

Notes: (1) Based upon data in *An Analysis Of The Accounts Of The Principal Chinese Banks* published by the Research Department of the Bank of China.
(2) Including notes issued for account of other banks.

TABLE F-XXVIII. SILVER STOCK IN SHANGHAI*
Unit, $1,000

Year	Chinese Banks	Foreign Banks	Total
1925	62,233	71,817	134,050
1926	73,494	73,859	147,353
1927	79,342	62,907	142,249
1928	102,760	68,781	171,541
1929	144,196	96,064	240,260
1930	166,293	95,663	261,956
1931	179,305	86,883	266,188
1932	253,289	185,050	438,339
1933	271,786	275,660	547,446
1934	280,325	54,672	334,997

*Taken from *Financial & Commercial Monthly Bulletin*, being the December figures of the respective years.

TABLE F-XXIX. BANK CLEARINGS IN SHANGHAI
Unit, $1,000

Period	Clearings Through Joint Reserve Board		Clearings Through Native Bankers Association	Mutual Clearings	Total
	Dollar (1)	Transfer Dollar (1)	(2)	(2)	
1926	——	——	15,273,234	——	15,273,753
1927	——	——	12,648,740	——	12,648,740
1928	——	——	14,775,784	——	14,775,784
1929	——	——	16,858,209	——	16,858,209
1930	——	——	21,573,523	11,720,246	33,293,769
1931	——	——	25,609,091	7,674,438	33,283,529
1932	——	——	16,830,849	6,211,999	23,042,848
1933	1,118,674	847,778	13,811,380	6,214,423	21,992.255
1934	1,582,374	1,639,743	14,560,783	7,269,800	25,052,700
1935	1,857,579	1,858,249	13,578,830	7,209,100	24,503,758

Notes: (1) Based upon reports of the Joint Reserve Board of the Shanghai Bankers Association.
(2) Based upon data in *the Native Bankers' Monthly*.

TABLE F-XXX. VOLUME OF TRANSACTIONS ON SHANGHAI EXCHANGES

In Units of One Thousand

Period	Government Bonds (1) dol.	(2) dol.	Gold Bar (3) bar	Cotton Yarn (4) bale	Cotton (5) 50 kg.	Wheat Flour (6) sack	Wheat (7) 50 kg.	Soy Bean (7) 50 kg.	Bean Oil (7) 50 kg.	Bean Cake (7) piece
1926	450,738[8]	*	72,136	5,533	13,251	163,115	*	*	*	*
1927	238,169	*	65,920	2,807[9]	5,751[9]	104,114	*	*	—	*
1928	370,487	*	53,819	3,132	17,465	121,562	15,746[8]	710[8]	—	8,062[8]
1929	1,320,555	977,703	62,092	5,385	17,403	98,480	14,430	758	273[8]	3,612
1930	2,341,820	90,615	58,299	5,053	15,373	165,889	38,736	5,308	10	5,383
1931	3,362,540	555,022	53,364	11,435	33,550	295,337	76,430	15,023	2,090	18,125
1932[10]	901,710	303,939	23,058	6,159	20,106	95,715	8,642	1,561	180	2,923
1933	3,182,685	230,090	34,498	9,738	29,599	154,566	15,791	594	6	6,278
1934	4,773,410	—	33,518	10,379	32,695	185,115	18,811	2,492	1,762	11,926
1935	4,909,980	—	19,625	8,943	27,024	168,640	10,818	3,509	1,779	10,255

(1) Volume of transactions in the Shanghai China Merchants Stock Exchange, before 1930 based on *the Commercial Monthly*, since 1930 based on materials supplied by the Shanghai China Merchants Stock Exchange.
(2) Volume of transactions on the Shanghai Stock and Merchandise Exchange based on *the Statistical Monthly* with the 1926-28 figures lacking. The figure for 1933 extends only to the end of May of that year after which the bonds section of the Shanghai Stock and Merchandise exchange was amalgamated with the Shanghai China Merchants Stock Exchange.
(3) Before 1933 based on materials supplied by the exchanges, since 1933 based on materials supplied by the National Tariff Commission. Both kinds of figures refer to the combined totals of the Shanghai Stock and Merchandise Exchange and the Shanghai Gold Bar Exchange until September 16, 1934 when the gold bar section of the former was amalgamated with the latter.
(4) and (5) Based on materials supplied by the Chinese Cotton Goods Exchange.
(6) Based on materials supplied by the Shanghai Flour Exchange.
(7) Based on materials supplied by the Provision Exchange, the 1926-27 figures for wheat, soy bean and bean cake being lacking.
(8) Total of eleven months only.
(9) Total of eight months only.
(10) During this year business on the stock and cotton goods exchanges was done for only nine months, that on the flour and provision exchanges for only eight months while gold bar transactions continued throughout the year.

TABLE F-XXXI. VOLUME OF BUSINESS DONE ON THE SHANGHAI STOCK EXCHANGE[1]
Unit, Share

Year	General Common Stocks	General Preferred Stocks	Rubber Stocks	Total
1931 (2nd half)	7,080,725	88,533	100,319	7,269,577
1932 (1st half)	—	—	—	2,230,739[2]
,, (2nd half)	—	—	—	2,107,729
1933 (1st half)	—	—	—	4,429,710
,, (2nd half)	—	—	—	4,104,876
1934 (1st half)	967,422	41,909	9,641,561	10,650,892
,, (2nd half)	534,162	30,898	7,236,685	7,801,745
1935 (1st half)	49,889	21,190	253,655	324,734
,, (2nd half)	—	—	—	573,587

Notes: (1) Based upon data supplied by Swan, Culbertson & Fritz.
(2) Transactions of four months only.

TABLE. F-XXXII. AVERAGE DEFLATED QUOTATIONS OF GOVERNMENT BONDS AND INDICES OF BONDS AND STOCKS

Period	Government Bonds' Average Deflated Quotation Balance Unpaid at Beginning of Period=100 (1)	Bond Indices		Stock Index Quotation at End of July, 1931=100 (3)
		Monthly Interest at 1%=100 (2)	Quotation at End of July, 1931=100 (3)	
1928	—	69.62	—	—
1929	—	80.95	—	—
1930	—	68.03	—	—
1931	—	62.29	85.62[6]	99.76[6]
1932	44.30[4]	49.05[5]	60.86[5]	80.28[7]
1933	55.25	71.35	78.48	71.36
1934	69.84	96.82	97.94	65.29
1935	70.25	92.43	98.25	57.11

Notes: (1) Based upon data in *Bank of China Monthly Review*.
(2) Based upon data especially supplied by the Singhua Bank.
(3) Based upon data especially supplied by Swan, Culbertson & Fritz.
(4) Average of May-December.
(5) Average of January and May-December.
(6) Average of July-December.
(7) Average of January and April-December.

TABLE F-XXXIII. SPINDLAGE OF COTTON MILLS IN CHINA, 1890-1935[1]

Year	Chinese		Japanese		British		Total	
	Number	Index	Number	Index	Number	Index	Number	Index
1890	114,721	17.60					114,712	11.67
1891	204,712	31.41					204,712	20.83
1892	204,712	31.41					204,712	20.83
1893	204,712	31.41					204,712	20.83
1894	204,712	31.41					204,712	20.83
1895	221,744	34.03	22,432	9.61	72,312	74.02	316,488	32.10
1896	324,116	49.74	123,480	52.89	72,312	74.02	519,908	52.90
1897	324,116	49.74	149,608	64.09	72,312	74.02	546,036	55.56
1898	324,116	49.74	149,608	64.09	72,312	74.02	546,036	55.56
1899	416,056	63.84	149,608	64.09	72,312	74.02	637,976	64.91
1900	416,056	63.84	149,608	64.09	72,312	74.02	637,976	64.91
1901	416,056	63.84	149,608	64.09	72,312	74.02	637,976	64.91
1902	416,056	63.84	149,608	64.09	72,312	74.02	637,976	64.91
1903	416,056	63.84	149,608	64.09	72,312	74.02	637,976	64.91
1904	416,056	63.84	149,608	64.09	72,312	74.02	637,976	64.91
1905	484,136	74.29	149,608	64.09	72,312	74.02	706,056	71.84
1906	507,336	77.85	149,608	64.09	72,312	74.02	729,256	74.20
1907	596,084	91.47	149,608	64.09	97,688	100.00	843,380	85.81
1908	622,676	95.55	149,608	64.09	97,688	100.00	869,972	88.52
1909	651,676	100.00	149,608	64.09	97,688	100.00	898,972	91.47
1910	651,676	100.00	172,648	73.95	97,688	100.00	922,012	93.81
1911	651,676	100.00	172,648	73.95	97,688	100.00	922,012	93.81
1912	651,676	100.00	172,648	73.95	97,688	100.00	922,012	93.81
1913	651,676	100.00	233,448	100.00	97,688	100.00	982,812	100.00
1914	687,964	105.57	307,048	131.53	153,320	156.95	1,148,332	116.84

TABLE F-XXXIII. Continued

Year	Chinese Number	Chinese Index	Japanese Number	Japanese Index	British Number	British Index	Total Number	Total Index
1915	687,964	105.57	307,048	131.53	153,320	156.95	1,148,332	116.84
1916	817,660	125.47	307,048	131.53	153,320	156.95	1,278,028	130.04
1917	837,628	128.53	397,448	170.25	153,320	156.95	1,388,396	141.29
1918	1,025,772	157.41	423,576	181.44	153,320	156.95	1,602,668	163.07
1919	1,173,012	181.00	455,640	195.18	153,320	156.95	1,781,972	181.31
1920	1,358,552	208.47	549,752	231.64	153,320	156.95	2,052,624	208.85
1921	1,749,468	268.46	902,960	386.97	153,320	156.95	2,805,748	285.48
1922	2,061,770	316.38	1,268,344	543.31	153,320	156.95	3,483,488(2)	354.44
1923	2,191,120	336.23	1,404,848	601.78	153,320	156.95	3,749,288	381.49
1924	2,205,684	388.42	1,553,120	665.30	153,320	156.95	3,912,124	398.05
1925	2,256,624	346.28	1,636,156	700.87	153,320	156.95	4,046,100	411.69
1926	2,277,104	349.42	1,636,156	700.87	153,320	156.95	4,066,580	413.77
1927	2,287,152	350.96	1,636,156	700.87	153,320	156.95	4,076,626(2)	414.79
1928	2,287,152	350.96	1,674,844	717.44	153,320	156.95	4,115,316	418.73
1929	2,304,592	353.64	1,674,844	717.44	153,320	156.95	4,132,756	420.50
1930	2,395,792	367.64	1,674,844	717.44	153,320	156.95	4,223,956	429.78
1931	2,730,790	419.04	2,003,388	858.17	170,610	174.65	4,904,788	499.06
1932	2,773,273	425.56	2,063,448	883.90	183,196	187.53	5,019,917	510.77
1933	2,885,796	442.83	2,098,176	898.78	187,628	192.07	5,171,600	526.20
1934	2,951,436	452.90	2,242,624	960.65	187,628	192.07	5,381,688	547.58
1935	3,008,479	461.65	2,284,860	978.74	233,508	239.03	5,526,847	562.35

(1) From H. D. Fong, *Cotton Spinning and Weaving Industries in China*. Detailed figures as well as the index numbers for 1931-35 are added and calculated by this Institute.
(2) These totals do not agree with the sums of the Chinese, Japanese and British spindles, but no data are available to correct the figures.
(3) The index numbers are computed with 1913 as the base year

APPENDIX G
SOCIAL STATISTICS
TABLE G-I. GROWTH OF POPULATION IN SHANGHAI[1]

Year	International Settlement		French Concession		Chinese Territory	Total
	Number	Rate of Increase	Number	Rate of Increase	Number	
1865	92,884	—	—	—	—	—
1870	76,713	—	—	—	—	—
1876	97,335	—	—	—	—	—
1880	110,009	—	—	—	—	—
1885	129,338	—	—	—	—	—
1890	171,950	—	—	—	—	—
1895	245,679	—	52,188	—	—	—
1900	352,050[2]	100	92,263	—	—	—
1905	464,213	132	96,963	—	—	—
1910	501,541	142	115,946	—	568,372	1,185,859
1915	638,920	181	149,000[3]	100	—	—
1920	783,146	223	170,229	114	—	—
1925	840,226[4]	239	297,072	199	—	—
1930	1,007,868[5]	286	434,807	292	1,702,130	3,144,805

Notes: (1) Data from page 21 of *Shanghai, as Shown in Statistical Tables* by C. Y. Lo with the exception of the 1930 figure for the Chinese Territory which is taken from Table F-1.

(2) This figure is chosen as the base because the International Settlement had its last extension in 1898.

(3) This figure is chosen as the base because the French Concession had its last extension in 1915.

(4) Including (a) 298 foreign residents in Pootung, (b) 7,097 foreign residents in External Roads Areas, (c) 10,381 Chinese residents in villages and huts, and (d) 14,082 Chinese residents in shipping and boats.

(5) Including 9,506 foreign residents in External Roads Areas.

TABLE G-II. SEX RATIO OF CHINESE POPULATION IN SHANGHAI

Year	International Settlement	French Concession
1870	290	—
1876	297	—
1880	277	—
1885	238	—
1890	227	—
1895	218	—
1900	197	—
1905	180	—
1910	175	197
1915	172	184
1920	160	173
1925	172	166
1930	156	149

Data from page 30 of *Shanghai, as Shown in Statistical Tables*.

TABLE G-III. AGE DISTRIBUTION OF POPULATION IN SHANGHAI CHINESE TERRITORY IN 1934

Age	Male	Female	Total	Percentage
Under 1	22,836	18,057	40,893	2.1
1- 5	99,599	85,781	185,380	9.7
6-12	128,025	89,517	217,542	11.4
13-20	175,468	131,295	306,763	16.0
21-40	422,861	301,625	724,486	37.9
41-60	223,380	155,829	379,209	19.8
61-80	30,532	27,338	57,870	3.0
81-100	1,156	1,394	2,550	0.1
Unknown		1	1	—
Total	1,103,857	810,837	1,914,694	100.0

Computed from material on page C-23 of *the Shanghai Year Book, 1935* published by the History Compilation Bureau of Greater Shanghai. All figures refer to Chinese residents only.

TABLE G-IV. NATIVITY OF RESIDENTS IN SHANGHAI CHINESE TERRITORY

Province or City	Number of Persons	Percentage
Kiangsu	751,531	39.23
Chekiang	358,364	18.71
Anhwei	86,510	4.52
Kwangtung	48,795	2.55
Hupei	34,211	1.79
Shantung	31,684	1.66
Hopei	30,294	1.58
Fukien	13,196	0.69
Hunan	11,401	0.60
Kiangsi	8,452	0.44
Honan	8,306	0.44
Szechuan	2,134	0.11
Kwangsi	1,129	0.06
Liaoning	536	0.03
Shansi	405	0.02
Yunnan	216	0.01
Shensi	202	0.01
Kweichow	130	0.01
Heilungkiang	47	0.01
Kirin	45	0.00
Kansu	37	0.00
Chahar	19	0.00
Suiyuan	4	0.00
Hsinkiang	2	0.00
Shanghai	488,631	25.51
Nanking	31,316	1.64
Peiping	6,466	0.34
Tsingtao	631	0.04
Total	*1,914,694*	*100.00*

Data from page C-24 of *the Shanghai Year Book, 1935.*

TABLE G-V. INCREASES IN LAND VALUES IN THE
INTERNATIONAL SETTLEMENT OF SHANGHAI, 1903-1933

District	Estimated Price Per Mow			Percentage of Increase in Value
	1903	1930	1933	1903-1933
Central	$13,549	$107,878	$132,451	978%
Northern	4,819	37,857	41,802	867
Eastern	2,539	11,864	15,385	606

Data from *Assessment Schedules* of Shanghai Municipal Council.

TABLE G-VI. COMMUNISTIC ACTIVITIES IN SHANGHAI

Year	Communists Arrested and Sentenced	Communist Organs Discovered	Copies of Red Propaganda	Secret Radio Stations	Pistols	Bullets
1933	233	174	7,160		11	1,155
1934	149	142	53,014	3	27	1,000

Taken from *Shanghai Municipal Reports*.

Appendix H

EXPLANATORY NOTES ON THE
VARIOUS SURVEYS

1. Notes on the Survey of 1928

The earliest and comparatively comprehensive survey of Shanghai industries was made in 1929 by the Bureau of Social Affairs of the City Government of Greater Shanghai and published under the title "Industries in Shanghai." Unfortunately items included in that book are very few in number, and the classification of factories is not satisfactory. Though the book includes many statistical tables and charts, there are several charts without corresponding tables. Even the figures appearing in the tables show discrepancies with those in the explanatory remarks on the classification of industries as appear in the body of the book. For each important industry, there are explanatory remarks, giving the names of factories in that industry, their addresses, capitalization, and number of workers, but if their totals be compared with those appearing in the statistical tables at the beginning of the book, the result shows great discrepancies. One possible explanation is that factories listed in the book are larger in size, small scale establishments being excluded. Sometimes, however, it is also found that the number of factories, capitalization and number of workers appearing in the explanatory remarks are larger than those in the statistical tables, and for this we are not in a position to risk any explanation. Often, also, there are duplications of factories or establishments in the lists when both the new name of a factory after its reorganization and the old name before it are given, and treated as two separate establishments. Furthermore, the method of classification of the industries in the body of the book differs from that in the statistical tables. This explains another difficulty in checking the figures of this survey.

This investigation began in October, 1927, by the Bureau of Industry, Agriculture and Commerce (農工商局) when the Municipality of Greater Shanghai was first established. After the reorganization of the Bureau into the Bureau of Social Affairs in August, 1928, the survey was completed, and according to the book above referred to items included in the survey were 20 in number, as follows:—

1. Name of factory.
2. Address of the factory.
3. Name of general manager or factory manager.
4. Date of establishment.
5. Ownership.
6. Capitalization: Chinese or foreign.
7. Amount of loan floated.
8. Number of workers: Male, female and child.
9. Age of child workers: Oldest and youngest.
10. Wage rates.
    a. Highest: Male, female and child worker.
    b. Lowest: Male, female and child worker.
11. Working hours per day.
12. Raw material: Variety, annual consumption, producing districts, recent prices.
13. Products: Variety, annual production, principal markets, annual value of output.
14. Trade marks.
15. Motive power.

APPENDIX

    a. Steam, number of boilers, h.p. of turbine or engine, average coal consumption per month, coal-stoking machine, consumption of coal per h.p. per hour.
    b. Electricity, number of motors, total h.p.
    c. Diesel, h.p. of engine, average consumption of the oil per day, consumption of oil per h.p. per hour.
    d. Manual labor.
16. Machinery, variety, makers, cost of machinery in a factory, total cost of factory premises.
17. Possibility of substituting domestic products for imported machinery and raw material, difficulties in using domestic products.
18. Possibility of exporting domestic products to foreign countries.
19. Are the products widely marketed? If not, why?
20. Any plan for the improvement of technique and machinery? Is any guidance required?

Many of these questions are not for statistical purposes, and all except a few items have not been statistically summarized and published in the book.

The scope of investigation was to include foreign as well as Chinese factories in the survey, but judging from the result obtained, a large number of foreign factories has apparently been left out. At the time of investigation the total number of factories was estimated at 1,781, and that actually surveyed 1,500, representing 84.2 per cent of the total. In reference to the 1,781 factories, we are not in a position to know whether the number was limited to modern factories or not, and if so limited, what was the standard chosen for the survey. Or was it merely the number of factories the names of which happened to be known to the Bureau at that time? Modern manufacturing establishments operated on a small scale, such as printing shops and leather goods manufacturers, are numerous in Shanghai, and their numbers in the book are much smaller. It could not be because the survey was limited to those in conformity with the standard set up by the Chinese Factory Law, as at that time the law had not yet been promulgated. For these reasons, the accuracy of the estimated total of Chinese and foreign factories is doubtful.

Statistical tables appearing at the beginning of the book include the following:—

1. Classification of Industries.
2. Distribution of Capital in the Various Industries.
3. Distribution of Capital by Class Intervals.
4. Number of Factories Established During Past Years.
5. Distribution of Workers in the Various Industries.
6. Working Hours.
7. Statistical Table of Average Highest and Lowest Wage Rates in the Various Industries.

In the statistical charts the kinds and quantity of motive power in the various industries and export and import trade figures are separately represented. The latter cannot be considered as "industrial" statistics, while the former is not supported by tables, the reason for which is hard to explain. Hence, in Tables C-I and C-II in Appendix C, we cannot include the data about motive power, and other statistics that are included are limited to the number of factories, capitalization, number of workers, wage rates and working hours. As before 1928 there were not even such statistics for Shanghai industries, these figures, though not satisfactory, are worth quoting.

2. *Notes on the Survey of 1929*

According to the "Wages and Hours of Labor of Greater Shanghai", published in 1929 by the Labor Section of the Bureau of Social Affairs of the City Government of Greater Shanghai, a plan to investigate into the various kinds of laborers in Shanghai had been drafted, but owing to lack of funds the work had not been started. To know the actual earnings of the laborers a special investigation was made in May, 1928, covering 1,504 factories and 237,522 workers. In the course of the investigation, attention was paid more to large factories than to small ones, and for this reason estimates for the latter were included. A

APPENDIX

second investigation was made in August, 1929, covering 1,593 factories and 275,027 workers, and if estimated figures were included, the total number of factories covered by the survey would be 2,326 and workers, 285,700. The following is a brief account of the method used in the investigation and estimation of the number of workers, taken from the "Wages and Hours of Labor of Greater Shanghai".

"In May, 1928, it was found as a result of our investigation that there were 1,504 establishments with a total labor force of 237,522 laborers in this city.[1] In this investigation, we had not been in strict adherence to the definition of a factory given in the Factory Law, which requires that a factory should have a labor force of not less than 30 workers. In 1929, the project of a labor census was still an unrealized hope. Nevertheless, our plan to compile statistics of wage rates demanded a better knowledge of the total labor force in this city. Therefore, another inquiry was made in August, 1929, to check up the result of the previous investigation. In this inquiry, the method of estimating was emphasized. Actual investigations, however, were made wherever accessible. The method employed in the estimation and investigation of the total number of workers may be summarized as follows:

"(1) Where employers' associations, labor unions, etc. exist, we are able to get hold of lists of establishments under the respective associations. With this information as our guide, direct inquiries are possible. As to those establishments which have not joined the associations, such information is lacking. Agents are sent by the Bureau to search the streets in the city for such establishments. This, however, cannot go very far as to cover every quarter and every crooked lane in this city. Investigations are not impossible where such establishments are of appreciable scale and well known to all. Small scale establishments, however, would inevitably escape our notice. Wherever direct investigation is impossible, a method of estimating has to be employed. The

---

1. Bureau of Social Affairs, City Government of Greater Shanghai: The Index Numbers of Earnings of the Factory Laborers in Greater Shanghai, July-December, 1928.

number of such establishments, the average number of laborers, and the proportion of male, female, and child workers are to be estimated, basing upon the information obtained by direct investigation. These estimated figures and figures obtained in direct inquiries, taken together, constitute the total number of laborers in the respective industries. Figures for workers in soap, silk reeling, cotton spinning, silk weaving, cotton weaving, knitting, bleaching and dyeing, and tobacco industries are obtained by this method.

"(2) Where no employers' associations exist, agents are sent to different districts of the city for direct investigations. Information regarding unknown or inaccessible establishments, however, can only be in the form of estimates. Such estimates are based upon the reports of labor organizations, known establishments in the same industries, etc. Figures for workers in foundry, machinery, glass, tanning, and printing industries are obtained by this method.

"(3) There are certain industries which contain only a few well known establishments of large scale. Information regarding such establishments can easily be obtained. Establishments in the sawing, shipbuilding, match, enamel, flour, oil, egg and egg products, and paper industries are of this type."

The investigation covers 17 districts and one special area. The Shanghai City Government covers 30 districts and one special area but at that time only the 17 districts of Lu Hang, Yang Sze, Yang Ching, Tang Chiao, Kao Hang, Kao Chiao, Hu Nan, Chapei, Kiangwan, Woosung, Ying Hang, Ying Siang, Fa Hwa, Pu Sung, Chen Ju, Tsao Ching and Peng Pu had been transferred to the administration of the City Government, while the special district consisted of the French Concession and the International Settlement. All industries in the 17 districts and one special area were included in the survey, particularly Nantao, Chapei, Kiangwan, Ying Siang, Yang Ching and the special administrative area, which are the main centres of industry. For this reason, special attention was paid to the survey of factories in these areas.

APPENDIX

Industries were selected according to their importance, namely, those which had factories operated on a comparatively large scale or had a large number of workers. Any industry employing more than 1,500 workers was considered important, and hence was included in the investigation. For compiling the statistics of actual earnings of workers, 30 industries were included, while for compilation of wage rate statistics, only 21 industries were included, the same number that was included in the investigation of the total number of workers. Only workers engaged in the manufacturing process in the factories were included, while staff members, technical experts and other employees were eliminated.

The investigation schedule was very simple and the period covered by the survey was short. From experience during two recent years in compiling statistics of the actual earnings of workers, it was found that the conditions prevailing in April, May, September, and October were most normal, and for this reason the wage account of September 25 was taken as the basis for the investigation of the wage earnings, while the number of workers was ascertained one month earlier. The report further says:—

In the course of our work we have decided to abandon the old system and to adopt a more comprehensive scheme of classification of industries and occupations worked out by the International Labor Office as a result of the International Conference of Labor Statisticians held at Geneva in 1924. The method of classification suggested by the International Labor Office is based upon three principles: the materials worked on, the process of manufacture, and the nature of the products. But, it is impossible to choose one of these principles exclusively as the basis of classifying. A classification may be based upon two or all of these principles. In the earlier stage of manufacture one raw material usually predominates. The material worked in might therefore be taken as basis. In the later stages of manufacture, however, the finished products generally require a combination of different materials and involve complex processes. In these cases, either the process or the nature of the products has to be taken as the leading principle. However, these three principles do not constitute the underlying factors behind such a classification. The real controlling principle lies in the nature of the industrial organization. Whether material, process or the finished product, either taken singly or in conjunction with one another, is sufficient as a factor in deciding upon a group depends upon whether it is distinctive enough to have resulted in a separate industrial organization. Fundamentally, therefore, it is the organization of a distinctive industrial group that has the final sway in classification. The system of classification of the International Labor Office for manufacturing industries is as follows:[2]

1. Wood Working.
2. Furniture Manufacture.
3. Metal Industry.
4. Machinery and Metal Tools and Utensils.
5. Construction of Boats, Ships, and Vehicles for Land and Air Transportation.
6. Manufacture of Bricks, Earthenware, Glass, etc.
7. Construction of Buildings, and Making and Repairing of Roads, Railways, Bridges, and Canals, etc.
8. Production and Transmission of Gas and Electricity, and Supply of Water and Water Power.
9. Manufacture of Chemicals and Allied Products.
10. Textile Industry.
11. Manufacture of Wearing Apparel.
12. Manufacture of Leather, Skin, and Rubber.
13. Manufacture of Foods, Drinks, and Tobacco.
14. Paper and Printing.
15. Manufacture of Clocks, Watches, and Musical and Scientific Instruments.
16. Other Manufacturing Industries."

There are many difficulties in calculating wage rates, which we have also experienced in our work. The 1929 survey paid special attention to the investigation of wage rates and earnings,

---

2. International Labor Office: Systems of Classification of Industries and Occupations.

APPENDIX

and for this reason its method of investigation and calculation is worth studying. The following is a quotation of the original text on the method of converting piece rates into time rates, and it also explains the way the wage earnings in the 1929 statistics were calculated.

"The most perplexing problem in the collection of wage data is that of the piece rates. Information regarding the basic unit of the products, the number of units of output per laborer, the rate of wages per unit of output, and the number of hours worked on the day of investigation must be secured. From this information, the piece rates are to be converted to a time basis by multiplying the number of units of output per laborer with the rate per unit of output, and dividing the product by the number of hours worked. Thus, the hourly rates of wages are obtained. Information regarding the unit of output and the rate per unit can be readily afforded by the managements. The units of output per laborer and the number of hours worked, however, have to be specially recorded for us by the staff and foremen in different departments of various establishments. This is undoubtedly a very painstaking task. We owe very much to the cooperation and assistance of the many officers, who helped us to realize our plan. Nevertheless, some of the records kept are not very satisfactory, and their accuracy is highly questionable. The result would be more reliable if we had enough agents to do the work of recording ourselves. In view of such deficiencies, we had, in the compilation of wage-rate statistics, treated the time workers and piece workers separately, such that the unreliability of the piece rate data would not affect the validity of the result as a whole."

Although the scope of the 1929 survey was limited to a few principal industries, the names of factories and the number of male, female and child workers were given for each industry in the statistical tables. In addition, the sources of information, and the number of factories and workers investigated were stated, and if there were estimated figures, they were also marked out. The method and basis of estimation were scientific, and for this reason, though the estimated figures represented one-third of the total number of factories, they did not affect the data collected by investigation. As to the total number of workers, the number estimated was only 40,000, representing one-sixth of the number investigated. Statistics of wage earnings were given separately and in great detail for each individual industry, differentiating between male, female, and child workers, the nature of their work, and time and piece rates. Piece rates were converted into time rates according to the method mentioned above, thus making it possible to combine the two and arrive at an average. Figures in the statistical tables of Appendix E are the average hourly and and daily earnings and working hours of male, female and child workers in the various industries, while other data of the 1929 survey are given in Appendix C.

3. Notes on the Survey of 1931

For explanation of the 1931 survey, it is best to quote the Explanatory Remarks of the Preliminary Report on Shanghai Industrialization.

From May to July, 1931, an extensive survey was made of Shanghai factories and workshops according to a standard to be explained later on, with the cooperation of six organizations—the Research Committee of the Chinese Economic Society, the National Government Directorate of Statistics, the Ministry of Industries, the National Tariff Commission,[1] the Bureau of Social Affairs of Greater Shanghai, and the Chiaotung University. The total number of men engaged in the work, including those who directed the cooperating staffs and edited the schedules, was 42 during the first three months of the survey.

After July, it was found necessary to keep on with the survey to include more factories and workshops, as well as to revisit others whose schedules were not satisfactorily filled. Many of these had to be visited several times, before their schedules could be used. Most of the cooperating organizations kept on with the Chinese

---

1. The Tariff Commission was invited to join the survey because it had trained investigators familiar with the industrial products and their prices.

APPENDIX

Economic Society in this work, although the number of their investigators in the field was reduced. It was agreed that this should continue for three more months till October, 1931, after which the Chinese Economic Society alone continued in the work, with the occasional help of the staff of the Shanghai Bureau of Social Affairs and the Chiaotung University Research Institute.

The cooperative survey was organized in the following manner. Each cooperating organization designated a representative to form a joint committee which supervised the work as a whole. At the same time each organization supplied two to four field workers to visit the factories and collect the data and two or three editors to edit the returns. Each organization bore the expenses of its own staff, but in the case of the Chiaotung University, because its investigators were especially engaged for this survey and put directly under the supervision of the writer[2], their salaries and expenses were fixed and paid by the Chinese Economic Society Research Committee with funds supplied by the University. The six organizations also jointly maintained an office on Peking Road in the down town district, and each contributed a sum towards its expenses. These sums, as well as the salaries and expenses of the cooperating staff (except those of the Chiaotung Univerity investigators), amounted to approximately $20,000, but they did not figure in the accounts of the Research Committee—later reorganized into the China Institute of Economic and Statistical Research—as contributions because the survey was considered a cooperative enterprise.

For the sake of the survey, Shanghai—including the International Settlement, the French Concession and the much larger territory under Chinese Administration—was divided into 8 districts, and two investigators were assigned to each district. They were given names of all factories and workshops on the streets in their districts arranged by streets, as a guide to their visits. If new ones were found which were not mentioned in

---

2. Through the courtesy of Mr. J. Usang Ly, President of the University and Vice-Chairman of the Research Committee.

the lists, they were to visit them and fill in the questionnaire just the same. Hence it amounted almost to a house to house survey. If a factory in the list could not be found, the investigator was to make inquiries in the neighborhood until it was located either in the same district or in another one to which it might have removed. In the latter case, it was assigned to the investigator in the other district. When the survey in one district was completed, the investigators there were transferred to another and assigned to a number of streets which had not been already surveyed by the investigators there.

The investigators were under the direction of a chief investigator and an associate chief investigator appointed by the joint committee. All of them reported daily at the office on Peking Road where an office staff was maintained to register and file the schedules and where the chief investigator kept in constant touch with all the investigators. He was also responsible for distributing the filled schedules to the editors of the various organizations and collecting them back.

Although the chief investigator had been trained by the writer over ten years in the former Bureau of Economic Information, the Bureau of Statistics of the Legislative Yuan, and the National Government Directorate of Statistics, the latter spent half of his time in Shanghai to supervise the work personally. A meeting was held at least once a week with all the investigators, at which the writer answered all their questions and helped them overcome whatever difficulties they might encounter during their investigation. The chief investigator also made all the necessary arrangements with the Chamber of Commerce, the industrial associations and sometimes the factories themselves so that the investigators would not be refused admission during their visits. Inspite of all such arrangements, some factories had to be visited several times before they would answer the questionnaires, and a few refused to answer entirely.

In editing the schedules, the editors of the various organizations were asked to point out all figures and information in the schedules

APPENDIX

that were apparently inaccurate or at least doubtful. These were written on small slips of paper attached to the questionnaires, and sent to the chief investigator, who would assign them to the various investigators who were carrying on the survey in the sections in which the factories were situated. One factory was often visited several times until the answer was finally found satisfactory.

When all the necessary corrections had been made in the schedules, five additional copies were made so that each cooperating organization might have a complete set. These were distributed among the organizations from time to time as the copies were made. When these reached the Directorate of Statistics in Nanking, Mr. C. Sun, who was then a division chief of the Directorate and at the same time a member of the Chinese Economic Society Research Committee, would examine them once again, and schedules containing any doubtful items would be sent back to the chief investigator at Shanghai for explanation. This generally meant renewed visits, and it was for these reasons that the field work continued till January, 1932, when the Japanese invasion of Shanghai made it impossible to go on.[3]

As for practical reasons it was impossible to cover all factories and workshops in Shanghai in a three-month survey as originally planned, it was decided after much deliberation in the Research Committee and the joint committee of the cooperating organizations to adopt the following definition of scope:—

    1. The survey should cover all factories and workshops employing 10 or more workers or using motive power in their manufacturing process. This was suggested by Dr. Ta Chen who was then in Shanghai making a study of the applicability of the Chinese Factory Law and adopted by the joint committee. While there were only about 700 factories in Shanghai which used motive power and employed more than

---

3. An investigator, G. G. Chu, who lived on North Szechwan Road, was probably killed in the first days of the invasion, since he has never been seen again by members of the Economic Society or his own family, after January 28, inspite of all their efforts to find him.

30 workers[4] the number covered by the survey was nearly 2,000.

2. Since the scope was so broad, it was realized that there was not enough time to cover the whole ground. It was decided that old-fashioned handicraft industries should be left out for the time being, although a few samples of those that afforded comparison with modernized industries were included. In other words, the survey did not try to cover all handcraft workshops employing more than ten workers.*

3. The original plan of the joint committee was to include foreign as well as Chinese factories in the survey, but prolonged efforts to make the necessary arrangements produced no results. An attempt was also made to cooperate with Dr. Ta Chen in his study of the applicability of the Chinese Factory Law which was initiated by foreign factory owners in Shanghai, by having our investigators fill his questionnaire for Chinese factories and the foreign factory managers fill our questionnaire at the same time they answered his. To this proposal the foreign manufacturers did not agree, and as their own questionnaire was not answered by all foreign factories in Shanghai, their agreement would not have helped our survey very much. Hence it was finally decided to limit the survey to Chinese establishments only.

With these limitations, altogether 2,001 factories and workshops were covered. However, some of these were visited in 1932 after the Japanese troops had withdrawn from Shanghai, and so much time had lapsed since the beginning of the 1931 survey that the data could not very well be included in the total. Again, although the investigators kept the original instructions in mind, they sometimes filled the questionnaires before they realized that the establishments did not come up to our qualifications. It took them so

---

4. According to the provisions of the Chinese Factory Law.
* There are in fact less than 50 such modernized workshops, which, due to some misunderstanding, have not been weeded out during the recent revision.

APPENDIX

much time to locate the factories and workshops in the first place, and get them to answer their questions in the second, that they could not always ask questions in a predetermined order so as to find out if the establishment should be included in the survey or not. Fortunately such cases were not many, and the number included in the following tables is 1,066.

After the number of establishments to be included in the summary has been decided upon, the next thing is to classify them into groups, divisions and sub-divisions. In forming the main groups, we follow the system used by the International Labour Office which has sixteen main classifications. For the various divisions of the main groups we also follow the suggestions of that office as far as they could be applied to the conditions in Shanghai. For instance, the clothing industry forms Group XI in the I.L.O. classification, and in explanatory remarks that office enumerates tailoring, dress-making, manufacturing of under-clothing including hosiery goods, millinery, manufacturing of hats, boots and shoes, dyeing and cleaning of clothing, etc. This classification is more inclusive than is generally adopted in any manufacturing census, since custom tailoring and cleaning of clothing are not considered as manufacturing industries at all, although they may be included in a classification of laborers. Again, as leather and rubber shoes in China are the direct results of introducing leather (referring to that which is tanned by modern chemical processes) and rubber into this country, they are better studied in connection with these raw materials in Group XII instead of Group XI.

The classification into sub-divisions and sub-sub-divisions is much harder than that into groups and divisons. In this we have to consider the actual conditions of the industries in Shanghai. For instance, since there are no Chinese milliners in Shanghai, there is no need of having that subdivision. On the other hand, knitted hosiery is now a very important industry here, and 101 manufactories of this article are included in our survey. Hence, there is necessity of a careful analysis for this industry. We start out by classifying the establishments according to the raw material used, namely, cotton, silk and rayon, wool, and cotton, silk and wool combined. This classification is not logical, but is based on actual conditions.

Again, under cotton there are establishments which use cotton yarn only, some cotton thread only, some both yarn and thread, and others with anything that may be supplied by the customer.[5] Under silk and rayon there are similar sub-sub-divisions. At the same time there are also establishments which specialize in the sewing of knitted hosiery for the knitting establishments, and others which make hosiery as well as other articles of apparel. These cannot be classified according to their raw material, but are added as two sub-divisions under knitted hosiery. The following will show the situation more clearly.

11. Clothing industry
11-1. Knitted hosiery.
11-1-1. Cotton hosiery
11-1-1-1. Cotton yarn only
11-1-1-2. Cotton thread only
11-1-1-3. Yarn and thread
11-1-1-4. Raw material supplied by customers
11-1-2. Silk and rayon hosiery
11-1-2-1. Silk only
11-1-2-2. Silk and cotton
11-1-2-3. Rayon and cotton
11-1-2-4. Silk and rayon
11-1-2-5. Silk, rayon and cotton
11-1-3. Woolen hosiery (pure wool)
11-1-4. Cotton, silk and wool combined
11-1-5. Sewing of knitted hosiery
11-1-6. Hosiery and other articles of apparel

On the whole the divisions represent separate industries, the sub-divisions establishments making different products in the same industry, and the sub-sub-divisions those using different materials or different kinds of machines for making the same product.

---

5. They are put in the cotton sub-division because their machines can only knit cotton hosiery.

APPENDIX

There are altogether 16 main groups, 88 divisions. For the sake of such classification, many of the establishments were visited several times again and a special investigation was made of 58 industries in Shanghai as industries to understand their process of manufacturing, how and why they were classified into industries and groups according to Shanghai usage.

An English version of the questionnaire used is appended to the end of the Silk Report. A few hundred copies of it were printed in 1931 for use with the foreign factories, but were later discarded when these factories were not to be included in the survey. As may be seen from this version, some of the data could not be summarized for all industries, for instance, the number of machines, the kind and quantity of raw material used, and the kind and quantity of goods produced. Most other data, however, are in terms of the same unit for all industries, and have therefore been tabulated and summarized.

A few questions are included in the questionnaire which should have been left out or differently worded, but such mistakes are often unavoidable in a cooperative enterprise. One of these concerns the style of the building, if it is new or old. What is meant is whether the building is one specially constructed for factory use, or an ordinary dwelling house in which machinery is installed. The wording is so indefinite that, in spite of repeated explanations to the investigators, the question was on the whole unsatisfactorily answered. As it is not an important question, the results are not tabulated.

A more important mistake is made in the wording of the quantity of raw material consumed. Instead of asking for the quantity actually consumed during the preceding year or month, the question calls for the quantity required every month. It was the opinion of the joint committee of the cooperating organizations that it would be very hard to obtain information on the actual quantity, and even were it obtained, it would most likely be the quantity of raw material bought during the specified period and not the quantity consumed. We would have to find out in addi-

SHANGHAI INDUSTRIALIZATION

tion the quantities of raw material left over at the beginning and the end of the period before we could attain our object, and these figures are seldom recorded in Chinese factories and never in the workshops. The quantity required could easily be estimated on the basis of the productive capacity of the plant, which experience during our survey has proved to be correct. Only the figure so obtained is a mere estimate, is related to the productive capacity, and is useless in ascertaining the raw material cost of the output, except in a few industries for which we have taken special pains to revise these figures.

Since the factories and workshops were very reluctant to answer our questions, which we very soon found out during our survey, it was later decided to leave some of the questions unasked so that the rest might be more fully answered. In the same way the editors also laid emphasis on the latter. In the following tables, only some of the latter are summarized, which are most general in character. These summaries were mostly prepared about a year ago, but they have not been published because it has been our intention to publish first separate reports on special industries in the nature of the Silk Report, and reserve the general report to the last. It has also been planned to include in the general report a description of the general economic and social conditions of Shanghai to show the effect of industrialization. However, as this may mean a delay of several years, the present preliminary report is prepared to give some of the results of the survey.

In connection with the following tables, a few general observations should be made.

In the original schedules certain figures are given in terms of Chinese silver dollars, others in Shanghai taels, and still others in various foreign currencies. These are all converted into silver dollars at fixed and uniform rates. All Shanghai taels are converted at the rate of 0.72 taels per dollar, which is higher than the market rate in 1931, but does away with many decimal figures and saves the calculation work considerably. For foreign curren-

APPENDIX

cies which only occasionally form the unit of value, the averages of the five monthly rates of May-September, 1931, as published in the Shanghai Market Prices Report, are adopted as our rates of conversion, because the survey was carried out mainly in these five months. These average rates are:—

    One U.S. dollar .... $ 4.64 silver
    One pound sterling .... 22.53 „
    One Japanese yen .... 2.29 „
    One Hongkong dollar .... 1.10 „

Except in the case of capitalization, where all sums are worked out to the nearest dollar, all other figures are worked out to the nearest cent. When more than one factory belongs to the same organization and has one single sum as its capital, this figure is set against the main or No. 1 factory, and the other factories are not assigned any part of it, to avoid duplication. This means that the total capital in some sub-divisions may be below the actual amount, because some factories of one organization belong to more than one sub-division, and their total capital appears only under one of them. In such cases foot-notes are generally appended to indicate the fact.

Many more complications are found in connection with the number of officers and workers. In the first place the term "officers" is adopted in preference to others because the kind of people included under that term, according to Chinese industrial usage, is hard to define, but is generally known as *chih-yuan* 職員, which is usually translated in other connections as "officers". For instance, the manager is of course a *chih-yuan,* and the clerks and apprentices who learn to be clerks are also considered as such. Those who deliver the goods to the purchasing firms, even though they perform manual labor, are also "officers," which term often includes also janitors of the factory. The scope of the term is not always the same with all industries, and in some industries like silk, the officers are further classified into "civil" and "military" as explained in detail in the special report on silk. Some factories, on the other hand, classify engineers as laborers, and whenever we

SHANGHAI INDUSTRIALIZATION

can ascertain the fact, we make corrections by transferring them to the officer class.

For the above reasons, ther are a number of factories which classify certain laborers as officers, and when we cannot get them to supply us with detailed figures for the sake of reclassification, footnotes are appended to the totals to indicate this fact. Sometimes, the number of male laborers are given but not the female or vice versa, although they have both males and females, the totals therefore do not represent the actual figures, and it is pointed out in the notes. Temporary help, though sometimes reported by the factories, is not included in the number of laborers. Although we distinguish between time rate and piece rate workers, some factories fail to supply these figures separately, as we have noted in Table III.[6] Laborers who do miscellaneous work are generally classified under male time rate workers.

Since many of the workshops surveyed are quite small, the owners often serve as the only officers, and in some cases they are also included among the workers because they generally do manual work themselves. As we cannot count one man twice, the owner is considered as an officer, and one man is deducted from the number of workers. Fortunately, the owners do not draw salaries, and this transference does not affect total salary or wage payments, as is often the case when other corrections are made in the classification of officers and laborers.

While apprentices who learn to be foremen or book-keepers are generally reported as officers, and are classified as such, those who learn to do manual work are classified as laborers, no matter how they are reported. The difference between apprentices and child workers consists in the fact that the former have to serve a fixed term of apprenticeship, and are usually furnished with board and lodging free, although otherwise they receive little remuneration.

---

6. These tables refer to those in the Preliminary Report. Their order has been changed in this volume. See tables in Appendix A.

APPENDIX

Table IV shows the amount of power employed in the Shanghai factories and workshops. The schedules originally require separate figures for steam engines, steam turbines, petrol engines, electric generators and rented electricity, but the first, fourth and fifth are more common in the Shanghai factories, and separate totals for the other items in our table are hardly necessary. Electric generators must be operated by the engines and turbines, and to include the kilowatt figures in the total of power supply would be double count. However, there are some cases where the factory gives only the kilowatt figure of the generator, and not the horsepower of the engine, and then we convert the former into horsepower and include it in the total. This accounts for the decimal figures in the horse-power totals. Rented electricity is also given in terms of horse-power because that is the prevalent practice in Shanghai. When electricity is generated in the factory or rented from outside for lighting purposes, that amount of power is not included in the total. However, the amount is often inseparable from that of power supply, and hence our total is larger by such amounts.

In the value of the output two kinds of figures are included. Where the establishment manufactures a complete product for the market, the value is that of the product. Where it manufactures with raw material supplied by customers, and the value of the material is not known to the manufacturer, then the value of the output is the value as added by manufacture. Hence, the totals often include both kinds of values, and sometimes one factory does both kinds of work. Such totals are naturally not quite satisfactory, but we do not consider it advisable to estimate the prices of the raw material and add it to the value as added by manufacture. Again, some factories and workshops can furnish figures only for their principal products, while the the value of their by-products either cannot be ascertained, or will not be furnished. These also affect the total value of the output.

Besides the value of the output, there are two other questions which call for figures of the preceding year, namely, the amounts spent on salaries and wages. Some factories which were established in 1931 had naturally no such figures to supply. Others that were reorganized during 1930 or 1931 generally supplied figures for one or several months, and we estimate the annual figures on that basis. In other words, we assume that the factory was running throughout the whole year of 1930 before the reorganization unless it is definitely stated in the questionnaire to the contrary. The same rule applies to the calculation of the value of the output.

After the results of this year's survey were presented in the Preliminary Report in July, 1933, a few changes have been made in the organization of the statistical data, as follows:—

1. Although the main groups are as before, some changes have been made in the divisions and sub-divisions. For instance, 4-3-1 formerly included electric bulbs as well as neon light tubes, but in the revised classification they are separated into two sub-divisions. Similarly 1-4-1-2 is split into three separate sub-sub-divisions.

New sub-divisions have been added when new factories are added to the 1931 data. For instance, the Shanghai-Nanking Railway Machine shop, the cotton ginning industry and a small steel works were due to some oversight at that time, not covered by the 1931 survey, but as they were then already in existence, their 1931 data have been later obtained and these factories have been added to the 1931 statistics during the revision.

3. Some factories originally classified under one division or sub-division have been re-classified under another, because later investigation has revealed more clearly the nature of their business. A foreign brick and tile factory was mistaken to be Chinese and included in the Preliminary Report; also a match factory in Nanhwei but very near to the border line of that *hsien* and Shanghai. These are now excluded.

4. Many additional statistical data which were not organized and presented in the Preliminary Report have been now included in the tables in Appendix A, such as the average number of years and months the factories had been in operation, the ownership

APPENDIX

of the factory buildings, the number of working hours a day, and the number of days in operation a year.

5. Forms of business organization were given in the Preliminary Report under four headings, but they are now given under six.

6. In the Preliminary Report, when data for all factories in any division or sub-division were not complete, the number of factories for which data were available was given in a subscript under the figure. As this involved too many figures and caused many mistakes in the printed report, the subscripts are now taken away, and instead an asterisk is attached to the data indicating that they are not complete for all the factories.

7. Many sub-totals were given in the Preliminary Report, which are now omitted, and only the totals of the 16 main groups are given. As the time for printing this report is also very short, it being necessary to send a few hundred copies to America before the I.P.R. Conference in August, all figures that are not absolutely necessary are left out.

4. *Notes on the Survey of 1933*

In 1933 the China Institute was entrusted by a Government Organization with the task of conducting an industrial survey of the whole country, limiting it to factories that came up to the standard of the Chinese Factory Law. Shanghai was to be included by making use of the Institute's data of 1931, to be supplemented with some investigation of new factories established since that date. Both the time and the fund for completing the survey were definitely fixed, without providing for a complete survey of Shanghai. However, by securing financial assistance from another source*, and the utilization of all available staff members of the Institute, an entirely new survey of Shanghai factories was carried out, the results of which are presented in Chapters III, IV and V of this volume and in the seven statistical tables in Appendix B.

---

* The Sun Yat-sen Institute for the Promotion of Culture and Education.

SHANGHAI INDUSTRIALIZATION

At the beginning it was learned that the National Goods Advisory Board had during the summer investigated over 600 factories in this city, but its budget for the purpose had been exhausted, and the work was not finished. This Institute therefore approached it with the suggestion that it would volunteer to complete the survey, and publish the results in the name of the two organizations without any further expenses to the Board. At the same time the Board should turn over to the Institute the 600 odd schedules that had been so far filled. An agreement was reached after some negotiations concerning c rtain minor points, but the main idea was the same as above suggested. In pursuance of the agreement, a Chinese pamphlet in the form of a directory, with one statistical table giving the capitalization, value of output and number of male, female and child workers of 1,036 factories was published in October, 1934. This did not include all the factories surveyed by the Institute, as the Board was anxious to have the pamphlet published, even before all the data had been properly analyzed. The directory however included over 1500 factories, many of which were covered by the Board survey and were below the standard of the Factory Law.

Besides the fact that many of the factories covered by the Board survey were below the standard, many of its schedules were not properly filled, and even when they were, some items in our schedule were not found in theirs. For these reasons all of the 600 odd factories covered by that survey and fulfilling the legal requirements were visited a second time by our own investigators to make the necessary corrections and additions to the data collected. The advantages gained from the cooperation with the Board were that its schedules served as a basis for the Institute investigators to go on with the new survey, and association with such an organization whose nature was more readily understood by the factories helped in facilitating the contact. This Institute had been known to many of the larger factories, but changes, especially in the smaller ones, were so frequent in Shanghai that it often took quite a little time to convince them that economic and statistical research was of any use to the practical business men. For the same reason, we were compelled to include a few questions in the

APPENDIX

schedule which were of no use to statistical analysis, but merely to show the factories that we were interested in their welfare. As most factories had to be visited twice or more than twice to get the schedules properly filled, the Board data saved us at least one trip in the case of the factories covered by their survey.

From the Board data, those of our own, as well as information from all kinds of sources, a list of Shanghai factories was compiled, first according to the industries to which they belonged, and then to the sections and streets in which they were located. The former served to check possible duplications and the latter was used as a guide to the investigators in the survey. Lest the list should still be incomplete, and in order to prepare the factory people for the visit by our investigators, a printed circular letter was distributed explaining the nature and aim of the survey, enclosing an investigation schedule, and a stamped envelop. Half a dozen office boys on bicycles were given the section and street lists to send these circulars to the factories in the respective sections, and they were instructed to mark on the lists if the factories had moved, if the street number had been changed—a common occurence in Shanghai—and if the factories were large or small in size, as far as they could see from the size of the factory buildings and site. A number of the factories even filled and mailed the schedule upon receipt of the circular. All this helped the investigators in their work, but as the time limit was definite, they were not able to wait till the whole ground had been so covered, but the survey was started while the distribution of the letters was still in progress.

At first most of the Institute's investigators were working in the various provinces, and only three men were in Shanghai to cover three small sections of the city. As the work went on, the rest began to return and joined the Shanghai survey The largest number engaged in it was seven, while five more in the office examined the schedules and analyzed the statistical data. Compared with the 1931 survey, the total number of office and field workers was much smaller, but they were more experienced in such investigation, worked under more centralized control, and the whole thing was better mapped out beforehand. Also the scope was more limited, because only factories coming up to the standard of the Factory Law were included. Consequently this second survey was completed in a shorter period than the first. It began in December, 1933, and ended in March, 1934, although some supplementary investigations were carried out till October when the filled schedules were found to be unsatisfactory in any respect.

To make the data comparable with those of the factories in other cities and provinces of the country, all information about Shanghai factories related to conditions existing in 1933, although the survey extended into the following year. For data of the preceding year, as value of total output, etc., those of 1932 were required. There was little misunderstanding on the part of the factories, for they were still accustomed to the old lunar calendar, and the survey was completed before the end of the lunar year. For these reasons we consider this survey as relating to 1933 and not 1934. All factories established in 1934 were excluded from the survey.

In the case of certain industries, use was made of data from other authoritative sources and direct investigation was obviated. For instance, the Chinese Cotton Mill Owners' Association had official statistics of all cotton mills in China, and its Shanghai figures were used in connection with our survey. Supplementary information required by our schedule but not obtainable from the Association was taken from the investigation reports of the Four Banks Joint Reserve Society, and the Social Research Institute of Peiping, both of which had recently made special investigations of the Shanghai cotton industry. Similarly, for the silk reeling industry, we used the available information of the Shanghai Association of Silk Filatures, with some additional data derived therefrom by estimates on the basis of our special study in 1932. The same procedure was employed by the Bureau of Social Affairs in estimating the number of workers in the filatures in 1929. In other industries, many factories had been covered by our 1931 survey, and their capitalization, form of organization, mechanical equipment, etc., had not changed. Only the changed conditions

APPENDIX

needed to be reported, and the investigator's work was therefore much lightened.

When the investigation was completed, and the results statistically analysed, a slightly different system of classification from that employed in 1931 was adopted. The main groups were still 16, according to the classification of the International Labor Office. The numbers of divisions in these groups were also about the same as those of 1931, but the sub-divisions were simplified. Some factories formerly classified under one division were transferred to another, due to a better understanding of the nature of its business. Similar corrections were, however, not made for the 1931 statistics, as such corrections were few compared with the changes in the sub-divisions themselves.

Certain items in the 1931 questionnaire were not included in that of 1933. The amount of reserve was omitted, as only the very large factories operated by registered corporations put aside every years some of their earnings as a reserve, and even in these cases the figures often had little significance unless we know more about their accounts. In fact, even the capitalization figures did not mean much, as many factories had lost their initial capital, and were operating on loans from banks or from further assessments on the partners. In America, for instance, partnership enterprises usually would not reveal their capitalization figures to outsiders. Although this is not the case in China the figures given generally represent the initial capital only. Our figures for either year, therefore, refer to such capital, and when we arrive at the conclusion that the Shanghai industries are insufficiently capitalized, we also have the initial capital in mind. To make further assessments on partners or loans from banks only when the initial capital is nearly exhausted is a short-sighted policy.

The number of workers required for full time operation was supplied by the factories in 1931, but it was found that the estimates were not always made on the same basis. In fact, many factories especially the small ones, were unable to make any satisfactory estimate at all, and the figure was unnecessary for our study. Hence the question was omitted from the 1933 schedule. The ownership of the factory building and the number of days the factories were in operation during the year were also omitted because it was thought that the results collected during one survey was enough for our purpose.

In 1933, besides a few questions which had no bearing on statistical analysis to which reference has been made a few paragraphs back, a few others were included which were analysed and presented in the tables. The area of the factory site and its ownership supplemented the information gathered in the first survey concerning the factory buildings. It was thought the factories could fairly accurately tell the number of holidays every month and every year as they had fixed rules about them. By substracting these, especially the latter, from 365 days, a figure would be obtained showing the number of days the factories were in operation unless such operation was suspended on account of bad business or regular seasonal influences. Such figures served as a check on the number of working days per year obtained in 1931.

A more important addition was the value of raw materials consumed during the preceding year in order to compare with the value of the output of the same year.

In 1931, the medians of the highest and lowest wage rates were separately computed and given in the Preliminary Report. Such a way of presenting the results was later considered as not quite satisfactory, and instead the actual maxima and minima were used for the 1933 figures. At the same time the 1931 wage rate figures have been omitted from the tables in Appendix A which present the modified results of that year. The number of officers in the 1931 data included general and factory managers, but these were excluded from the 1933 figures because the Government organization for which the statistics were compiled did not want their inclusion.

As the classification of the factories is different for the 1931 and 1933 data, it makes comparison difficult. For this reason a

APPENDIX

few factories have been reclassified in the Comparative Tables in Appendix D. The same applies to the 1931 data.

5. *Notes on the Survey of 1934*

This survey was conducted by the Industrial Section of the Bureau of Social Affairs of the Shanghai City Government in the spring of 1934, when our 1933 survey had not yet been completed. The Bureau survey was to cover a much larger ground, but the questionnaire was very simple, consisting merely of a few items such as the name of the factory, the address, the telephone number, the name of the manager, the kind of products manufactured, the nature of motive power used, the capitalization, and the number of male, female and child workers and apprentices. Such being the case, only the last two items involved statistical data. As the Bureau did not want to publish the capitalization figures of the individual factories, the only figures in the Directory, which was the final form in which the results of the survey was published, were the numbers of the various kinds of workers.

The factories were classified into a number of groups and divisions. Although the former numbered also sixteen, they did not exactly correspond to the classification of the I.L.O. The manufacturing of furniture and construction material was not put into separate groups by themselves, while instead the manufacture of machinery and metallic wares was split up into three groups: machinery, electric machinery and metallic wares. The public utilities group was renamed the motive power group, and included, in addition to electric and water supply, such other things as the English gas works, and a Chinese and a French factory which produced oxygen, acetylene, etc. It is a little difficult to understand how the waterworks, gas works and manufacturers of oxygen should be considered as suppliers of motive power.

No totals were given for any group or division in the Directory, but at the beginning of the volume, a very simple statistical table was inserted which gave the number of factories, capitalization, and number of workers, classified into male, female, child, apprentices and unclassified, as well as their total number, for the 16 main groups. These totals generally do not agree with what one may arrive at by adding up the figures of the individual factories in the respective groups, as given in the Directory. Here, in the table, the total number of factories was given as 5,418, of which only 2,540 supplied capitalization data, amounting altogether to $478,293,341, and 3,893 factories supplied data about their workers, who numbered altogether 299,585. In our Comparative Tables in Appendix D, figures for 1934 are based on the statistical table, with the main groups modified to agree with those for the 1929, 1931 and 1933 surveys. Although the industries classified also differ somehow from those for the three other surveys, we have not been able to make the required corrections for lack of necessary data. Besides, in the three other surveys too the classification does not always coincide.

The Shanghai Year Book of 1935 published some more detailed statistical tables on the basis of the Directory. Figures were given not only for the main groups, but also for the divisions. However, these figures often agree neither with those in the Directory nor with those in the summary table of that publication. It is apparently due to miscalculations. As they are in greater detail, we have included the Year Book tables in Appendix C, in which may be found the general summaries of the five surveys.

According to the explanatory remarks in the Directory, the 1934 survey covered all factories and workshops which either employed some kind of motive power or at least five workers working with the help of "machinery or other kind of instruments." Both Chinese and foreign factories were included. The scope was therefore very wide, and rather vague, as all handicrafts use some kind of instruments. When the Bureau had nearly completed its survey, we borrowed their data and checked over the names and number of factories with our own records. We also supplied them with the data we had collected and which they needed. In our judgement, the number of Chinese establishments of all sizes, exclusive of handicrafts, were less than 4,000 at that time.

APPENDIX

The remaining included a few hundred foreign factories and a larger number of semi-modernized handicrafts.

The Chinese monthly publication of the Bureau of Foreign Trade has also published certain statistics of Shanghai industries in 1935, said to be obtained from the Shanghai Bureau of Social Affairs. Inquiries at the latter office, however, have elicited the information that the figures are incorrect, as they apparently are. Request for the correct data has not yet been complied with when this goes to the press, and we are obliged to leave them out. All figures are said to be much smaller than the corresponding ones for 1934.

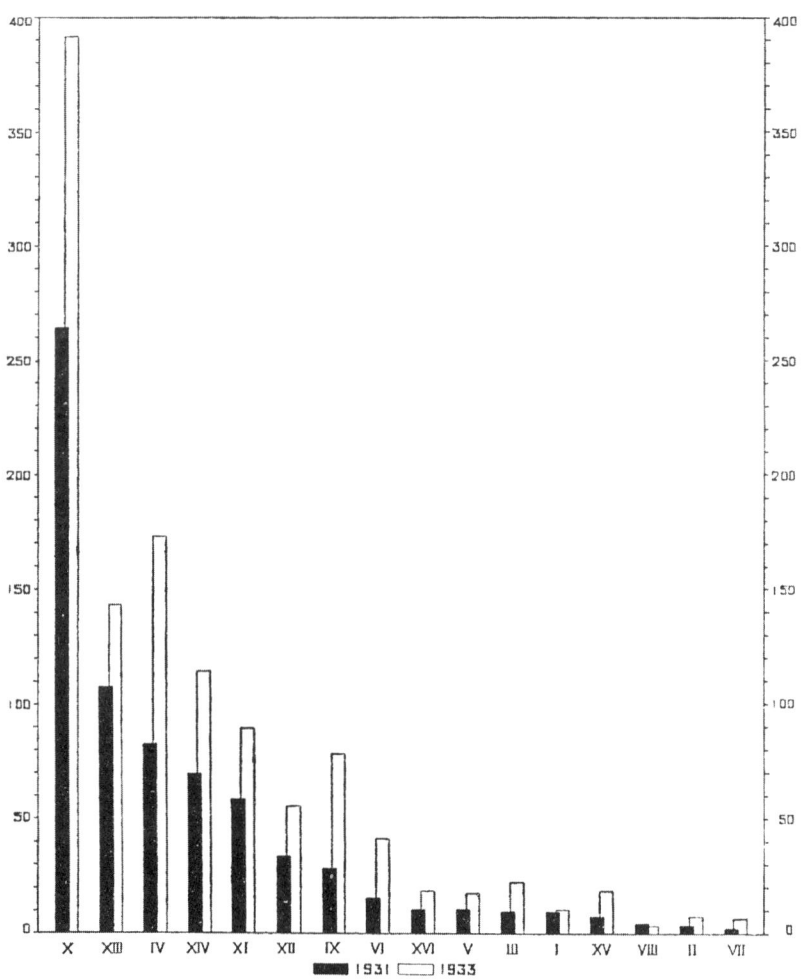

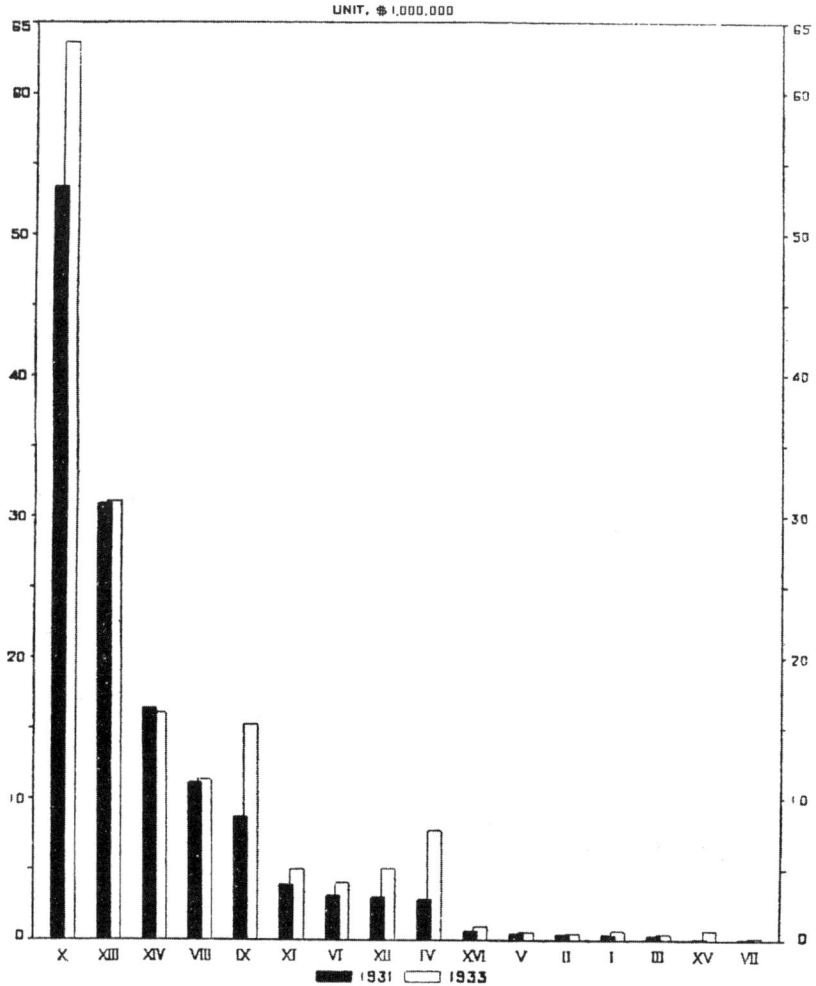

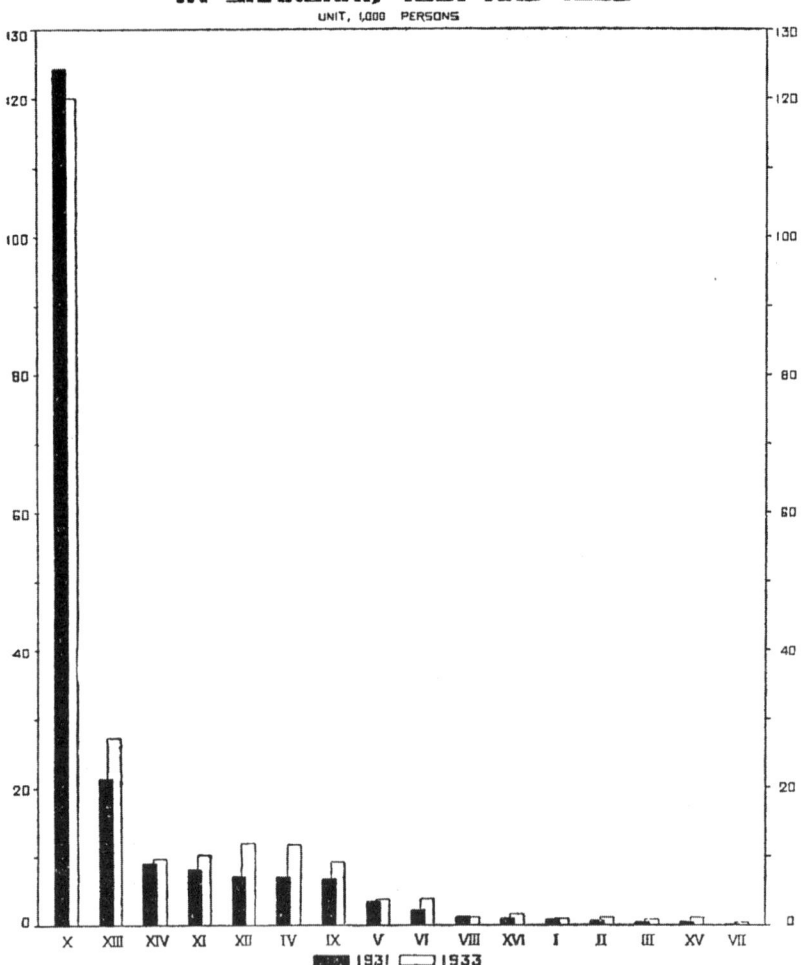

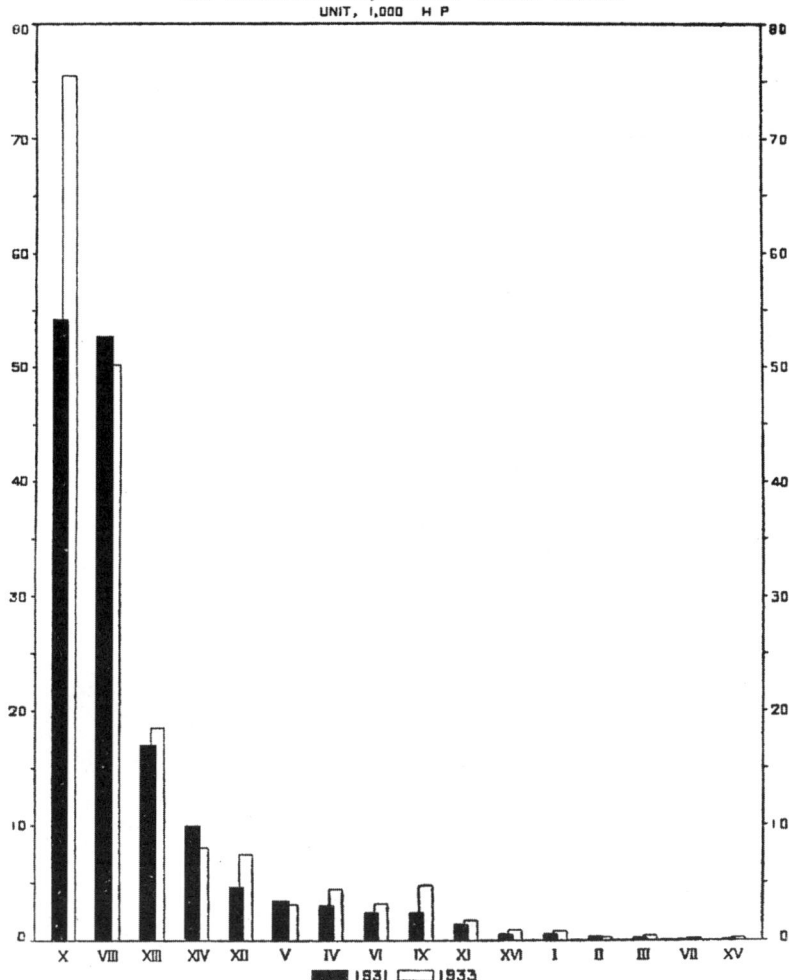

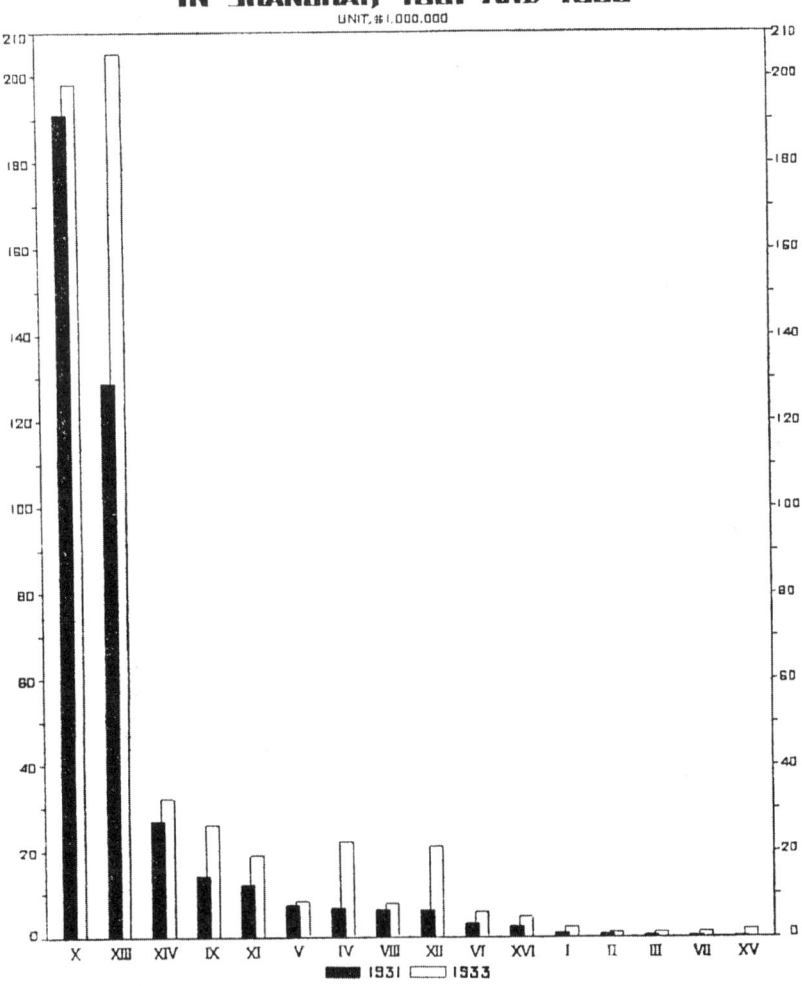

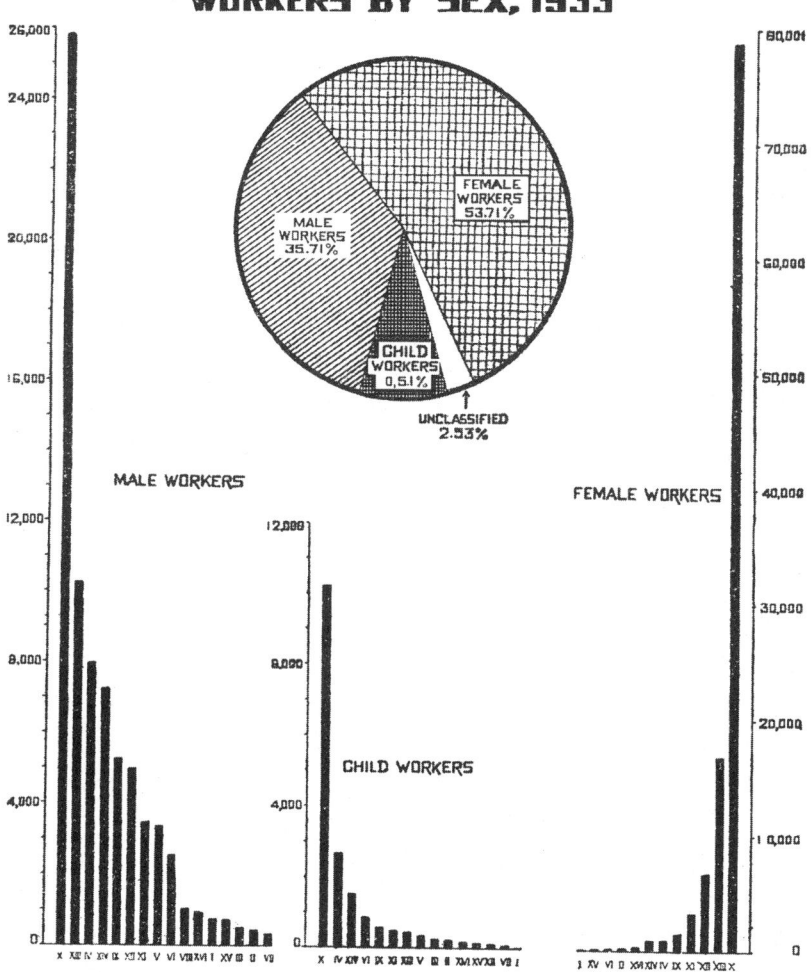

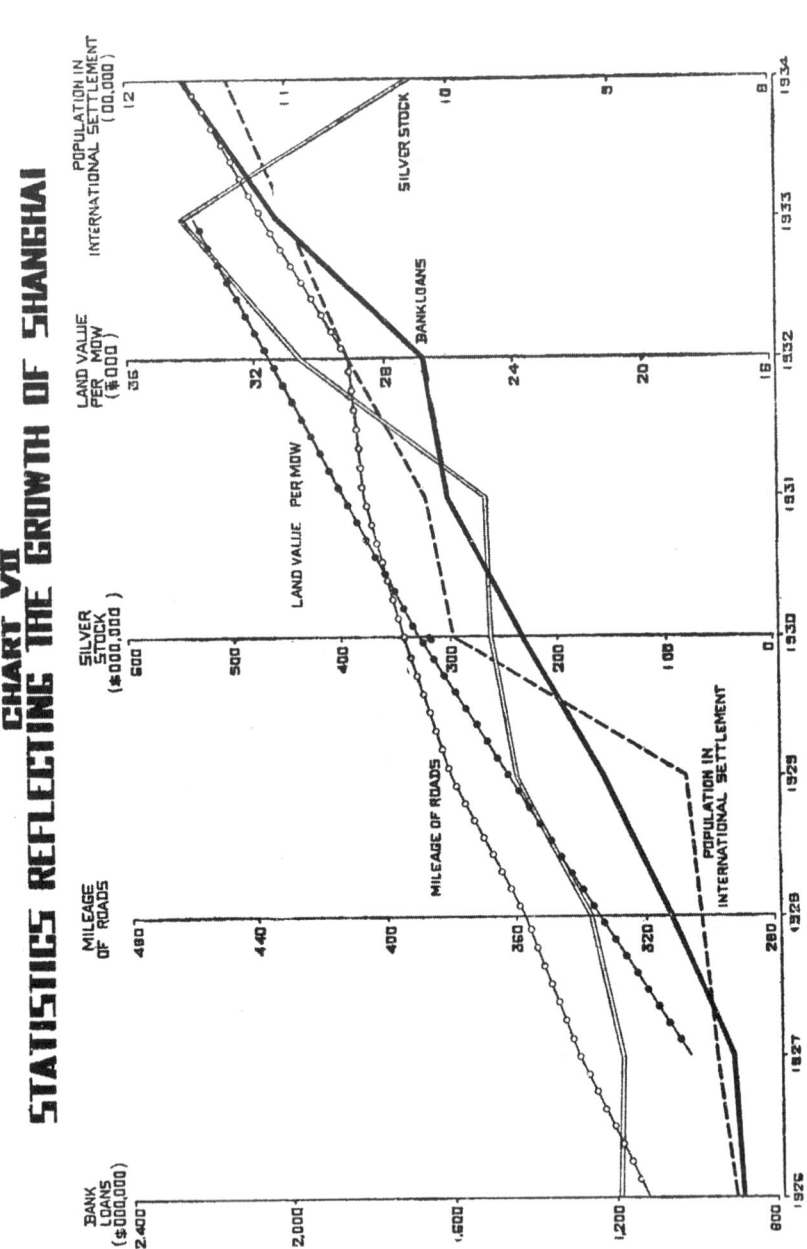

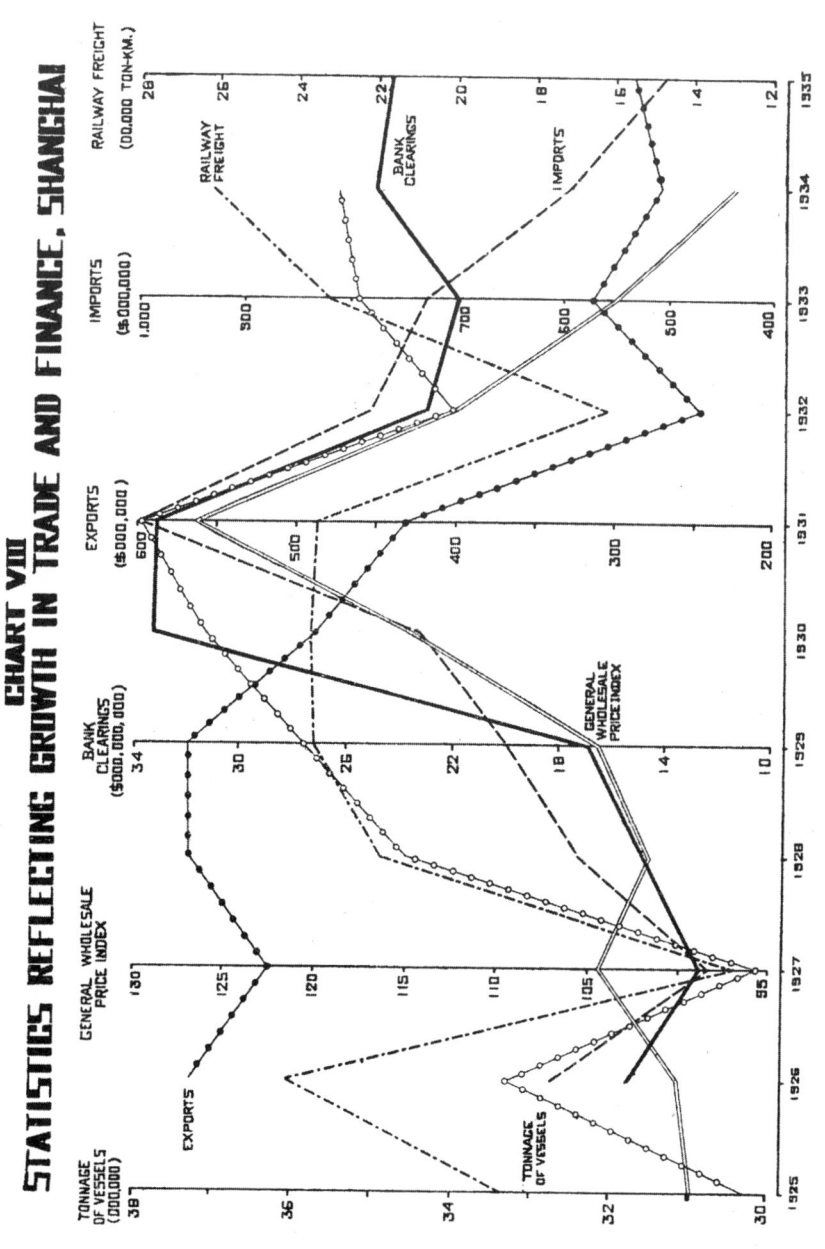

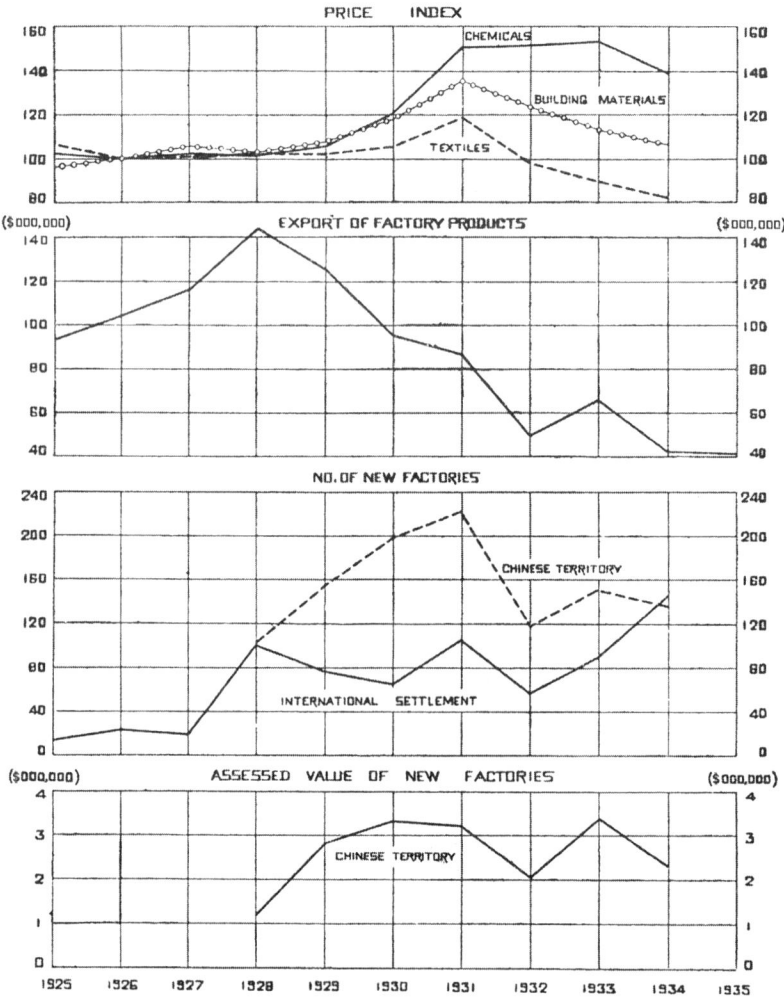

INDEX

A

Acids, manufacture of, pp. 79, 111, 122.
Adulteration, p. 10 .
Age distribution of population, p. 166.
Agriculture and agricultural products, pp. 8, 9, 69, 154, 156.
American Economic Mission, p. 141.
American silver purchase program, pp. 27, 158, 182.
Apparel maufacturing industries, pp. 41, 92.
Apprentices, pp. 4, 121.
Artificial silk, p. 39.

B

Bank clearings, pp. 158, 187.
Bank deposits, p. 158.
Bank loans to industries, pp. 73, 81, 94-98, 157, 159.
Bank note issue, p. 158.
Banking and industrial development, p. 30.
Banking business, growth of, pp. 158, 161, 186.
Banks, modern, pp. 8, 158 et seq.
Bonds, Government, p. 159.
Boycotts, pp. 24, 25, 46, 52, 55, 71, 81, 106, 128, 177, 181, 182.
Bricks, tiles and crucibles, manufacture of, pp. 78, 122.
Building construction, pp. 143, 146, 161, 187.
Bureau of Social Affairs, Shanghai pp. 63, 66, 100, 113, 121, 125, 127, 131, 15, 1 6, 147, 185.

C

Canton, p. 15.
Capital and labor, pp. 4, 129, 131.
Capitalization, average, pp. 94, 95, 184.
Capitalization, insufficiency of, p. 93 et seq.
Capitalization of cotton mills, p. 96.
Capitalization of industries, pp. 15, 47, 51, 67, 75 et seq, 92 et seq, 148, 183.
Capitalization of silk filatures, p. 94.
Cement, manufacture of, pp. 12, 78.
Chemical industries, pp. 79, 87, 92, 111, 148, 182.
Chengchow, pp. 10, 11.
Chiaotung University Research Institute, p. 65.
China Institute of Economic and Statistical Research, pp. 15, 16, 66, 121.
Chinese Economic Society, p. 64.
Chinese Factory Law, pp. 15, 47, 65, 75, 113, 130, 184.
Chinese Statistical Society, p. 65.
Cities, industrial, see industrial cities.
Collective bargaining, pp. 133, 135.
Communications, pp. 132, 136, 166.
Communist activities, pp. 129, 134, 176.
Competition, pp. 23, 86, 105, 153.
Concentration of industries, p. 5.
Concentration of residents from the same native town, p. 168.
Construction material, manufacture of, pp. 78, 122.
Construction of factory buildings, pp. 146, 161, 187.
Consumption goods, pp. 68, 87, 183.
Cost of living, p. 182.
Cost of living index, pp. 123, 124, 147.
Cost of production, pp. 38, 39, 69, 81, 82, 88, 95, 106, 109, 111, 122, 124.
Cottage industries, pp. 7, 84.
Cotton Control Commission, p. 33.

Cotton import, pp. 151, 154.
Cotton mills, pp. 7, 9, 15, 22, 23, 25, 28 et seq, 104, 154.
Cotton mills in China, British, pp. 23, 29.
Cotton mills in China, Japanese, pp. 29, 31, 80, 88, 96, 107.
Cotton mills, number of workers in, p. 116.
Cotton Mill Owners' Association, Chinese, p. 32.
Cotton yarn import and export, p. 151.
Cotton yarn market, p. 32.
Cotton spinning industry, pp. 22, 28 et seq, 72, 80, 88, 119, 127, 151, 165, 182, 185.
Cotton weaving industry, pp. 22, 34 et seq, 80, 122, 165, 187.
Crime, pp. 172, 179.
Custom work, p. 103.
Currency inflation, p. 68.
Currency System, the Chinese, pp. 27, 159.

D

Demand, elasticity of, pp. 37, 150, 151.
Depression in China, pp. 41, 62, 71, 81, 98, 147, 161, 179, 181, 187.
Depression, World, pp. 8, 17, 27, 32, 38, 67, 72, 94, 139, 141, 148, 150, 155.
Differentiation of industrial process and responsibility, p. 102.
Diseases, communicable, p. 176.
Diseases, veneral, p. 173.
Dyeing industry, pp. 119, 122, 148, 185.

E

Economic organization, old Chinese, p. 5 et seq.
Economic units, self-sufficient, p. 5 et seq.

Efficiency, productive, pp. 10, 31, 105.
Electric machinery, manufacture of, pp. 77, 122.
Employer and employee, p. 4.
Employment of laborers, pp. 133, 136, 139, 161, 186.
Enamelware industry, pp. 54 et seq 79, 122, 125.
Export of commodities, see under names of commodities.
Exposition, Chinese Home Products, p. 26.
Exposition, Nanyang Industrial, p. 24.

F

Factory buildings, construction of, see under construction.
Factory buildings, rented, pp. 101, 184.
Factory Law, see Chinese Factory Law.
Factory management, p. 10.
Factory products, pp. 7, 161.
Factories in China, number of, pp. 15, 26.
Factories in Shanghai, number of, pp. 15, 64, 75 et seq, 100, 144, 184.
Factories involved in labor disputes, number of, p. 135.
Factories involved in strikes, number of, p. 135.
Factories, small size of Shanghai, pp. 100, 183.
Family, breaking up of, p. 169.
Family, size of, p. 164.
Fires, p. 176.
Flour import and export, pp. 45, 152, 187.
Flour mills, pp. 7, 23, 43 et seq, 107, 109, 117, 122, 124, 125, 153, 183.
Foodstuff industries, pp. 43, 84, 87, 90, 91, 133, 136, 182.

INDEX

Foodstuff industries, number of workers in, p. 116.
Foreign factories in Shanghai, pp. 10, 12, 29, 31, 35, 43, 45, 48, 51, 54, 55, 57, 59, 61, 62, 75, 79, 88, 110, 129, 134, 136, 153, 181.
Foreign trade, pp. 12, 13, 148 et seq, 156, 161, 181, 187.
Foreign trade index numbers, p. 149.
Foundries, pp. 77, 95, 107, 111, 117, 122, 125.
Furniture manufactories, p. 76.

G

Glassware, manufacture of, pp. 78, 125, 185.
Gold bar transactions, p. 159.
Government and industrial enterprises, pp. 22, 26, 33, 109.
Government enterprises, pp. 22, 28 et seq, 100.
Growth of Shanghai and its industries, pp. 62, 70, 74, 85, 139, 140, 146, 157, 161, 163, 181, 188.

H

Hand vs. power driven machines, pp. 42, 83, 108.
Handicrafts, pp. 4, 6, 28, 43, 48, 51, 91, 113.
Hangchow, pp. 34, 42, 105, 171.
Hankow, pp. 10, 15, 42, 46, 53, 54.
Heavy industries, the, pp. 76, 93, 95, 110.
Highways, p. 167.
Holidays and rest days, p. 127.
Home made goods, encouragement of, pp. 24, 26, 46, 55.
Home Products Exposition, p. 26.
Housing, p. 142.
Housing problem, p. 173 et seq.

I

Import of commodities, see under names of commodities.
Index numbers, see under cost of living, foreign trade, price and wages.
Industrial centers, pp. 9, 11, 12.
Industrial cities, pp. 5, 7, 9, 139, 140, 145, 179.
Industrial development in China, pp. 11, 18 et seq, 62 150, 154.
Industrial development in Shanghai, pp. 17, 61, 68, 69, 77, 104, 140, 161, 180, 187.
Industrial history of China, p. 20 et seq.
Industrial raw materials, pp. 5, 69.
Industrial Revolution, p. 5.
Industrial survey of Shanghai, pp. 63 et seq, 139.
Industrialization, definition, pp. 1-3.
Industrialization effects on Chinese economic organization, p. 9 et seq.
Industrialization of China, pp. 5, 18 et seq, 150.
Industrialization, process of, pp. 5, 15, 16, 61, 87, 92, 109, 138, 169, 183.
Industries, classification of, pp. 15, 73.
Institute of Pacific Relations, p. 11.
Interest rate, p. 157.
International Committee for the Improvement of Sericulture, p. 37.
International Labor Office classification, p. 73.
Iron works, pp. 6, 9, 13, 76, 93, 110.

J

Japan, see under Manchuria, Shanghai Incident, boycotts, competition, cotton mills, etc.

K

Knitting industry, pp. 41-43, 83, 122, 125, 182.
Kuomintang, pp. 129, 134.

L

Labor and Capital Mediation Committee, p. 136.
Labor disputes, pp. 135 et seq, 177, 186.
Labor feuds, p. 179.
Labor movement, pp. 127 et seq, 176.
Labor revolution, p. 176.
Labor trouble, p. 40.
Labor Union Law, p. 130.
Labor unions, pp. 128 et seq, 179.
Laborers, see under workers.
Laborers, number of, see under workers.
Lancashire, p. 10.
Land values, Shanghai, pp. 69, 98, 141, 143, 161, 174, 187.
Large scale production, pp. 3, 53.
League of Nations, pp. 8, 171.
Leather industry, pp. 50 et seq, 84, 88, 92, 125.
Limited liability companies, pp. 94, 99, 100, 184.
Lockouts, pp. 130, 131 et seq.
Looms, number of, p. 35.

M

Machine-making industry, pp. 22, 23, 42, 48 et seq, 77, 87, 92, 105, 111, 122, 125, 182.
Machinery, import of, pp. 5, 151 et seq, 155, 161, 186.
Manchuria, Japanese occupation of, pp. 27, 32, 71, 72, 116, 131.
Man-days lost during strikes, p. 134.
Manufactured goods, import of, pp. 7, 12, 150, 155, 186.
Market towns, pp. 6, 7.
Match industry, pp. 53, 54, 79, 120, 122, 125.
May 6th Movement, pp. 25, 127, 134.
May 30th Incident, pp. 26, 46, 55, 106, 127, 134.

Mechanization, extent of, pp. 102, 107, 183.
Metal industries, p. 76.
Ministry of Industries, pp. 26, 58, 64.
Ministry of Industries and Commerce, p. 26.
Mob psychology, p. 177.
Money market, the, pp. 67, 138, 157 et seq.
Motor cars in Shanghai, p. 146.

N

Nantung, pp. 11, 23, 96.
Nanyang Industrial Exposition, p. 24.
National Directorate of Statistics, p. 64.
National Economic Council, p. 31.
National Government, the, pp. 24, 33, 130.
National Tariff Commission, pp. 8, 64, 147, 155.
Night shift, pp. 32, 126.

O

Oil mills, pp. 23, 85, 122, 125.
Output, value of, see under value.
Ownership of factory and site, p. 100.

P

Paper industry, pp. 22, 56 et seq, 85, 92, 125, 183.
Partnership, pp. 20, 99, 100, 184.
Period of ammunition manufacturing, p. 21.
Period of commercial commodities manufacturing, p. 22.
Period of cooperation between Government and people for industrial development, p. 26.
Period of flourishing private enterprises, p. 24.
Period of foreign industrial enterprises in China, p. 23.

INDEX

Period of general depression, p. 27.
Period of Government encouragement, p. 24.
Periods in Chinese industrial history, p. 19 et seq.
Population, pp. 138 et seq, 144, 161, 163, 186.
Population, mobility of, p. 167.
Power, average quantity per factory, pp. 107, 183.
Power consumption, pp. 75 et seq, 104, 148, 183.
Power, motive, pp, 75 et seq, 100, 107, 184.
Power plants, pp. 12, 79, 121.
Power, quantity at command of one laborer, pp. 107, 183.
Power, rented electric, pp. 13, 75 et seq, 104, 106, 183.
Price index numbers, pp. 8, 67, 123, 147, 149, 155, 187.
Price level, the, pp. 8, 67, 68, 123, 161, 187.
Prices of commodities, see under names of commodities.
Printing industry, pp. 59 et seq, 86, 92, 118, 120, 122, 125, 127, 132, 134, 181, 183.
Produce exchange transactions, pp. 156, 161, 187.
Production goods, pp. 69, 87, 182.
Productive capacity of average worker, p. 117.
Proprietorships, pp. 20, 99, 100, 184.
Prostitutes, number in Shanghai and other cities p. 173.
Prostitution, p. 171 et seq.
Public utilities, p. 79.
Purchasing power, pp. 140, 143.

R

Railways, pp. 10, 146, 156, 161, 167, 187.
Raw materials, pp. 7, 70, 73, 93, 95, 98, 108 et seq.
Raw materials, import of, pp. 73, 106, 150, 153, 159, 184.
Raw materials, prices of, pp. 38, 60, 68, 72, 81, 82, 108.
Reeling basins, number of, pp. 36, 37, 82.
Relative positions of Shanghai industries, p. 89.
Rickshas and ricksha coolies, number of, pp. 113, 115, 146.
Road construction, pp. 145, 161.
Rubber goods industry, pp. 51 et seq, 84, 92, 107, 117, 182.
Rural bankruptcy, p. 9.
Rural districts, pp. 7, 154, 179.

S

Seduction, p. 172.
Sex morality, pp. 169, 179.
Sex ratio, p. 164.
Shanghai, pp. 5, 11, 12, 14, 15, 18, 27, 28, 35, 110, 138, 149, 154, 160, 171, 180, 188.
Shanghai City Government, pp. 63, 100, 136, 145, 176.
Shanghai, Sino-Japanese Conflict in, pp. 32, 39, 52, 58, 60, 71, 127, 131, 134, 139, 140, 145, 152, 159.
Ship-building industry, pp. 48, 77, 121, 122, 125.
Shipping, pp. 155, 161, 167.
Silk export, raw, pp. 36, 72, 151.
Silk filature, pp. 23, 35, 82, 102, 105, 117.
Silk price, pp. 37-39.
Silk piece goods export, p. 39.
Silk reeling industry, pp. 22, 35 et seq. 72, 81, 88, 90, 117, 123, 147, 151, 182, 185.
Silk weaving industry, pp. 20, 38, 82, 118, 122, 125, 147, 182, 185.
Silver export duty, p. 33.
Silver, price of, pp. 67, 148, 150, 155, 181.
Silver purchase program, American, see under American.

Silver standard, the, pp. 67, 139.
Silver stock in Shanghai, pp. 8, 158, 161.
Small scale industries pp. 104, 109, 108.
Small size of Shanghai factories, pp. 10, 183.
Smuggling, p. 162.
Soap industry, pp. 122, 125.
Social strata, changes in, p. 169.
Soda, manufacture of, pp. 79, 92, 110.
Saw mills, pp. 75, 122, 125.
Speculation, pp. 142, 159, 160.
Speculative nature of Shanghai industries, pp. 32, 73, 106.
Spindlage statistics, pp. 22, 25, 30, 34.
Squatters, p. 175.
Standardization of manufactured products, p. 5.
Stock exchanges, pp. 106, 142, 160.
Strikes, labor, pp. 128, 129, 131 et seq, 177, 185.
Strikes, sympathetic, p. 133.
Sugar refinery, p. 85.

T

Tariff, the, pp. 25, 29, 67, 79, 179, 182.
Terms of exchange, p. 7.
Textile industries, pp. 28 et seq, 80 et seq, 87, 90, 132, 136, 147, 182, 185.
Textile industries, number of workers in, p. 116.
Tientsin, pp. 12, 15, 42, 46.
Tobacco industry, pp. 15, 24, 45 et seq, 110, 117, 120, 125, 153, 183.
Traffic in women and children, p. 171.
Transportation, p. 155 et seq.
Treaty ports, pp. 7, 8, 12, 29, 181.
Treaty, Shimonoseki, pp. 23, 29, 181.
Tsingtao, pp. 12, 15, 42.

U

Unemployment in Shanghai, pp. 80, 82.
Units, economic, see economic units.

V

Value added by manufacture, p. 109.
Value of output, pp. 16, 67, 75 et seq, 90 et seq, 124, 148, 183.
Value of output, average per factory, p. 112.
Value of output, average per worker, p. 117.
Value of output in relation to capitalization, p. 95.

W

Wage earnings, pp. 117 et seq, 185.
Wage index numbers, pp. 123, 124, 147.
Wage payments, pp. 95, 124.
Wage rates, pp. 110, 121 et seq.
War, Opium, p. 181.
War, Sino-Japanese, pp. 23, 29, 181.
War, World, pp. 24, 30, 35, 36, 42, 43, 46, 49, 96, 181.
Wood working industries, p. 75.
Wool spinning and weaving industries, pp. 22, 40, 41, 82, 122.
Workers, child, pp. 90, 116, 135, 185.
Workers, female, pp. 90, 116, 135, 165, 185.
Workers, male, pp. 90, 116, 135, 165, 185.
Workers, number of, pp. 16, 62, 67, 75 et seq, 90 et seq, 111 et seq, 148, 164, 183, 185.
Working hours, pp. 124 et seq, 133, 185.
Wuchang, pp. 34, 42.
Wusih, pp. 11, 15, 23, 34, 42, 170, 172.

Y

Yangtze flood, great, p. 39.

图书在版编目(CIP)数据

上海工业化研究＝THE GROWTH AND INDUSTRIALIZATION OF SHANGHAI：英文/刘大钧著．—北京：商务印书馆，2015
（中华现代学术名著丛书：英文本）
ISBN 978-7-100-10490-6

Ⅰ.①上… Ⅱ.①刘… Ⅲ.①工业化—研究—上海市—民国—英文 Ⅳ.①F429.51

中国版本图书馆CIP数据核字(2013)第286599号

所有权利保留。
未经许可，不得以任何方式使用。

中华现代学术名著丛书
上海工业化研究
（英文本）

刘大钧 著

商 务 印 书 馆 出 版
（北京王府井大街36号 邮政编码100710）
商 务 印 书 馆 发 行
北 京 冠 中 印 刷 厂 印 刷
ISBN 978-7-100-10490-6

2015年12月第1版　　开本 700×1000 1/16
2015年12月北京第1次印刷　印张 30¼ 插页 1
定价：90.00元